Marilyn French

SHAKESPEARE'S DIVISION
OF EXPERIENCE

First published in Great Britain by
Jonathan Cape Ltd 1982
Published in Abacus 1983 by
Sphere Books Ltd
30–32 Gray's Inn Road, London WC1X 8JL
Copyright © Marilyn French 1981

Some of the material in the section on *Macbeth* first appeared in
somewhat different form in *Soundings: An Interdisciplinary Journal*,
Spring 1975, Nashville, Tennessee.

Reproduced, printed and bound in Great Britain by
Hazell Watson & Viney Ltd, Aylesbury, Bucks

To LeAnne and Hilde

Contents

I wish to thank Harvard University for its grant of a Mellon Fellowship, which made possible a year of research for this book. Gwynne Evans generously read the entire manuscript and made many good suggestions. Morton Bloomfield, Maureen Quilligan, Hilde Hein, and LeAnne Schreiber read parts of the manuscript and made helpful comments. Thanks also to Patty Lipman for her help in preparing the manuscript, and to Mary Solak of Simon and Schuster whose painstaking attention and help were deeply appreciated. And my delighted gratitude to Robert French III for preparing the index.

Quotations from Shakespeare refer to the Riverside edition, ed. G. B. Evans (Houghton Mifflin, Boston and London, 1974).

Introduction

The basic distinction in human social order since the beginning of recorded history has been gender. Beyond any other characteristic, gender has determined role and function. As Benjamin Whorf asserted, gender has been "a standing classificatory fact in our thought-world."[1] It has determined division of labor, value, the structure of our languages and the structure of our lives. Above all, gender difference has influenced the way we think, the way we perceive reality.

Whorf believed that humankind has a "habitual consciousness of two sex classes."[2] The double consciousness which attended the awareness that women become pregnant and give birth and men do not led to a division of labor along gender lines. Although identical tasks may be performed by either gender in different communities, the two genders usually perform different tasks in any one community. Thus in one tribe, it is considered natural that women farm and men fish; in another, that men farm and women fish. Eventually, these divisions are accorded divine sanction, and social roles are abstracted into principles seen as imposed by both nature and deity. "Masculine" and "feminine" principles thus become expressions of natural law embracing not only the world but the cosmos.

However, this distinction in human social order is not itself fundamental. This is to say, it does not in fact arise out of nature. There are no forms of labor impossible to either gender except child carriage, birth, and nursing. A different musculature may make some tasks easier for the average male than for the average female, but men can be parents as loving and nurturant as women, women can perform heavy labor and aggressive physical acts. It is conditioning and training that are responsible for the division of labor presently considered "natural" in most of the Western world.

The fundamental split in human thinking is not gender, but a perception of humans as separate from, different from nature. This perception was probably responsible for the survival of a species lacking the special physical or perceptual equipment possessed by other surviving animal species. Humans, rooted in and subject to natural environment and natural processes to the same degree as other animals, stood up on their hind legs, and used what they had—a brain more powerful than those of other animals, and a retractile thumb—to attempt to control an environment they were not especially adaptable to. Some animals—bees, beavers—also make attempts to control nature, or to alter its workings. But no other species has made as concerted and insistent an effort to lessen its vulnerability and subjection to nature. This effort has taken hundreds of thousands of years—if not more—and was made by both females and males.

To people uncertain of their food supply, their shelter from the elements, and their relation with other animals, control over these things had to seem a good. But it also had to entail a sense of loneliness, isolation, exclusion from the thoughtless, "happy" participation in nature enjoyed by other animals, and perhaps retained in a "racial" memory as an Eden once possessed by humans as well. This loneliness may have been assuaged, as loneliness so often is, by transformation of it into superiority: different is better. Unquestionably, there was a sense of inferiority as well—there still exist myths and rituals in which people attempt, through ingestion or imitation, to appropriate certain animal excellences. The belief that humans could do this, however, is a belief that humans had powers not given to other animals, and was an additional sign of superiority.

Humans domesticated earth through farming, domesticated or hunted animals and fish and birds, domesticated themselves with clothing and shelter. They made tools and vessels, and most important of all, they made language. Yet they remained subject to natural catastrophe, and remained identical to animals in their physical functioning. Human digestive, excretory, and reproductive processes are similar to those of larger (more easily observed) animals. But only certain humans menstruated, conceived, gave birth, and produced milk to feed the newborn. Because of these involuntary but very visible functions, women came to be seen as "closer to nature" than men— especially in times before male participation in procreation was recognized.

The indications are that at some time this seeming greater closeness to nature was worshipped as divine; remnants of this attitude still remain. But eventually, the hard circumstances of human life led to a valuing of control over and separation from nature as an absolute good and a defining human characteristic. As this sense of things developed, women's supposed closeness to nature became a stigma rather than a miracle, and women began to be seen as lower than men; being part of nature in a way men were not, they were also part of what must be controlled.

The foregoing is, of course, a hypothetical explanation for the almost universal derogation of women, but it is not mere web spinning. The written word, the best record we have of attitudes of earlier times, supports the associations I have described. The Adam's-rib story in Genesis (which is considerably older than the opening explanation of the origin of the world and of humans) shows an already developed misogyny and oppression of women. Like the Greek myth of Pandora, it attributes to a woman introduction to moral knowledge and to the pain and sorrow and loss such knowledge entails; like the Greek myth, the Genesis story blames Woman for the human condition. The first chapter of Genesis also makes explicit the value structure we still live by:

> And God said, Let us make man in our image, after our likeness; and let them have dominion over the fish of the sea, and over the fowl of the air, and over the cattle, and over all the earth. . . .
> And God said to them, Be fruitful, and multiply, and replenish the earth, and subdue it.[3]

The sign of human dominion is naming, language, for "Adam gave names to all cattle and to the fowl of the air, and to every beast of the field."[4] Clearly, although the later, more sophisticated and abstract account grants humanness to both males and females, in the older account, Adam is man, he, the human. "And Adam called his wife's name Eve; because she was the mother of all living."[5]

The value structure is clear. Man is the image of the human; he is granted control and labor (tilling); his control extends over all of nature including Eve, she, woman, seen totally as the bearer of children, who, like the other animals, is given her name, according to her function, by dominant man. Above all, the proper relation between man and nature (which includes woman) is dominion, control, power over.

Now, of course, all of this is absurd. In the first place, women are not closer to nature than men. Menstruation and conception are no more involuntary than nocturnal emissions, or the unpredictable and uncontrollable operations of the male sexual organ. And apart from generation, male and female physical processes are identical. Variables, like a higher male infant mortality rate, tendency towards certain diseases, and overall life-span, are tied to environmental and role influences, and are inessential compared to the similarity of our fates. We are born, we hunger, we get sick or injured, we die. Pregnancy and nursing do constitute· major differences in functioning, but they are not an impediment to women (as proven by the behavior of women in certain cultures, who do hard physical labor up until the moment of birth, and immediately afterwards), but rather an additional ability of women.

Nor, at the time Genesis was spoken or written, did humans have control over nature. Even in our own highly developed technological culture, we cannot make such a claim. Humans have only two forms of control over nature: to tame or domesticate or crossbreed it, which is a form of ownership; or to kill it. But earth, the elements, and even certain animals (especially insects) resist those two rather crude manipulations. Human functioning within nature works best when it is done in a cooperative manner, taking and giving back, nurturing it as it nurtures us, and understanding and abiding by nature's facts. Full subjugation of earth can mean only its destruction.

The claims of the myth of human dominion are absurd. But they are also potent. The attitudes explicit in Genesis were not a local manifestation. They became, in one form or another, the dominant myth of human civilization, and they have been the impetus behind human behavior ever since.

Although all cultures which have survived and flourished have exercised some control over nature, dominion, mastery, has been emphasized mainly in the Western world, that world influenced by Judaic-Hellenistic-Christian thinking. Whether as owning, knowing, or destroying, power-in-the-world, power over, has been the directing value of this tradition for over three thousand years. It is echoed in the very structure of Western languages, in the relation of subject-verb-object.

The basic relationship between humans and nature is intended to make humans less vulnerable, less subject to nature's power. And control over nature has made life easier and more pleasant for many people. Poverty does make people vulnerable; wealth and luxury can lessen as well as mask that vulnerability: thus ownership is a good. Because ownership is a good and nonownership precarious in an owned world, hostility and aggression, the power to take, become a value. And since nature's ultimate power cannot be totally vanquished, humans have used their powers to create structures that will not die— or so it seems. Monuments, dynasties, emperies, poems, and institutions, things that can *weather* the flux of life within nature seem to console us for the inevitable loss of our own lives. The erection of "permanent" structures makes the alien feel at home. Men have gone so far as to attribute to an eternal realm the structures created on earth, and to claim the power of the keys of that kingdom. Although men created the intellectual structure of Christianity, and claim all its power, women as well as men believe in it.

Despite the warnings of poets, despite "myths" like the stories of Midas, King Canute, and Faustus—all of whom claimed or had superhuman powers over nature—dominion over nature increasingly became the proper moral relation to it. And inevitably, given the association of women with nature, as power over nature increased, polarization between the sexes also increased. Deborah (eleventh to tenth century B.C.) was a judge in Israel, but by the time of Proverbs, several centuries later, women were expected to be servants, virtuous and subservient.[6] Pythagoras lived in the sixth century B.C.; he and his followers developed a numerical symbology. According to this symbology, the number *one* was the number of godhead and of maleness; the number *two* was the number of divisiveness and femaleness. One, God, man, were associated with light, order, good, right, rights, and the right hand. Two, divisiveness or chaos, woman, were associated with darkness, evil, magic, and the sinister, the left hand. To this day, the buttons on men's shirts are on the right, on women's, on the left; to this day, members of a wedding party arrange themselves in a place of worship in accord with these associations: groom's party on the right, bride's party on the left. The term *legitimate* has no meaning in nature: a child who is born and lives is a living child. A child is labeled *illegitimate*, however, if no male takes credit or responsibility for that child by conferring upon it his name. In past times, noble bastards wore the bar sinister on their family emblems.

Throughout Western culture, thinkers and poets have reminded

us that male and female, yang and yin, are complements, and conceptual equivalents for qualities found in all people. This insistence is
futile, however, and will remain so as long as the value placed on the
two poles is unequal. Our culture and our tradition place extremely
high value on light (white), order, unity, and right (which is always,
when combined with power, pluralized into *rights*) and a negative
value on darkness, disorder, and magic (magic being remnants of old
religions gone underground, and associated with control of an "illegitimate" sort). Naturally, then, it values the genders identified with these
qualities in the same way. Power (god) and stability (permanent order)
have become the two highest values on earth. With certain fluctua-
tions, they have been for millennia.

I call the two opposing poles the masculine and feminine principles. I use these terms not because I believe they are accurate descriptions of human capacity or human experience, but because there are
no other terms as precise in describing how humans have *conceptualized* their experience for the past three millennia. The problem with a
conception like yin and yang is that it presumes a wide difference of
capacity and expression in the two genders—a difference for which
there is little proof. That women and men think, speak, and act differently is unquestionable, but is clearly linked to cultural programming.
It is more significant that men sometimes act "like women"—that is,
they can be tender and nurturing and compassionate; and women
sometimes act "like men"—they are aggressive, cruel, tyrannical. Such
seeming crossovers are even more significant in view of the fact that
no one raised in Western culture, even in our own "enlightened" century, is free of the associations of the gender principles. Whatever
people themselves may be, they know what is properly masculine,
what is properly feminine.

The definitions of the gender principles and our categorization of
experience in accordance with them can be traced in every human
tradition: in language, law, religion, art, philosophy, and science. But
the fullest and most easily accessible expression of these ideas is found
in literature. And the most realized expression, the most complete
awareness of these ideas are found in the greatest artists. Shakespeare,
the greatest poet to use the English language, in fact deals continually
with these poles and with the implications of polarization.

This is not to say that Shakespeare thought in terms of a feminine
or masculine principle. But he did unquestionably think in terms of
men and women, male and female, not as similar members of a single
species, but as very different creatures, subject to different needs and

desires, capable of different kinds of action, and judged by different standards.

Shakespeare began his career with profound respect for "masculine" qualities and profound suspicion of "feminine" ones. In very short span—by the time he wrote *The Two Gentlemen of Verona*—he had come to admire "feminine" qualities. By the end of his career, he had come to fear and deplore the power and capriciousness of the masculine principle, and to idealize certain aspects of the feminine. Nevertheless, he never abandoned belief in male legitimacy or horror at female sexuality, and these continued to color all his thinking. He did not, it seems, think abstractly about morality; certainly he did not think about moral principles in terms of gender division. But his work represents a lifelong effort to harmonize moral qualities he did associate with the two genders, and to synthesize opposing or seemingly opposed states and qualities.

This book is a study of the gender principles as I see them existing in Shakespeare's work. I did not bring my theory to the work; rather, the work of Shakespeare, when contrasted with the work of some twentieth-century authors (who will be dealt with in a later study), brought me to see as I do.

There are some who will perhaps call this study *ideological* in order to dismiss some of its more discomfiting conclusions. Insofar as the study is concerned with ideas and issues from a writer with a point of view, it is ideological. But so is every book that is concerned with ideas. Studies of Shakespeare written from more traditional perspectives are no less ideological: that an ideology is accepted by most members of a culture, that it constitutes the received wisdom of its time, does not make it less an ideology. Those who exalt reason over passion, or order and degree over social flexibility and democracy, are making ideological, moral choices they assume to have been Shakespeare's, but which I hope to demonstrate were not. Many critics judge the characters in a narrowly moral way, assuming that Shakespeare did so as well, in accordance with the Aristotelian notion that tragedy involved possession of a "fatal flaw" in the protagonist.

In fact, what I have attempted to do in reading the plays is something I believe Shakespeare did in writing them: I have tried to keep my mind morally neutral. This is to say, I have not clamped it down like a set of teeth, excluding certain actions from the attributes of humanity. To write a play in which a man murders, and is destroyed because of his murder, an author has to have more in mind than simply the notion that murder is evil. Most people believe that murder

is evil: it requires no extended proof. It is far more daring and interesting to write a play in which one asks *why* murder is evil, what happens
to a murderer as a result of his action.

Thus, I have presumed no pregiven good or evil. I have attempted
not to be swayed by the rhetoric surrounding characters like Richard
III, Coriolanus, Goneril, or Joan de Pucelle, in order to examine their
actual performances, their actual speeches. I have done this because it
is impossible to analyze a morality when one participates in it. It would
be impossible to deduce what incest meant to Shakespeare, for instance, if the very word conjured horror to the moral imagination. Any
absolute evil is an unexamined evil; any absolute good is an unexamined good.

Finally, some may complain that the real interest of this study is
not Shakespeare but traditional Western attitudes and values, or they
may insist, as many Shakespeare scholars have insisted, that it is not
possible to deduce Shakespeare's politics from his work. Insofar as
politics are morals (and I believe they are identical), I disagree with the
second. As for the first, there is a long and honorable tradition of using
literature and other disciplines and interests to illuminate each other.
A reading of Shakespeare can illuminate our knowledge of Western
attitudes; an analysis of values can also illuminate some dark corners
in Shakespeare's work. For Shakespeare, unlike some of his critics, did
not unthinkingly adopt the received wisdom of his time. He really
probed, dramatically, the subjects of power and legitimacy, his own
attitudes towards sex and women; he struggled all his life for a vision of
a proper ordering of society. The approach to Shakespeare taken in
this book is certainly not the only way of reading the poet. But it is a
fruitful way, both for our understanding of Shakespeare and for our
understanding of our own lives, our own thinking.

I

THE GENDER PRINCIPLES

1

The Gender Principles

The whole notion of dividing experience into gender principles is a "masculine" one. (This is not to say only males created and perpetuated it. The gender principles as I describe them are not necessarily identical with gender.) It is "masculine" because it originally arose as a form of control. Because it is "masculine," it is linear, which is to say it has a fixed, stipulated goal.

Because the notion is linear, the gender principles may be laid on a gamut. The poles of this gamut are masculine and feminine. At the center are qualities which are not gender-specific, which are valued in both genders. The extreme of the masculine side is the ability to kill; that of the feminine side is the ability to give birth: the two most profound of all human activities. Clustered about each pole are qualities which support the extreme.

The masculine principle, predicated on the ability to kill, is the pole of power-in-the-world. It is associated with prowess and ownership, with physical courage, assertiveness, authority, independence, and the right, rights, and legitimacy. It claims to be able to define and administer justice; and it supports law and order as an arrangement imposed and maintained by force.

Its energies are directed at making permanent, fixing the flux of experience. It exalts the individual (who wants to transcend nature and natural oblivion). It values action over feeling, thought over sensation. Its ultimate goal is transcendence of nature; its immediate goal is the attainment and maintenance of power-in-the-world, whether as force or authority. In principle, it is conceived of as a means of protecting and ensuring the continuation of the human race and its felicity.

The masculine principle is linear, temporal, and transcendent, for it aims to construct something in the world and within time that will enable the individual to transcend nature (which is cyclic), time, and mortality. The thing erected is a sort of immortality. It may be a tribe bearing the father's name, or a dynasty; it may be a noble act recorded in legend and poetry. Or an institution or tradition such as a religion, a school of thought, a school of art. Or it may be an artifact, Stevens' jar in Tennessee which imposes human significance on the impersonal and undifferentiating cycles of nature.

The masculine principle is thus profoundly threatened by and antagonistic to impulses towards acceptance of simple continuation, of present pleasure, of surrender to mortality. These impulses are associated with the feminine principle, which is identified with nature. Defying the power of nature, the masculine principle is the standard of hu(mankind), and identifies the human with the male.

The divisiveness associated by the Pythagoreans with the number *two*, the number of femaleness, may be connected with parturition. But it is certainly connected with the perception of a duality in nature. Nature has two aspects (although they are not always easily distinguishable): a benevolent (nutritive, regenerating, supportive) and a malevolent (destructive, subversive of human constructions, and more powerful than any human constructions—up until the atomic age, anyway). Because we die, nature always, inevitably vanquishes us. Human effort has always been to diminish this power, whether through belief in control of an afterlife (supranatural) or through erection of cultural traditions and artifacts that carry on our lives.

As far as I can deduce, the two aspects of nature were taken as a whole in pre-Christian thought. Identified then as now with the female, nature was a powerful lover and a powerful hater. Eve the instigator of the fall was also Eve the mother of all living; Aphrodite was a goddess of shifting weather, of the fruitfulness of spring and the withering of autumn, the goddess of sexual desire and of wedded love and fruitfulness; Kali incarnated both natural creativity and temporal destructiveness. The goddess was at least dual, and sometimes triple in her manifestations as nubile virgin, mother-whore, and wise old hag.

But all those manifestations were *male* perceptions of female power. In such a conception, the feminine principle has great power, but it is also very threatening to the "masculine" drive towards control.

The later myths of Aphrodite and Athene as having been produced by the immaculate conception of their fathers' brains or sperm are attempts to harness the powers of the feminine principle into service to the masculine. But these attempts were not notably successful. They drove female goddess-worshippers underground; the old religions were denigrated as mere magic; the goddesses gave up their names to the new gods; the character of the Erinyes was changed from agents of justice to avengers; and the father was declared the true parent of the child, the mother being merely a vessel. Zeus (power) and Apollo (light and order seen as harmony) superseded the older, more earthy deities. Flesh, body, was declared inferior to mind, and the two were perceived as antagonists inhabiting a single entity. Word was declared prime, and the nature of deity; while spirit, which is feeling, was ignored. In the beginning was the word, and the word was with God, and the word was God.

These efforts to establish a new hierarchy of value were intermittently successful until Christianity. It was the architects of the early Christian church who first understood *divide and conquer* in the moral realm. Christianity succeeded in defeating the supremacy of the feminine principle by splitting it in two. The Eve who was responsible both for the fall from unity with nature and for the continuation of the race becomes a subversive figure "redeemed" by the Mary who accepts that she is *ancilla*, ancillary, a handmaiden, only a vessel in the transmission of a male line. This split in the principle of nature, the feminine principle, still exists in our perception of actual women; there is the mother madonna, and the whore; the nourisher and the castrator.

This split in the feminine principle I call inlaw and outlaw aspects of it. The outlaw aspect retains the characteristics of femaleness described by the Pythagoreans. It is associated with darkness, chaos, flesh, the sinister, magic and above all, sexuality. It is outlaw because it is subversive, undermining of the masculine principle. It claims both poles of the gamut, the ability to give birth and the ability to kill, both of which actual females possess. Its sexuality is dynamic and nearly irresistible; it is sex as abandonment (as opposed to "masculine" sexuality, which is possession or aggression—rape) and a power like that of nature to destroy. It has no end, no goal beyond the pleasure of being. Its rebellion against the masculine principle is based not in the desire to set up controlling structures of its own, but in the desire to eradicate such structures completely. It is tremendously threatening to the masculine principle because it does not respect the constructs attendant on that principle, and because it is vital and attractive. It is vital and attractive because it contains fundamental human energy and will, and because it sees the end of life as pleasure.

Pleasure of all sorts, but especially sexual pleasure, is a threat to the masculine principle, the energies of which must be directed towards transcendent goals. Aggression and usurpation are part of the masculine principle, but beneath any "masculine" hostility is a respect for structure, hierarchy, and legitimacy: revolutions may place different people or classes or races in the chairs of power, but the chairs of power remain. Permanency is the greatest good. The outlaw feminine principle is a rebellion against any permanency except the cyclic permanence of nature. These two principles comprise a dichotomy of their own: the masculine principle, the pole of power, is the pole of the individual who dedicates his life to a suprapersonal goal; the outlaw feminine principle, the pole of sex and pleasure, is the pole of people destined for oblivion who dedicate their lives to personal satisfaction.

There is, however, a third "pole." It is the inlaw feminine principle, the benevolent aspects of nature "purified" of their malevolent side. Since most of the power resident in the feminine principle as a whole is attributed to its outlaw aspect, the inlaw feminine principle is rather wispy. Its great strengths are castrated by its scission from its other half. The inlaw feminine principle is an expression of the benevolent manifestations of nature. Founded on the ability to give birth, it includes qualities like nutritiveness, compassion, mercy, and the ability to create felicity. It requires volitional subordination, voluntary relinquishment of power-in-the-world. It is impersonal, or suprapersonal, or altruistic, totally: it values above all the good of the whole, the community. It exalts the community above the individual, feeling over action, sensation over thought. *It is not passive:* it actively reaches for subordination for the good of the whole and finds its pleasure in that good rather than in assertion of self.

The split in the feminine principle was designed to guarantee the subordination of the benevolent aspects of nature to the human need to transcend nature, and cast into a no-man's-land the outlaw feminine principle, which could then be destroyed without scruple. Each quality of the inlaw feminine principle was seen as connected to, and supportive of, a quality in the masculine principle, but always as subordinate. Mercy may only temper justice; compassion may only temper authority; feeling is essential, but must defer to thought; nutritiveness must bow to power.

What developed was a value system in which the masculine principle, originally designed to be the means to protect and foster the true ends of human life, procreation and pleasure, became instead its own end. The philosophy of Jesus became the Catholic church; the ends of Christianity—volitional subordination of self to attain human harmony, meekness and tolerance as Jesus preached them—were taken over, preempted by the church which preached them, a church dedicated above all to power, control, and transcendence. And a church which has, for the past two thousand years, dominated Western thought.

Because it abjures power-in-the-world in favor of what may be called the quality of life, the feminine principle is (in both aspects) circular, atemporal, and accepting (as opposed to transcendent). It is associated with the cycles of nature, eternal recurrence, with eternity and the present moment. It does not admit the possibility of transcendence, nor the need for it. However, when it is split in two, its inlaw side is pressed into the service of transcendence. Sometimes the outlaw aspect is given a word of praise for the same act: the whore with a golden heart is its symbol.

The only way the masculine principle can control the feminine principle is by fission. In its inlaw aspect, the feminine principle which supports and nourishes the masculine principle is associated with civilization; thus, occasionally, women (identified with the feminine principle by most literature) are identified with culture, control of the animal man, and morality (seen as oppressive). At other times, the inlaw feminine principle is seen as divine, as a moral touchstone, as lifting man from his essential bestiality. The outlaw feminine principle is sometimes seen as threatening, as castrating and destroying the masculine principle; at other times, it is seen as a source of energy and force. What remains still, stable amid this fluctuation, is the masculine principle, the human image, subject to or overcoming the overwhelming "feminine" force surrounding it.[1]

The imagery associated with the feminine principle is natural imagery: the moon and the sea, menstruation and menopause, the seasons' difference and their eternal recurrence; fruitfulness; and sex. The imagery associated with the masculine principle is both natural and civilized: thunder and lightning, of the heavens or of human warfare; cities, industry, human occupation, from farming to weaving to making art, mining and fishing and governing: every form of control.

The associations of the gender principles are not without consequence, on moral, political, and philosophical levels. The masculine principle is, through most of literature, identified with males. When one is dealing with a field of males alone, only certain males possess full legitimacy: the rest are "women" to the males with rights (prerogatives). When one is dealing with a field of males and females, all males have right (prerogative). The male is the image of the human, the standard, in the moral, political, or philosophical dimension. The male is judged ethically, expected to conform to the laws laid down by other men, expected to take his place in the hierarchy of males without demur.

Females can never fully enter this dimension. They represent the nonhuman; they are superhuman (inlaw aspect) or subhuman (outlaw aspect), but they are differentiated from the human. They are judged mythically. Females may be saints and goddesses, or they may be whores and witches; they may be the martyred mother or wife, or the castrating bitch. In either case, they are seen only in relation to males and the male (human) standard. Autonomy is impossible in females because they are not seen as human, but as parts of the dimension (nature) with or against which humans operate. They are therefore invariably seen as trying—successfully or vainly—to exert control over the male, the human.

In actuality, of course, all people manifest qualities associated with all aspects of the gender principles. However, literature, history, theology, and philosophy, all "masculine" since they all aim to erect permanencies, tend to reflect not actual experience but traditional conceptualizations of it. In fact, we cannot talk about actual experience, because we are incapable of knowing it beyond our conceptions of it—although sometimes those conceptions are shattered enough that new conceptions can enter our minds.

In literature, therefore, males act out the human role, erring and correcting, experiencing the gamut of emotion and behavior, while females act out the type, standing as static poles in human (male) experience.[2] Some forms of literature contain no human figure at all: the human is the confluence of a set of types. This is the case in allegory, and in miracle and morality plays. The difference between the human and the type is that the former has the possibility of change, and the latter does not. Types, whether archetypes or stereotypes, represent moral positions not amenable to change.

Human figures in a work are the major characters; most works contain only one. They are mobile and dynamic; they make mistakes of judgment, of values; they grow, learn, change, and fail or succeed. They possess moral excellence and moral fallibility. Their moral flexibility is what makes their experience interesting and significant. Although Antigone is the dominant figure in Sophocles' play, it is Creon who is the human figure. Antigone is absolute, static, inflexible; it is impossible to imagine her behaving in any way other than she does. She is an archetype in Creon's moral life, a symbol of a way of thinking with which he must come to terms.

Female figures may suffer unjustly, like Cordelia, Hero, and Hermione; they may inflict suffering, like Goneril, Regan, and a host of nameless or faceless or characterless female figures in Shakespeare: but their experience does not change them. There is no residue of anger or resentment in Julia, Kate, Titania, Hero, Cordelia, Desdemona, Imogen, Hermione, and others.

Male figures, on the other hand, may survive or not, but they are changed by their experience. Oedipus and Orestes must suffer through the consequences of their actions, but they are changed by that suffering and thus exemplify a human pattern. Lear and Gloucester are transformed by their experience, as are Leontes and Prince Hal and even Macbeth. That consummate villain, Edmund, has a change of heart as he lies dying, and tries—vainly—to do some good.

On the other hand, Medea, Elektra, and Clytemnestra perform actions that change their worlds, but they themselves do not change. Their actions are the inevitable consequence of their characters, and their characters are one-dimensional, they are fixed. Lady Macbeth is psychologically destroyed by her actions, but that destruction was implicit in her statements at the opening of the play, and does not change her character. Macbeth, on the other hand, grows to larger awareness, even though he also is destroyed.

Spenser's Una does not turn against Redcrosse for his abandonment of her, nor does Duessa learn from her humiliating public exposure. Spenser's characters are allegorical, and therefore types, but his male heroes, who exemplify human undertaking, do err and grow and learn. It is significant that his female hero, Britomart, does not make any serious error in her quest, and is the only knight in *The Faerie Queene* who does not require rescue by Arthur. This is not, however, because Spenser necessarily saw females as morally superior to males. It is because, according to the traditional division of experience, females *had to be* morally superior to males. Females were not permitted to err: had Britomart made the errors of Redcrosse or Guyon or Artegall or Calidore, she *could not have been* redeemed. She is the knight of chastity; had she fallen into unchastity, what could save her?

Females are inevitably bound inside the feminine principle in traditional—and even untraditional (consider Blake)—Western thought and literature. Even when female figures begin to act as human figures, in eighteenth- and nineteenth-century novels, they are tightly constricted within a type. Their problem is still to adjust to a male world, to male needs, desires, and power. Female figures have little power-in-the-world, and what power they do possess, they are likely not to use because of the onus on female power-in-the-world. When oppression moves out, guilt moves in. But not only do these figures have narrow physical and political room: they also have little moral room.

Because of the very effective split of the feminine principle created by Christianity, and because in both the actuality and the written records of the Western world, males voted themselves the economic and political power, females have been, and still are, under great pressure to conform to the image of them entertained by Western culture. Not only are they expected to fit themselves into the narrow category labeled "feminine," but they are expected to use only a fragment of their capacities—the inlaw feminine principle, the aspect that supports the dominant male establishment.

The split in the feminine principle precludes the slightest error in the females associated with it. Females are seen as untrustworthy; like Chaucer's Cressida, all women are susceptible to "slydyng." They must therefore be, like Caesar's wife, beyond reproach, beyond even suspicion. They must renounce any quality which is threatening to the more powerful masculine principle. Any error can plunge them into an abyss of darkness from which they cannot arise again. Even the rumor of an error is enough to destroy them—in literature generally, but even, sometimes, in life.

A character like Shakespeare's Prince Hal can experiment with elements of misrule (outlaw feminine principle) and return enriched to rule, right, and legitimacy. Henry V is admirable for his "feminine" qualities—his democratic movement among his men, his charming deference to his future wife. But female figures who attempt to move into the masculine principle, like Queen Margaret, Joan, Lady Macbeth, Goneril, and Regan, are condemned as fiends, witches, and devils: the most usual term applied to them is "unnatural." In Shakespeare (as well as other poets of his time), males are urged to incorporate the inlaw feminine principle, but females who attempt to incorporate the masculine principle—to exercise authority, to show physical prowess, to kill—fall inevitably into the outlaw feminine principle. It is not mere chance that St. Joan became, in Shakespeare's first tetralogy, and in popular British imagination, not only a witch but a whore, or that Jezebel, whose crime was worshipping foreign gods and influencing her husband, is remembered as a fornicatress. The door between the gender principles opens only one way.

Females may incorporate some of the capacities of the masculine principle if they do so in disguise and continue to accept the constrictions of femaleness. Thus Rosalind and Viola are able to move about in the world in male dress (something they could not do in upper-class female dress), but both are shown to cling almost lovingly to their female limitations, suffering from physical weariness, or terror at the thought of a duel. In fact, female limitations are so severe in Shakespeare's work that despite their charm and unshakable good values— or perhaps precisely because of their unshakable good values—females are rather static. They do not change: they are either utterly good or utterly evil because if they are not utterly good, they become instantly utterly evil.

Stasis of character is found in female figures throughout literature. It is impossible to imagine Circe growing old like Odysseus; Antigone as a happy pregnant wife; Dido returning stoically and with bitterness against men to her duties as governor of Carthage; Lavinia complaining that she likes Turnus better than Aeneas—as well she might. Niobe and Hecuba weep through eternity, and Helen is always young.

Because the two gender principles occupy different conceptual realms—the human and ethical versus the type and the mythical— they cannot be synthesized. They cannot be equal because they are not like. But because both principles are abstractions from universal human experience, representing urges and needs found in all of us, they desperately need synthesis. And much of the thought and literature of the past has been devoted to attempts to produce a synthesis.

The most common form of arrangement is to see the masculine principle as dominant. Its power makes it legitimate, and right and rights are its prerogatives. It accepts the feminine principle (and usually, the women associated with it) insofar as that principle is inlaw, insofar as it volitionally subordinates itself to the nourishment and support of the masculine ends of control and transcendence. In this arrangement, the outlaw feminine principle is feared and condemned. Utterly illegitimate (the inlaw aspect may borrow legitimacy from the masculine principle when it operates under a masculine aegis, but can never possess it independently), it is subversive of legitimacy. However, the masculine principle requires the energy and freedom of this pole, and therefore tolerates it in nonthreatening forms. Nonthreatening forms are those in which males maintain control; thus, sexual freedom is permitted to men in the form of concubinage or prostitution. A degree of sexual freedom in males is in fact seen as admirable (although not by late Shakespeare). But too much abandonment to sexual pleasure is deplored. The onus of sexuality is placed entirely on the women involved, who are, in almost every Western culture, looked down on as subhuman and entitled to absolutely no rights.

A more religious synthesis of the gender principles places the inlaw feminine principle above the masculine; its ends, procreation and the good of the whole, and its qualities of subordination (humility, meekness), compassion, and nutritiveness are seen as ideal. However, in this synthesis, the masculine goal of transcendence is absorbed by the inlaw feminine principle, and the realm in which it is supreme is placed beyond worldly human life, in some sort of heaven. The inlaw feminine principle is seen as divine, and the masculine principle is urged to uphold it. In this arrangement, the outlaw feminine principle is utterly beyond the pale, for men or women.

This kind of synthesis varies from religion to religion, but in Christianity, the divine element is actually a fusion of feminine and masculine qualities (always omitting the outlaw aspect). Dante's *Paradiso* fuses love (feminine) with power (masculine) to create justice which is also love. But his heaven, like the structure of the church which holds its keys, is hierarchical and legitimate. The feminine principle suffuses the power structure with love that is light, thus combining the two.

The greatest poets of the English Renaissance—Shakespeare, Spenser, and Sidney—all attempted to synthesize the gender principles in more earthly locales, in a similar way. Their visions involved male (human) figures assimilating, absorbing the qualities of the feminine principle through education and through suffering, becoming in the process good governors, good men, or not doing so, and being destroyed. Shakespeare's nightmare visions always involve the destruction of the qualities of the feminine principle by masculine abuse of power. But occasionally, as in Spenser's Bower of Bliss, or Cleopatra's Egypt, the outlaw feminine principle vanquishes the masculine, leading to indolence and shame. The attractiveness of the outlaw feminine world is probably best seen (by our biased eyes) in males like Falstaff.

These visions of synthesis are invariably visions of male figures. It is never suggested that any female figure should or could absorb the masculine qualities of power, authority, or right, or should or could claim legitimacy in her own right. But these conceptions have little to do with actual life, actual women and men. They rest on perceptions that have been forgotten by the conscious mind, but which are perpetuated by the conventions of our literature, art, and language. Men insist that the word *man* is generic, and includes women. Women know better. For centuries they have been conceptualized as static figures operating in male experience, and denied entrance into full humanity.

Many critics have perceived in Shakespeare polarities of the sort I will examine. In *The Wheel of Fire*, G. Wilson Knight claims that the two primary values for Shakespeare are love and war, and the two primary aspects of humanity are intuition/emotion, which leads to faith, and intellect/reason, which leads to cynicism.[3] He adds that for Shakespeare, good is love, and hate is "an awareness of the world of actuality unspiritualized, and shows a failure to body infinite spirit into finite forms, and a consequent abhorrence and disgust at these forms." The dualism in Shakespeare is between "actuality" and "spirit."[4] Terence Hawkes writes, "since the nature of genuine and desirable 'manhood' and 'womanhood' must inevitably be one of the most potent and formative notions held by any group of people, it is not surprising to find it as a central concern of Shakespeare's drama."[5] E. M. W. Tillyard discusses Aristotle's assertion that poetry answers two profound human instincts: imitation, which is connected with the desire to learn, and harmony or rhythm. Tillyard interprets the former as form, which offers order, the latter as richness, offering expansion of range of experience, and finds these two approaches in varying balances in Shakespeare's work.[6] And John Wain suggests that Shakespeare "had the kind of mind that seeks always to reduce multiplicity to unity, to take the widest possible spread of material and weld it together into a whole." Wain believes that Shakespeare wrote out of a world view, not about character.[7] So do I.

More than any other poet, Shakespeare breathed life into his female characters and gave body to the principle they are supposed to represent. Yet his dis-ease with the sexuality supposedly incarnate in women grew, as he aged, into a terrified loathing. More than any other poet of his time, Shakespeare was tormented by the consequences of power. Yet he could not imagine the world being run in any way so that power could be checked and restrained, except by the internalization, in a governing class, of the qualities of the feminine principle. The problems for the world inherent in each gender principle, and in the relations between or among them, continued to fascinate him to the end of his career.

2

Formal Equivalents of the Gender Principles

The characteristics of the gender principles pervade the literary forms that depict them.

Works concerned with the masculine principle—in Shakespeare's time, and in later works as well—are dominated by a male figure. Such works are linear and transcendent, that is, they contain a narrative which progresses chronologically and a protagonist who has a specific worldly goal which will, when attained, place him in a transcendent position. He may aim at living happily ever after, ruling in security forever after, or performing an act of vengeance that makes him an agent of "heavenly" justice. He may wish to win a war or establish a dynastic line or secure his throne; or he may wish to marry the girl, or make a fortune and marry the girl, or become legitimate by discovering his paternity and receiving his proper inheritance (place in the world). Although the real end is transcendence, that is, becoming invulnerable in a permanent way, this transcendence is always to be achieved through worldly means. The story is the description of his progress, which is located in space and time; his success or failure in reaching his goal (which may be ironic—success that is failure, failure that is success) is the conclusion and ends the linear time of the narrative. In cases where a "good" male is defeated, some transcendent substitution is arranged—a tomb or monument will be erected, a ceremony will be performed, or a story will immortalize him.

In such works, a clear cosmic order hovers in the background, an order which sanctions the masculine claim to legitimacy and right (right as both power and moral right). English literature, from Shakespeare to the mid- to late nineteenth century, is dominated by "masculine" works.

Literature concerned with the feminine principle is circular and eternal: it juggles time or ignores it. It presents incidents which have no apparent causal (rational) connections. Cause and effect and chronology may be entirely suspended in favor of psychological, emotional, associational links. "Feminine" works are not mainly concerned with progress towards a goal, but with depiction of the texture of life, its quality. They focus on interior experience, on sensation, emotion, and reflection, and are synthetic rather than analytic in their thinking. In Shakespeare and his contemporaries, "feminine" works are built around a central female figure, although she will not dominate the action as male figures do in "masculine" works.[1]

In "feminine" literature, there is no great external goal to be achieved because there is no purpose to human life beyond continuation and pleasure. Only the living matters, moving into a tomorrow which will be much like today. Therefore there is also no strong cosmic order hovering behind the action, and indeed, even power-in-the-world is largely nullified. Power may be evaded, mocked, parodied, or converted; it does not deeply affect the life that is being lived before our eyes. In addition, "feminine" worlds are essentially anarchic. A coronet does not carry with it legitimacy in a world where no one is legitimate. People simply *are*: the very term *legitimacy* has no meaning in feminine worlds. Characters may be more or less likable, more or less morally acceptable; but they cannot be more or less legitimate.

Thus, feminine literature is outlaw literature: it challenges, however subtly, masculine worldly structures, power, and permanence. It shows a different side of life: it celebrates flux, the moment, sensation, and emotion. It is likely to be concerned with love and sex rather than power or justice. Literature dominated by the feminine principle is found mainly in the medieval period, the sixteenth century, and the twentieth century.

Most literature, perhaps all, combines the two principles, but one usually dominates. The progressive structure of Books I, II, and V of Spenser's *Faerie Queene*, with their heroes, their quests, and their attainments, are "masculine." Books III and IV, which center about

Britomart and a set of damsels in distress, are "feminine." The structure of these central books is interwoven; it juggles time, place, and
characters. No single figure dominates in the way Redcrosse, Guyon,
and Artegall do. And they are concerned with love and desire (although they are denominated the books of chastity and friendship)
rather than with holiness, temperance, and justice, which are transcendent virtues. Book VI is a true synthesis, focusing on Calidore but
also forgetting him for long periods, and giving much loving attention
to the shepherd world and Pastorella. Courtesy, the virtue addressed
in Book VI, is a synthetic virtue, a combination of hierarchy/status/
decorum with democracy/concern for the whole/affection. The climax
of the book, Calidore's vision of the Graces dancing, is a "feminine"
vision, having to do with the inner life and the beauty of experience.

Although it is centered on two male figures, Sidney's *Arcadia* is a
"feminine" work—loosely structured, with incidents and characters
seeming just to pop up and disappear. It is mainly concerned with love
and sex. Appropriately, Pyrocles and Musidorus are disguised in the
dress of illegitimates—one as a woman, the other as a shepherd. Although there are battles and fighting, the action is often comically
described. The heroes seem to have a goal—to marry the princesses,
and then, ostensibly, to return to their own kingdoms and rule, having
learned by then how to be a good prince. But one's sense of the work
is that they are having far too much fun even to think of returning
home, and that their real goal is sexual consummation with the princesses (desire, outlaw feminine) rather than marriage (marriage is a
permanence, and masculine). In fact, no goal is attained in this unfinished work.

The work of Shakespeare may be roughly divided into gender
categories by division into comedy and tragedy. In most of his plays,
however, he attempts either a synthesis of the principles, or an examination of the kinds of worlds that result when one or the other principle is abused, neglected, devalued, or exiled.

The comedies are held in less esteem than the tragedies by critics
of earlier centuries, and some of our own. This is the result of a tradition in which only drama of character is considered *serious* (read legitimate, masculine). Drama of character is always "masculine," even
when its main figure is a woman—as sometimes happens in drama of
the late nineteenth and the twentieth centuries. It is "masculine" because the very notion of individuality is "masculine": the feminine
principle is concerned with community more than with any individual.[2] But Shakespeare never really wrote drama of character, although

Hamlet and *Lear* and *Macbeth* come close. This seems to have been acknowledged in the last few decades.

The comedies and tragedies deal with identical material, as do those plays which are difficult to categorize. The important difference in the two modes is that in tragedy, events are irrevocable; in comedy, they are revocable.[3] Both modes are true to actual experience: we undergo many deaths and departures in our lives before others and we ourselves actually die. We lose, but we replace, we substitute: we go on. This is as profound a truth as that we lose and cannot replace, we die. In tragedy, the loss of a handkerchief results in a death sentence; in comedy, that which is lost will be found.

Shakespeare's comedies and tragedies have similar events. In tragedy, a woman unjustly maligned (Desdemona) dies; in comedy, she (Hero, Hermione) seems to die. In tragedy, a child (Macduff's son) is murdered; in comedy, a child left to die (Perdita) returns. In tragedy, insensitivity and arrogance lead Lear into an irrevocable error; in comedy, heroes may do penance for such qualities, as do the lords in *Love's Labour's Lost*, or Leontes in *The Winter's Tale*. There are conversions and forgiveness in the comedies, rather than bodies strewn about the stage: and which is truer to actual experience? Macbeth and his wife eradicate the inlaw feminine principle from Scotland, which becomes a nightmare state. The values of Venice ignore the inlaw feminine principle, but some of its inhabitants are nevertheless saved by it.

The irrevocable world is one of action; the revocable world is one of language.[4] In actuality, of course, some actions are revocable and some words are not. But the tragedies present mainly actions, like murder or warfare, which cannot be changed, and within the tragedies, language functions as action. What Goneril and Regan *say* to Lear is equivalent to what is *done* to Gloucester. *King Lear* focuses on Lear's sufferings in a way that makes it impossible to forgive those who caused them. Iago's words to Othello have the force of acts, and cannot be undone. Lady Macbeth's words to Macbeth not only fix his determination to kill Duncan, but fix her character irrevocably. The Capulets' words about Juliet when she refuses to marry Paris are instances of dramatic irony, but no less irrevocable for that.

In comedy, on the other hand, the focus is on other parts of experience. Imogen is as badly treated as Lear, and by a variety of characters, but the play focuses on her hope and love and faith, so some of the authors of those sufferings may be forgiven. In comedy, acts are as revocable as language. Indeed, the early comedies concentrate on language as a theme, language as the subject of language.

Through word play, equivocation, malapropism, and imitation and parody of literary styles, the comedies turn language into a major focus. Play with language is equivalent to challenging the masculine principle. "Masculine" minds (even in our own day) believe that words have fixed meanings, that there should be a unity of "heart and tongue," and thus, implicitly, that feelings as well as words can be fixed, made permanent, irrevocable.

Play with language denies all this. It implies doubleness, even duplicity.[5] To say two things at once, or to say and unsay a thing simultaneously; or to pursue words, homonyms, or puns continuously is to deny that there is any right, absolute meaning to words. Play in itself, of any sort, denies the "masculine" faith in purpose and permanence and seriousness; it turns life upside down and mocks the beliefs that are the foundation of Western culture. Language as theme thus suggests that things are not as people say they are; it suggests relativism and ambiguity in human life. And relativism and ambiguity function to permit revocability. There are many conversions, forswearings, penances, and forgivenesses in the comedies, in which even actions of a dire nature are able to be circumvented, and character too is not fixed, may be changed.

Critics sometimes point to an ideal world, in which acts and words and feelings would always be at one, to a union of "heart and tongue," or of appearances and realities. Such ideals ignore the actuality of human experience in a way Shakespeare never did. If every word had the irrevocability of action, if every action were immediately effective, the human race would be largely—and wisely—silent and still. Feelings are rarely—perhaps never—single and simple. No word can be utterly true, no statement beyond the assertion of mortality absolute. No word or act uttered or performed today can be guaranteed to be a true expression tomorrow. And the world would be a grimmer place than it already is if this were demanded of humans.

The early comedies of Shakespeare delight in, exploit, and celebrate the flexibility of language, its multivalence, and the confusions attendant on this. Truth, as defined by a "masculine" culture, is that which stands, which is permanent, which endures. The two poles, the extremes of the gender principles, giving birth and murder, represent actions which cannot be changed although they can be concealed. They are in this sense absolutely true. The tragedies concentrate on words and actions which are true *because* they are irrevocable, and those words and actions lead inevitably to death, the ultimate truth. Comedy, on the other hand, exploits not a linear truth, but a vertical or circular one, inner truth. Through disguise, word play, revocable utterance, and changes in feeling and behavior, comedy presents the multiple truths that make up a human being, a human community. Thus tragedy is constrictive, comedy, expansive.

Shakespearean comedy is feminine: it aims at continuation, procreation; it is concerned with an entire community more than with one individual; it is accepting rather than transcendent, for although it ends with marriage or the promise of marriage, which is a masculine permanency, transcendent in its guarantee of happiness ever after, the plays end with the moment of exaltation, the moment of communal harmony, and do not depict the actual marriage situation.[6] Comedy is circular, tied to nature and eternal recurrence.[7] Northrop Frye and Susanne Langer have described all comedy as circular, tied to nature and community.[8] But all comedy is not the same. Satirical comedy is far less "feminine" than Shakespeare's romantic comedy. Ben Jonson's comedies have linear plots, the male protagonists have stipulated goals, and although a community of people may be focused on, the interest is in their discord rather than their harmony.

In Shakespeare's comedy, the multiple figures have a multiplicity of goals: Toby Belch wants to go on enjoying himself; Bottom and company want to put on a play; Rosalind wants to marry Orlando; Don John wants (like Kierkegaard) to cause difficulties everywhere. On the whole, comic figures want to have pleasure and to survive. No one figure, no one class, dominates the comedies, which present an anarchic world despite the hierarchical class structure within which the characters live.[9] Jaques and Touchstone are as important as Celia and Orlando to the design of As You Like It; the artisans are more important than Theseus and Hippolyta to the design of A Midsummer Night's Dream.

Because they are circular rather than linear, the comedies do not have strong plots. A plot is a causal sequence, one step leading irrevocably to another. The comedies move by elaboration, like bits of mosaic slowly accumulating around a central image or idea. The two plot lines of A Midsummer Night's Dream—that surrounding the four lovers, and that concerning the power struggle between Titania and Oberon—provide only an armature for the real action of the play. (This is true also of Hamlet, in which the plot, Hamlet's obligation to avenge his father's murder, occupies less attention than the events and reflections it gives rise to. The four "problem plays" are all written in mixed modes, which is one reason they are problems. The tragedy, Hamlet, contains much circular material; the comedies—Troilus and

Cressida, All's Well That Ends Well, and *Measure for Measure*—all
contain an amount of plotting unusual for a Shakespearean comedy.)

In tragedy, even those tragedies that focus on a love story, the
focus and the weight are on power.[10] Different kinds of power may
war against each other; or the major figure may have an external goal
that requires power or authority; or various figures or factions may
make war on each other fighting for the single seat of power. Tragedy
has plot.[11] It may also have subplots, but these are parallels or illumi-
nations of the major plot, rather than elaborations around themes.
And because tragedy is linear, externally oriented, and concerned with
the individual (individualism is the extremest form of transcendence of
nature), it is necessarily disintegrative. The paradox lies within the
masculine principle itself, which, cherishing the individual and his
transcendent goal of establishing something within time that will outlast time, inevitably leads to death.

The world of tragedy is hierarchical, both in the political structure
which is a backdrop to the characters, and in the interest taken in the
characters. One figure dominates, the others take their places in ranks
beneath him. The major figure acts out and suffers the whole range of
human feeling possible to him, thus exemplifying human fallibility,
capacity, and suffering. He is the image of the human in a discordant
world. Because he is individual, he does not and cannot fit comfortably
into comedic community. Even when a tragic hero is an ultimate
embodiment of the values of his community, as is Coriolanus, he finds
himself at odds with it.

Comedy is expansive. It permits entertainment of the most serious
questions without necessarily entailing serious consequences. It operates to open up, to allow a terrible thing to be, then not to be, and so
permits consideration of the terrible without the terror that usually
accompanies it. Tragedy is constrictive. It concentrates on a single
course of action, a single mode of being, and therefore presents a more
sharply defined world than comedy, the multiple focus of which makes
for luminosity, like concentric haloes around a sun. Tragedy presents
the terrible consequences of actions or feelings which might not, in
other circumstances, lead to such consequences, and therefore arouses
the terror involved in being alive. That terror is alleviated by the
knowledge that these terrible consequences are happening to someone
else, and a fiction, at that.

The history plays are primarily "masculine" because their subject
matter is power-in-the-world. But they contain more "feminine" elements than the tragedies because they are not concerned only with

one character but with the ongoing life of a society which does endure. The problem plays are also mixtures, as I said earlier. But mixed modes were not comfortable for Shakespeare, raised in a world in which the gender principles and their formal equivalents were seen as widely separated.

II

RECEIVED IDEAS

———————————

3

Power:
The First Tetralogy

Henry VI, *Parts One, Two,* and *Three*;
Richard III

To trace a conception or conceptual framework through an author's work, it is well to begin where he began (as far as we can determine that). The *Henry* VI plays were among the first that Shakespeare wrote, and were unquestionably his earliest extant noncomedic dramatic efforts. Thus, they are important in providing clues to the value structure with which Shakespeare began his playwriting career.

The subject of the tetralogy as a whole has been a matter of debate. Since no hero dominates all four plays, and indeed, none dominates even one of the *Henry* VI plays, the idea has arisen that an abstract respublica is the true "hero" of the play.[1] But John Danby argues that in all Shakespeare's work, "character as such must be subordinated to the 'idea' which ensures the organic coherence of the whole."[2] There is a single idea animating all four plays—the idea of legitimacy.[3]

In traditional ways of thinking about government, a basic assumption is that one person, class, or group must take command or a state will fall into anarchy, which is seen as chaos. These people are the full legitimates: they make the law (in their own favor) and enforce it. They possess the power of force and authority. But to some degree, neither force nor authority is really theirs—it must be granted to them by others. No one can maintain rule unless this basic deference occurs; no one can rule long without the assent of the people, whether this assent is gained through fear or approval. (People, in this context, does not necessarily mean the masses of people; it can refer to the lesser legitimates who uphold the king or president or oligarchic group.)

Different cultures have different standards for determining what constitutes legitimacy. In Biblical times, direction was given by people with moral force and vision, like Deborah and Samuel. In the time of Abraham or Odysseus, legitimacy accrued to those who owned more than others—more sheep or goats, more weapons. Often, legitimacy was seized by those with physical power, the war leaders. But eventually, as cultures became more stable, legitimacy became a matter of bloodlines. It was inherited, not earned.

But inherited legitimacy offers the poorest guarantee that leaders will have the qualities valued by the society they govern. It is also lamentably subject to biological failure: a ruler may die without an heir, with an incompetent one, or with only an infant, as is the case in 1 Henry VI. When this happens, how do humans decide to confer legitimacy? The first tetralogy is an examination of this question.

The question is one Shakespeare continued to probe throughout his life. L. C. Knights writes: "a wholesome political order is not something arbitrary and imposed, but an expression of relationship between particular persons within an organic society."[4] He adds, in a different work, "order—especially order dependent on absolute rule and unquestioned value: essential order, simultaneously political and more-than-political, was something that needed [Shakespeare's] full mature powers to define and assert."[5]

The proper or happiest way to order a society, whether approached from the top down (power, government) or the bottom up (the family, community), is the major concern of Shakespeare's work.

1 Henry VI

1 Henry VI opens with a lament. It is on one level a lament for the death of Henry V, who was a great warrior, a king, and a father. But the lament hardly fits a mere mortal, albeit an important one: the language suggests that what has died is legitimacy itself. (The shaky origins of Henry's legitimacy are not touched on in discussion of him, in this play.) The lords who commemorate him are the most powerful

men in England, and what they demand is that the cosmos itself recognize the catastrophe this death represents: "Hung be the heavens with black, yield day to night!" (I, i, 1). Bedford demands that the "bad revolting stars" that allowed Henry's death be "scourge[d]." Such references imply analogues: the death of Jesus and the fall of the revolting angel Lucifer from heaven.

More has died than just a man. An age that miraculously combined power with virtue has ended: "England ne'er had a king until his time: / Virtue he had, deserving to command; / . . . He ne'er lift up his hand but conquered" (I, i, 8–9, 16). The nobles question the reason for this unhappy termination: is it mere mischance, or is it the French who have toppled the giant by "magic verses" recited by "subtile-witted . . . Conjurers and sorcerers" (I, i, 26, 24, 25)? This language associates the French with the "revolting stars"—the devil—and with magic. Within twenty-seven lines, the battle lines of value are drawn.

The English represent a moral position in which God, power, prowess, courage, virtue, and legitimacy are identified: the masculine principle. The French undermine, are subtle and devilish, and use magic: outlaw feminine principle. The war is between the two most powerful areas of the gender principles. But there are two wars: one against France, and one within England. The latter is, on a philosophical level, a struggle to define legitimacy.

Within two more speeches, this struggle becomes overt. Winchester, the Bishop, draws an explicit parallel between Henry V and God, and between the French and the forces of ungodliness, and claims the power of the Church empowered Henry. Gloucester scoffs, claiming that the Church undermined Henry because it likes only "an effeminate prince" (I, i, 35), one it can dominate. Winchester retorts that Gloucester's wife dominates him more than either God or Church. Gloucester attacks, accusing the Bishop of loving "the flesh" (I, i, 41). Bedford tells them both to cease, lest only weeping women and babies be left in England.

There is considerable mention of women and feminacy in these speeches, more than one imagines there would have been in actuality. But it is part of, and develops, the value structure that will dominate the play. What Gloucester and Winchester are accusing each other of is being under domination of either a woman or the feminine principle. Whenever the feminine principle dominates (has *worldly* power) in Shakespeare, it is outlaw. Bedford reminds the men of the other aspect, the inlaw, the supposed end of power struggles.

The remainder of scene i brings in wave after wave of news of English defeats, reinforcing Bedford's warning. The way the news is delivered and received makes us feel as if England were in danger from a foreign invader, and were not the invader itself. The English are in dire straits: the ideal father (God) is dead, and with him the supreme power (force and righteousness) of the masculine principle. He has left only an infant son. The two most powerful men in the kingdom, Gloucester and Winchester, are to some degree subject to the feminine principle, and thus lack the legitimacy of a sovereign. The enemy, France, possesses the outlaw power of magic. The next scene, in which Joan introduces herself to the Dauphin, expands the associations.

Shakespeare's handling of Joan is troubling. It is true that the British of the Renaissance saw Joan as an enemy (and most unforgivably, a successful one) and a witch. But this does not fully account for Shakespeare's treatment of the character.

An important way of deducing Shakespeare's intentions in these four plays is to study his departure from his sources. There are many, which is significant since he was writing history plays. Such embroidering on fact was of course not uncommon in the Renaissance; nevertheless, Shakespeare's departures and inventions are not mainly stylistic—that is, compressions or omissions made for the sake of dramatic unity and force. They are, rather, ideological, creating associations he wished to make.

Shakespeare departed from his sources in depicting not only Joan, but also Gloucester and Winchester. Gloucester had a wife noted for her pride, but he also had a tumultuous sexual life, which does not argue domination by his wife. Shakespeare wished to play up the "good Duke Humphrey": thus he made the man meeker than he was, and omitted the lurid facts of his sexual life. He is a good man, but under the domination of a woman, which is to say, not good enough.

Neither Hall nor Holinshed suggests any hint of sexual corruption or bribery about Winchester (nor any remorse on his deathbed beyond sorrow over not attaining more power—in contrast to Shakespeare's depiction of his guilt-ridden death in 2 *Henry VI*, III, iii). But the playwright wished to show villainy in the Catholic prelate, so invented a sexual tarnishing. Sex is clearly a sign of evil.

Promiscuous sexuality is one of the major characteristics of Shakespeare's Joan, whose portrait, says Geoffrey Bullough, "goes far beyond anything found in Hall or Holinshed or in the Burgundian chronicler Monstrelet."[6] Both Hall and Holinshed declare Joan a virgin, although there is some sarcasm in Holinshed's description of her as having "great semblance of chastitie both of bodie and behaviour, the name of Jesus in hir mouth about all hir businesses." [7] The act of Joan's which seems, from Holinshed's account, most to have outraged her English captors and her chronicler is her wearing of men's clothing. [8]

Shakespeare's Joan is coarse and crude in language and sensibility. As soon as she appears, sexual innuendoes begin. She temporizes with the Dauphin's instant desire; Alanson comments, "Doubtless he shrives this woman to her smock" (I, ii, 119). Although he suspects the Dauphin's sexual intentions, he places the responsibility for them on Joan: "These women are shrewd tempters with their tongues" (I, ii, 123). Talbot no sooner hears her name than he puns on it: "Pucelle or puzzel" (I, iv, 107). At his first encounter with her, he conjures her as "devil or devil's dam" and as "witch" (I, v, 5–6). Burgundy calls her a "trull" (II, ii, 28). The continuing alignment of the French with magic, the British with God and righteousness, could be written off as understandable patriotism, or chauvinism. The British lost their war: some explanation is necessary. But the magical, diabolical means used by the French are also continually associated with women and with sex. (This continues even after Joan is dead.) The subsurface, "mythic" war waged in this play is a war against women, identified with sexuality: it is a war against the outlaw feminine principle. It is a paradoxical war, as well, for the gender principles, as they are divided, insist that women *cannot* possess physical prowess and courage. The only battle Joan is shown as winning is a duel with the French Dauphin. We are told that Joan vanquishes the English, but we never see her doing it. In her first encounter with Talbot, she flees to help the Dauphin; during the night attack, she and her party flee at the mere mention of Talbot's name. At Rouen, she wins by "policy"; and when Talbot challenges the French to combat after the loss of Rouen, he pointedly excludes Joan from the discussion, refusing to speak with a "railing Hecate" (III, ii, 64). Joan's persuasion of Burgundy is essentially a verbal seduction which feels to him as if he'd been "bewitch'd" (III, iii, 58). And although we are told that it is Joan with her magic who has changed the English fortunes, Talbot, when he exhorts himself to action, and lists his enemies, omits Joan's name.

That this handling has a peculiar bias, and certainly clouds historical reality, could also be written off. Humans still write this way. War movies frequently show American enemies in World War II, whether German or Japanese, to be stupid, silly, fanatic, and absurd, to the point where one wonders why it took so long to win that war. But this paradox—the attribution of great power to "feminine" figures, simultaneous with the denial of any worldly power—is the pattern of treatment of all the female figures in the *Henry* VI trilogy.[9] The real enemy is not France, or even dominant women: it is sexuality and "anarchy" —the urge located within the outlaw feminine principle to overthrow all hierarchies, all legitimacy. Thus, it functions organically in a play which seeks to define the grounds of "true" legitimacy.

The allusions surrounding Joan associate her with what is pagan, dark, and female.[10] But her character is most denigrated by two scenes that have nothing to do with witchcraft or whoredom. Both of these scenes are Shakespeare's inventions, and one of them totally reverses the known facts. In actuality, Bedford presided over Joan's trial and her execution by burning. But Shakespeare shows him sitting in a chair, ill and dying, being taunted from the walls of Rouen by a crassly triumphant Joan. The second invented scene is one in which Joan repudiates her father. The father is shown as loving and heartbroken: he offers to die with his daughter. Joan denies his parentage, claiming a "gentler" descent. The father's final curse and consent to her execution place an almost divine seal on the justice of her fate.

One point of both scenes is to stamp England's enemy with every moral obloquy possible. But both scenes involve an identical act: the denial of the authority, legitimacy, and worthiness—lovableness, even —of the father figure. Joan challenges the very notion of legitimacy, like the outlaw feminine principle of which she is a part. That such challenge is in some way connected with females in general is supported by two scenes which have frequently been seen as extraneous to the play as a whole.[11]

The first is the encounter between the Countess of Auvergne and the hero Talbot. The Countess, comparing herself with Tomyris, a barbaric queen who killed Cyrus in battle, attempts to destroy Talbot, not in battle, but by treachery. So generous is the hero that he forgives her. Since one does not readily forgive enemies who offer real threat, this is another example of simultaneous attribution and denial of power. It is also another example of a woman attempting to challenge and destroy the "father."

The second is the scene between Suffolk and Margaret.[12] Within it, Margaret appears as a beautiful, spirited, modest, and proper young woman—an exemplar of the inlaw feminine principle. The irony of her behavior does not function within 1 *Henry* VI; it does not appear until 2 *Henry* VI, in which Margaret takes over the role Joan plays within this part of the trilogy. The implication—even young women who appear "inlaw" are not to be trusted—is evident. And this scene is in turn paralleled by 3 *Henry VI*, III, ii, in which Elizabeth Grey appears, acting as virtuous and modest as Margaret had earlier, aware of her place in a way Edward is not.

Not just women, but love and marriage are seen as corrupting. Margaret claims she has a "pure unspotted heart, / Never yet *taint* with love" (V, iii, 182–183); the young Henry VI sees marriage as "wanton dalliance with a paramour" (V, i, 23), and explains that he was "never yet *attaint* / With any passion of inflaming love" (V, v, 81–82). (Italics mine.) It is Gloucester, who believes a royal marriage should be a political and commercial arrangement, who will prove to be right, rather than Suffolk, who (for whatever purposes) argues that marriage should be "a matter of more worth / Than to be dealt in by attorneyship" (V, v, 55–56), and urges the pleasures of the nuptial bed. And it is the lust aroused in Henry by Suffolk's words that causes him to insist on the disastrous alliance.

The external war fought in this play, then, is waged by the masculine principle against the feminine. But the nourishing and supportive qualities of the latter principle are essential to human felicity and stability. If women are false, sexual, and aggressive, the compassionate qualities they are supposed to uphold must be taken over by men. Thus the external war is connected to the internal one. For the problem of legitimacy is connected with the relations between men and women. Since Shakespeare's women can never attain legitimacy, they are given to undermine it. In doing so, they betray their inlaw aspect. But both (male) legitimacy and the inlaw feminine principle can be upheld by men operating in a tradition of father to son.

The father-son relation is central in *1 Henry VI*.[13] In this relation is found the core of legitimacy, the passage from one male to another of virtue, courage, and prowess. There is a set of father figures in the play: Salisbury, Bedford, and Talbot, the hero warriors, and Mortimer. Each of them is free from the taint of female domination; each supplies in himself the necessary "feminine" qualities: "A braver soldier never couched lance, / A gentler heart did never sway in court" (III, ii, 134–135), Talbot says of the dead Bedford. Bedford has remained with his men, ill as he is, to hearten them; he suffers silently Joan's mockery. Salisbury's death is mourned in terms as hyperbolic as those used about Henry V; exequies are promised Bedford as well. Each warrior is a "father" to his men, and to the other warriors, who seem to gain strength from each other's heroism.

It is Talbot, however, who is the greatest hero, and who unites the gender principles most fully. Some critics have seen the opposition of Talbot and Joan as the major one of the play. Such a reading is inadequate to support all five acts, but there is no question that the major opposition of the play is between the principles the two represent. Talbot is the central and exemplary figure. He is the standard, the sturdy Briton whose patriotism, courage, control, and implicit sexual purity never waver. His main scenes occur near the center of the play, surrounded by the demise of Henry V, and the foreshadowed ascendency of Margaret. Those scenes are framed by the squabbling of his countrymen (IV, i) and the mockery of the French (IV, vii), and function much as what C. S. Lewis, writing about *The Faerie Queene*, called the "shrine" cantos, emblematic episodes which enrich and illuminate the surrounding material.[14]

Leo Kirschbaum—and others—have pointed out that the scenes from IV, v, 16, in which Talbot and his son begin to argue about John's remaining in the battle, through to IV, vii, 32, when both father and son are dead, are written in rhymed couplets.[15] The verse form sets off this section and raises it to a different level from the surrounding material, indeed from the rest of the play. Its formality turns the scenes into ritual.

This "shrine" section makes explicit one form of true legitimacy, the succession from father to son of courage, honor, and heroic ideals. The relationship is similar to that of God and Jesus; the woman who provides it is, like Mary, a vessel, passing from father to son an identical spirit. If anything other than the identical spirit is passed, the honor of the woman is impeached. John proves his legitimacy—he urges his father not to make a "bastard and a slave" of him by ordering him from the battle—by saving his father, and dying in the act. Both are eventually wounded, and Talbot (like Aeneas carrying his father out of the flames of Troy) carries his son in the womb/tomb of his arms, and dies with him, although not before predicting for himself and his son, transcendence of mortality like that of Daedalus and Icarus.

The importance of this segment of the play to Shakespeare's intentions is underscored by the wide deviations in his version and that of his sources. The battle in France was fought by Talbot and two of his sons—one a bastard, the other, possibly a stepson or son-in-law.[16] The bastard son was killed at Bordeaux; the other son died twenty years before Talbot. And there is no basis in fact for the English failure to relieve Talbot.

Shakespeare's departures from his sources function to "purify" the warrior-hero, and to sacramentalize the relation between father and son, to define one sort of legitimacy.

There are other father-son successions in the play. The gunner has a true son, who obeys him eagerly and uses initiative, and is successful in killing Salisbury. Because they are French, however, they operate from ambush rather than in open encounter: this time his sources and Shakespeare's associations are in accord. Henry VI, son of a French mother, does not have his father's quality, and is destined to lose all that "Henry born at Monmouth" gained.

Another father-son succession is the oblique one of Mortimer and York (who, like other survivors, promises Mortimer proper funerary ceremonies). Mortimer's long recital of his titles and successions emphasizes that York is as legitimate through bloodlines as is Henry VI. The ambiguity of legitimacy is underscored by Shakespeare's placing of the scene between Mortimer and Richard immediately after the disputatious Temple Garden scene.

And the consequences of disputed legitimacy are the loss of clear authority and thus the loss of civil peace. The rebellious outlaw feminine principle is rampant throughout England and France. A resentful, insubordinate sentinel is responsible for the success of Talbot's night attack; at its conclusion, the French nobles bicker about blame. Winchester and Gloucester (as well as their servingmen), York and Somerset, Vernon and Basset all quarrel because when there is no clear authority, every man is his own rabbi. Henry VI, still young in this play, can only "prevail, if prayers might prevail" (III, i, 67) and offer "sighs and tears" (III, i, 108).

As *1 Henry VI* ends, the hero-fathers are all dead, and a son has attained maturity. But it is already clear that this son is not at all like *his* hero-father.

2 Henry VI

Although father figures exist in this play, something is wrong in their relations with their sons. And it is sons—brothers—who are the focus of *2 Henry VI*. Henry is beginning to function as king, but like his uncles (fathers), he is tainted by subjection to a woman and by his own "effeminacy," his piety.

The play opens with the celebration of a marriage which is supposed to produce "England's happiness" and a "contracted peace" (I, i, 37, 40) with France. But peace itself is called "effeminate" at the conclusion of the preceding play, by York (*1H6*, V, iv, 107). And this peace is denounced by Gloucester as shameful: British losses in France are made to seem entirely consequent to the marriage of Henry and Margaret. Again, as in the opening of *1 Henry VI*, the British identify themselves and their cause with Jesus: "Now by the death of Him that died for all, / These counties were the keys of Normandy" (I, i, 113–114), Salisbury cries, and Warwick grieves, swearing "Mort Dieu!" (I, i, 123).

In this section of the trilogy, the trend begun in the middle of the first part is continued: not only women, but lower-class men rebel against "authority," and peers contest against each other. Although there are two main factions, Henry's and York's, each person is really a faction to himself. Various characters combine and ally, then abandon their allies, announce private purposes. The males bicker among each other in "masculine" self-assertion; the women challenge male supremacy; the commoners rebel against the nobles. What is under attack by all of them is either legitimacy itself or the legitimacy of another rather than the self: for most of the characters, the latter is nearer to the point.

The sons in this play are either spurious or unlike their fathers. Henry VI is his father's opposite; despite allusions to God and Christ, Aeneas and Anchises, Cade's claim to a relation to Mortimer is false and ludicrous; and Clifford, whose father was a hero like Talbot, has none of the Talbot delicacy, and vows a cruelty like that of Medea in revenge for his father's death. (Since Medea is female and not noted for preserving members of her family, she seems an inappropriate allusion for Clifford to make. The allusion serves, however, to link Clifford's rage for revenge to the outlaw feminine principle.)

Horner and Peter are another destructive "father-son" team, as are Winchester and Gloucester, whose avuncular relation is stressed. Something has gone wrong in the line of transmission.

The action whirls around the still center that is Henry VI. Some readers believe that Shakespeare saw the King as a saintly ideal.[17] It is true that Henry VI is an exemplar of the inlaw feminine principle: he urges harmony, piety, meekness, and is himself often willingly subordinate to others; it is also true that elsewhere Shakespeare upholds as divine this gender principle. But it is impossible that Shakespeare could have intended Henry as an ideal figure. He is weak, easily swayed, mealymouthed, whining, and uses his piety to evade responsibility. Until his final scenes, he lacks totally the authority of a Cordelia, the enduring steadfastness of a Hermione. At the end of the play, he represents a moral ideal, perhaps, but not a political one.

The scene in which Simpcox appears claiming to have been cured of blindness is usually interpreted as intending to show Gloucester's wisdom. It also, however, shows the King's real blindness. Henry believes Simpcox utterly and instantly. Henry's pious mouthings are insistences on noninvolvement. In the midst of a furious argument among Gloucester, Suffolk, and the Queen, Henry says: "I prithee peace, / Good Queen, and whet not on these furious peers, / For blessed are the peacemakers on earth" (II, i, 32–34). He professes great love to Humphrey, yet holds himself apart when the Queen and the nobles attack the Duke in I, iii. He claims his conscience tells him Gloucester is innocent of the charges brought against him, and weeps when Gloucester is taken away, but again he refuses to involve himself in the power struggle. And after the emotional discovery that Humphrey has been murdered, in the middle of a tumultuous argument between Suffolk and Warwick, Henry pronounces piously and self-approvingly, "What stronger breastplate than a heart untainted!" (III, ii, 232).

Shakespeare does not paint a respectful portrait of Henry VI (although he omits mention of Henry's mad periods), but he also darkens York's character somewhat.[18] There has been considerable discussion of the playwright's views on kingship, assertions that he found the murder or overthrow of an anointed king a crime of cosmic proportions.[19] Careful analysis of all the plays in which such an act occurs, however, seems to indicate that he slanted his attitude towards such acts according to the central idea of his drama.[20] In this case, it seems, he implies that Henry's overthrow was inevitable. Softening Henry's inadequacies, but making him sound like a dithering idiot, darkening York's character somewhat, but presenting the Duke's claim to the throne without scant or irony, Shakespeare avoids bias. There is truth in York's claim that he would be a better king than Henry. What Shakespeare is working towards in this tetralogy is a definition of legitimacy that is not limited to, but synthesizes claims based on bloodlines, prowess, or morality. True legitimacy consists in possession of all three. Neither Henry nor York possessess all three: neither does anyone else in the play.[21]

The character who comes closest is Humphrey. He is in some ways a parallel to Henry: he is dedicated to the "public good" (I, i, 199), "the profit of the land" (I, i, 204), and he has a faith in earthly justice that parallels Henry's faith in divine justice—he tells his wife, "I must

offend before I be attainted" and insists he is not in danger because he
is "loyal, true, and crimeless" (II, iv, 59, 63). Like Henry in 3 *Henry*
VI, Gloucester is willing to die if his death "might make this island
happy" (III, i, 148). Humphrey is more forceful and more irritable than
his nephew, and might be a better king. However, Humphrey (also like
his nephew) is under the power of a woman.

Although Eleanor's downfall in fact preceded Gloucester's by
some years, Shakespeare links the two. Andrew Cairncross finds the
mention of Eleanor's pride and Gloucester's earlier affair(s) in *1 Henry*
VI "dramatically unnecessary," but they foreshadow the events of
2 Henry VI, and provide added texture to the struggle of gender principles in the first play.[22] The influence of women is seen throughout
the trilogy as invariably malign. Eleanor is no sooner condemned than
Henry asks Gloucester to give up his staff of office. (Indeed, Eleanor
not only dabbles in magic, but utters treasonous statements; Gloucester chides her for this, but is quickly brought back into line: see I, ii.)
Eleanor is an outlaw, like Lady Macbeth, ambitious for power-in-the-
world. Her presumption, like Joan's, is explicit:

> Where I a man, a duke, and next of blood,
> I would remove these tedious stumbling-blocks,
> And smooth my way upon their headless necks;
> And, being a woman, I will not be slack
> To play my part in Fortune's pageant. (I, ii, 63–67)

Shakespeare's handling of Margaret is similar to his handling of
Eleanor, but more extensive. As he did with Joan, he frequently departs from his sources in depicting her. Hall praised Margaret highly,
and described her as the true ruler of the country.[23] There is no suggestion beyond mutual respect and affection in the relation of Margaret and Suffolk. Shakespeare's elaboration of an affair is based on
one phrase—that Suffolk was the Queen's "dearling."[24] As he did to
Joan, Shakespeare omits reference to Margaret's real power and ability, and he "taints" her with sexual "impurity." Margaret is powerful,
but she is not powerful—she works through treachery and "policy,"
much as Joan worked through magic and policy.

And again, it is difficult to understand why Margaret, as she is
depicted, should constitute such a threat. She nags the King; she tries
to speak for him and is reprimanded by Gloucester; her force is shown
mainly in nasty remarks in support of Suffolk. Such behavior is hardly
that of the authoritative and commanding woman Hall describes. Hall
asserts that it was Margaret who excluded Gloucester from power, but

Shakespeare makes Margaret a mere shrill echo to Henry in II, iii. Since it is Henry who removes Gloucester from power, his grief over Humphrey's later arrest and his attack on Margaret for causing it (another unhistorical addition) are somewhat undercut.

Nor can Margaret work alone: she seems a groupie to Suffolk's party. In III, i, Winchester, Suffolk, York, and the Queen conspire to murder Gloucester. As they seal their pact, York says, "and now we three have spoke it, / It skills not greatly who impugns our doom" (280–281): since they are four, one is being overlooked. It is surely Margaret. Warwick later dares to order her, the Queen, to silence. Nor can she defend herself: Suffolk does it. The picture of Margaret that emerges from this play is that of a shrewish busybody who likes to imagine herself as moving events. However, her portrait deepens after Suffolk's death, as her contempt for the King grows more obvious.

Women who dare to move into the masculine principle—power-in-the-world—are dangerous, but they are not. The same is true of the commoners (men illegitimate in a world of men). One difference in the Queen-Suffolk faction and Gloucester lies in their treatment of the poor and humble. Gloucester has offered respect and compassion to the commoners' petitions: "Pity was all the fault that was in me; / For I should melt at an offender's tears, / And lowly words were ransom for their fault" (III, i, 125–127). The Queen and Suffolk tear up the petitions and dismiss the pleaders. It is the commoners' rage that causes Suffolk's banishment, and his own arrogance is largely responsible for his death. The rebellion of the commons and the execution of Suffolk by the pirates are morally, ideologically connected with Jack Cade and his rebellion.

The Jack Cade scenes are the center of this play as the Talbot scenes were the center of 1 Henry VI (and they occur in approximately the same place). Again, Shakespeare departs widely from his sources. Hall describes Cade as "sober in communicacion, wyse in disputyng, arrogant in hart, and styfe in his opinion." He was "subtill": and promised those who followed him "libertie (which the common people more affect and desire, rather than reasonable obedience, and due conformitie)." When Cade entered London, he prohibited "to all men, Murder, Rape, or Robbery."[25] In spite of this, Lord Say and James Cromer were killed; the rebels did take over and set fire to houses.

Shakespeare's Jack Cade is as coarse and presumptuous as Joan; he is also a buffoon, stupid, ludicrous, and deluded. The very men who follow him make jokes at his expense. He promises that "all the realm shall be in common . . . when I am king" (IV, ii, 68–70). He kills a man simply because he can write, and promises to kill all lords, all gentlemen (all legitimates). Like Joan, he repudiates his true parents and pretends to be of noble birth.

The warring elements of 1 Henry VI are extended and elaborated in 2 Henry VI, but they are the same elements. The father figures in this play are less noble, and all of them die—Winchester, Gloucester, and Clifford. In place of the exalted eulogies of 1 Henry VI, however, there are only Henry's tears for Humphrey, his pieties over the body of the guilt-ridden Winchester, and young Clifford's ugly vow of revenge. Suffolk too is dead, and the civil war in progress: war between "brothers" is now physical as well as verbal. The masculine principle is in contest with itself.

At the same time, the feminine principle is in revolt. Women strive for mastery (ominously but unsuccessfully); the lower classes rebel (ominously but unsuccessfully). And the proper leader, Henry, cannot deal with this situation.

The scene in the garden of Alexander Iden is sometimes seen as providing the mean in this play; sometimes it is Gloucester's, sometimes Henry's beliefs.[26] All three do provide a mean of sorts, but all three are ineffectual. Iden kills the intruder, but his pastoral ideal is fragile, and can be invaded. Males who uphold the inlaw feminine principle in this play, like the females who uphold it (sometimes with male assistance) in later plays, are seen as morally excellent, but politically inadequate. The "shrine" scenes are those featuring Jack Cade, who is exemplary in a negative way in 2 Henry VI as Talbot is exemplary in a positive way in 1 Henry VI. When clear legitimacy is doubted, when authority is not granted respect, even the worms rebel. In 1 Henry VI, Shakespeare provided a model for proper grounds for legitimacy in Talbot and his son. In this play, he demonstrates with increasing force, the necessity for such a quality.

3 Henry VI

An ideal and exemplary father-son tradition, postulated in 1 Henry VI, gives way in 2 Henry VI to a contentious rivalry in which the political "sons"—the lower classes—rebel against the upper classes, which are supposed to be benevolently paternal, like Gloucester, but are not. Father figures dies, brothers war on each other. In the final part of the trilogy, not only brothers but even fathers and sons battle against each other. The basic unit of legitimacy has turned murderous. *3 Henry VI* is a play in which, as Tillyard points out, all decencies are abandoned, and even children are murdered.[27] David Riggs demonstrates that there is no longer any talk of justice and rightness (although there is of rights), no more praise for heroism: "the chief oratorical forms are the *vituperatio* and the lament."[28]

In fact, Shakespeare shows the characters of the drama as behaving even worse than they actually did.[29] *3 Henry VI* presents a nightmare world so hideous it is capable of breeding a Richard, who will incarnate its values and take it to its full degradation in the last play in the tetralogy.

The first scene is an argument about legitimacy and succession. Henry insists he will retain the crown, but agrees to make York his heir, cutting off his son. (This, although in *2 Henry VI*, Henry has protested he longs to be a subject, not a king.)

This wrong to his son enrages Clifford, Warwick, and Northumberland, who calls the act "unmanly" (I, i, 186). Henry himself sees it as unnatural, but shrugs it off: "Be it as it may" (I, i, 194). Margaret immediately accuses him of being an unnatural father and divorces herself from him.

Henry's failure to maintain proper succession is immediately followed by a contrast, as York's sons insist that he break his oath and press his claim, and that is followed by Clifford's hideous murder of a child, Rutland, in vengeance for his own father's death. The next scene shows Margaret taunting the captured York with a handkerchief stained with Rutland's blood, and the ugly murder of York. Thus the entire first act, as cruel a set of scenes as can be found in Shakespeare, focuses on parents and children, on succession and lack of it.

Henry continues to act the wimp, wringing his hands over his broken oath while Margaret and Clifford prepare to attack the town of York. But when Clifford urges him to fight for his son's right, Henry answers, for the first time in the trilogy, with dignity and force. He asserts that ill means poison their ends, and that some ends are not worth the means used to achieve them. This is a turning point in his characterization, although not a complete one: Henry goes on being blind and self-absorbed to some degree right until the end of his life. For instance, late in the play, Exeter warns Henry that Edward may be able to seduce enough soldiers away from Henry to defeat his forces. The King responds with his usual blind complacency: he insists that his "meed" has won him "fame"; his pity, mildness, and mercy, he claims, have been extended to the unworthy people. "Why should they love Edward more than me?" (IV, viii, 38–47) he asks. But within three lines, Henry's forces are vanquished and he himself captured by Edward. This is a clear comment on his statements: the virtues Henry represents are admirable, and without them there is tyranny. But they are inadequate.

The "shrine," or emblematic scene in this play is Henry sitting on the molehill. It is a molehill rather than a throne—a molehill like the one York stood on when he was killed. Henry watches the alternations of the battle with total detachment: "To whom God will, there be the victory" (II, v, 15). He expresses the wish that he could relinquish his position and live as a shepherd. The pastoral tradition in England always opposed the country to the court. The pastoral ideal is a moral arrangement which makes the inlaw feminine principle dominant over the masculine. It assumes relinquishment of power, wealth, and personal assertiveness, setting in their place the humble contentment of life close to nature, love, and the reflective life (usually expressed in song). Henry's speech emphasizes the atemporality of the feminine principle, for although he concentrates on time ("How many hours, How many days, So many hours, So many weeks, So many years") he really asserts timelessness, the cyclical time of nature, simple continuation.[30]

Henry's speech explicates the ends of life—continuation, felicity, the pleasure of sensation (shade of a hawthorn bush), and the ability to trust which guarantees the ability to "rest" and to "contemplate" (II, v, 23–40). It is also, however, totally self-involved: around him swirl the events of the battle, which will perhaps determine the fate of his son, as well as many other sons, and Henry sits thinking about his own idyllic dream.

Rudely bringing him face-to-face with reality, the set piece that is an emblem for the civil war shows a son who has killed his father, a father who has killed his son. Henry's reaction is typically self-involved, but it seems to change him, for in the next scene in which he appears, having returned from Scotland out of love of England, he is a somewhat different man. He has a quiet dignity; he accepts that he is "a man at least" (III, i, 57), using a different definition of manhood from anyone else in the play. A little later, he acknowledges his inability to govern, and gives the reins of the kingdom over to Warwick and Clarence.

He shows an ability to see through the surfaces of events, and prophesies accurately. He sees Richard's intentions and predicts his malevolent future. Yet, poor man, even this is undercut by Richard's spirited, mock-surprised comment as the King's blood flows: "What? will the aspiring blood of Lancaster / Sink in the ground? I thought it would have mounted" (V, vi, 61–62).

The shift in the characterization of Henry is pivotal in the play. The first part of the trilogy has a clear standard, the legitimacy of the heroic, masculine line as exemplified by Talbot and John. It is undermined by destructive, underhanded women and by "effeminate" or contentious men. There is clear knowledge of right (and thus, of rights): honor is a greater good than power, but the greatest good is the two combined.

2 Henry VI shows a world unsure of right—and therefore of rights. Authority (Henry) is undermined by evil, destructive women and its own "effeminacy." Henry is virtuous, but cannot handle power; those who can are not virtuous. Humphrey emerges as the most admirable figure in the play, suggesting that a new set of values is being introduced—humanitarianism combined with willingness to hold power. But even he is too naive, too "feminine" to gain control, for he is a man who, like his nephew, can be dominated by a woman.

In 3 Henry VI, among all the competing claims of legitimacy, in fact only power matters—power as might, force, rather than authority. Thus in the three plays, three different standards for legitimacy are tried—and found inadequate. In the world of might, there is no mercy, no concern with moral right, no thought of "feminine" ends (thus the emphasis on the murder of children).

In the midst of this, Henry takes on a higher stature. He begins to assert real values, rather than utter pious formulas of disengagement, and to maintain them in the face of force. His values are the opposite of those the world around him holds. He is destroyed, but he will remain in memory. His values will combine with Gloucester's humanitarianism and the values of the hero-warriors of 1 Henry VI to produce the fully legitimate king: Richmond, the first Tudor king.

There are important shifts in the conception of women in this play, also, as shown in the character of Margaret. No longer the shrewish, sexual, intruding busybody she was in 2 Henry VI, now that Suffolk is dead, she has moved into some authority and control. She openly announces her contempt for Henry and divorces him (verbally). She is concerned now only with the future of her son: she has become a full mother figure. But since she also dares to move into the realm of power-in-the-world, she is steeped in the evil Shakespeare associated with such behavior.

To see Shakespeare's attitudes, it is helpful to examine his sources.

Hall reports that the nobles in unison worked out the Henry-York agreement, and that only the Queen objected, and mounted an army. York decided to fight because the war was being led by only a "scolding woman, whose weapon is onely her toungue, and her nayles." According to Hall, and Holinshed as well—although the latter does say there is another version of events—Clifford did not kill York, but found his dead body, chopped off its head, put a paper crown on it, and presented it to the Queen and her party, who laughed.[31] But even in the second version, the Queen is not present when York is killed. The taunting of York with the bloody handkerchief is pure invention.

Warwick did break with Edward, but not until five years after his abortive embassy to France to attempt to arrange a marriage for Edward. And when Margaret, returning to England, heard of Warwick's death, she collapsed and retired to a monastery. Even after support for her arrived, she was "drouned in sorowe."[32]

Shakespeare's changes function doubly, as they do with Joan. On the one hand, he removes Margaret from any direct political power or action, although by depicting the actual events, he could have laid responsibility for the war entirely on her. However, that would also show Margaret to be a very powerful woman, able to muster an army on her own, and fight against a union of the most powerful nobles in the land (which she was, and did). Instead, he shows the nobles—Westmoreland, Northumberland, and Clifford—rejecting the compromise. Margaret—and her child (she is seen as mother rather than governor)—enters only afterwards, and Margaret's act is a personal one, the divorcing of herself from her husband. Shakespeare shows the King winning back the lords by writing to them.

He places the words of contempt for a woman general in the mouth of Richard rather than York—he must have already had Richard's intensely misogynistic character firmly in mind. He invented the terrible scene with the pinioned York and the bloody handkerchief: he made Margaret the instigator and Margaret the killer, but not as the general, the warrior. She is aggressive in a vile and insidious and indirect way. The scene also permits him to put into York's mouth words, like those of Talbot to Joan (about her taunting of Bedford), excoriating women who move out of their proper sphere, and defining women's place and function: to be "soft, mild, pitiful, and flexible" (I, iv, 141).

Margaret's gloating over York about the death of the child Rutland is equivalent to Lady Macbeth's avowal that she would dash out an infant's brains had she sworn to do it. It constitutes the final stamp of

"unnaturalness" on her, just as Joan's repudiation of her father constitutes hers. York calls Clifford, who actually murdered Rutland, *fell*; he
calls Margaret *false*. But there is nothing false about Shakespeare's
Margaret: she is openly horrible. Her only "falseness" is that she is
female but does not behave as women are supposed to: she is false to
her skin. She has a "tiger's heart wrapp'd in a woman's hide" (I, iv,
137). She is not called *cruel* or *wicked* like the men. Because she has
not behaved better than the men, but rather, has acted *like* them,
Margaret has become a "she-wolf of France, but worse than wolves of
France" (I, iv, 111): renouncing the inlaw feminine principle, she has
inevitably slid into the outlaw aspect, into the subhuman, into the
"bestiality" of nature.

   But again, like Joan, her power is not "legitimate": it resides more
in her tongue than in any other faculty. Warwick leads her army;
Henry is its standard; Prince Edward is the cause. Even the "haught"
Northumberland weeps for York as she taunts him; she is called (like
Joan) a "trull," a "callet." At the same time, she is not fearsome: "A
woman's general: what should we fear?" (I, ii, 68). Still, when Margaret
and Henry are captured, the York faction places the blame for the war
upon her: her bridal poverty lost Henry his kingdom; her sedition
caused the broil. (This, although we have seen these princes incite the
elder York to war. The York party is not known for its honesty, but the
emotional weight of the scene is with them: Edward treats the royal
pair as if what he was doing was rescuing the King from the Queen:
"Since thou deniedst the gentle king to speak. / Sound trumpets!" [II,
ii, 172–173].)

   By placing the time of Warwick's break with Edward at the moment when he is suing the French King for the hand of Bona, and
receives news of Edward's marriage to Lady Grey, Shakespeare again
manages to place responsibility for the continuation of the war on a
woman and a marriage, for the way events are presented makes Margaret appear without a champion until Warwick turns to her aid. Lady
Grey is graceful and proper in her first interview with Edward, much
as Margaret appeared in her first introduction. Nevertheless, she here,
as again, later, in *Richard III*, changes her mind easily, moving out of
her proper station into the queenship. She is to this play what Margaret is in *1 Henry VI*, a foreshadowing of the future.

   Shakespeare alters his source again, in his depiction of Margaret
after she hears the news of Warwick's death. She is courageous and
valiant and not at all "drouned in sorowe." Her behavior is admirable,
but her insistence on carrying on the war makes her responsible in

some way for her son's death, which occurs in the next scene. It also prepares for a shift in Margaret's role. In her speech, she claims the aegis of the usurped king, justice, and God's name; she concludes in tears. She has not appeared thus before. Within moments, her son is dead, and she begs the Yorkists to kill her too. With the death of her son, her own life is over.

Like Eleanor in 2 *Henry VI*, Margaret has learned too late that her power is not really hers, but resides in the male. Women have only two choices—to undermine that male power, or to support it. All Margaret is capable of now is "to fill the world with words" (V, v, 44). The death of her son means her death as well, because children, procreation, are the end of the feminine principle Margaret has, throughout this trilogy, repudiated. When she appears again (in *Richard III*), she will be a walking curse, a walking lament, still fierce, but powerless except for her words.

In his alterations of his source, Shakespeare makes explicit some of his attitudes towards women. They are as split as the split in the feminine principle. Women are powerful, capable of sorcery, pride, sexual promiscuity, and atrocity; but they are not powerful in the world, they can fight only in underhanded ways. When women attempt to move into the pole of power, they necessarily attempt to dominate men, which was for Shakespeare at this point in his life, abhorrent. When women connect themselves with power, they can will only evil and their effect is malign, because they cannot extirpate from themselves the outlaw aspect of the feminine principle. Thus, they are fundamentally antistructure, fundamentally underminers of masculine legitimacy.

Characters like Joan and Margaret crop up again in later plays— Goneril, Regan, Lady Macbeth, for instance. But these later versions have more dignity than their predecessors; they are less shrewish, coarse, or unpolished. In terms of moral position Joan's and Margaret's closest relatives in Shakespeare are actually Adriana of *Comedy of Errors* and Kate of *The Taming of the Shrew*, two early comedies. As Shakespeare grows older, he concentrates on a different kind of female character, one who accepts the limitations of her role, and finds ways to assert herself (mildly) within it. These characters are compounded of the inlaw feminine qualities *purified* of the sexual taint that makes the unified feminine principle terrifying and threatening.

Although at some periods of his life, Shakespeare seems to have felt a degree of tolerance for sexuality, fear and loathing of it surfaces in the middle of his literary career and remains through to its end—

although he had found mechanisms to control it by the time he wrote the romances. It is not a new development after 1600, as Dover Wilson suggests.[33] It exists in full expression in this first tetralogy.

Shakespeare will, however, never again treat male legitimacy with quite the same respect and reverence he shows in these plays. He seems to have thought it through in this tetralogy, and decided that legitimacy is not a sacred and sacrosanct gift conferred by God, but an earthly necessity that carries a heavy price. Even his portrait of the nearly ideal Henry V is hedged about with shadows and misgivings. Hal's rejection of Falstaff is the emblem for what legitimacy costs. In later plays, Shakespeare will build up positive female characters who stand as reproaches to the legitimate men around them; in the trage-dies, Shakespeare probes the consequences of power unmodified by the feminine principle. And in his later life, it would seem, to judge by the romances, Shakespeare was in despair about humanity in general, delighted by neither man nor woman, but only by moral ideals.

At the conclusion of 3 Henry VI, Gloucester departs for London "to make a bloody supper in the Tower" (V, v, 85), and argues with Henry, alluding to the Icarus myth which Talbot had alluded to just before he died. Richard disposes of the myth with his usual mocking humor and in doing so, lays the father-son theme to rest. It will appear in Richard III only as a litany, a funeral dirge. Legitimacy requires more than bloodlines, virtue, or force, and the old traditional personal passage of power from father to son is part of a myth as lost as that of Daedalus and Icarus.

Richard's crowing also provides an ironic contrast to the last scene, with its emphasis on hopes for Edward's new son and for "last-ing joy" (V, vii, 46). Richard's image of Daedalus as a peevish fowl has squashed such hopes even before they are uttered.

Richard III

Shakespeare spent considerable time and trouble preparing for this last play of the tetralogy. Building and shattering different ideals, he is able without underscoring to suggest an integrated ideal legitimacy. And the character of Richard is prepared for throughout 3 Henry VI.

At first, Richard is shown as courageous and loyal: "Richard hath best deserv'd of all my sons" (3H6, I, i, 17), York says after the battle of St. Albans (at which time, as Shakespeare knew, the real Richard was three years old). Richard urges his father to break his oath to Henry

VI, but does this in his father's interest. He is courageous on hearing of his father's death, and immediately transfers his loyalty to his older brother and Warwick.

However, he has another side: he has contempt for women ("A woman's general . . .") and for sex. When Edward interprets the three suns as a promise and decides to bear the emblem on his shield, Richard quips: "Nay, bear three daughters . . . You love the breeder better than the male" (3H6, II, i, 41–42). The contemptuous reference to women as the "breeder" is reinforced by his contempt for other qualities of the inlaw feminine principle: "Tears then for babes; blows and revenge for me" (3H6, II, i, 86). Richard's taunts of Prince Edward imply the boy's bastardy and his inheritance of his mother's contemptible nature. Richard and Clarence make locker-room jokes during Edward's interview with Lady Grey, and it is after this, in the middle of 3 Henry VI, that Richard reveals his character and desires.

He wants to be king, but between him and the crown stand Henry VI, Prince Edward, the "lustful" Edward of York, and Clarence. He considers giving up his ambition and seeking "pleasure" in the company of ladies. But love is impossible: "Why, love foreswore me in my mother's womb"; he is bodily deformed and cannot be beloved. Better to "command, to check, to o'erbear such / As are of better person than myself" (3H6, III, ii, 153; 166–167).

The surface arrangement is clear: because he is deformed and therefore unlovable, Richard chooses power alone as his aim. But this is absurd.[34] Richard's shape does not impede his courting of Anne Neville or his marriage to her; he persuades Queen Elizabeth that he can have children by her daughter and persuades her also to grant him her daughter in marriage. His deformity does not at all make him unlovable. And, oddly, it is never suggested that his deformity might impede him as a warrior, which is far more likely than the former.

Richard's deformity is an emblem, a symbol for an inner perverseness. Richard represents the masculine principle completely unmitigated by any tinge of the feminine. (As such, he is the first of a series in Shakespeare.) His nature was predetermined; he came into the world "legs forward" (3H6, V, vi, 71) and with teeth; with a shriveled arm and a hunchback. Because he was determined from birth to this role, because he is a hopeless outcast at life's feast, he feels no connection to the community—no responsibility to it, and no need for it:

I have no brother, I am like no brother;
And this word "love," which greybeards call divine,

Be resident in men like one another,
But not in me: I am myself alone. (3H6, V, vi, 80–83)

Feeling determined and isolated in his role, he suffers from no
guilt about it, and his freedom from that oppressing and inhibiting
emotion gives him the energy, gaiety, and irreverence that make him
appealing. His attractiveness, even as he is bent on horrid business, is
an important element in the play.

Richard III opens with a restatement of the themes associated
with Richard in 3 Henry VI: his contempt for love (approved by one
critic, who says that "Richard gains sympathy by his Puritan withdrawal from 'the idle pleasures of these days' "[35]), and his superiority
in this regard to his brother Edward.[36] Richard's attitudes are shared
by Clarence as the two crack sexual jokes in 3 Henry VI, III, ii, and in
the opening of Richard III. Edward, Richard claims, is ruled by his
wife: the Queen is the King. Richard alarms Brakenbury by bantering
with the lord about Shore's wife, Edward's mistress. In his dialogue
with Hastings, Richard again (less flamboyantly) places the blame for
Clarence's arrest on the Queen's faction.

All of Richard's comments are of course politically manipulative:
Richard uses his own and his society's misogyny to destroy the men
around him. Nevertheless, the net effect is that almost the entire first
scene is given over to disparagement of women. That scene concludes
with Richard's announcement that he intends to marry Anne Neville.
The next scene shows him in a virtuoso performance, winning her
over. The conclusion of this scene defines Richard's sense of sex or
love—it is an exercise in power, and the joy it brings is not one of
harmony and unity, but of triumph and conquering: "Was ever woman
in this humor woo'd? / Was ever woman in this humor won?" (I, ii,
227–228).

But his conquest is pervaded with contempt for his victim for
forgetting where her fidelity should be: "Hath she forgot already that
brave prince, / Edward, her lord, whom I, some three months since, /
Stabb'd in my angry mood at Tewksbury?" (I, ii, 239–241). Richard
wants Anne, as he will later want Princess Elizabeth, to consolidate his
power base. (Women = territory in this period as well as in the time of
Virgil.) He takes pleasure in winning her against her will, and has
contempt for her because he can. He castigates her for her lack of
fidelity, although in other places he brags about his own. But there is
a difference: his lack of fidelity has a purpose. His actions are performed in the name of self and are directed towards possession of a

crown. Anne's wavering loyalty seems to have no aim beyond perhaps the gratification of vanity. Anne's behavior reinforces Richard's contempt for the worldly and intellectual powerlessness of women.'

Nevertheless, at the very moment he is crowing with elation at his feat, he is also praising Prince Edward at his (Richard's) own expense, and is granting that Anne has "God" and "her conscience" on her side. He utters these terms as if they had meaning for him. He will continue to do this throughout the play. Shakespeare's Richard is made in the image of Satan, the rebel thrust out of a heaven whose supremacy, righteousness, and legitimacy he affirms. As Satan is the proof of God's right, Richard is the proof of the rightness of those who oppose him.

Richard III is the most rhetorical of the plays in this tetralogy, and possibly the most rhetorical play Shakespeare wrote. God and heaven are always on Richard's lips; he seems to accept the Christian view of sin and punishment. He will not curse Margaret in I, iii, lest he curse himself; he prays that God will take Edward's soul; Anne says that Henry was "gentle, mild, and virtuous," and the immediate response of Richard, who murdered him, is "The better for the King of Heaven that hath him!" (I, ii, 105). At the end of his hallucinatory and prophetic nightmare, he prays: "Have mercy, Jesu!" (V, iii, 178).

In other words, Richard damns himself. Now this is most improbable, psychologically, and does not sit well with Richard's apparent freedom from guilt. But Shakespeare is attempting in this play a most difficult feat: to create a hero who integrates all the qualities necessary to "save" England, a hero who was the founder of the current ruling house of England. To accomplish this, the young playwright uses a series of devices.

By showing Richard as a moral monster of epic proportions, he legitimates Richmond's usurpation. By having Richard himself damn himself, he legitimates Richmond's righteousness. By building, in the last three plays, a foundation for judging legitimacy, and giving Richmond the benefit of those qualities—prowess and courage, virtue, humanitarian ideals, as well as respectable bloodlines—he draws the audience into the drama, having already given them the ideas they will need to approve Richmond. There are several other devices.

One is rhetorical: the language used by the characters of this play is strong semantically (if not perhaps as poetry). It is also morally judgmental, black and white. God and justice are invoked continually; Richard is associated, by many characters, with hideous images like cockatrices and rooting hogs, with the devil, with utter evil.

The second is stylistic and structural, and draws on the first three plays of the tetralogy. Gradually, the struggle has changed from the war between the masculine and outlaw feminine principle of 1 Henry VI, to a war within the masculine principle (with the outlaw feminine aspect a mere abettor) in 2 Henry VI, to a war in which the weeping widows and babies mentioned by Bedford in the opening scene of 1 Henry VI are a full reality. 3 Henry VI presents a world in which not the outlaw and powerful aspect, but the inlaw, powerless feminine principle is being destroyed. The symbol for this is the murder of children. Gradually, the war has become one between the (abused) masculine principle and the *inlaw* feminine principle.

With the death of their sons, the women of the play lose all their worldly power, and slide back into their proper role, upholders of the feminine principle. (This is not to say they are morally absolved of what they have been: implicit in their role as lamenters is the knowledge that they are effectively dead, and that their sufferings are to some degree deserved.) Gradually, in *Richard III*, those who support the inlaw feminine principle gain unity with each other, placing their opposition to Richard above their squabbles with each other. Richard becomes the single standard-bearer of the unmitigated masculine principle: those who support him, even Tyrrel, who murders the two princes in the Tower, grant importance to "feminine" qualities like pity and mercy.

The gradual alignment of the forces opposed to Richard is a structural principle of the play, which alternates between sections of active plot and sections of reflection (lament or vituperation). The reflective passages comment on the overall action (of the entire civil war) in terms of human society as a whole, that is, on human ends. This strand neither advances nor affects the plot. It is involved with emotion, prophecy, and dream; it centers on children, continuation, England's future. And it is pervaded by guilt, remorse, grief, and helplessness. It is an expression of a defeated inlaw feminine principle.

Against this helpless faction is the character of Richard, who wins every battle, every contest. With joy at his own dexterity, he cons first Clarence, Hastings, and Anne; then, interrupting the Queen's party worrying among themselves, he is able to use their characters against them. In time, he destroys Clarence, Hastings, the Queen's party, and the princes. He seems unstoppable. He also seems incredibly malevolent.

But, as John Danby has pointed out, Richard really is an expression of "the consciousness of his time." Like the much later Coriolanus, Richard is a kind of scapegoat, carrying to their ultimate the values of his culture, and being rejected by that culture: "he is the logical outcome of his society, and yet a pariah rejected by that society."[37]

There is not much difference in Richard's behavior during the war, and Clifford's. Richard has killed a "father"—Henry VI—and a "son"—a child, Prince Edward; Clifford has killed a father and a son (although not a king). Richard (essentially) murders his brother Clarence, but Clarence once fought against his brother Edward. Edward, who comes off as least opprobrious of the three (in another alteration of Shakespeare's sources[38]), is tainted by being under the domination of a woman, and so emasculated. The difference between Richard and Clifford is that Clifford really is a conscienceless brute and Richard is not. But there is little moral difference among the survivors of the civil war. Richard is only the fullest manifestation of the type. But it is Richard who makes continual reference to terms that apply to conscience: it is Richard who is certain of the right. Those who oppose him are contemptible, but have God on their side. He therefore adds, to the powerless females who oppose him, his stamp of certitude in their cause, and in a subtle way, adds his force (worldly) to theirs (moral).

The "feminine" scenes alternate with "masculine" ones. The first "feminine" scene is Anne's combined lamentation and imprecation over the corpse of Henry VI; the second is Richard's speech about Prince Edward, in which he affirms the excellence of what he has destroyed. In I, iii, Margaret glides in like a patient fury and utters her prophetic comments and curses. Momentarily, her appearance unifies Richard with the Queen's party, as she points out. But in time this unification will grow tighter, and in opposition to Richard.

Clarence's dream is part of the meditative strand, as are his remorse and guilt about his broken loyalty and his murder of a child. Brakenbury, trying to soothe the Duke, draws a moral that is reminiscent of Henry VI's meditations on the molehill. Henry compares the fortunes of war to the time when one "can neither call it perfect day nor night" (3H6, II, v, 4). Brakenbury also suggests moral ambiguity, which "makes the night morning and the noontide night" (R3, I, iv, 77). He adds: "Between their titles and low name / There's nothing differs but the outward fame" (I, iv, 82–83). Thus the entire scene functions to challenge the standards of the masculine principle, to challenge the very notion of legitimacy.

The ambiguity of moral right (and thus of all other "rights") is emphasized by the comic dialogue of the two men about to murder

Clarence. They argue about conscience, and with Clarence. Both sides call on God. Clarence, begging God to stop the murderers, has murdered; the murderers urge the Duke to "make peace with God" (I, iv, 249). Thus doubts about legitimacy lead inevitably to doubts of the divine being and divine sanctions which shelter it (as Dostoevski pointed out in *The Brothers Karamazov*). The rhetoric of *Richard III* leads to a cosmic conflict: if there is a deity, and he indeed supports the "masculine" and patriarchal establishment and its values, why does he not step in to stop the slaughter: "When didst thou sleep when such a deed was done?" (IV, iv, 24), Elizabeth challenges God. If God does not manifest himself on earth in this dire situation, there is no God.

The scene which follows Clarence's murder presents the first chorus of women. The women have given up their (foolish) hopes for power and legitimacy, although not their self-assertiveness. They alternately curse and bicker with each other, and make lament, in overwhelming sorrow, demanding justice. In later appearances of the chorus, the bickering and imprecation against each other and the past give way to a mutual hatred of Richard. As they give over concern for self and unify in concern for the future of the country, its continuation, and their desire for divine retribution against Richard, their passages become more ritualistic, incantatory. They become, notably in the first half of IV, iv, the "shrine" scenes of this play.

Richard in himself (and not in his aspect as the bearer of one standard of value) is completely impervious to the women. The chorus does not provide a dramatic antagonist for him any more than Joan provides one for Talbot or Margaret for York. Dramatic antagonisms in this tetralogy occur only among the men. The chorus functions rather to uphold a value structure opposed to Richard's.

Richard's contempt for the women is too complete for their tears or curses to touch him. Even his mother's curse does not make him flinch; he turns away casually and immediately begins to bargain with Elizabeth for her daughter's hand. This is a strong contrast to his behavior with men. When Buckingham shows reluctance to agree to the murder of the princes, his one moment of hesitation touches Richard so deeply that he completely repudiates his former partner, thus risking his rebellion. Richard cares what men say and do because he respects and fears them.

He neither respects nor fears women. His misogyny is not simply one attitude among many, nor a peculiarity of his character. His misogyny—misogyny itself—is raised in this play into a general attitude towards life. Since Shakespeare, as well as most of his culture, associated genders with the qualities of the gender principles, devaluation of women had logically to lead to devaluation of the qualities of the feminine principle. Implicitly, Shakespeare blames women for this as well as men: the ferocious Margaret, the crude Joan, the lowborn Elizabeth have not upheld the virtues they represent. But their defeat is the defeat of the ends of society.

The third act concludes with Richard in triumph: he has attained the crown, the object of all his action. It is followed by the chorus of women unified in hate and hopelessness. And after the murder of the princes, the chorus of women makes explicit that England's problem is also a cosmic one, that divine justice must manifest itself to reestablish a clear right if England (the world) is to continue.

But Richard, as I said before, is insouciant; he shrugs them off and turns to Elizabeth and is even able to persuade her to give him her daughter—although she knows what he is. There is no suggestion that Richard, like Joan, uses witchcraft to persuade. The implication Richard draws (and many critics as well) is that women are indeed a sliding, wavering lot, ignorant of their own wishes and well-being. Richard sneers "relenting fool, and shallow, changing woman!" (IV, iv, 431). (And in this case, Shakespeare was following his sources.)

But the scene presents a problem. It is long, which is to say, it occupies considerable valuable space and attention. Yet it seems a duplication of the scene in which Richard seduces Anne, which is also long. The pair of scenes comprise the longest one-to-one dialogues in the play, and if we include the matter surrounding the dialogue, they are among the longest scenes in the play. Yet neither has much relevance to the plot, the backbone structure of Richard's rise and fall. Once Anne is won, she effectively falls out of the action—we never learn the real reasons for Richard's desiring to marry her, nor why he decided to kill her, or any other surrounding emotions. He wants her, presumably, because her connection with Edward brings him some of Edward's legitimacy; he kills her, presumably, because he is after bigger game, an alliance that will consolidate more fully the Lancastrians and the Yorkists. But why should Shakespeare spend no time at all on Richard's motivations, and so much on his wooing of Anne?

By the same token, once Elizabeth is persuaded, she and her daughter fall out of the action: the desiderated marriage to Princess Elizabeth never takes place. Indeed Elizabeth also has promised her daughter to Richmond; her thinking is never explained. Tillyard comments that the scene with Elizabeth is "far too elaborate and weighty for its effect on the action." [39]

If Shakespeare wished to convey contempt for women's vacillation or weakness, or Richard's contempt for those things, or even to show Richard giving a virtuoso performance, one of these scenes would have sufficed. They are similar in effect, although Richard's approach to the two women is slightly different. It is necessary to examine these scenes to deduce Shakespeare's intentions.

Anne is full of hate and loathing for Richard for approximately 135 lines. What disarms her is Richard's offer of his sword, and his challenge that if she cannot forgive him, she should kill him. He offers, finally, to kill himself if she should say the word. Anne is too credulous, clearly, but this ploy wins her. She finds herself unable, like a Joan or a Margaret, to move into the sphere of worldly power. Richard, indeed, insists that he has moved into her sphere of power, and has killed for love of her. He is claiming that his "masculine" values are dedicated in fact to "feminine ends." Thus Anne represents both the strength and the weakness of the inlaw feminine principle: she can trust, she upholds "feminine" ends, she repudiates worldly power, and she is terribly vulnerable. As punishment for her failure in endurance (the strength permitted the feminine principle), however, she is miserable with Richard and foresees her own murder.

The scene with Elizabeth is vastly different. She too curses Richard for a long time, heaps every blame on him. But Richard finds an argument that sways her. He claims that if he does not marry the princess, the civil wars will continue: "Without her, follows to myself and thee, / Herself, the land, and many a Christian soul, / Death, desolation, ruin, and decay" (IV, iv, 407–409). This argument, coming after the lamentations of the early part of the scene, has great force. The women agree about the futility of struggles of right for right: what is important is the children, the future. And indeed, if there were no Richmond, or if Richmond had lost, such a marriage might indeed have been the only way to heal the divisions in the kingdom. The voluntary submission of Elizabeth and her daughter might be the price of harmony.

Harmony is restored, however, in the person of Richmond. With all the thought and preparation that have gone into creating him, he remains a wooden figure. Perhaps this is so precisely because of the stylistic and rhetorical means used to heighten his role. He enters the play as the synthesis that has been called for, and as the agent of divine justice: it is clearly too much for any mortal to bear. He validates divine and worldly legitimacy, bringing power dedicated to the ends of the whole society yet strong enough to defeat power dedicated to itself.

Richard fights in "the King's name" (V, iii, 12), Richmond fights "in God's name" (V, ii, 22); Richard is peremptory, edgy, and suspicious with his subordinates, Richmond is gentle and trusting; Richard's last act before sleeping is to give an order, Richmond's to pray.

Hall gives a fairly long recounting of the two men's orations to their armies. Shakespeare departed rather widely from these: his intentions are in line with the interpretations of these characters suggested above.

In Hall, Richard concentrates on the beggarliness of the English invaders (many of whom are exiles like Richmond) and their French cohorts. He claims Richmond is cowardly and inexperienced in battle. He admits freely that he has done wrong in getting the throne, but insists he is going to keep it. His only mention of women is to claim that the invading forces wish to "distroy us our wyfes and children."[40]

Shakespeare's Richard harps on the lowliness (of status) of the opposing armies—they are vagabonds, rascals, runaways, scum. He uses Hall's word "mylkesoppe" to describe Richmond (implying effeminacy) but omits any mention of military inexperience. He tries to raise his soldiers to an emotional pitch, however, by mentioning women and sexuality. The invaders, he says, want the men's land and their "beauteous wives," and cries, "Shall these enjoy our lands? lie with our wives? / Ravish our daughters?" (V, iii, 336). In keeping with his character throughout the play, Richard is obsessed with the very sexuality he scorns.

It is Richmond, according to Hall, who did use such arguments. Richmond claims that Richard "hath not only murdered his nephewe beyng his kyng and sovereigne lord, bastarded his noble brethren and defamed the wombe of his verteous and womanly mother, but also compased all the meanes and waies that he could invent how to stuprate and carnally know his awne nece under the pretence of a cloked matrimony."[41]

Hall's Richmond is concerned above all, however, with money. "While we were in Brytaine [Brittainy] we had small livynges and lytle plentye of wealth or welfare, now is the time come to get abundance of riches and copie of profit which is the rewarde of your service and merite of your payne."[42]

Shakespeare's idealized Richmond concentrates on the unity of his "loving countrymen" under "God and our good cause"; he calls Richard "God's enemy"; he promises an ability to "sleep in peace" (V, iii, 237; 240; 252; 256), and gratitude from wives and children. None of these phrases appears in Hall, but all are linked to the rhetorical creation of "right" which pervades this play, and to the defense and well-being of the feminine principle. There is only a passing reference to money: "Your country's fat shall pay your pains the hire" (V, iii, 258). Had Shakespeare emphasized the money-conscious side of Richmond and his army, he might be a more realistic character, but would not be a divine agent, would not legitimate legitimacy.

Since he is, and does, Shakespeare omits the abuses performed on Richard's corpse. And he shows Richard defeated from within as much as from without. The villainy he has performed with cheery wit all through the play suddenly overwhelms him with guilt. Although at the end of 3 *Henry VI*, he repudiated "pity, love, and fear," he does not sense until the end of *Richard III* the consequences of that repudiation. Suddenly he realizes he has not loved, is isolated and unloved. He ruminates: "I shall despair; there is no creature loves me, / And if I die no soul will pity me. / And wherefore should they, since that I myself / Find in myself no pity to myself?" (V, iii, 200–203). His repudiation of and contempt for the feminine principle is a renunciation not only of women and children, but also of the "feminine" qualities they (supposedly) represent: friendship, trust, love, human society, any dependence at all upon others. His pride, his isolation, his lack of a sense of a trusting community (a thing that is emphasized in Richmond's address), demoralize him.

Geoffrey Bullough, speaking of 1 *Henry VI*, writes: "It seems best to regard the play as built around the opposition between two forces or principles, one patriotic and constructive, the other destructive and selfish."[43] I agree that the tetralogy as a whole is concerned with opposition among forces, principles, but unfortunately, they are not so simply describable. Virtue, like Henry's, can be an ill; power can be an ill; legitimacy is never clear. As Ronald Berman has pointed out, rights of inheritance are not enough, and "legitimacy itself is ambiguous."[44] Don M. Ricks, writing about the Shakespearean history play, claims it "carries a very real . . . complex of ethical meanings in the juxtaposition of its scenes and characters, in the emotional coloring of its image patterns, even . . . in what was adopted and what omitted from its sources. . . . Shakespeare's judgments upon his material are everywhere implicit. . . . [and] the kind of thinking they embody is essentially moralistic."[45] Since *moralistic* implies a judgmental and nonprobing kind of thought, I would prefer to say *moral*, as does James Winny: "The early history plays are . . . directed by a close concern with man's moral identity." Winny adds that Shakespeare's implication is that "man's moral consciousness . . . cannot be tied off if the individual is to survive."[46]

The problem is that the moral cannot be differentiated from the political and aesthetic dimensions of life. The holding of power is a moral as well as a political act. Those qualities most people identify with moral life are the elements of the inlaw feminine principle, which, when separated from its power—sex—is totally helpless. And the elevation of qualities which are associated with a despised gender creates a schizophrenia that cannot be overcome. That schizophrenia is implicit in the division of moral qualities into gender principles in the first place.

Moreover, the morality of the tetralogy is not as clear as it seems in critical redactions, because most of these omit an essential element in the plays. It is obvious what we are to *think* of the witch Joan, the ludicrous Cade, the menacing Margaret, and the wicked Richard. What is not so obvious is what we are supposed to *feel* about them. In fact, much of the energy of these plays resides in these outlaw figures (just as much of the energy of medieval moralities resided in its outlaw or devil figures): *Richard III* would be dreary and mechanical without Richard's joyous liberated breaking of every moral delicacy, every moral sanction. He acts with impunity, as, if truth be told, we would all like to act. Joan's crudeness undercuts Talbot's complacent and self-aggrandizing dying words at a crucial moment, and brings in what we may well feel—with one part of ourselves—to be a breath of fresh air. Cade's silliness is no worse than that of Henry VI, and a good deal less cloying. When virtue is cut off from its roots, it is stultifying—and the true roots of virtue are the very vices it is supposed to transcend. When virtue is stultifying, aggression is fun, malice is delightful, and both can renew a stodgy world. No account of the morality of these plays is complete without a perception of the way they are enriched and energized by the very outlaw feminine values the surface action of the play strives towards overcoming.

Leslie Fiedler, in *The Stranger in Shakespeare*, described women, Jews, blacks, and Indians as existing on and defining "the limits of the human." These borderline figures are the strangers in a culture whose values, Fiedler says, Shakespeare basically shared. Fiedler points out that there are no women present in the final moments of *Richard III*, as if Shakespeare "can imagine no final reconciliation, no hope of peace except in an all-male world."[47]

Fiedler's perceptions seem to me acute. But he too overlooks the fact that the driving energy in this tetralogy, as well as in other Shakespearean plays (consider *Othello*), comes from precisely the "outlaw" elements the "masculine" establishment deplores.

Another important point is that Shakespeare's major sources for these plays, Holinshed and Hall, are explicitly misogynistic. They both fear, look down on, and have extremely rigid standards for the behavior of women. In addition, the tetralogy seems to me indebted for its aims to *The Aeneid*, which aimed to exalt the ends of empire and derogate its means. *The Aeneid* is also a misogynistic book—extremely so in its second half.[48] And Shakespeare's culture was misogynistic, despite being ruled (and well) by a woman. Shakespeare began to write these plays with a coherent set of received values in his mind.

Nevertheless, he began at some point to see where such values inevitably led, and places them, these values he shares to some degree, in his villain. One of Richard's defining characteristics is misogyny (so too, Iago). Shakespeare did not unthinkingly adopt the ideas of his culture: he saw something profoundly lethal about misogyny, and tried to find another way to deal with the traditional arrangement of morals implicit in the gender principles.

At the bottom, psychologically, his situation was probably fairly common: he was highly sexual, extremely guilt-ridden about sex, and associated sexuality with women—ergo . . . For women to possess worldly power in addition to their already overwhelming sexual power (as he saw it) led—in his imagination—to the annihilation of the male. His state is not at all outdated.

4

Marriage

The Comedy of Errors and
The Taming of the Shrew

The Comedy of Errors is probably Shakespeare's first comedy, perhaps his first play. *The Taming of the Shrew* was probably written after the *Henry VI* plays. I will discuss them together because they have a number of features in common.

These two plays (and *The Merry Wives of Windsor*) are Shakespeare's only farces. Farce is action comedy, and action being a "masculine" quality, these plays are linear, strongly plotted, and are concerned with marriage rather than with love.[1] (Because it is a structure, a permanency, marriage is "masculine"; sex and affection are "feminine.") All three of these plays are concerned with property, a form of power, and all focus mainly on male characters, unlike the "feminine" comedies. And interestingly, *Comedy of Errors* and *Taming of the Shrew* contain the only female figures in Shakespeare who change. Other females—Queen Margaret, or Lady Macbeth, for instance—may suffer and may be in some way destroyed, but their natures do not change. Only the fate, not the moral character, is subject to change in Shakespeare's women. But Adriana and Kate were conceived in human terms, and are permitted fallibility and repair.[2]

Action is associated with the tragedies because it is more irrevocable than language. But comedy deals with what is revocable. Thus, the major interest of these plays is not language, but disguise, which makes action revocable. Disguise in some form—including mistaken or changed identity—is more rampant in these plays than in the other comedies.

The Comedy of Errors

Comedy of Errors is set in Ephesus. This is important because Shakespeare changed the city from the Epidamnum of his source. He had to have a reason for this. Ephesus is identified with witchcraft, worship of a goddess, and sexual freedom—the outlaw feminine principle—as well as with St. Paul's discussion of the properties of marriage.[3] The rebellion and sexual energy and fury that roar through the first tetralogy characterize the subsurface life of Ephesus, and are connected with one of the plots: the rebellion against the constraints of marriage of both Adriana and Ephesian Antipholus. It is appropriate in a setting whose ambience is outlaw feminine, that the dominant imagery centers on man as a beast.[4]

The surface life of Ephesus, however, is firmly in the control of the masculine principle. The political background is a power struggle between two cities which has resulted in a law which is inhumane but legitimate, and is thus an example of that principle in an oppressive form. Aegeon's lack of money (power) traps him in the law, and as a result, his life is forfeit. The Duke, who represents this set of values, is moved by Aegeon's story, but insists he "may not disannul" (I, i, 144) the law. Nevertheless, at the end of the play he does precisely that: there is no mention of the fine at the end. This change cannot be attributed to a psychological shift in the Duke; it is a result of the moral revision of the entire society that develops from the events of the comedy.

The two gender principles appear at their worst at the opening of the play. The feminine is outlaw, connected with sorcery and rebelliousness; the masculine is oppressive, inhumane. And the world depicted is an unhappy one: a husband and wife quarrel with each other; a husband is unfaithful; a wife is jealous and rebellious; servants are brutalized; greed and competitiveness imbue male relationships. The bonds linking this society are codified into law, but law does not keep E. Antipholus from frequenting a courtesan, Adriana from feeling resentment, masters from beating their servants.

The two plots work in a complex manner. The frame story—Aegeon, who was seeking his son, now waits only for death, impoverished in a strange city, bereft of human connection—provides the basic terms, the fundamental condition of human life. Within this, Syracusan Antipholus seeks his brother (in a parallel to his father), and when a series of (seemingly) fortunate events occur, is frightened. He several times attempts to flee the city.

Through the disguise convention, S. Antipholus commits adultery with an attractive stranger, and falls in love with his "wife's" sister; E. Antipholus discovers his wife's affair and is outraged into planning to beat her. E. Antipholus, who suffers the unhappy half of events, discovers the basic (vulnerable, powerless) state of man as he is stripped of his wealth, perceived as illegitimate (mad), and hauled off to be locked up. Given the right combination of elements, this could happen to anyone.

The problem of the unified Antipholus is to discover and accept his proper place within a society dominated by oppressive political, economic, and social structures, and undermined by powerful inner urges. This problem is paralleled in Adriana, who (subtly) threatens to repay her husband's infidelity with her own, and who balks against the subordination of the female role. Adriana must learn her true "identity," which in this play means her proper role, just as Antipholus must learn his.

The disguise convention of the play functions doubly. On the one hand, it permits the performance of irrevocable actions, transforming them into revocable ones. On the other hand, it destroys the stability of the characters. The implication of the confusions and bewilderments is far more subtle here than in *Taming of the Shrew*; it is that unacceptable acts (adultery, loss of property, madness) lead to terror and isolation. Terror within, isolation from the social structure, are so serious as to be tantamount to loss of personal identity. The males in particular suffer: they feel themselves going mad, they are sexually overwhelmed, they are threatened with imprisonment. The social structure on which they have unknowingly depended suddenly repels or suddenly, strangely, accepts them. In time, the entire society is sucked into the whirlpool of their confusion.

The focus of the play is multiple. Although the main point of view lies with the Syracusans, especially Antipholus, the Syracusan pair is onstage only slightly more than the two Ephesians. Adriana and Luciana, who appear almost always together and may be read as complementary halves of the unified feminine principle—outlaw and inlaw—are onstage more than any single male. The "insanity" of these major pairs spreads to the secondary characters as well, and eventually strikes even the Duke (who always appears with Aegeon, another pair representing opposing aspects of the masculine principle—one in service of law, the other in service of love) and the Abbess, who is the only figure who is immune to the general madness.

S. Antipholus is in a condition of freedom. He has power (money), and companionship (his slave) but he is miserable, feeling like a drop of water in a sea, searching for a "fellow." He wants a brother, which is to say, an equal, a like. He wants community. The major worldly blessings fall upon him—sexual satisfaction, money, and eventually, love—but he reacts with terror and wants to flee. In his freedom, he does not know who he is. He begs Luciana to enlighten his "earthy, gross conceit," or else, since she seems to him more than human ("divine"), to make him new, "transform" him (III, ii, 32–40). He asks, in short, that she certify his place in the world; he feels he is going mad.

E. Antipholus is in a condition of bondage. Married to a jealous woman, he desires sexual freedom; secure in prosperity, he is nevertheless subject to loss of wealth and status and the legitimacy those confer. Wanting a place on earth (as S. Antipholus wants a place in the world), he makes a break for freedom in his relation with the courtesan. In the swirl of events, he does attain the freedom he has desired, but in the process loses his identity and his legitimacy. He does go mad.

Comedy of Errors comes out firmly on the side of bondage as opposed to freedom, but as its confusions unravel, it "renews" bondage, transforms it into *bonding*. Social order can be changed only by altering the inner condition of the characters. This is accomplished in the comedy by subjecting the characters to the bruising and disconnection that are implicit in freedom.

The nightmare the characters undergo in the time of confusion terrifies them into grateful acceptance of limitation—the cost of external order. Ephesian Antipholus must restrain his power and govern his wife with love (or she will remain jealous and perhaps be unfaithful to him); Adriana must accept her powerlessness and subordinate herself to her husband with love (or he will be unfaithful to her, and treat her cruelly, beat her).[5] Both must contain their sexuality within a sanctified (legitimated) form—marriage. S. Antipholus discovers his place by finding a "brother" and a wife, that is, an equal and an "other self," a partner who represents the "higher" or divine self but is simultaneously subordinate.

Both brothers, in discovering each other, discover their parents, thus swelling the group into a full community. The kind and loving Aegeon replaces the inflexible Duke as "father": in this new state, new ambience, the law dooming Aegeon may be suspended.

The saintly Abbess has the power to overcome Ephesus' outlawry: she is able to unravel the confusion wrought by the nature of the city and the urges of its inhabitants. Thus she brings the inlaw principle to breathe through the city's structures, making them flexible. Her saintly wisdom is predicated on her voluntary renunciation of not just power but the world itself, as well as of sex. Thus a flexible and expressive order supersedes the oppressive one because the extremes of both gender principles have been brought into restraint.

Within the play, Luciana functions as a parallel to the Abbess. Together, these two women combine to form a symbolic image that will be significant to Shakespeare for the rest of his career. The super-human (divine) inlaw feminine principle with its insistence upon voluntary subordination of self to the whole, and on voluntary renunciation of both worldly and sexual power, enables true identity to be discovered.

The central concern of the play is the marriage relation. Not only the design of the play, but Shakespeare's alteration of his sources, indicates that this was his major concern. His granting to Adriana her deeply felt speeches, and his probing of an unhappy marriage from the point of view of the wife, are distinctly un-Plautine. The laundering of E. Antipholus' relation with the courtesan, the addition of the ideal romantic love of S. Antipholus and Luciana, the comic "love" of E. Dromio and his large wife, and the addition of the parental love of Aegeon and Aemilia all emphasize the subject.

Roman and English satiric comedy is totally "masculine": it is highly plotted, it aims at an external goal (money and/or marriage), and female figures are mainly objects—like money—within it. It involves an outwitting, tricking, or overpowering of elders in order that continuation may occur, that the young may live. It uses "masculine" means to defeat a male establishment, that is, essentially, to usurp it.

Shakespearean comedy, on the other hand, even this "masculine" comedy, is devoted to the ends of the inlaw feminine principle. The action leads to voluntary relinquishment of oppressive power, or at least, an agreeable acceptance of its loss. The end of Shakespearean comedy is not just continuation but social harmony. Control is necessary to human life, but Shakespeare urged domestication (taming, internalization) rather than destruction. It is this bowing of many selves to the whole that gives Shakespearean comedy its great sweetness.

Although the design of *Comedy of Errors* leads to a regeneration of society by reeducation of the characters, the values of the play are ambivalent. For on the mythic level, the play deals with serious disruption: a man neglects his wife for his prostitute; a woman locks her husband out of the house while she entertains a lover; a man attempts to seduce his wife's sister; slaves are blamed for everything and continually beaten. Such events could lead to domestic melodrama or even tragedy.

The play is saved for comedy by the convention of disguise, which permits these events to be revocable. The film is run backwards: a man did not neglect his wife for his prostitute; a man did not make love to his wife's sister; a woman did not lock her husband out of the house while she entertained her lover—it only seemed so. Nevertheless, on some level, the audience has had to accept that these things *did* happen. The audience's acceptance of the disguise convention is an acceptance of revocability; because of affection for the characters, and a consequent desire that things work out well for them, the audience accepts behavior that it perceives to be immoral, and forgives it. This process is an acceptance by the audience of the feminine principle with its emphasis on the good of the whole, and on moral flexibility.

The imagery of the play—*chain* and *gold* are very frequent—reinforces metaphorically the theme of bonding within a propertied community.[6] There is general critical agreement that the major theme of the play is "finding of one's self by losing one's self and the freeing of one's self by binding one's self."[7] One critic writes: "At the centre is relationship: relationship between human beings, depending on their right relationship to truth and universal law: to the cosmic reality beneath appearance, and the cosmic order."[8]

What is noteworthy to those of us less certain about cosmic order is that at this point in his life, Shakespeare believed that one's identity is largely a matter of one's place in the world. This is in contrast to his later belief, given utterance in *King Lear*, that one's identity is defined by one's place on earth, which is mere lonely vulnerable mortality. Legitimacy, status, and wealth were necessary to maintain men (and the women dependent upon them) in the face of the terrifying freedom of the void. The play insists that no matter how we protest, we are what we are socially perceived to be, that outer structures determine inner ones, to a greater degree than people raised to worship individuality and transcendence may be willing to admit.

The Taming of the Shrew

Like *Comedy of Errors*, *Taming* is concerned with defining the proper relationship in marriage. But whereas *Comedy of Errors* focuses on marriage as the root relation from which all others grow, as the nucleus, the foundation of an entire society, *The Taming of the Shrew* focuses on marriage as the foundation of a happy and orderly life. *Comedy of Errors* looks outward; *Taming* looks inward. Thus, in *Comedy of Errors*, many characters rebel against the social structure or experience a degree of freedom from it. Only two characters in *Taming* fully rebel against the social structure—Katharina and Petruchio (and on one occasion, Grumio)—although several experience some freedom by changing their social status (role). At the conclusion of *Comedy of Errors*, all strata of society are represented, and its lowest members, the Dromios, decide that equality, rather than hierarchy, is the happier relation. The conclusion of *Taming* is severely stratified, and more narrowly. The guests at the dinner are mainly husbands and wives; the servants—even the wonderful Tranio—are limited to serving; and Katharina gives a long sermon asserting the dependency of women (implicitly the inlaw feminine principle) upon men. In other words, the conclusion of *Comedy of Errors* emphasizes freedom and flexibility within social limitations; the conclusion of *Taming* emphasizes social limitations on freedom.

Disguise pervades this play and is used for a variety of purposes. That it is fundamental is indicated by the Induction, which is both keynote and satiric comment on the play. Sly's insouciant adjustment to his new identity and his treatment—he is given comfort, fine clothes, good food and drink, and an obedient spouse—are in direct contrast to Kate's inability to adjust, and her treatment by Petruchio. At the same time, Sly's ludicrous notions about how noblemen behave intimates that leopards cannot change their spots. Thus, those who can change were not true leopards in the first place, and Kate was not really a shrew.

The subject of Sly's first conversation with his "wife" also points to an important assumption of the play. Marriage is a sexual relation, as Sly is eager to prove, but above all it is a social, functional relation. Wives properly address their husbands as "husband," "goodman," or "my lord"; husbands properly address their wives as "Madam," rather than as Al'ce or Joan. This insistence on the functional definition of marriage underlies Petruchio's "chattel" speech, which is central to the play. All the procedures of the comedy depend on it. Marriage is a purchase made between men: whatever gaps exist in his control, Baptista has unchallenged political, economic, and social power over his daughters. He may be outwitted or overwhelmed psychologically or emotionally, but his worldly power is never in doubt.

In parallel to this, it is Petruchio's political and economic power over Kate that makes his "taming" of her possible. Audience sympathy for him and his position is essential if the play is to be seen as comic and agreeable. Given audience acceptance of the principles of the "chattel" speech, Petruchio's treatment of Kate is humane and restrained—he doesn't beat her. Without audience assent to those principles, Petruchio's treatment of Kate is nothing less than torture of the sort now called brainwashing. Denial of food and sleep and freedom of movement is outlawed even in most prisons. Thus the comedy of the play depends on assent to the legitimacy of Petruchio's claim to "own" his wife.

Petruchio's disguises—as a beggarly madman at the wedding and as a cruel madman afterwards, all the while pretending to kindness—operate much like those in *Comedy of Errors*. Petruchio violates the decorum Katharina is accustomed to: he removes her from familiar ground, violates the customs and structures she is used to, and pretends, throughout, to think she is someone other than she thinks she is. As the characters in *Comedy of Errors* are brought into line by being thrust into the terror of freedom, disconnection, Kate is brought into line by total oppression, imprisonment. She is forced, for the sake of her sanity and any gratification at all, to bow to the new structures Petruchio provides.

However, like *Comedy of Errors*, the play runs its course in two ways: it describes the taming of the shrew Kate and the shrew Petruchio. He is able to cease abusing his power once Kate is able to accept volitional (internalized) subordination. Only in the earliest plays does the movement work in this way—the surrender of the female makes possible the surrender of the male.[9] In later comedies, females (except for Beatrice) do not presume *not* to surrender (that is, they do not rebel against male supremacy in general, although they may attempt to evade the power of a particular male), and the design focuses on reeducation of the males.

Kate's transformation is explicitly an education in upholding the inlaw feminine principle, and she is taught this by being punished by oppressive "masculine" power. Thus, watching Petruchio abuse Grumio and a servingman, she, who used to strike Bianca, is appalled, and prays "who never pray'd before" (IV, i, 79) for mercy for his victims. She urges Petruchio to be patient with "a fault unwilling" (IV, i, 156). Her eventual acceptance of the inlaw feminine principle, her renunciation of its outlaw aspect (Kate's rebellion is not rooted in her desire to supplant "masculine" power, but in a desire not to accommodate herself to it), lead to her acceptance of the role defined for her by the social structure. She becomes "conformable as other household cates" with the result of "peace . . . and love, and quiet life, / An aweful rule, and right supremacy" (V, ii, 108–109). The *right* in that verse is crucial. Northrop Frye says "When we first see Katharina she is bullying Bianca, and when we take leave of her she is still bullying Bianca, but has learned how to do it with social approval on her side."[10] It would be more accurate to say with *male* approval on her side, and in male terms.

All the events of *The Taming of the Shrew* tend towards a definition of proper marriage. The two plots are reversals of each other. Bianca, the sweet docile woman, is in great demand on the marriage market. To woo her, Lucentio and Hortensio demean themselves socially, making themselves subordinate: thus, they move into the feminine principle. *Taming* may well be Shakespeare's rebuttal of Sidney's *Arcadia*, in which the princes also subordinate themselves to their lovers, and learn to feel. The expansion of their experience to include "feminine" subordination, victimization, and emotion is designed to make them whole. Shakespeare suggests quite otherwise.

Kate, the intractable, insubordinate woman, is also "wooed"— mainly after her marriage—by Petruchio, who, with his political and economic power, is able to overmaster her. The power relations of the two married couples—Bianca and Lucentio, who exclaims he is willing to be "a slave, t'achieve that maid" (I, i, 219), and Kate and Petruchio —remain forever in the mold in which they are originally cast.

Despite his lifelong examination of the "feminine" side of experience, and his later apotheosizing of the inlaw feminine principle, Shakespeare clearly believed in a difference in rank so strong as to be a class difference between men and women, and that this difference was natural and ineradicable. After all Petruchio's abuse of Kate, some of which Hortensio has witnessed, and even assisted, he makes no comment until Petruchio addresses Vincentio as if he were a young girl. Then he says, " 'A will make the man mad, to make a woman of him" (IV, v, 35–36). As in *Comedy of Errors*, role is dictated by gender and station, by the requirements of the external world. It must therefore be learned, and it never permits full expression of the self.

Thus, disguise is the very core of the play. In such a rigidly determined structure, disguise alone permits the expansion of the experience of the characters. Tranio makes a better Lucentio than the original; the pedant, a more generous father than Vincentio; and Sly surely a more amusing lord than most. Kate as shrew lives out her outlaw aspect; Lucentio and Hortensio disguised express their "feminine" aspects. Human possibilities are unlimited; but we can wear only one set of clothes at a time.

There are other disguises as well. Bianca is "disguised" in a sweet docile role, as Kate is in a rebellious one. Petruchio "disguises" himself as a capricious tyrant. Vincentio is cast into disguise by Petruchio's "mis-taking" of him. Thus, even as disguise functions in the plot to allow Lucentio to woo Bianca and Petruchio to woo (tame) Kate, and thus establish a proper, stable, and satisfying order, it also functions to overturn proper, stable order. As in the first tetralogy, the vitality and gaiety of the play issue mostly from the abused masculine and outlaw feminine principles, from assertion of self and rebelliousness. We enjoy the play not for its delineation of ideal marriage, but for Kate's and Petruchio's defiance of accepted manners, for Grumio's taunting, equivocating insubordination, and the devious practices used by Lucentio, Tranio, and Hortensio to deceive the elders. The established order may confer role and social identity, but it also constricts; challenges to it, as C. L. Barber has shown, are felt as liberating, and allow the expansion of personal identity.[11] *The Taming of the Shrew* concludes with a harmonious synthesis of unabused masculine and inlaw feminine principles, but it celebrates the outlaw aspect, defiance and rebellion.

III

THE INLAW
FEMININE PRINCIPLE

5
Constancy

The Two Gentlemen of Verona,
Love's Labour's Lost, and
A Midsummer Night's Dream

The Two Gentlemen of Verona

Controversy remains over *Two Gentlemen of Verona*, despite strong defenses made by a number of critics. John Danby has looked directly at its value structure, pointing out that character and psychological realism are less important than the central idea—that love is a discipline and the lover an initiate.[1] This is unexceptionable: all the elements of the play cluster about this notion, including comic contrasts and parallels such as Launce's love for his dog and his subhuman woman.

Like *The Comedy of Errors* and *The Taming of the Shrew, The Two Gentlemen of Verona* has a multiple focus, that is, no single character totally dominates the action. But in all the comedies, there is one major character with whom the audience's sympathy primarily resides. In *Comedy of Errors*, that figure is S. Antipholus; in *Taming of the Shrew* it is Petruchio. In *Two Gentlemen of Verona*, that figure must be Proteus—the play opens and closes with his point of view.

Shakespeare seems to have set out to write a play about friendship. The essential quality of friendship, wrote Sir Thomas Elyot, is constancy, and the play does examine that virtue.[2] Proteus' inconstancy, his failure in both friendship and love, and his reeducation in both could have made him the most interesting character, and perhaps the most sympathetic one as well, if midway through the play, Shakespeare's sympathies hadn't moved elsewhere—to Julia, Launce, and Speed. These characters have a charm, a magnetic power that Proteus lacks. Magnetic power, the power to draw others to one (rather than the power to impose on others), is "feminine" and may be called the power of beauty—which is what it is called when it appears in women.[3] It is the complement to masculine power-in-the-world.

In creating characters endowed with magnetic power, Shakespeare opened up new possibilities for himself, and his handling of the inlaw feminine principle. Locating inlaw qualities in a female hero, and outlaw qualities in a clown (or clowns), he could incorporate in his drama the full range of human moral qualities without the threat that the unified feminine principle held for him. Placing these qualities in illegitimates who accept their illegitimacy (instead of insisting, as do Queen Margaret or Joan, on "masculine" power, or, like Adriana and Kate, on "masculine" rights), he defused the feminine principle.[4] This in turn made it possible for him to level radical criticism at "masculine" structures without fear of really toppling them.

Invariably, the human urge to permanence goes too far: it turns everything it touches into gold—or dead bone. Thus it is always in need of expansion, flexibility, of an infusion of spirit or feeling, of allowance for flux. An important presence of illegitimates in a play signals criticism of legitimate establishment, sometimes through parody of that establishment, as with Dogberry and company, sometimes through illegitimate imitation of legitimate behavior, as with Touchstone and Autolycus. This class of character appears in all the comedies written after *Two Gentlemen* and is most important in those written entirely from a "feminine" (illegitimate) point of view.[5] The criticism this presence represents is explicit in *Two Gentlemen* when Launce takes on himself the blame for his dog's physiological impertinence, and asks the audience "How many masters would do this for his servant?" (IV, iv, 29–30), or when Julia, a mere woman, is able to uphold the standard of constancy to which Proteus merely gives lip service.

The political attitude inherent in the feminine principle is anarchy, the lack of a single dominant force, and an important presence of illegitimate characters creates an anarchic social world even though the social structure in which the characters live is hierarchical. Launce and Speed in *Two Gentlemen* are more important dramatically than the Duke and Antonio, rulers of their worlds; the same thing is true in *Comedy of Errors*, in which the Dromios are more important to us than the Duke and Aegeon. In *Two Gentlemen*, however, the illegitimates function almost autonomously, and are more than wryly good-humored victims.

The slaves in any society, no matter what they are called, are always in the best position to comment on its pretensions. Lacking the power to rebel and sometimes even the power to comment openly, this class offered Shakespeare a tool for assimilating into the whole the vitality, rebellious truth, challenge, and reminder of sexual freedom and personal desire contained in the outlaw feminine principle. In *Two Gentlemen*, both Launce (as shown in his love for his dog) and Julia possess the virtue that is central to the play—constancy.

"Were man but constant, he were perfect." But man is not, nor woman neither, as Shakespeare no doubt knew. *Two Gentlemen* is the first of his plays to exalt this quality; it is important to *Love's Labour's Lost* and *A Midsummer Night's Dream*, as well. In later plays it is merged with chastity to become a single absolute good, the fragile virtue on which depends the weight of the entire social structure. It therefore requires some analysis.

Constancy is a superlunary virtue, possible only in the undecaying realm above the moon. Below, all is transient, corruptible matter. Shakespeare embodies this superhuman virtue in characters depicted as mortal and somewhat realistic, and we accept them and their emotion without demur. Perfect heroines are, of course, a tradition dating back to medieval saints' tales and the romances, but we can still accept Julia or Viola or Rosalind in a way we can no longer accept Griselde. The reason for this is partly Shakespeare's brilliant characterizations, but it is also because of the organic importance of constancy within his total value structure.

Constancy is central to Shakespeare's vision of human harmony. It functions in a number of ways. First, it validates language, otherwise easily "corruptible," variable, flexible, able to be stretched, wrenched out of meaning in the way Beatrice frights the word *foul* "out of his right sense." Constancy is an attitude that insists words have fixed referents, that they be rooted in a single and unambiguous reality. And this single, unambiguous reality is Shakespeare's ideal. He idealized human beings less than human *possibility* in envisioning a condition in which all of a person's emotions and desires were fused and focused on one thing or person (something that does occasionally happen in human life), and *remain* that way forever with no second thoughts, no bitter aftertastes, no conflicting impulses.

This notion is fundamental to all of the plays; it is fundamental to Shakespeare's way of seeing. Constancy fuses the gender principles: it is feeling, thus "feminine" (although its singleness is not. Single unambiguous feeling is not gender-related—it occurs only in madness, fanaticism, or infatuation); but it is permanent, thus "masculine." The core of Shakespeare's vision synthesizes the gender principles, and the beauty of that union as he saw and felt it irradiates the comedies. Where this synthesis is lacking, it is palpably lacking, and edges the play towards or into tragedy.

The ideal of constancy functions in the comedies as a moral standard; it also acts to connect the two major interests of the comedies, language and sex. Constancy involves the spoken word, the vow; it involves sexuality as well. The positing of constancy as a human possibility suggests that beneath the wonderful ambiguous play of words, beneath the vacillation in sexual desire, there is something firm and certain, the world as it should half be. The core of the comedies is this synthetic standard; the aim of the comedies is marriage, another synthetic standard (the making permanent of love, a feeling): the comedies are thus ringed on the inside and the outside by union of the gender principles.

Constancy is rare indeed in actuality. What passes for constancy is often patience, grim weariness, tedium, the disbelief in alternatives, despair, constricted horizons. Yet we believe in it as it appears in Julia or Viola or Perdita or Marina. In fact, constancy is not as hopelessly ideal as it seems. It is unrealistic when demanded of one person but it is an actual virtue of the human race. We believe in it because it is true of our *racial* experience. Constancy lies at the heart of our desires; it is a symbol of the continuing, unvanquishable, unquenchable drive towards that which binds without bonds, which binds up in restoration, towards qualities like nutritiveness and compassion and unoppressive supportiveness. Steadfastness in devotion goes largely unrewarded when it occurs, but it makes bearable the life of the human race. Because it is a value stronger in the race than in most individuals, it partakes of the eternal world, the realm that lies on the dark side of the moon.

Julia's constancy is cast in the Griselde mold: she follows Proteus to Milan and remains constant in her love even after overhearing him woo Silvia. She consents to woo her for him in her page's disguise, and offers Silvia the ring she had given Proteus. She follows him to the forest and hears her beloved threaten to rape Silvia. Still she loves him, and her constancy is given a magical power by Shakespeare: it alone wins back Proteus' love.

Constancy is magical, however, only in female characters. Males who are faithful, like Valentine, Orlando, or Troilus, lack the luminous, potent haloes possessed by Julia, Marina, or Hermione. That it is a female virtue is significant.

Love's Labour's Lost

Constancy is the subject of two other comedies, *Love's Labour's Lost* and *A Midsummer Night's Dream*. In *Love's Labour's*, constancy is abused as it is in *Two Gentlemen*—the lords forsake their vows for the ladies, then forsake "their" ladies for "other" ladies, being unable even to recognize their own loves.

In *Love's Labour's Lost*, Shakespeare makes events revocable not so much through disguise—although that is an element—but by focusing on language as theme, on language that embodies the inconstancy of the characters.[6] The play contains a whole gamut of characters with idiosyncratic approaches to language, most of whom are in some way castigated for their language. The ladies stand largely as the ideal; Moth (one of the most illegitimate males) parallels them on a different level; and Jaquenetta, who is not only illiterate but largely unvocal, and the most illegitimate character in the play, escapes unscathed. All other characters are in some way reproached for their language. Although the play is sometimes seen as a satire on pretension and pedantry, not all of the castigation is directed at the pretentious: the nonpretentious Dull and Costard mock and are mocked throughout the comedy.[7]

Love's Labour's has a multiple focus: the village people comprise not a subplot to a main action, but fragments of a world which are gradually integrated into a whole through the interweaving structure of Shakespearean comedy. In the conclusion, Holofernes becomes simple and dignified, Costard and Armado obliquely and surprisingly profound; and the Princess is gracious, as usual. But the pompous verse of the pageant and the cruel and brisk heckling of the lords provide the discordant note found in any group of humans.

Shakespeare knew what is sometimes forgotten, that the problem in ordering a society is not how to eliminate discord, but how to contain it, allow it to exist freely without disrupting the whole. His symbol for this *discordia concors* is music, which appears sometimes as allusion, sometimes as theme, sometimes as song itself breaking into or—as in this play—ending the drama. Music, a permanent, transcendent, highly formal structure, celebrates the fluid, the transient, the recurrent. Just so, the play celebrates the beauties and humiliations of nature and the transiencies and variety of the characters.[8]

Despite the pervasive criticism of the others' language by almost all the characters, Nathaniel knows that society is the happiness of life and dull Dull is not excluded from the feast. The world would be poorer without the extravagances of Armado and the village crew, without the comic absurdity of Holofernes and Nathaniel perusing a forbidden love-letter and seeing only a literary style in need of their evaluation. The theme of language operates like the convention of disguise to permit stretching of identity and morality: it permits expressions of aggression and sexuality that would not be acceptable in action.[9]

Ralph Berry, who believes the play is about language, traces three approaches to it: that of the lords, Armado, and Holofernes, for whom words are ends in themselves; that of the clowns, for whom words symbolize things; and that of the ladies, for whom words symbolize reality.[10] The play celebrates a dual process. Like the earlier comedies, it takes its pleasure in what is not fixed, what is ambiguous and shifting and duplicitous and playful; and at the same time it suggests an ideal of constancy in which word and spirit are identical, heart and tongue are one.[11]

Disguise permits unusual or conventionally immoral acts to occur by making them revocable. Language as theme permits unusual or conventionally immoral statements to be made; language is revocable because it is being uttered in *play*. Bawdy jokes and hostile remarks function in all of the comedies as means for expanding experience, and as safety valves: one can say in play what one cannot do, or say, seriously. *Love's Labour's Lost* is Shakespeare's freest comedy, the one most completely set within the feminine principle. The park is outside time, out of reach—through most of the drama—of the structured world of power.[12]

The ideals enunciated in the opening speeches are indeed "masculine" values—transcendence, knowledge, and accomplishment—but they are unworldly forms of power, possession, and prowess. Bobbyann Roesen points out that the King's first words associate Fame, Time, and Death. But, she adds, Berowne realizes within the first scene that the only way to deal with time and death is "to accept it, to experience as much of life's sensory loveliness as possible."[13] Political and economic power are negligible in Navarre. It is a world of pure play, despite its threatened punishments, because the motivations of the lords are so openly shaky and unrealistic. Berowne's objections to Navarre's pronouncements cast on them a light that makes it difficult to take seriously threats of tongue excision.

The abuses in this world are abuses against the feminine principle, with its anarchic or at least democratic insistence on the validity of all things. The lords' treatment of their social inferiors is not courteous, as the masculine principle properly handled would enjoin. Berowne expresses considerable misogyny; he is arrogant with Costard in III, i, calling him *slave*, *knave*, and *villain*. Armado's conception of himself as King Cophetua and Jaquenetta as the beggar is also arrogant and pompous. Both the schoolmaster and the curate make disdainful remarks. All of these involve setting oneself up as superior to others—hierarchy—and they foreshadow the cruelty and scorn which ruin the pageant. All the legitimate males abuse their privilege; all suffer as a result of this general tendency, this mode of thought and behavior in male circles.

The victorious principle in the play is nature seen as insistent, undeniable sexuality, and the need for bodily and mental pleasure, for play. This involves submission to nature as well: what ends the drama is the announcement of death and a song about sex and weather. The grease of Joan in the lyric that concludes the comedy is a homonym, in Shakespearean pronunciation, with grace.[14]

Love's Labour's Lost is the only comedy, indeed the only play of Shakespeare's in which the chastity of a heroine is impugned without serious consequences. Rosaline is deemed light by Berowne in language which adumbrates the serious speeches of Claudio and Iago. He sees her as:

> A whitely wanton with a velvet brow,
> With two pitch-balls stuck in her face for eyes;
> Ay, and, by heaven, one that will do the deed
> Though Argus were her eunuch and her guard.
> (III, i, 196–199)

Boyet also charges Rosaline with loose sexual morals. The charge is neither denied nor admitted: like power, sexual constraint is negligible in this park. It is not the waiting women but the ladies themselves who indulge in bawdy jokes.

In addition, of all Shakespeare's works, *Love's Labour's* has the most "feminine" conclusion. No transcendent marriage ceremony concludes its events; no legend or monument is erected. "Feminine" works are open-ended; in the eternal focus of the principle of nature, monuments are built to Ozymandias. Such works presume only continuation—the world will go on as it has always gone on. No external goal is as important as the magical, haloed present moment. The sojourn in the park has been beautiful indeed, and its conclusion is large and rich and sure enough to contain pomposity and cruelty and even death without losing its overall harmony.[15]

The ladies will return home; the lords will spend a year learning what life is like when one does not have privilege. So will Armado if he can stick it. The rest will go on as they were. The design of the play operates less to change the characters than to find a social-aesthetic form broad enough to contain them all.

Shakespeare did not continue in the path begun by *Love's Labour's Lost*. He moved away from its freedoms with both language and sex, and moved his female characters to a realm "untainted" with the latter. In addition, he did not again turn his back so firmly on "masculine" power. Although the comedies may take place largely in a "feminine" green world or place apart, they are also firmly set within a realm of political and economic power (except for *Twelfth Night*). And the value which underlies the later plays is a development of the value foreshadowed by *Two Gentlemen* and *Love's Labour's Lost*: constancy.

A Midsummer Night's Dream

Shakespeare gives constancy its fullest utterance in A *Midsummer Night's Dream*, where is it set against, opposed to, imagination. There is critical agreement that the comedy is about imagination, but disagreement on the moral value of this quality.[16] Imagination in *Midsummer Night's Dream* is the mental power to shape reality; it is mode of perception. The way one sees can one day endow a woman with radiant beauty and the next day cover her with pitch; it can make a place feel like heaven one day and hell the next; it can make an ass appear desirable.[17]

Constancy, of course, implies an ultimate reality, an ultimate truth: Athens is really either heaven or hell; a woman is really beautiful or she is not. Imagination vacillates like all human minds; constancy remains, like a divine standard. The symbol for the intersection of the two qualities is the moon, the Renaissance emblem for the intersection of two realms of being—the sublunary, with its decaying matter and transient life, and the superlunary, with its eternally lasting planets and divinities.[18] *Midsummer Night's Dream* synthesizes the two realms not through metaphor (as in Spenser's *Mutability Cantos*), but through its design.

The major convention of the play is transformation, a cousin to disguise, but subtler, for transformation is the result of imagination, mode of perception, rather than changed clothes.[19] The notion of transformation and the symbolic moon are associated in the first lines of the play: imagination can make the moon seem an impending step-dame or a huntress's bow.

Theseus wooed Hippolyta with power which is now being cere-moniously transformed to love. Hermia's challenge to her father's power has transformed his love for her to hate, and his opposition to her choice of a husband has transformed the heaven of Athens into a hell. Helena plans to follow her friends to the forest in an attempt to turn *her* hell into heaven. And of course Oberon uses power to trans-form Titania's loyalty to the dead mother of the changeling boy, and her love for him, into sexual love for an ass. He thus transforms her challenge of him back into submission.

These transformations are more complex than disguises; they are not simple alternations, but syntheses. When Cambio removes his mean clothing, he is Lucentio again (albeit, perhaps a bit stretched); when the lords of *Love's Labour's* remove their Russian disguises, they are again themselves. But transformation includes all manifestations of a thing. Thus, Theseus' present love for Hippolyta does not annul or eradicate his victory or his power over her; rather, it contains them. The quarrel of Oberon and Titania does not annul their essential rap-port. The inconstancy of Demetrius and the enchanted Lysander is an expression of the ambivalence of love. The reawakened Titania vaguely recalls that she loved an ass. The conclusion of the play, then, includes all its preceding events, synthesizes polarities of heaven and hell, love and the fading of love, just as the moon symbolizes both constancy and inconstancy.

Thus the play presents a dream that is able to include everything. It has been shown that the imagery, which gives a first impression of beauty and harmony and fruitfulness and great delicacy, includes many elements that are grotesque, threatening, ludicrous, and ugly.[20] The sorts of love that are shown in the play also include the absurd, the grotesque, and the foolish. Romantic love is made absurd by the circular madness of the four young mortals; it is parodied in the artisans' performance of Pyramus and Thisbe; and idealized (with considerable subversion, however) in Theseus and Hippolyta. Titania's passion for Bottom is grotesque; Oberon's desire for the changeling boy has a tinge of the perverse, of Jove's love for Ganymede. And, as in *Love's Labour's*, there are intimations of considerable sexual freedom in the fairy folk without any concomitant suggestion of evil or pollution. Both Oberon and Titania accuse each other of varying affections, and Theseus' sexual history, as recounted by Oberon, sounds like something Shakespeare might condemn in a different play, as it includes broken vows, abandonment, and outright rape.[21]

Because it is so inconstant and can take many forms, love is associated with the moon. The moon is seen multivalently, even contradictorily—it is a stepmother checking desire, a bow; it is cold and fruitless; it governs floods, it is chaste and inhibiting. But it is also horned, and laments "enforced chastity." The final vision of the moon is the one held up by Starveling: although the man is supposed to be in the moon, the moon is in the man's hands. It is an emblem here for the power of human imagination to create what it sees.

Nevertheless, through all its varieties and inconstancies, the moon returns, month after month, to proceed through its same phases. And so too love. Mortal, and even immortal love may be folly: but love is part of a larger design.[22] In *Midsummer Night's Dream*, love is a principle of the universe, Empedoclean Eros. Like the moon, it is inconstant only within a larger pattern of constancy. Regardless of the foolishness or vacillation of individual approaches to love, the earth goes on being replenished. The play asserts the supreme power of love seen from an overarching point of view, from eternity. David Young discusses the panoramic imagery, used especially by Titania and Oberon, as a device for creating "perspective and distance."[23] However, the design of the play also contributes to this distance.

The design of the comedy presents a series of actors and witnesses. Theseus and Hippolyta begin as spectators to the cosmic panorama, then become witnesses to a domestic quarrel. Groups act in seeming isolation, but they are integrated with other groups without their full knowledge. The suggestion of a larger perspective is thus always present. In the final scene, the three mortal groups converge, although there are still "actors"—the artisans—and witnesses—the reunited lovers and the court group. But unknowingly, the humans are being watched by the fairies. And all of the groups have parallel qualities. Thus, Theseus' ultrarationalism is parodied and paralleled by the literalism of the mechanics; the sexual inconstancy of Theseus, Oberon, and Titania is paralleled by that of the two male lovers. The same things exist on the low, middle, and high human ground, as well as in the divine realm.

Nor is power disregarded in this play about love. Theseus has heroic power (prowess) and political power—he is a duke. He has conquered Hippolyta with both. Hermia's father has political and economic power over her. Oberon uses magical power on Titania. Magic in this case is acceptable because it is in the control of a male. Power operates both to hinder or destroy, and to foster love: it is as ambivalent as anything else in the play.

But constancy provides the wide outer framework for all qualities, holding within it the many inconstancies and inadequacies and foolishnesses of mortals and immortals alike. On earth it is imagination that dominates: the moon is in the man. But if these two forces—constancy and imagination—are antagonistic to each other, they are also synthesized in the play as perfectly as any human creation can synthesize experience. The moon is in the man. But the man is in the moon, too.

6

Money

The Merchant of Venice and
The Merry Wives of Windsor

A *Midsummer Night's Dream* establishes love as a power in the universe, transcending the variables, the inconstancy of natural processes, in the same way that the constancy of lunar processes transcends their inconstant variables. To explore and examine this power, Shakespeare pitted it, in two comedies, against one manifestation of "masculine" power-in-the-world, economic power, money. In the problem comedies, he will weigh it against political power as well.

In *Midsummer Night's Dream*, love is primarily erotic; in *The Merchant of Venice*, the notion of love is projected beyond sexuality, as a force for harmony, acceptance, and flexibility in general human life. In *The Merry Wives of Windsor*, love is posited both as sexual desire and the binding qualities of the inlaw aspect, but in fact, so dominant are the terms of its environment that love appears in this play merely as possession. With *Much Ado About Nothing*, these two comedies contain the only clear, recognizable villains. (Malvolio cannot be counted as one of these because he has too little effect on the action.) In each of these cases, the character of the villain represents the nature of the threat posed to the play-world. C. L. Barber has claimed that Shylock is a scapegoat, that he bears, solely, responsibility for values entertained by his entire community.[1] The same is true of

Falstaff and Don John. These figures cannot, however, be neatly categorized simply as misrule figures, as representative of the emotion
that overthrows reason and order. They are associated with the opposite gender principles. Shylock, who cares about possession for its own
sake, is an example of the masculine principle when it has forgotten
the ends for which it exists. The Falstaff of *Merry Wives* and Don John
have the rebelliousness and interest in sexual freedom that characterize the outlaw feminine aspect.

This chapter analyzes the first two of these comedies in which the
power of the feminine principle is pitted against that of the masculine.

The Merchant of Venice

A bonding by love holds together the entire universe in *Midsummer
Night's Dream*; the same kind of bonding occurs in *Merchant of Venice*, but it influences not the universe or even the entire play-world,
but only half of it, Belmont. Venice is dominated by the masculine
principle, Belmont by the feminine, but the two are related to each
other, dependent on each other, and share certain concerns.[2] The
meaning of Venice is understood by the Belmonters, by Portia, at
least, but the meaning of Belmont is not even suspected by true Venetians.

The opening scene depicts the values of Venice: the city is entirely
absorbed by money and manners. Manners are "feminine" when they
are dictated by the self-subordinating desire to please or to set another
at ease; they are "masculine" when they are dictated by a desire to
assert the self, to show superiority or rank, or to make an impression
on another person. In Venice, manners are tied to "masculine" values
like honor, reputation, and fame. Although such things can be important, the play suggests they are barren unless they are tied to true ends
—pleasure (play) and procreation, seen in this play as fruitfulness.

Antonio is sad, but replies "O fie!" when asked if he is in love.
Love is not a value in this world in which women are "vendible." Portia
is described merely as a way of acquiring wealth. She is "richly left,"
"nothing undervalued," having "worth"; her hair is a "golden fleece,"
and she can provide Bassanio's "thrift," making him "fortunate."
These terms are double-edged, and can apply to moral as well as financial wealth, but the base of the metaphors is economic.[3] They are the
best one can do in Venice, which understands only economic language.

Salerio and Solanio are infatuated with money and possessions, and rise almost into high poetry just talking of these things. Gratiano and Lorenzo are concerned with money and manners, with making an impression on the wealthy Antonio. Antonio himself and Shylock are deeply connected. Both are wealthy merchants, both are Venetians, both lend money. But money is an end in itself for Shylock, who is a Jew, a characterization no doubt intended to plug into Renaissance notions and prejudices, but whose behavior is more accurately described as puritanical. Shylock's house, according to both Launcelot Gobbo and Jessica, is joyless and sparse; sensuous pleasure is forbidden, whether it be food or drink, music or dancing, or even watching others at pleasure. Shylock lends money to make money, thus forcing it to bear fruit, but its fruit, Shakespeare suggests, does not feed the inner person. Antonio, on the other hand, lends money to earn love. Nevertheless, the love he holds most precious is that for Bassanio, which, because it is a same-sex love, is as barren a love as Shylock's. Antonio is able to enter Belmont—imaginatively and physically—because he can feel love. It has been claimed that he too is a usurer, because he gives in order to receive.[4] If, as Shakespeare suggests, Shylock is "unnatural" because he is a usurer, clearly Antonio *feels* unnatural too. He calls himself a "tainted wether of the flock" (IV, i, 114).

Shylock rules out pleasure; Antonio, by his proclivities, is ruled out of sex. Money and its concomitants (possession, structured manners) are the governing values of Venice. For Shylock, willfully, and for Antonio perforce, money is the equivalent of love. In this world, Bassanio is a failure, and that is his main virtue.

The dialogue between Portia and Nerissa, which follows immediately the scene delineating Venetian values, opens with a discussion of Portia's sadness. Like Antonio, Portia is sad because she lacks love. Like him, she will use her wealth to purchase love in the form of a husband. (Harley Granville-Barker claims that often in Shakespeare, love is buying and selling and that most often the woman is bought for her property. But a propertied woman would seem to be not the bought but the buyer—as indeed Portia claims to be.[5]) Since money is so important an element in middle-class Renaissance marriage, it is a (to us) deflecting or vulgar factor in what would otherwise be pure romance. But given the class structure of the time, it would be naive to insist that money should not matter. It matters in the plays because it mattered in the life. The point is not who buys or is bought, but the intention of the people involved. Once Portia has "bought" her hus-

band, she gives herself and all she owns to him; and Bassanio is chosen
because he conceives of love as pure giving.

Portia and Nerissa, at their first appearance, discuss morality and
the ambiguity of human conduct. This is another way of talking about
moral flexibility, implicit in the feminine principle. Conversations in
Belmont frequently focus on this subject. Despite the fact that there is
only one "right" answer to the choice of caskets, in all other matters,
the Belmonters are free-swinging in their views. Then Portia offers a
set of satiric sketches of her suitors: it is not just the mercantile world
which is being satirized here, but "masculine" values in general. Portia's suitors are insensitive, pompous and artificial, narrow (loving only
horses and drinking), arrogant, egotistical, and ignorant of the meaning of love.

The movement of the play is a gradual emigration of characters
from Venice to Belmont, a reversal of this as many of them go back to
Venice, and a final sorting out which is equivalent to a moral categorization. The departure of Bassanio from Venice is a loss to Antonio;
the elopement of Jessica is a loss to Shylock: but both emotional losses
are *felt* essentially in economic terms. Antonio's lost ships are symbolic
of his loss of Bassanio, and threaten him with the loss of his life.[6]
Shylock cries out for his ducats and his daughter. Different as they
are, the two men understand each other, speak the same language,
and entertain similar values, although with an importantly different
emphasis: Antonio gives his love for Bassanio priority; Shylock puts his
ducats first.[7]

The world of Belmont is shown as graceful and harmonious; one
of its main characteristics is moral flexibility. It may seem paradoxical
that the dimension of experience concerned with morality—as opposed to law—should also be morally flexible, but a true morality is
one which is rooted in human needs and desires, and attempts to
contain them within a balance so that people may breathe freely, and
yet live with each other. Moral law, on the other hand, is a fixed code
that is imposed on people from outside. Moral flexibility means mercy
(not justice), compassion (not judgment), and support (not discipline).
It also includes revocable expressions of hostility and sexuality, especially in wordplay and banter. (Wordplay, as suggested earlier, always
indicates a degree of moral relativism.)

Thus the scene that immediately precedes the trial of Bassanio
and Shylock is totally irrelevant to the causal sequence. III, v, is occupied with banter among Jessica, Launce, and Lorenzo—among the
least legitimate of the characters—that contains both hostility and

sexuality, but includes both in fluid acceptance. Thus, too, the con-
cluding scene, the return to Belmont. These scenes frame the legal
rigidity of Venice with the moral flexibility of a "feminine" world.[8]

Portia's disguise, like those of all the transvestite heroines, allows
her to enter the masculine principle. The essential element in these
disguises is not whether the Renaissance held such dress to be wicked
or a sign of sorcery; in Shakespeare, what matters is *why* a woman
adopts male dress. Joan adopts it in order to use her power to kill;
Portia adopts it in order to use her power (knowledge) to save. Dedicated still to volitional renunciation of power-in-the-world and to the
support of the masculine establishment, a disguised woman might exercise a degree of independence and assertiveness. If her goal, her
aim, is "feminine," male dress does not compromise her natural female
identity.

Portia's disguise is essential to her purpose, for in her own identity
she could not act in Venice. Venice hardly recognizes what she represents—the feminine principle—and could not be convinced of the
legitimacy of it. She must appear speaking the language, bearing the
appearance of the world of power, money, and law. Law is an attempt
to use language precisely, to codify shades of meaning, to fix morality.
The courtroom discussion is an attempt to define terms, an attempt
that contrasts strongly with the moral ambiguity of the wordplay of
Belmont which surrounds it. Although Portia uses Belmont values in
her "mercy" speech, this gains her nothing. She must use Venetian
values to win. "Neither the Venetians nor the laws and customs of
Venice are vindicated by Shylock's downfall," writes J. W. Lever.[9]
Whatever degree of sympathy we grant to Shylock, he is clearly guilty
of inhumaneness. But he loses everything he values except his life; no
one else loses anything. In the trial scene, it is not only Shylock, but
Antonio, Bassanio, and Gratiano who are tested: none passes.

It is frequently remarked that there are two kinds of love shown in
the play. Sometimes these are distinguished as friendship (between
males) and love (between male and female). But Shakespeare indicates
rather clearly, I think, that love is one thing—giving.[10] Flexible and
fluid as giving is, it cannot be fixed by a code; it is "feminine." Love of
male for male can easily have this nature, as does Kent's love for Lear,
say, or Horatio's for Hamlet. It is above all a giving of the self in the
way Portia gives herself to Bassanio. (This can have political overtones,
suggesting that Portia has control over her own life, choice of husband;
but it is primarily emotional.) This is the kind of love Bassanio chooses
when he selects the leaden casket. Despite his selection, however, he
understands it improperly.

He understands it improperly because he has not been educated in it, but rather in the "masculine" love found on the Rialto. "Masculine" love is codified love; it becomes a code of honor or fidelity, the laws of marriage, or a code of manners. It is not a free gift made out of overflowing bounty or because of the need of the receiver: it has other ends. These may be the maintenance of honor or status or of a social structure perceived as a boundary between humanness and savagery. Thus, Antonio's love for Bassanio is "feminine"—given purely, with no hope of return or gain. His "love" for Balthasar is, understandably, another kind of thing. He urges the giving of the ring out of shame at being found ungrateful. In doing so he demonstrates that he too lacks understanding of the kind of love that exists between Portia and Bassanio. Both men grant a higher value to "masculine" love than to the insubstantialities of the other variety. Indeed, one critic agrees with this priority.[11]

During the trial, and in the hearing of their wives, Bassanio and Gratiano subordinate their "feminine" love to their "masculine" one. It is easy to do this, partly because the latter form has connections with power and possession that the first lacks, and partly because their "feminine" love is for females, who are subordinate in this society, and whose loyalty and fidelity can be taken for granted. Bassanio claims he would sacrifice Portia to Shylock if that would help Antonio; Gratiano wishes Nerissa dead so she could intercede for Antonio in heaven. Even Shylock is shocked: "These be the Christian husbands" (IV, i, 295). Having returned to Venice, the two men have forgotten the insubstantial—the spiritual, or emotional—values of Belmont, and slide back easily into their old ones. The statements made at the trial are the first steps in the giving up of the rings.

The last act returns the characters to Belmont and the final working out of the power struggle. Belmont is filled with music—the dominant image of the play.[12] The scene opens with a discussion of failed loves which nevertheless stand as affirmations of the power and value of love—moral relativism affects love too. Portia and Nerissa open the battle. Gratiano, still Venetian, insists that Nerissa's ring was of little value, and that it was inscribed with a silly verse. Neither husband understands the meaning of his act until the women equate the symbolic rings with an emotional stance—chaste constancy, an invisible and unenforceable bond of love.

The moral flexibility which is one of Belmont's characteristics permits revocability, forgiveness of the words which have been spoken, the actions performed. It also permits the sexual banter which ends the play. The victory of morality over legalism is a victory of pleasure and (ceremonialized) sex over puritanism and power as its own end.

Nevertheless, Belmont and Venice are ultimately related. They need each other; they share more than they separate. They are two complementary realms: on the most basic level, the same money that Venice is obsessed with protects and maintains Belmont. But the division between them, and Venetian blindness to the nature of Belmont, its supposition that its values are the *only* values, will provide material for Shakespeare's tragedies.

The Merry Wives of Windsor

The Merry Wives of Windsor is a farce, an action comedy, with a linear plot, heavy use of disguise, and a male "hero" who is also the villain. The ambivalence of the central character resembles that of Petruchio, who is both hero and villain (for Kate, at least), and the split between the twin Antipholuses, who each unwittingly become the antagonist of the other. The difference between Falstaff and the two other figures is that they win and he does not. Petruchio is able to discard his shrewish side once Kate has subordinated herself to him; both Antipholuses accept happily their given places in the moral-social structure of their world. But Falstaff has set out to violate the core virtue in the Shakespearean value structure; the part of him that willed such an act must be, like Don John, exorcised from the community.

The setting is bourgeois—settled, prosperous, and imbued with a moral complacency lacking even in the puritanical Shylock. Its terms are overwhelmingly "masculine": the play opens with Shallow and Slender listing the former's claim to legitimacy in the form of titles and prerogatives, anciency of house, coats of arms. Because the characters are so foolish, this discussion acts to challenge the notion of legitimacy. Thus, as usual in Shakespeare, the opening of the play sets forth its terms: they seem familiar—legitimacy versus challenges to it. But in this case, the challenge arises (at first) not from outsiders, illegitimates, but in our minds, as a result of the inanity and self-satisfaction of the legitimates. There arc further challenges quickly: Falstaff kills Shallow's deer, illegally; his men pick Slender's pockets. And we know by now that Slender is intending a kind of theft: he agrees to marry Anne Page for her money.

The major themes of the play are the cornerstones of bourgeois life: possession of property, possession of women, and fear of theft. There are two plots, each containing a stranger who is a down-at-heels aristocrat (foreigner) who is attempting to "steal" from the propertied men of Windsor. The action concerns the efforts of Falstaff and Fenton to get what they want, and the efforts of the Windsorites to thwart them. The outsiders are perceived as thieves, like the "Germans" who do steal the host's horses.

But in keeping with the suggestion that the legitimates are not any more legitimate than anyone else, the insiders are also busy thieving. The host cheats his customers; Mistress Quickly cheats anyone who will pay for her help; the host intends to cheat the "Germans" who cheat him first. Evans and Caius intend to duel over a piece of property neither of them owns—Anne Page—but are cozened by the host and cozen him in return. Slender and his adherents intend to cheat the Pages by offering a false devotion to Anne in return for her person and her property.

Falstaff, supposedly the major cozener, is cozened into giving money to Mistress Quickly, is cozened by the wives, and is betrayed by his own servants. Ford is cozened by Falstaff into paying for his own cozening. Both Pages cozen each other in their attempts to have Anne stolen away, but she and Fenton cozen them instead. Everyone in the play (except William) cozens, is cozened, or both.

For the most part, the disguises operate similarly—they fool the person who adopts the disguise. Both Falstaff and Ford become the victims of their own disguises.

Merry Wives is a play about property. One reason for its unpopularity may be that property is *all* it is about. Even the "feminine" elements of the play—chaste constancy in the wives, love in Anne, and Falstaff's outlaw feminine sexual rebellion—become mere counters in a conflict over property.

Falstaff is set up as an example of the outlaw feminine principle (as he is in the *Henry IV* plays). He wishes to undermine or challenge the established order: he has a reputation for drinking, sexual freedom, and petty crime. But very quickly, in this play, a different note enters: his intention in crime and cozening is not primarily the fun of it—it is for survival. He has an edge of desperation in this play that makes him at once more pathetic and less fun—because he is less free—than the Falstaff of the histories.

And here, his opposition to the established order is less a rebellion against its constrictions and hypocrisies, less based in a need to assert other values, than it is an effort, however odd, to win a place within it.

He cheats and steals and strives to seduce in order to find a place within the society he is victimizing: he wants money to play the gentleman. Originally, he claims that his intention in attempting to seduce the wives is to get at their husbands' purses; but in his meeting with the wives, particularly that in the last scene, he expresses genuine desire for sexual or perhaps merely affectionate love. In his pathetic longing for esteem and affection, he is a sad scapegoat. He wants what everyone else in the play wants—and however unacceptable his means of attaining it, he is more morally acceptable than Mr. Ford. What keeps Sir John an outsider in Windsor, despite his status, is his lack of wealth.

The pathos built into his character would not preclude him from being a villain—it does not do so for Shylock—if his goal were really what it seems—to destroy chaste constancy, the emblem of the feminine principle. But money values override everything in this world. The wives respond to his letters with an outrage similar to that one would feel at an attempted robbery. Their language and their behavior demonstrate that they, like their husbands, see their bodies and reputations as possessions of which Falstaff is trying to defraud them. Their revenge is motivated by the sense that in writing to them at all, he has stolen something from them, and it is calculated in the same terms: they will lead him on until he is forced to pawn his horses to the host.[13]

The host is jealous and possessive about his property; Caius is jealous and possessive about his house and closets; Ford is jealous and possessive about his wife. Page is jealous and possessive about his daughter, whom he sees as property to be disposed of as he chooses: Caius, Evans, and Slender see Anne the same way. (No wonder she speaks so little in the play.) Even Fenton confesses to her that his original intention in courting her was to gain control of her wealth.

Cuckoldry means something quite different to Mr. Ford than it does to Claudio in *Much Ado About Nothing*, or to Posthumus. For them it is a failure of the pivot on which the rest of human life turns. For Mr. Ford it is theft: "My bed shall be abus'd, my coffers ransack'd, my reputation gnawn at" (II, ii, 292–293). He is not concerned with his wife's affections, her relation with him. Nor is he primarily concerned with his reputation—he drags the whole community into his house to witness what he conceives of as *his* degradation. His fear of cuckoldry is a fear of theft.

On the mythic level of this play, a married woman has an affair right under her husband's nose, with the assistance of a woman friend and a village nitwit; and a young woman being courted by two village nitwits defies her parents and elopes. What keeps this underplot from gaining force is that everyone in the community except Anne Page and possibly Fenton, perceives all events in terms of money, possession, and theft.

The disguise convention revokes the adultery and operates to punish Falstaff to the point where he can be assimilated in the community. The marriage is irrevocable, but it too seems to be forgiven and accepted by the elders in the conclusion. *Merry Wives* also concentrates on language-as-theme. Like *Love's Labour's Lost*, it is filled with characters who speak idiosyncratically and who criticize the speech of others: Evans, Pistol, Bardolph, Caius, Slender, and Quickly.

The significance of the language theme is indicated by a short scene which is otherwise extraneous.[14] IV, i, is a discussion of language among Evans, William Page, Mrs. Page, and Mrs. Quickly. There is comedy in Evans' pedantry and Quickly's misunderstanding, but that does not seem reason enough for its existence.

The four characters represent four approaches to language, each dictated by the inner world of the speaker. William, whose mind is still flexible, translates *lapis* as *stone* and *stone* as *pebble*, an understandable progression. He has not yet learned to think in circles. Evans has milked all the life out of language: *lapis* is *stone* and *stone* is *lapis*. Mrs. Page has a greater understanding than anyone else of what is going on, but her interest, in keeping with her place in the community, is strictly material: the *profit* her son is obtaining in school. Evans' scolding of Quickly is, like the disguises in the play, self-delusive: with his accent, he is in a poor position to criticize others' lack of comprehension. And Quickly's horror at the drunkenness and lechery Evans seems to be teaching the child is ironic, since it is her own associations that lead her to this conclusion.

The mutual incomprehension of the residents of Windsor is reminiscent of that of the residents of Navarre, but this short scene with its few characters enunciating their attitudes towards language—rigid pedantry and unimaginativeness; learning for profit; and associations with lechery and drunkenness (and food)—underlines the constriction of atmosphere in which this child is growing up.

Despite the difficulty in comprehension of the Windsorites, despite their mutual censure, hostility, and thievery, there is some sense of community in the town. The two wives are loyal to each other; people dine together; the host prevents the duel between Caius and Evans because the community needs both the "terrestrial" and the "celestial" (III, i, 106). Individual idiosyncrasies are overcome in the masque scene, in which all the characters speak "perfect" English in their united attack on Falstaff.

Fenton, who is in some ways Falstaff's other half, succeeds.[15] He wins Anne Page and proves his love by marrying her even though her father has threatened to cut her off. Falstaff is another case. He is attacked because of his sexual improprieties, mainly, but there is only one value in this town, and Falstaff is no more of a threat to the property of its men than is the host. He is, at the conclusion, accepted as an "insider," but he cannot be an insider because he has no money. Falstaff is an eternal outsider; as a sexual threat he is a poor devil. Neither his defeat nor his acceptance is quite satisfying: a play about property is fun only when the cozeners win.

7

The Realm of Emotion

As You Like It and Twelfth Night

Shakespeare's finest comedies contain a synthesis that is elegant, flexible, and comprehensive. They envision worlds that are able to contain in some degree of freedom, separate elements—the aggressive and rigidifying structures of the power world; the impulse to giving and sacrifice; subversive, intractable sexual and political rebelliousness; and idiosyncratic self-assertion, which makes life interesting but can also fragment a community. The balance arrived at is different in each play, according to its central concern. The central concern of As You Like It and Twelfth Night is the same: the emotional dimension of experience. As You Like It is mainly about love; Twelfth Night is mainly about life—that is, vitality.

As You Like It

The point of view of As You Like It is from the underside of society, made up of women, exiles, outcasts, the poor, the eccentric, and the low in status. From such a perspective, power usually seems oppressive, and its possessors tyrants: both Duke Frederick and Oliver fit the

pattern. The play opens with a complaint at a deprivation of legitimacy. Although the complaint is particular and justified, it also suggests the point of view of the entire play. Because Orlando is a younger
son, his legitimacy is tenuous: it depends on his father's will—in both
senses of the word. That will is known, but is not law, and is not being
acted upon.

Celia and Rosalind, being well-born but women, have the same
fringe status, although they do not complain about it. For them, illegitimacy is built in. Celia does, uniquely in Shakespeare, criticize her
father for his abuse of others. She and Rosalind are witty and assertive
with each other, the fool, and Le Beau—another fool. But with the
Duke they are subdued and subordinate, and protest his decree tear-
fully, meekly.

Orlando, by contrast, fights against Oliver, explaining that it is his
father's spirit within him—a legitimate spirit—that mutinies against
servitude. Nevertheless, the power world overwhelms him too. What
is established in these opening scenes is that these characters are not
illegitimate deservedly, and that their exile is not a result of outlaw
feminine rebelliousness in them.

All three characters are shown to be androgynous. Rosalind and
Celia can act with independence and courage; Orlando not only fights,
but treats Adam with compassion and democracy. He finds as soon as
he enters Arden, however, that "masculine" forms are not acceptable
or necessary here. To get food, one need merely ask. Arden is a feminine world.[1]

The wood is outside timespace. And, although status is formally
retained—the lords defer to the Duke, Touchstone treats the country
folk with disdain—the way of life of the characters as well as the form
of the dramatic design are anarchical. Such anarchy obtains when one
is secluded from, beyond the reach of the world's power structures:
anarchy is a fact of emotional life. Each person or group in the forest
is alone and separate, yet all live together easily without domination.
Only Touchstone, who has the lowest status of any of the court folk,
attempts to dominate anyone, and even that is done for love, or at
least, desire. As You Like It has the most multiple focus of any of the
comedies.

Language as theme is important here. There is banter among
Rosalind, Celia, and Touchstone, and a bit of mockery of Le Beau,
that implies the moral relativism of banter found in Merchant or Love's
Labour's. So does Touchstone's equivocating conversation with Audrey about honesty and poetry and his conversation with Corin. But

much of the language theme centers on literature—honesty vs. poetry, or honesty and poetry. Just as love is central to emotional life, and thus the central theme of this play, attitudes towards love are central in poetry—or were, once upon a time. Rosalind's comments on Orlando's verses, her arguments in the testing of Orlando, Jaques' cynicism, Corin's palinodic comments, and the postures of Phebe and Silvius provide a running commentary on literary renderings of love.[2] This commentary is accompanied with a set of postures in the characters that seems to offer the reality on which that literature is based. Altogether, the characters' seemingly real and seemingly received ideas and feelings comprise a vision of love-in-the-round, a multivalent view.

Disguise too has a slightly different purpose in *As You Like It* from most of the comedies. Rosalind's transvestism, designed at first, like Julia's and Viola's, for protection, operates to other ends once the party is safely in Arden. In court, Celia and Rosalind have a completely equal, give-and-take relationship. However, once they enter the forest in their disguises, Celia's part diminishes. Partly this is because Rosalind's involvement with Orlando is central to the design, but partly it functions to allow Rosalind to live out a freer, more assertive and independent role than she could otherwise. This tendency is observable in II, iv, before the women are aware that Orlando is in the forest too. In male garb, Rosalind automatically becomes the dominant figure of the two. It is she who deals with the outside world, who can meet and converse with men, speak and act assertively, even authoritatively. And she is listened to seriously, bantered with, without the deferential, complimentary, and essentially trivializing address that gentlewomen receive from gentlemen in Shakespeare's plays. She is thus able to develop and demonstrate areas of her personality that could not, according to the stage conventions Shakespeare adhered to, be gracefully revealed if she were in female apparel. She restrains Touchstone's arrogance and disparages Jaques' melancholy; she chides Silvius and Phebe; she is flip with her father. Above all, she is able to speak to Orlando about love without coyness or concealment, without having to defend against romantic or erotic attitudes or demonstrations. In short, she can be a person.

At the same time, Shakespeare is careful to disarm the audience, to keep Rosalind from offending. She makes constant references to her femaleness, references located in a belief in "natural" and basic differences in the genders. Like Orlando, who, weary and hungry in the forest, nevertheless heartens Adam and promises him food—and even carries the old man—Rosalind, weary and hungry, wants to cry but forces herself as "doublet and hose . . . to show itself courageous to petticoat" (II, iv, 6–7). She attacks Celia: "Dost thou think, though I am caparison'd like a man, I have a doublet and hose in my disposition?" (III, ii, 194–196); "Do you not know I am a woman? when I think, I must speak" (III, ii, 249–250).

Her speech and behavior emphasize that for Shakespeare, the difference between female and male was as profound as the difference in other polarities in this play—fortune and nature; court and country. Indeed, Rosalind is often a spokeswoman for "male" values. Her testing of Orlando consists partly of an assertion of the misogynistic maxims of the day. Her chiding of Phebe comes completely out of a male point of view, a sense of women as objects for sale.[3]

Rosalind's charm, her confusions, her swoon, and her references to her womanhood protect the audience from the notion that a gentlewoman could be taken as seriously, could function as effectively in the world as a man. On the other hand, however, and even as he asserts them, Shakespeare questions gender constrictions.

Phebe's passion for "Ganymede" (like Olivia's for "Cesario") permits a comic—revocable—examination of same-sex erotic love. So too do the loves of the two Antonios for Bassanio and Sebastian, although these require no disguises but much more subtlety. In *Merchant*, erotic love of man for man is repudiated because it cannot breed naturally; in *As You Like It*, erotic love of woman for woman is repudiated on grounds of physical impossibility.

Nevertheless, the inclusion of such a love in Arden rounds out the multivalent portrait that is given. The tested, tried, romantic and erotic love of Rosalind and Orlando is the central ideal in a broad group. There is also the idealizing romanticism that binds Silvius; the sudden violent passion of Celia and Oliver; the humiliating vanquishment of a wryly embarrassed Touchstone by intense desire; Phebe's love for a (disguised) woman; the understanding renunciation of Corin; and the skepticism of the former libertine Jaques. All these exist together; the sea of possibilities includes the forbidden, the forgotten, the weary, and the disappointed.

Through delving into the "feminine", pole of their experience, nature as opposed to fortune, the characters discover their inclinations, the inner drive and need. Unaffected by considerations of status, economics, and power structures—and in Phebe's case, even gender —they discover a different sort of identity than that found in *Comedy of Errors*.

Harold Jenkins complains of the lack of cause-and-effect plotting in *As You Like It*; he writes "nothing happens that changes the course of [the characters'] lives."[4] But the play focuses not on the course but on the texture of the characters' lives, of their relation to earth, not the world.[5] Hierarchical structures like plot, possessions like kingdoms and estates, are irrelevant to this dimension of human experience. And what the characters find in their investigation of this part of themselves sometimes surprises them. The Duke finds sweet the uses of adversity; Touchstone, the snob, is helplessly attracted to an ignorant and unseemly shepherdess; Oliver believes he is giving up wealth and power to settle down with a country girl. Jaques, who is primarily "masculine" in his continual search for significance in experience, and who meditates on human claims to significance, human claims to virtue, human claims to be different from other animals, decides to remain in Arden, that "feminine" world, in order to learn from the converted Duke Frederick. It is ironic that Jaques and Touchstone, who are the two intellectuals of the play, are most profoundly affected by the nonintellectual, "feminine" environment. Touchstone falls victim to an eroticism powerful enough to overcome his strong sense of status; Jaques, who insists men are nothing but the roles imposed on them by a social structure (the Shakespeare who wrote *Comedy of Errors* has not completely vanished), intends to continue in the meditative life, and cannot join in the (comparatively) mild structuring of a wedding ceremony. He vanishes into relativism, skepticism, and denial.[6]

Touchstone's famous speech on degrees of aggression, uttered just before the marriage ceremony, is a gloss on the technique of comedy and a gloss on the play. Aggression, in keeping with its "masculine" nature, is stratified, hierarchically categorized. Touchstone describes a form of war as it appears "in print, by the book"—thus, codified, fixed. All these degrees of aggression can lead to irrevocability unless one appends an "If." "Your If is the only peacemaker; much virtue in If" (V, iv, 102–103).[7]

This speech, directly preceding the transcendent hymn of Hymen, casts the light of relativity upon the proceedings, just as Jaques' parting speech, predicting but two months' wrangling for Touchstone's marriage, looks backwards at the events. The kinds of marriages that will develop from the ceremony vary as greatly as the kinds of love that led to them. The extremes are Touchstone and Audrey, with their exclusively erotic bond, and Phebe and Silvius, whose bond lacks an erotic element (for Phebe, anyway). At the center is the ideal love of Rosalind and Orlando, and (implicitly) that of Celia and Oliver. But if Jaques will not stay to celebrate, he attends the ceremony; Corin is not present except in memory.

If: were humans but constant, life were perfect. *As You Like It* does not blink the multivalent truth of love; at the same time, it insists, like *Midsummer Night's Dream*, that all foolish or transient mortal emotion is part of a larger process, the binding by the cosmic force of love.

Albert Gilman discusses the frequent suggestions of relativity in *As You Like It*—Touchstone commenting on the shepherds' life, or Rosalind on time, for instance. But he concludes: "The relativism of the play's discourse is bounded by a set of moral absolutes that cannot be taken as you like it."[8] Some of these are sickness, as Corin describes it, or natural facts like cold and hunger.

In fact, the events of the play are doubly bounded—by the power structures of the world on the one hand, and the constrictions of nature on the other. Both impinge on the characters, both are "causal." But neither is terribly important. Arden is not, despite the associations that underlay Shakespeare's division of experience, the realm of nature, but the realm of emotional life, which is subject to nature no more than it is to the world. In actuality, it is subject to both: nevertheless it continues to live free.

Twelfth Night

On the mythic level of this play, a sensitive person (in comedy: therefore a female) is thrown up by the sea on a land of emotion to which she is a stranger, and in which she does not know how to behave. She has no identity because she has no role; she lacks even gender identity. She is beloved by Antonio (her social inferior, and composite with the captain who aids her in the beginning of the play), Olivia (her social equal and like), and Orsino (her social superior), among whom she finds it painful to choose. Finding herself in an impossible emotional bind, she does not herself attempt to act, but rather leaves the situation to time. Events themselves and her own unconscious feelings lead to a choice among Antonio, who loves her in a subordinate way, serving and caring for her; Olivia, who loves her with passion and demands requital; and Orsino, who loves her in a superior way, for her charm, her subordination, and her fidelity.

The world of *Twelfth Night* is often viewed as mad.[9] Its title indicates such a condition, but the madness of Illyria resembles that of Ephesus: it has the frenzy and disconnection attendant to emotional life not structured by role. *Twelfth Night* is, in a sense, a reseeing of the problems first approached in *Comedy of Errors*.

As in *As You Like It*, love is the central fact of emotional experience, but *Twelfth Night* is concerned not only with forms of sexual love (and its denial and repudiation), but with forms of love of life (and its denial and repudiation). Insofar as the play has a norm, it is Viola, but she represents essentially an absence, the searching, uncertain part of the self. All of the sensitive characters suffer some impediment to wholehearted embracing of life. That Orsino and Olivia seem to derive pleasure from feeling pain does not change the fact that they feel that pain. Viola suffers from complete disorientation, a loss of home and sibling that amounts (as in *Comedy of Errors*) to loss of place, and therefore identity.

Sir Toby and his cohorts have no such impediment: they love life totally because they are unconscious of irrevocability—of tragedy, of death. Thus, they are incarnations of the spirit of comedy unmodified, undisciplined by a power principle. It never occurs to them that their games might cause Malvolio *real* suffering, or end with Andrew or Toby or Cesario suffering a broken head. Although Toby's motivation is given as a desire for money, the intention to bilk, such efforts simply peter out (as do Falstaff's economic motives in *Merry Wives*) in the face of a motive more pressing. Falstaff's is sexual desire; Toby's is fun.

Toby and his crew are exemplars of the outlaw feminine principle. They abandon themselves to sensuous pleasure—eating, drinking, jokes, and encounter with Maria. They defy the proper order of a polite household; they do things for no reason beyond the fun of doing them. Despite their continual drunkenness, they are lively and witty and provide the energy of the play. They love life in a basic, childlike way. As rebels against the established (or any) structure, they are related to Falstaff and Don John, but they are not severely humiliated or promised "brave punishments"; rather they are knocked about a bit, forced to learn that some actions, some words, are indeed irrevocable. They take part in the final scene, if not its final moments; thus, although it is eccentric, their behavior can be tolerated, assimilated in this community.

The important thing in the comedies is not what is done but why it is done; emotional state, not action, is important. Thus Oliver's conversion at the end of *As You Like It* can eradicate his former cruelties to Orlando. The jokes of Toby and his crew could indeed have serious consequences, but the group is accepted because their motive is less malice than love of play. The "villain" in this comedy is not the outlaw feminine principle, not Toby or Andrew, but Malvolio, the denier of life and joy.

All of the major characters except Malvolio are connected through love or love of pleasure with the feminine principle. Maria, that opaque figure, is sensitive to other people—she *sees* them. So she understands Olivia's needs and Malvolio's delusions. She seems to suffer from a love that has not been legitimated; nevertheless, she revels in Toby's world.

Orsino and Olivia are "feminine" because they exist totally in feeling. Orsino drowns in his own emotion. Depsite his passion for Olivia, he does little to show it: as Viola points out, if *she* loved Olivia, she would build "a willow cabin at your gate, / And call upon my soul within the house" (I, v, 268–269). Olivia drowns in mourning.

Illyria is often seen as the kingdom of misrule; if it is one, the misrule is not parody or abuse of power, but no dominant power at all —anarchy. This is true on the communal and on the personal levels. Worldly power is not important to most of the characters. The Duke is courteous to his inferiors, and is not feared; Toby and his group ignore Olivia's rank and position in the house. As *As You Like It* provides a "feminine" atmosphere by removing the characters from the world of power, status, and legitimacy, *Twelfth Night* does the same thing by removing concern about power, status, and legitimacy from the characters. (In many ways, the two plays are complements, emphasizing opposite positions in the same argument.) Like Arden, Illyria is a place where all live their own way, yet manage to live together. And Illyria too seems to exist outside of time.

The only characters who are concerned with or even aware of worldly power are Malvolio, Feste, and Antonio, who make up the "subversive" or minority voice in this play.

These three characters represent the masculine principle in Illyria. Appropriately, all feel like outsiders in the "feminine" atmosphere, all are illegitimates in a "masculine" sense.

Malvolio desires decorum and formality, self-control, and denial of sensuous pleasure. He longs for rank and power, and insists on law and order in the house. He wants Olivia's trappings rather than her company. If he had power, he might be a puritan like Shylock, or perhaps like Angelo. Without it, he is not threatening, is an annoyance rather than a tyrant. He values (seeming) permanencies like possession and status rather than pleasure and love because he knows nothing about feeling. Since egotism and love of status are isolating qualities, and the inability to feel pleasure and love is like being cut off from light and warmth, his "punishment"—being isolated in darkness and treated as if he were mad—is an emblem for his emotional state.

Feste is an outsider because his experience has damaged his capacity for joy. He is a reminder of the constrictions that exist both in the power world and in nature. Sylvan Barnet points out that he, whose name "signifies" that he is the very incarnation of festivity— stands apart, calling attention to the hardships of life." [10] Life is hard, and love does not last, he insists. He is right. But it is an error, I think, to find his truth the central truth of the play. [11] It is one truth among many in this round view.

Antonio is an outsider because he mixes the gender principles in an unacceptable way. He is or has been a warrior, and is therefore a threat to the emotional world of Illyria. But he is also giving, nutritive, and subordinate; he loves. Like that of his namesake, his love is doomed to barrenness. The bitterness of his reproach of Cesario has far more force than is necessary for the plot. It is a strong statement about the misery and disappointment of one who is deeply emotional and thus belongs in the world of emotions, but who is a misfit there: even emotions can be declared unacceptable. Nevertheless, there he is—providing another true but partial view of experience.

The major characters, then, are all floundering in feeling—the revelers because they choose to, and are not aware of possible consequences of their behavior; Orsino and Olivia because of their natures; Viola because she has been set adrift and does not know how to structure her life. In the terms of the play-world, she has no identity because she has no place, but she is in a way the psyche or searching mind of all the characters. It is perhaps impossible to live with anarchy of the soul: something(s) has to be more important than others, which is to say, structure is probably necessary. But a happy structure—one which merges the gender principles—cannot be imposed, must be discovered. For the revelation of this, Viola trusts to time. And just as she represents a part of all the characters, Viola becomes pivotal in the discoveries they make, as well. Her place, when discovered, determines theirs.

The structure, or design of the comedy, reiterates this movement on another level. The design is intricately interwoven, and demonstrates a gradual and complex integration. The first three scenes present Orsino and his court; Viola and the Captain; and Toby, Maria, and Andrew Aguecheek. In the next scene, Viola is integrated into

Orsino's court. Then Olivia, Malvolio, and Feste are brought together with Toby and Maria, and the scene concludes with Viola's introduction into this world. II, i presents Sebastian and Antonio, providing the audience early in the drama with an "if," a device for revocability. Thereafter, there are encounters between Viola and Malvolio, Feste and Orsino, and Viola and Feste. The complex III, iv integrates Viola with Toby, Fabian, and Andrew, and its conclusion places Antonio among them. Sebastian runs swiftly through the course of Olivia's people in IV, 1. The last scene integrates the whole as Orsino finally confronts Olivia, and Sebastian and Viola appear together. In each place she goes, Viola changes the mix, becoming openly important to Olivia, and to Orsino for different reasons, and comically important for Toby's crew.

The moral design of the play is concentric-circular, and exemplifies kinds and degrees of life denial, life acceptance. At its center are Toby and his circle, vital, amoral, irresponsible, joyful—in Freudian terminology (which is appropriate to this play), libido figures. At its outer rim stands Malvolio, the superego, the force that would leash, repress, muzzle, or, if it could, eradicate that vitality. Orsino/Olivia hover listlessly below Malvolio; both are possessed of vitality which neither can use. Between them and Toby's group are Viola/Sebastian, coming up courageously and with mirth from near death into survival and final joy. Outside the whole figure, looking in, are the starving dispossessed, Feste and Antonio. Neither is a restrainer or potential oppressor, but both have been prevented, by the circumstances of their lives and natures, from being part of the general dance.

C. L. Barber writes that "the most fundamental distinction the play brings home to us is the difference between men and women."[12] Gender is indeed crucial in a play that assumes one's identity is partly, perhaps mainly dictated by one's place in society, a society in which gender difference is primary.

Orsino cannot realize (make real, fulfill) the pleasure he takes in his page because of Cesario's apparent gender; Olivia cannot realize the pleasure she takes in Cesario because of his actual gender. Viola, a still center in this hurricane, cannot act. Viola is *emotionally* androgynous, something Rosalind and Portia, despite their "masculine" qualities, are not. No matter how much she disclaims Olivia, Viola's wooing of her is fervent—far more so than that of the Orsino whose work she is supposed to be doing. Indeed, it is the passion and genuineness of that wooing which are partly responsible for Olivia's passion. Viola woos Olivia assertively—like a Renaissance hero. With

Orsino, on the other hand, she is patience on a monument, she is diffident and deferential. She woos him with patient chaste constant adoration so subtle as not to appear to be wooing.

All of this functions workaday well in the plot—close scrutiny of revocable plots does not do, isn't fruitful. On the mythic level, however, it provides an extraordinary glimpse into the predicament of an androgynous gender identity. Olivia is irresistible in her passion; the Duke's sensibility is charming, taking, his treatment of subordinates admirable. Viola herself is utterly *sympathique*.

Yet Shakespeare does to Viola something he does to no other heroine: he humiliates her and makes her the object of group mockery.[13] The seemingly comic threat of having to fight a duel operates in this play as the bruises of the various characters of *Comedy of Errors* operate on them: to force a recognition of *natural* identity. In actuality, most men would be as frightened as most women at having to engage in physical aggression. And some women would be able to handle that as well as some men. But in Shakespeare's division of experience, this is not true: men are aggressive *by nature*; women cowardly and gentle *by nature*. Viola is forced to recognize that she is a woman by nature, and therefore by nature loves men, not women. At bottom, she must depend not on her feelings but on natural distinctions to teach her her identity, her place.

The situation at the beginning of the final scene of *Twelfth Night* is an impasse, and has led to critical questions about logic (plot). Why does Viola not question Antonio when she hears his protest? It must suggest to her that Sebastian is alive, and in actuality (could such a situation occur in actuality), she certainly would. Why does she not speak up immediately when Sebastian appears? He is her lost, beloved brother, and it violates realism that she remains silent. Suppositions, based on Shakespeare's sources, about fictive pasts, the original home of Viola/Sebastian, or her prior knowledge of the Duke, are irrelevant. What is being played out is the myth.

Thus, Viola stands silent in V, i, as both the Duke and Olivia lay claim to her, and Antonio regards her with bitter disappointment. The implications of ambiguity about gender are pushed to the limit—indeed, to the (also unrealistic, given Orsino's character and his previous relationship with "Cesario") threat of death.

The comic resolution, however, makes the situation revocable by splitting Viola into two genders. She, with her other half, Sebastian, are able to live out two kinds of love, leaving only Antonio the outsider he has been. However, as in *Much Ado About Nothing*, the central problem is so serious that the joyousness of the conclusion is a bit dampened. For the final resolution of all these relationships suggests that love of life, vitality and joyousness, is not fully a personal matter, something people would prefer not to believe because it diminishes the control they prefer to believe they have over their lives. It suggests that hardship and poverty, an unacceptable gender identity, or confusion about one's desires can destroy one's chances of sitting at life's feast.

All of the characters appear in the final scene: in the world of emotion, every tendency is valid, even the denial of Malvolio. But the ending is abrupt, and there is no final ceremony: not everyone can be included in the rites of pure joy. There is room for everyone in the world of the emotions, but the table is stratified: some people get much to eat and some get almost nothing.

The conclusion is "feminine": Toby and Andrew have been forcibly taught that irrevocability exists: they suffer real injuries. But there is no suggestion they will change their ways. Neither will Malvolio: he will endure and threaten with his rules and regulations.[14] Feste and Antonio are doomed to live out their deprived lives. The rest move, it is intimated, into transcendence, happiness ever after.

Nevertheless, as M. C. Bradbrook observes, the characters seem to be viewed "at the end of a long perspective; their sentiments are dream-like, without the stab and sparkle of life at first hand."[15] She points out that the lovers never speak directly to each other, and that their wooing is oblique. *Twelfth Night* presents the opposite situation to that of *As You Like It* in that the latter comedy emphasizes the primacy of individual feeling in determining one's place in a community. *Twelfth Night*, like *Comedy of Errors*, emphasizes the primacy of communal structures and codes in determining one's place in emotional life. There is a formality, a stiffness at the end of *Twelfth Night* which seems to recognize possibilities abandoned, renounced, roles accepted that are constrictions of the full self. *Twelfth Night* is a far more aware, profound play than *Comedy of Errors*, which suggests that acceptance of societal role will bring contentment and joy. *Twelfth Night* suggests that societal role is determining and necessary to structure the still terrifying freedom of emotional life, but that the price is high.

Love of life, love of another, remains the bond that links the world. But it is and will continue to be restrained and repressed—not by Malvolio, but by the organization of *nature* and society (seen as identical in assumptions). Emotion, inclination, is not enough to confer identity: gender, role, class (and in *Merchant*, even color), must be properly matched up. Constancy is required; love must lead to marriage; and marriage must lead to procreation. That is the law.

In the end, Malvolio wins.

8

Chaste Constancy

Much Ado About Nothing

Constancy, as defined in chapter 5, is a synthesis of the gender principles that stands as the ideal center of the flux and rigidity of human experience. It attaches language to unambiguous meaning, thus uniting heart and tongue; it unites appearance and reality.

Shakespeare associated constancy with women. Since, insofar as it is a permanency, it is a "masculine" quality, we may question why he did so, but the reason is surely that constancy had come by Shakespeare's time to refer exclusively to the sexual dimension of life. In other dimensions, constancy had different names—loyalty, fidelity, or steadfastness, for instance.

No Shakespearean heroine could, like Romeo, shift her affections from one male to another even before betrothal or marriage. Heroines in the comedies love at first sight (even when, like Beatrice, they deny it), chastely, and forever. For this reason, they are often seen as a moral standard, and as wiser than their men. But the fact is they show no sexual vacillation because Shakespearean heroines are permitted no sexual vacillation. Their utter chastity—emotional as well as physical—*must* be unimpugnable.

Although at times Shakespeare suggests that constancy in a male is also a virtue, he evinces considerable skepticism about its achievement. In addition, it is not an *important* virtue in males; it may even be dispensed with before the marriage—Ferdinand will cheat and Miranda will forgive him. Female constancy, on the other hand, is essential, and is usually linked with chastity.

Chastity was considered a virtue in some pre-Christian societies —for women, again. Although one suspects it has always held more importance in literature than in life, it becomes, in literature, a complex symbol. Northrop Frye suggests that it became important in the Hellenistic period as a concomitant to the male notion of honor: possession of a hymen indicated that a woman was not a slave.[1] This hypothesis does not, however, explain why virginity was essential to the much older figures of Artemis and Athene.

For the goddesses, virginity was a sign of power and dominance. Loss of virginity makes a woman *pregnable:* that is, subject to the natural processes of pregnancy, childbirth, and child care, and perhaps also, subject to domination by a male. Thus, in a much later period, many sermons and pamphlets warned women of the brutality of men and the slavery of marriage, and urged the convent as an alternative. When women are locked out, by societal restrictions, of independence legal or financial or both, maintenance of virginity is their only form of autonomy.

Thus chastity can be seen as a symbol of female integrity: as such, it is the notion underlying *Measure for Measure*, Richardson's *Clarissa*, and Charlotte Brontë's *Jane Eyre*. "A woman's chief obligation is to protect the honour implicit in her chastity, for she is incapable of positively gaining honour by performing virtuous deeds."[2] Chastity in such a case is an active, not a passive virtue. In time, the very word *virtue*—when applied to women—meant chaste constancy.

On the other hand, chastity is a deference to male ownership of females, male assurance of paternity for property rights (which have throughout recorded history been entailed mainly to males despite a division of labor that was at best equal, at worst heavier for women). The maintenance of chastity in a world of aggressive supremacist males requires also relinquishment of freedom of movement, and has led sometimes to virtual imprisonment of the female. Protecting chastity "is often thought possible only if the woman remain obedient to appropriate male authority."[3]

St. Paul declared chastity a prime virtue, marriage a decent alternative to "burning." In Christianity, chaste constancy is enjoined on both genders, but it has been taken seriously mainly for women. For women in some cultures and in Shakespeare's view, loss of virginity (or failure in constancy after marriage) "was an irreparable injury which includes the loss of all other possibilities of virtue."[4] Shakespeare, like Spenser before him, makes constancy within marriage as elevated a virtue as chastity before it.

For most of Shakespeare's heroines, anything other than chaste constancy is unthinkable: so says Desdemona, so thinks Hamlet. In *The Merchant of Venice*, Portia and Nerissa tell their husbands that their chaste constancy depends on the men's granting their wives and their marriage the proper importance and respect. The conclusion of the play suggests that the men will remember to behave properly for fear of their wives' infidelity. *The Merchant of Venice* thus adumbrates what is to become a major tendency in Shakespeare's thinking—that society is founded in marriage, that marriage is founded on female chaste constancy and male respect for it. In *Much Ado About Nothing*, he posits chaste constancy as the foundation of civilization.

The reasons for placing so much importance on this quality are more profound, or at least, more complex, than just property rights and the guarantee of paternity, important as those have been to men over the millennia.

In certain religious sects, and in priestly and monastic groups, chastity is required of males. The attainment of holiness—being like god—is held to depend in part on the denial of the body and its physical needs: thus, asceticism. Chastity is the most difficult but possible of these denials. One may survive on locusts and honey, but one must eat; one may drink the stale of horses, but one must drink; some protection of the body—through clothing and shelter—is also necessary for survival. But sexual life, although essential for the continuation of the human race, is not necessary for individual survival. In transcendent value-structures, holiness is equated with renunciation of nature, seen as control.

However, since the male is not defined as essentially sexual, for him abjuring sex is an accidental attribute. "Masculine" values involve rejection of experiences that subordinate the self. Thus sex, which is a (momentary) loss of self (not so much to another as to feeling, abandonment), is redefined as power *over* nature—rape—or abnegation of it as immoral, as a regression into nature. But sex is supposed to be the very essence of femaleness; thus its denial for a woman is tantamount to giving up the one power she is supposed to possess.[5] "Female chastity," writes Northrop Frye, "in all pastoral romance down to Milton's *Comus*, is an attribute of the higher order of nature."[6] Nevertheless, and this is indicative of the relative respectability of the two genders, denial of the one power they are assumed to have is demanded of *all* women (not just nuns) as their duty; whereas when men remain chaste they are seen as saintly and exalted.

Because of the visibility of female sexual functioning—menstruation and pregnancy—which led to the association of women with nature, sex, and the flesh: "The flesh is . . . the female principle"[7]: it is deemed more difficult for women to attain transcendence. (That all thinking on this subject is contradictory, paradoxical, and absurd is one reason for the existence of this study.) Throughout Western culture, women have been seen as the vehicles of sexuality. No matter what form it takes, women are held responsible for it: the raped Lucrece kills herself, not her attacker. Women are admonished in many medieval—and even some twentieth-century—tracts to keep themselves covered up lest they tempt men. In Moslem countries, women are expected to keep not only their bodies but their differentiating faces hidden, and are sometimes physically attacked if they do not obey this injunction. It seems never to have occurred to the writers of such edicts that males should be held responsible for their own sexual behavior. In our own country, raped women are often blamed for their victimization because they were out alone, or because of the manner of their dress. To this day it is prostitutes who are—not whipped, as in Shakespeare's time, but—arrested and imprisoned and fined. *Women are the guardians of the sexuality of the entire human race.*

Thus Mistresses Ford and Page wonder what they did to provoke Falstaff's attempted seduction; Angelo dallies with the idea of blaming Isabel for his sudden erotic desire; and Alanson assumes that if the Dauphin is sexually drawn to Joan it is because she has tempted him.

The reason for this absurd and unworkable attribution of sexual responsibility is the division of experience into gender principles and the association of males with the human, females with nature. The association of women with nature leads to a sense of all "bestiality"—a term that conveys considerable shame and guilt about sexuality—projected onto the sex that supposedly incarnates sex. There are underrunning fears involved in this: one, that women are voracious, insatiably sexual, and would devour men if they were allowed to. The other is basic male insecurity about the operations of the penis, and the desire not to be compared with other men, male competition being another facet of this set of attitudes. Clearly, for Shakespeare, female sexual power was above all *political:* free, autonomous sexuality in a woman is the equivalent of treason in a male, and is called revolt, or rebellion. The male sexual organ is seen in Shakespeare's work far more as a weapon than as an instrument of love—consider, for instance, the opening scene of *Romeo and Juliet*, the discussion between Sampson and Gregory. The penis is seen as an instrument of power: one uses a sword to subdue men, a penis to subdue women. Just so, the words for orgasm in the Renaissance were different for women and men: for a male, orgasm was *to kill*; for a female, it was *to die*.[8]

Men who surrendered themselves to sex were seen as unmanly, bewitched, enchanted by the power of an outlaw feminine figure— Antony, or Spenser's knight in the Bower of Bliss, lying abandoned in Acrasia's lap. The female incarnates sexuality, which is probably why there is no English word meaning *woman* that has not at some time had sexual connotations. Female figures who are remembered in history or literature are defined by their sexual natures. Those who are associated with the masculine principle are praised for their denial of sex, their virginity. The Queen of Sheba, Cleopatra, and Dido are not remembered for their political power or administrative ability. Boadicea, who was a great warrior but has no sexual legend, is remembered by London tour guides for shrewishness. Penthisilea, Zenobia, and Deborah, who were great figures but have no sexual legend, are forgotten. Esther, Delilah, and Susanna, all of whom have a sexual dimension, are remembered for that alone.

Women = sex = nature. Control over nature means control of sex and control of women.

In addition, insistence on female chastity grants to the male the one thing women do have by nature that men do not—the ability to know their own children. Close possession of woman is an attempt to allay the doubt and uncertainty involved in "masculine" emphasis on the self, since only by close possession can a male be certain that *his* spirit is the one being passed on in a child. A son is supposed to be a reincarnation of the father—even daughters do this occasionally in Shakespeare, as when Lear grumbles when his daughter will not give him what he wants: "I never got her."

The most elaborate attempt to create a male line similar to the natural female one is the Trinity posited by Christianity, which can be seen as the ultimate victory won by the masculine principle over the feminine, and implicitly, by males over females. The Father God utters the Word which is the Son and also God; the transmission is absolute—the female body used to perform it is mere vessel—virgin, and *ancilla*, ancillary. Father and Son love each other and the fruit of their love is the Holy Spirit, referred to as "He." This male line, which is necessarily composed of spirit rather than flesh, is then postulated as higher, more exalted, than any mere natural transmission. On earth, an assured masculine transmission can occur through insistence on female chaste constancy; the same is erected theoretically and projected to an afterlife, and seen as the central mystery of Christianity. Mystery indeed.

With the possible exception of Rosaline (*Love's Labour's Lost*), all of Shakespeare's heroines are, on the surface level of the play, unquestionably chaste. Inconstancy is suggested only in male characters— Proteus, Oberon, Demetrius, Theseus (in his past), and by intimation, Benedick, Orsino, and Ferdinand. Unchaste female protagonists like Cressida or Cleopatra are seen as often as not as villains rather than heroines.

Nevertheless, the sexual jokes which pervade the comedies, and occur in some of the tragedies as well, are obsessed with one subject: cuckoldry. There is an occasional pun on standing, on tools and yards, the functioning and size of the penis. But they are infrequent compared to references to cuckoldry, which expand to mean any loss of prerogative by a male. Manhood is partially defined by the ability to control one's wife, daughters, and mother.

But this obsession with cuckoldry is strange in a world full of chaste constant women. Aside from the threat of death, rare in the comedies, cuckoldry is the worst possible threat to a male, and its intimation, the worst possible insult. There are a few sexual jokes directed at women—puns on bearing, and lying. But in general, when women are teased, it is with the *same* threat: that they will make their husbands cuckolds. The point of view is totally male: if a woman is sexually free, she will injure not herself but her husband. What men do sexually may upset their wives—as in *Comedy of Errors*—but it is not crucial to the overall structure of society. It is women's disposition of their genitals that determines male legitimacy, guarantees male control, and upholds male structures. In this way, female chaste constancy is the lynchpin of the basic contract of civilization. Through chaste constancy the female (nature) promises the male (human) not to use her full (presumed) powers. Thus the enormous power felt to be resident in sex/nature will not be brought to bear against the shaky erections of the male establishment. The female will use only the benevolent aspects of the nature she represents to uphold and support male lines, male traditions, male legitimacy. One critic, writing about *The Winter's Tale*, sees marriage (the basic contract between the gender principles) explicitly in this way: "Dissolution and restoration of the marriage relationship [is] the disintegration and integration of man's relationship with Nature."[9]

In the world view developed by Shakespeare, the two great threats to human civilization were abused power and sexuality.[10] Female chaste constancy could castrate human sexuality and thus defuse its threat—but only if *every* woman adhered to it. Thus, as Juliet Dusinberre notes, "The capacity for virtue of men as a sex is not threatened by specific examples of vice; in women it is."[11] If a male performs an unacceptable action, he may be reproached or punished or destroyed for it, but at no time do the people of the play extend his viciousness to males in general; his sin is his own. When a woman performs an unacceptable action—notably, fail in chaste constancy—blame is almost always extended to *all women*. Hamlet does not just blame Gertrude; he assaults Ophelia as well, and cries out "Frailty, thy name is woman." Thus prostitutes, who lack this virtue, are seen as subhuman, entitled to no human rights, no human respect. Chaste constancy (and the childbearing whose "purity" it is supposed to ensure) comes to be not just the only virtue women are capable of, but their only function, their only reason for existence, and their only ground for claiming from males a share of the goods of the world.

A quality with so much dependent upon it naturally comes to have a magical property, as it does in medieval legends about capturing unicorns, for instance, or in Spenser's heroines. The play in which Shakespeare first explores the almost magical power of chaste constancy is *Much Ado About Nothing*.

Much Ado About Nothing

On the mythic level of *Much Ado*, a young woman who is betrothed engages in a sexual act of some sort before her marriage, is discovered and confronted with her behavior in a public and humiliating way, and dies of shame. She is already suspect before her engagement, having been wooed and won by a great nobleman prior to this betrothal. No heroine is permitted to vacillate in affection, even before a betrothal.

As a result of her death, however, the community of which she was a part is utterly disrupted. One of its males turns against the feminine principle, and repudiates love and women. One of its females turns against that man and demands he be killed. Everyone feels a sense of loss. In time, those males who injured the young woman are brought to regret, and even repent their action. They agree that the feminine principle has importance and engage to trust it once more. A new bride is found who is identical to the old one in all respects, and a new marriage enables the community to reintegrate to some degree.

Although disguise and wordplay are pervasive in *Much Ado*, and operate to make the action revocable, so serious is the crack in the foundation of society that the conclusion does not integrate all its elements, and the play ends on a somewhat discordant note.

Beatrice is the most balanced of Shakespeare's heroines. She is self-assertive and has the authority of intelligence and wit. She accepts formal, but not actual subordination: she does not break decorum, but she does urge her cousin to choose a husband of her own liking. She herself resents marriage because it will subordinate her and she would not be "overmaster'd with a piece of valiant dust" (II, i, 61).[12] Like Eleanor of Gloucester and Lady Macbeth, she wishes she were male and she moves far into the masculine principle when she orders Benedick to kill Claudio. Yet she is neither humbled nor condemned for this behavior. Her behavior coupled with the jokes and prophecies of the conclusion suggests that Beatrice breaks through the constrictions normally placed on women.

Beatrice is a Rosalind who has taken a step further into freedom: she thinks about marriage, not love, and finds it too constricting. She thinks about men, and finds them wanting. The next step in such a process is to challenge male supremacy entirely—to abandon chaste constancy.

But such a movement would take Beatrice into the threatening power of the united feminine principle; or perhaps the stage conventions of Shakespeare's time would not permit such a character. Therefore, that step is left to Hero. Beatrice, whose independence is remarkable to the members of her immediate world, suffers no imputation against her "honesty": it is the docile and faceless Hero who acts out this part of the action.

As she stands, Beatrice is a force for anarchy—democracy—in Messina. When she appears in social situations, the conversational formalities and barriers between sexes, ages, and classes diminish. She mocks male pretenses and male prerogatives, male pompousness and misogyny. Nevertheless, she is sensitive and compassionate, as her response to the treatment of Hero demonstrates.[13]

Benedick is also somewhat balanced. He has been a soldier and is respected within the male world, so he must be aggressive to some degree. He is assertive; he is legitimate. But he too shows compassion and sensitivity in his response to Hero's defamation.

Claudio and Don Pedro, on the other hand, despite their social grace and the older man's charm, are located firmly within the masculine principle. They stand on ceremony, rule, and right. So rigid are their codes that Don Pedro woos Hero by proxy for Claudio, and when Claudio discovers (mistakenly) that Don Pedro has won the woman for himself, he is hurt and angry, but remains polite and respectful to the Prince. Within the hierarchies of legitimacy, Don Pedro has the right to overpower Claudio, and Claudio must accept this gracefully.

On the other hand, when he is confronted with Hero's (apparent) betrayal—the two acts are directly parallel—he and his patron express their outrage at what they feel to be a betrayal not just of themselves, but their standards—right, rights, rule, legitimacy itself. Claudio is swift and vicious in his determination to punish her, and in his method of doing so. He and the Prince stand for the codes of the masculine world, in which women have essentially no part. The difference in value accorded that world and the world of females is emphasized when Claudio, after his engagement to Hero, offers to leave immediately after the wedding ceremony to accompany the Prince back to Aragon. It is these aspects of the masculine world that Beatrice is referring to when she replies to the Prince's playful suggestion that he become her husband, "No, my lord, unless I might have another for working-days" (II, i, 327–328).

The characters of these two men are essential to the theme of the comedy, which is a testing of the limits of female behavior against the codes of the male world.[14] Antonio and Leonato are less effectual, less powerful parallels to Claudio and Don Pedro. The four men, with Benedick's occasional assistance, have the majority voice in this play.

There are two minority groups: the Watch; and Hero, Beatrice, and Don John. The two women and the bastard represent rebellion. Don John has fringe legitimacy—he is a bastard, but is allowed to call himself Don. He has attempted to overthrow his brother, so has, at least in the past, commanded some power. But he must accept subordination to his brother and that makes him rebellious. He feels muzzled and clogged: he will not accept his position gracefully: "I have decreed not to sing in my cage" (I, iii, 34). He is outlaw feminine. His opposition to the established order is feminine at this point because it is not motivated as his previous rebellion was, by the desire to usurp his brother's power. His revolt is the revenge of the impotent.

Rebellion that emerges from the outlaw feminine aspect is often terrifying because it comes out of a sense of powerlessness and seems to want nothing. It wants to overturn for the sake of overturning. It is an inarticulate, incoherent challenge of the very notion of legitimacy and establishment, a fury inexplicable even to those who feel it.

In the plot, Don John arranges for Hero to be slandered. But the plot is, as many people have noticed, full of holes. Among them are the blankness of Hero, the unbelievable behavior of Margaret, and the apparent lack of motivation of Don John for the particular act he chooses, which hurts Don Pedro in fact very little. Don John is the incarnation of the spirit that makes Beatrice so lively and (acceptably) rebellious, the spirit that inflames the docile Hero to break the rules and play with sex.

As a noncharacter, the obedient and silent Hero exemplifies the inlaw feminine principle at its most acceptable: but like Bianca in *Taming*, she wears the disguise society demands of her, but harbors other thoughts under her impeccable exterior. On the mythic level of the play, Hero and Beatrice are one: two aspects of female independence. On the mythic level, Don John's attack goes to the very core of what he hates—male legitimacy and prerogative—by demonstrating the dubiousness and fragility of the chaste constancy on which it is based. Thus it is also appropriate that he be a bastard: it was his mother's lack of chaste constancy that made him what he is.

The minority voices express, mainly through language-as-theme, a challenge of the masculine establishment. The interchanges of Beatrice and Benedick cast a sour light on marriage. It may be the basic contract between representatives of the gender principles, and it may often be romanticized, but it is also a yoke, a commercial exchange, a burden, an overmastering by mere dust. It threatens a woman with loss of freedom and a man with cuckoldry. Beatrice's wit and charm enable her to challenge many assumptions of the establishment: her frighting words "out of . . .[their] right sense" (V, ii, 56) suggest the dubiousness of "right" in any sense.

Dogberry and Verges have a similar function in the play. Almost as illegitimate as the women, they ape legitimate language and behavior, and manage to suggest, through their mistakings and mispronunciations, that the legitimate world is not what it claims to be. They turn usual ("right") ways of thinking upside down by claiming that to "suffer salvation" may be "punishment," or that the most "senseless" and "desartless" man is always put in charge. Borachio's play with the notion of fashion is part of this set: fashion may not make the man but it makes his image. Fashion can make a man's "codpiece [seem] as massy as his club" (III, iii, 137–138). Deformation of truth is also truth: appearance is reality.

Disguise sometimes operates similarly to the language theme.[15] It permits deviation from societal norms, allowing Borachio to attempt to seduce Margaret, and Ursula to disparage Antonio during the masked dance.

Strong as is the minority voice in this play, the act with which it deals still seems to Shakespeare so serious that it cannot be countenanced in a harmonious society.

Claudio's language to Hero in the church, and Leonato's condemnation of her as she recovers from her faint, are stronger by far than any other statements in the play.[16] Claudio speaks with a contempt and hatred that seem extreme: Hero is a "rotten orange," knowing "the heat of a luxurious bed" (IV, i, 32, 41). She is "more intemperate" in her blood "than Venus, or those pamp'red animals / That rage in savage sensuality" (IV, i, 59–61). This seems strong language to describe *any* sexual behavior; it adumbrates the language of Hamlet, Iago, and the mad Lear. The implication of such language in this situation, however, is that it is horrifying for women to feel sexual desire at all: sex is permissible to them only as duty. Yet it is Claudio who makes most of the bawdy jokes in the play.[17]

Claudio's outrage and the terms in which it is couched and the strength of his attack on Hero require us to see Hero's (apparent) act as a wrong much deeper than personal betrayal, as an act that defies "sacred" laws. Leonato's approach to Hero is similar. He is concerned with his daughter's reputation—ultimately, with his own—more than with her morality, but his imagery casts on her the accusation of a crime of tremendous magnitude. He wishes her dead; he declares that "she is fall'n / Into a pit of ink, that the wide sea / Hath drops too few to wash her clean again, / And salt too little which may season give / To her foul tainted flesh" (IV, i, 139–143).

Hero's crime is so great that after her "death" she is completely disregarded. What emotion rages is (aside from Beatrice's) male to male. Leonato and Antonio speak ludicrously of revenge on Don Pedro and Claudio, who themselves feel pity—not for Hero, but for the two older men. They see Hero's father and uncle as injured parties like themselves. Beatrice demands that Benedick kill Claudio; Benedick's relations with his former companions are strained. Thus the entire community is disrupted and split.

The Watch presents an inverted example of the values of the establishment. Claudio (like Hamlet) renounces not just Hero, but love, all women—implicitly, the feminine principle entirely. Everyone is raw. And although we and some of the characters know that Hero is not really dead, the events and emotions expressed proceed *exactly* as they would if she were. Hero is symbolically dead, and, exemplar of the inlaw aspect that she was, her death means the glue, the harmonizing element holding the world together, is gone. The fragmenting that results from her loss forces certain questions to be asked. Is loss of virginity before marriage a crime serious enough to deserve death? Claudio and Don Pedro have no qualms in answering such a question. For them, Hero's crime is *worse* than treason: after all, Don John committed treason, and Don Pedro did not publicly humiliate him; he allowed him to live, and even at some liberty.

Claudio and Don Pedro do eventually feel some grief about the events, but only after they have heard proof of Hero's innocence. At that point, they lay the blame for what has happened on "slanderous tongues" (V, iii, 3) and do not even then question their own behavior. "Only the most pampered and therefore the most spoilt members of a society could be so immune as Claudio and Don Pedro from self-questioning and misgiving," writes James Smith.[18] But legitimacy encourages just such blindness and self-assurance.

The mourning of the two men contains no iota of self-reproach, nor does it really show much affection for Hero. What it does is express a willingness of the men to try again to trust the feminine principle, to have faith in it despite their essential contempt for it. Chaste constancy *does* exist: thus Claudio will marry, with no questions asked, no evaluation of her beauty or their rapport. She does, however, come with the proper family and financial credentials, and she will be granted the "right" Claudio "should have giv'n her cousin" (V, i, 291).

Thus, on the mythic level of the play, prevailing values are maintained without change; the only movement that occurs is that the powerful masculine establishment agrees finally to take some responsibility for keeping alive the essential but powerless feminine principle even when one of its participants has failed to attain the utter perfection (from one point of view) demanded of it.

Despite the minority voice, so vocal in the play; despite the disguise convention, which permits Hero's resurrection, nothing suffices to eradicate all memory of what has occurred. The conclusion of *Much Ado* does not show a reintegrated and enlightened society. The conclusion is less joyous than any of the other middle comedies. Two groups —Don John and his cohorts, and the Watch—are excluded from the final scene. The denouement is swift, almost curt, and the final speeches, although bantering, contain an ominous note. The voluble Borachio's confession does not entitle him to forgiveness, to acceptance granted even to the once hateful Oliver, the defeated Falstaff, and the outraged Malvolio. In a fully integrated world, the rebelliousness Don John shares with Falstaff, the comic criticism shared by the Watch and many other Shakespearean clowns, should be able to be assimilated, tolerated. The war of the masculine legitimates on the feminine principle ends this play as it began it. Words and disguises make things revocable—but only up to a point.[19] This community is utterly concerned with status, possession, and legitimacy; and to such a community, female sexual freedom constitutes a threat as great as natural catastrophe.

What ends the play is a set of speeches that bring up again the dominant images of the comedy—fornication and cuckoldry.[20] Claudio banters with Benedick with some hostility and a wry acceptance of the yoke of marriage, and intimates that Benedick has in the past enjoyed considerable sexual freedom (as is hinted also by Leonato's teasing in I, i, 107–108). Then Benedick advises Don Pedro to marry because "there is no staff more reverent than one tipp'd with horn" (V, iv, 123–124), which is a parallel to his speech early in the play equating marriage with cuckoldry. The suggestion is that both Beatrice (presumably the cuckolder) and Benedick will indulge in sexual freedom; yet the final lines concern Don John and the "brave punishments" that shall be devised for him. In the men's banter, in the playing of pipers (probably bagpipers—in medieval iconography, symbols of male sexuality), and those final lines, the point is clear: Don John is alive and well and living everywhere.

Looked at this way, the play is less problematic than it has appeared. Realistic problems such as those mentioned before, and such as the unpleasantness of Claudio and his seeming lack of feeling, and the absence of reproach for Claudio or Don Pedro, diminish. The characters are emblematic of moral positions: *Much Ado* is close to the romances. And despite his honesty in questioning the behavior and attitudes of the legitimate males, Shakespeare does find the abandonment of female chaste constancy the worst crime in his comedic cosmos. Without the magic of that virtue, sex is impure, marriage cannot be sanctified, legitimacy cannot be assured. The bargain between men and women, which is essential when experience is divided on gender lines, is broken. It is because of the enormity of Hero's supposed crime that Don Pedro and Claudio are let off so lightly at the end of the play; indeed, they are called *innocent*.

It may be objected that Don Pedro and Claudio do not literally kill Hero, and that therefore the two crimes, sexual freedom and murder, are not being weighed in the same scale. But they are in *Hamlet* and *Measure for Measure*. And there too, the crime of female sex is found the worse.

IV

IDEALS QUESTIONED

9
The Problem Plays

Hamlet, Troilus and Cressida,

All's Well That Ends Well, and

Measure for Measure

The four plays—*Hamlet, Troilus and Cressida, All's Well That Ends Well,* and *Measure for Measure*—have frequently been lumped together and segregated from the rest of Shakespeare's work. Frederick Boas wrote that these plays share "general temper and atmosphere."[1] Caroline Spurgeon notes a similarity in the imagery of *Measure for Measure, Troilus and Cressida,* and *Hamlet.*[2] W. W. Lawrence, in an attempt to delineate the problem comedies from other Shakespeare comedies, mentions that in them, Shakespeare shows more interest in the "complications of the action rather than its resolution."[3] E. M. W. Tillyard believes *Hamlet* should be included with the problem comedies because all four plays have a serious to somber mood, and in them Shakespeare is concerned with religious dogma, abstract speculation, or both. In addition, he says interest in character is not subordinated to the overriding theme.[4]

In discussing the problem comedies, A. P. Rossiter observes that all three show a deflation of commonly valued "nobilities," and make or are counterstatements of the ideal. He concludes that in these plays, "the accepted code itself may be on trial."[5]

The elements of these four plays are similar to those of others. Two have folktale sources, like some of the romances. War, a murdered father-king, heroines who go off alone in disguise, the issue of justice—all these are found elsewhere in the canon. But the events and characters of these four plays are questioned by critics with a depth, and an anguished perplexity not found in criticism of most of Shakespeare's work. Aegeon's (*Comedy of Errors*) arrest and threatened execution are based on grounds as fundamentally unjust and inhuman as those that threaten Claudio (*Measure for Measure*), yet no one has ever, so far as I know, found it necessary to defend Aegeon, or dredge up legal justification or condemnation for *his* behavior. Helena's pursuit of Bertram to Paris is no more aggressive than Julia's pursuit of Proteus, yet Julia is not condemned for behavior unbecoming a female. Many characters who are guilty of offenses as severe as those of Bertram and Angelo are forgiven at the end of Shakespearean comedies, but apart from Claudio (*Much Ado*), none cause as much critical consternation as the pardons of these two men.

Part of the difference in our reception of the characters of the problem plays is no doubt, as Tillyard points out, a result of the greater psychological realism and depth of these figures as opposed to those in the other comedies. But part is also a consequence of the facts that these plays share an unusual donné, and are all written in mixed gender modes.

Although from the beginning of Shakespeare's career, sexuality, associated with the feminine principle and with women, is an important theme, and often a problem, it is usually handled with a light touch. Failures in chaste constancy—like those of Adriana, Hero, or Mistress Ford—are revoked by the disguise convention. The "looseness" of Rosaline (*Love's Labour's*), and possible future looseness of Beatrice, are merely brushed in jest. Although sexuality appears in many different forms, from the simple bodily hunger of Touchstone for Audrey or Armado for Jaquenetta, to the romance of Rosalind and Orlando, and includes less "comic" kinds—resignation to the inconstancy of erotic love, cynicism about romance, same-sex erotic love, and renunciation of it like Jaques'—it always appears in a romantic context. The prevailing mood is lightheartedness, even in *Much Ado*. (This does not appear in my discussion of the play because I have concentrated on the failure of chaste constancy, and thus on the Hero-Claudio plot. But much of the play is devoted to the comic machinations of the characters who try to get Beatrice and Benedick together, to that couple themselves, and to the comic Watch.)

In the problem plays, however, even if there is a romantic attachment, it must breathe in an atmosphere of sexual disgust and loathing.[6] In these four plays, sex is degenerate, debased, and contaminating;

only the most arduous efforts can lift it from the mud. And these efforts either fail or are so costly as to seem hardly worthwhile. Sexual disgust dominates the ambience in these four plays and only in these four plays. This is not to say that it does not crop up elsewhere; it occurs in the first tetralogy, in *Titus Andronicus*, in *Venus and Adonis*, in the later sonnets, in *Much Ado About Nothing*, in *Othello*, in *Lear*, and in the romances. But in those works, it is an element; it does not provide the very ground, the donné of the plays.

The sense that sex is filthy, degenerate, and disgusting is an inevitable consequence of the insistence that what is human is not animal, transcends the animal. Since humans are obviously animal and tied to nature, this insistence is unrealistic, and the shift people took to deal with that is to divide people by gender, projecting onto one the qualities of "nature," and onto the other the qualities of the "human."

Although it would seem that aggressiveness, the ability (and willingness) to kill, presents the greatest danger to humankind in Western culture, aggressiveness has never been as severely condemned as sexuality. It has been condemned circumstantially, but exalted as well. Books about war and murder are not censored; items concerning sex are. Now, killing per se is as animal as sex: but murder is not. That is, animals kill for food, but they do not seem to kill gratuitously. Humans kill, essentially, for one reason: control. The control may be delusory or foolish: one kills one's wife because one cannot control her, or a nation of people because they do not think as one wants them to think, or a religion because one has projected certain uncontrollable and despised qualities upon its adherents and wishes to eradicate them. But killing is permitted because it fits into the dominant principle, it fosters real or illusory control.

Sex, on the other hand, requires the giving up of control. Of all human activities, it most involves a surrender that appears to be surrender to another (it is really a surrender to feeling). Sex is deeply connected to those despised things, the body, and emotion. It is also, for some men, connected with women, a despised species. In addition, it is compellingly attractive. Thus, for the masculine principle to win its complete victory over the feminine principle, sex had to be illegitimated, degraded, and diminished. It was permissible only in "masculine" terms—sex as control: possession of women for the purpose of breeding, and rape. "Feminine" sexuality is abandonment of self (ego), nakedness, vulnerability. It opens, exposes the self to another. It is antithetical to the im*pregn*able and transcendent ideal of the masculine principle.

As I suggested earlier, there are only two methods of control:

killing and domestication. Domestication can take many forms. With animals (and sometimes with people as well) it can involve severe bodily clogs, constrictions of freedom of movement. To control the sexuality of certain male animals, for example, an iron ring is placed on the penis. To control the sexuality of women, certain cultures perform the clitoridectomy. Segregation of female animals and people, physical abuse of women, and most potent of all, education into a "masculine" and male supremacist morality all are forms of domestication, training in obedience to male control.

But "masculine" codifications, structures, do the same thing. A man's personal power—prowess—is codified into political power when he is named king; if that kingship is passed in a dynastic line, the control of a single man (expanded to include his sons) is made permanent. Ability is codified into rank; influence into position; fairness and mercy into a legal code; and murderous aggression into ceremonialized execution, codes of honor, and war. In our own time, murderous aggression has been translated into game—since we no longer permit codes of honor involving killing. Sex has been codified into marriage, but marriage has never been adequate to the task. Other forms have therefore been permitted, forms which, like marriage, guarantee male control and female subservience. Thus, slavery, concubinage, or prostitution has flourished in every culture in which marriage is the desiderated norm for sexual activity. In all of these, it is essential that women be permitted few or no rights. In the second group, the general sexual contempt of the culture is projected onto the women alone: slaves, concubines, and prostitutes are viewed by the culture as a whole as subhuman, and entitled to no rights whatsoever.

This value system has been inherited by all our generations, and was inherited by Shakespeare too. No writer in English—to the present day—has examined its divisions, its assumptions, and its terms as deeply as he did. Nevertheless, the emotional associations of these divisions were deeply implanted in the playwright. He does, in the first tetralogy and in *Hamlet* and *King Lear*, question the very idea of legitimacy. He does, in *Macbeth*, examine *why* murder is evil. And in the problem plays, he does examine the nature of incest, its implications. But he does not, in any play, question *why* sexuality is such an evil when it is not severely restricted. Sexuality is ringed around for him with images of such violence and pollution that they overwhelm the reader: in the face of these associations, there is no room to ask just why sex is evil.

Merely to feel this way about sex is an oppression. Thus, for

Shakespeare to plumb the consequences of his own sexual disgust is an act of particular moral courage. He probed, like a surgeon with a metal pick, the raw painful foundations of his own moral being. The agony and strain of this effort are reflected in the plays.

In the *Henry VI* plays, and in *Much Ado*, feminine and masculine elements are in conflict with each other. In the problem plays, they are in a state of open warfare. The war is waged on a ground of sexual disgust and loathing. And most important, and part of what makes these plays problems, *neither principle dominates*. This is true of no earlier play: in all of them, one principle dominates, the other carries the minority voice. It is true, however, of the romances, which are sometimes associated with the problem plays.

The Comedy of Errors, *The Taming of the Shrew*, and *The Merry Wives of Windsor* are comedies, but are dominated by the masculine principle. *Hamlet* is a tragedy, and should be so dominated, but it contains as teetering a balance of the gender principles as *The Winter's Tale* or *The Tempest*. A work that gives equal attention to the two principles will inevitably confuse because it brings two different standards to stand in the same space. "Masculine" and "feminine" areas are supposed to be complementary, but they are not because they have different ends. Unless one bows to the ends of the other, they are mutually exclusive. When they are brought together with similar or somewhat equal power, the situation is war. Such a situation is frequently found in actual life, in personal, not public situations. And it is upsetting in art precisely for this reason.

In the four problem plays, Shakespeare scrutinized his two main ideals—female chaste constancy and male legitimacy—and finds them both in some way wanting.[7]

Hamlet

The play opens in murky light, on a cold battlement, and its first line is a question. Soon, a ghost appears, but he does not speak. He speaks to no one, throughout the play, but Hamlet. By revealing the ghost to eyes others than Hamlet's—indeed to the audience—Shakespeare establishes its objective reality, validates its existence. The presence of the skeptical, rational Horatio emphasizes that the ghost is not a figment hallucinated by a fevered mind. The ghost is as real as a ghost can be.

What is ambiguous is the import of the ghost, not just whether it is a "spirit of health or goblin damn'd," but what its message really means. Maynard Mack and Harry Levin have pointed out that the entire play occurs in an atmosphere of ambiguity, irony, and interrogation.[8] Doubt is the prevailing emotion.[9] All the major characters except Horatio are at some time or in some way acting a part: even Horatio is being careful not to show what he knows or feels.[10] All the other characters manifest inconstancy; they are continually checking up on each other—probing, eavesdropping, spying, even betraying.[11] The world of *Hamlet* is a world of incertitude.[12]

Generally, the incertitude that informs the play is attributed to some split—between seeming and being, appearance and reality; between an ideal good and a real evil; between a false ideal that is really an outmoded traditional code, and a perversion of that code; between intellect and action; between inside and outside.[13] The incertitude is sometimes seen as afflicting Hamlet alone, sometimes as the sickness that is polluting all of Denmark.[14] But the incertitude of the entire drama clusters around, flows out of the ambiguous figure of the ghost who speaks only to Hamlet. It is necessary to examine his message.

The ghost begins by telling Hamlet about purgatorial punishments that sound more like hell. This is odd. Although he was killed without time for "reck'ning," the terrible torments he implies and describes sound severe for a man who, we are told over and again, was perfection itself—a Hyperion, a Jove, a Mars, a Mercury, a great soldier and a loving faithful husband. One wonders what he can have done to deserve such torture.

The ghost lingers on the horrible nature of the place where he now resides, and then announces, briefly, the horrible truth of the place where he used to reside: man is murderous, woman is unchaste. He dwells rather differently on these two facts, giving each a different amount of attention and a different rhetoric.

First he recounts the overall fact of the murder, and the cover story given out. In this section, he calls Claudius a *serpent*. But quickly, the focus of his attention moves elsewhere—to Claudius as an *incestuous, adulterate beast*. His treachery and "witchcraft" are damned, not because of the murder, but because of Claudius' seduction of Gertrude. And, within a few lines, the ghost is attacking not Claudius, but his queen—and with considerable self-congratulation: "what a falling-off was there" (I, v, 47). In haste, the speech moves to a passionate climax, as the ghost describes Gertrude as lewd and lustful, sated in a "celestial" bed, and declining from it to "prey on garbage" (I, v, 56,

57). This is strong language indeed. What on earth could make a bed *celestial?* And the Claudius we have seen does not seem to be garbage, nor Gertrude, a predator.

The ghost returns to his tale for five and a half lines. The remainder of this section focuses on the horrible sensation of being poisoned, and the ugly look of a poisoned body. This is the longest segment of all the ghost's speeches. In this segment, Claudius is referred to as 'thy uncle," and "a brother." Nothing more. Then the ghost returns to his present condition of torment and rises to his second climax: "O horrible!" (I, v, 80).

At the opening of the ghost's dialogue with Hamlet, after his first description of hell pains, the ghost several times commands Hamlet to revenge his murder. Nevertheless, in the rest of the speech, Claudius and his act are given negligible attention. After his outburst—"O horrible!"—the ghost returns to the sexual element—*luxury* and *damned incest*. Then he forbids Hamlet to take action against Gertrude, and in moments, he departs.

This is a strange speech for a man who was deprived of life in his full vigor and power. He does order revenge against Claudius, but his real fury is directed against Gertrude and his outrage at the "pollution" of his bed, that is, the royal bed of Denmark. Although we must accept that the ghost speaks the truth, since it is confirmed in the course of the play—that Claudius seduced Gertrude and killed King Hamlet, and strongly suggested that Gertrude had an affair with Claudius while her husband was alive—it is still difficult to decipher precisely what the ghost is saying. It is difficult because his priorities are contradictory to his explicit orders. His orders are: revenge my murder; leave your mother to heaven. The priorities of his speech are: (1) and first in attention—his own sensations in the torments he is now undergoing, the ugly and unpleasant sensation and appearance of being poisoned; (2) and first in fury—Gertrude's lustful inconstancy; (3) and first in outrage—Gertrude and Claudius enjoying themselves in "his" bed. Then, more or less equal in importance or attention—the recounting of his murder, the orders of revenge and restraint, and self-praise of a rather high order.

In fact, the ghost's major priorities are identical to Hamlet's, both in his immediate response to the spirit and throughout the play. Hamlet's highest value, his primary response to experience, is to "feel" it—through sensation, emotion, or reflective thought. His response to life, then, is "feminine"—to experience it, and to articulate it (which would be masculine [a structuring] if it were expressed to others and thus became a form of action). As it is, he articulates his feeling-thoughts mainly to the audience—himself. Thus, after the ghost leaves, Hamlet devotes thirteen lines to expression of his feelings. His second priority is hatred for his mother; and he moves immediately from his own feelings to "O most pernicious woman!" (I, v, 105). Only finally does he arrive at Claudius, and calls him *villain*. Under the circumstances, it seems a weak word, and its etymology suggests the view of him Hamlet will take throughout the play: he damns Claudius not because he is evil or wicked or hateful, but because he is a diminishment of an ideal (explicitly a diminishment from his predecessor). Claudius is damned because he is illegitimate.

Hamlet has already given us a similar set of priorities in the first soliloquy, in I, ii. He spends ten lines describing his own emotional/ intellectual state, which is extremely depressed, even despairing. It is not his father's death that has shaken him: he grants that only a phrase —"But two months dead" (I, ii, 138). He spends only a phrase considering the difference between Claudius and his father. He then moves to the real object of his outrage: Gertrude. He cannot bear his mother's remarriage, but it is the speed, rather than the deed itself— remarriage—that he harps on. Haste in remarriage might, in an ordinary way, bother a person who is very conscious of social forms, of ceremony and ritual. But Hamlet is not elsewhere shown to be such a person; it is Laertes who cares about ceremony, and protests his father's and sister's scant burials.[15] The speed of Gertrude's remarriage violates Hamlet's sensibilities because of what it betrays: sexual desire in Gertrude, desire great enough to lead *her* to ignore standard social forms. The horror and shock he feels at the fact that she can feel desire at all is evident later, in his speech to her in her chamber, but it underlies all earlier references to the marriage. For Hamlet, sexual desire in a woman is a posting "with . . . dexterity to incestious sheets" (I, ii, 157). The phrases he uses here and elsewhere to describe sexual acts have the same ugly fascination of the abomination, the same fastidious revulsion, found in Iago's description of sex between Desdemona and Othello, Desdemona and Cassio. The haste of the marriage suggests Gertrude's desire existed before King Hamlet's death. Any remarriage by Gertrude shows her inconstant; hasty remarriage suggests she may also be unchaste.

And for Hamlet, there is no mean between chastity—pure, cold, and holy—and depravity in women. In addition, for Hamlet as for his ghost-father, men are divided into gods, the celestial, falling off into garbage, the ideal and the perversion.[16] Hyperion lacking, the satyr appears: men and women are gods or they are beasts. For Hamlet, there is no realm of the human, no masculine principle. There is the superhuman and the subhuman, and his categories apply to both genders. Hamlet's values are thus absolutist: one must have very fixed, firm standards so to categorize human behavior. Hamlet's thinking is very *young* thinking. And the young man has suddenly been thrust by events into a situation that is not easily understandable, and not at all manageable by absolute thinking. He, like the rest of us, lives in a world where the ideal exists, but only at moments, and only in certain areas of people's behavior. Like us, Hamlet has "declined" into an ambivalent and ambiguous world.

The second scene of the play presents the earthly dimension of the cosmic ambiguity which the ghost will later present. Claudius opens it with mixed grief for death and joy for marriage, an "auspicious and a dropping eye." He proceeds to state business with authority, intelligence, and benevolence of manner. He is not a king debilitated by lack of assurance, intelligence, or corrupted by egoism. He is concerned with the welfare of his country, seeking peaceful means to secure it. He is generous to Laertes and kind to Hamlet. He maintains his equanimity even after Hamlet's surly response to him: "Why, 'tis a loving and a fair reply" (I, ii, 121).

In general, the world that surrounds Hamlet is as morally ambiguous as the actual world. Claudius is a good ruler; he loves his wife and is patient and kind with her difficult son. He is also a murderer and an adulterer, according to the ghost. Gertrude is a loving concerned mother, a compassionate queen, a loving wife (to Claudius, so far as we see her), who is also able to comment with force and intelligence on Polonius' tediousness and the Player Queen's protestations. She is also inconstant.

Polonius is a more complex figure than either the King or the Queen. He seems to love his children; he seems to have the welfare of the kingdom in mind. His means of action, however, are totally corrupt. In I, iii, both Polonius and Laertes tell Ophelia that the words and actions of Hamlet that she has taken as "holy" are mere seemings. The nature of the male is lustful and deceitful, they inform her: she must not honor her love lest she dishonor her father. She must guard her chastity closely, for men are inconstant, their blazes "giving more light than heat, extinct in both, / Even in their promise" (I, iii, 117–119). Nature itself is dangerous: "the chariest maid is prodigal enough / If she unmask her beauty to the moon" (I, iii, 36–37).

The assumptions of Ophelia's "guardians" are that females are responsible for human sexuality, but that the world is full of aggressive lecherous men out to destroy utterly desirable, utterly helpless women. Female virtue is identical with chastity; thus, Polonius, who has carefully trained his daughter to be obedient and chaste, is able to use her as a piece of bait for his spying without any sense that he has compromised her—after all, her hymen is still intact.

The viciousness that both Polonius and Laertes attribute to men underlies another scene, in which Polonius gives orders for his son to be spied upon and even slandered, sure that Laertes is engaged in some vice, and willing to defame him in order to discover a truth he believes he already knows. And Laertes, who rushes home like an obedient son to avenge his father's murder, is willing to resort to treacherous and underhanded means to accomplish it.

In a sense, *Hamlet* is a fulfillment of the Old Testament verdict that the imagination of man's heart is evil from his youth. A sense of human nature as incorrigibly vicious leads to a code enjoining self-control and assumed virtue as necessary if humankind is to live together in society. But the irrationality of paradox underlying such a set is emphasized in the family scene. In the very middle of that scene, and juxtaposed with the two men's warnings to Ophelia, occurs Polonius' sermon to his son advising proper male behavior—moderation, self-control, and calculation for effect. Yet the old man ends: "To thine own self be true." To which self? The moral schizophrenia which is the real disease of this play is capsulized in this scene.

The eavesdropping, setting of traps, and spying which are Polonius' notions of statecraft come in time, because of Hamlet's odd behavior, to characterize the entire Danish court. Rosencrantz and Guildenstern are really awed by the King and Queen, and are, like Ophelia, obedient to the proper authority. They thus sacrifice the bond of human friendship to a social propriety. So too Laertes, later, obeys Claudius' suggestions as to how to revenge the murder, and in suggesting the poisoned rapier, sacrifices the code of honor he has been trained in. Obedience to constituted authority has sometimes been seen as one of Shakespeare's articles of belief, but in this play as well as the other problem plays, such obedience leads inevitably to corruption.[17] Hamlet's sense of Claudius as illegitimate can lead us to believe that it is Claudius personally who is to blame for this, but surely the play has a more universal significance than that. It is difficult to find in Shakespeare (outside of some rather cardboard figures in the history plays) a man who is both legitimate and powerful. Except (perhaps) for Henry V, the fully legitimate figures in Shakespeare are invariably dead and haloed by memory.

And to repeat: the Claudius who opens scene ii appears as legitimate as it is possible to be. Indeed, Hamlet's response to the courteous, patient, cordial King could lead a newcomer to the play to decide that Hamlet is a sullen resentful young man hugging his own untested virtue while accusing his parents of hypocrisy, and the soliloquy which follows it could reinforce our sense of Hamlet's priggish self-righteousness. But it does not. This is not because at this point in the play we believe Hamlet's feelings or judgments to be correct, but because of the power of his outrage. It overwhelms us, we are impelled into sympathy with him because the dramatist has so magnificently articulated his anguish and his hate. G. Wilson Knight has remarked that we see Denmark largely through Hamlet's eyes, yet they may not be trustworthy.[18] It does not matter, however: Hamlet's feelings are the most powerful things in the play, and they sweep us up.

The Prince has several responses to what he sees around·him. His intellectual response is to question the whole notion of legitimacy—as his creator did in the first tetralogy. At first, he questions only the legitimacy of his world, and finds everywhere hypocrisy, mere seemings. Lacking chaste constancy to guarantee male transcendence, the world falls back into mere nature, is an "unweeded garden" possessed by "things rank and gross in nature" (I, ii, 135, 136). The masculine principle, based on control and transcendence of nature, becomes a mockery in the face of an amoral, engulfing, animal nature. Since the masculine principle is the pole that attempts to deduce or impose significance on human life, the undermining of legitimacy also undermines whatever significance an age has attributed to *bios*. Without the guarantee of female chaste constancy, life loses all meaning.

The young idealist is thrown into despair by this perception. He has believed what he was taught too (like Ophelia and Laertes), that women were chaste and constant, males legitimate and noble, that both genders bent to the support and protection of the other in the face of the rough winds of heaven.

But the truth he discovers is other: no man should 'scape whipping. Thus, quickly, Hamlet's questioning of male legitimacy extends to his own. The "vicious mole of nature" infects him as well as other humans. His own flesh is—perhaps—sullied; he is rogue, slave, peasant, whore, drab, an arrant knave crawling between earth and heaven, a sinner who now believes that all humans are depraved. And this belief, conveyed to Hamlet by the ghost's information, becomes a self-fulfilling prophecy.

Hamlet harps on his major concerns throughout the play. His dialogue with Polonius in II, ii contains three main themes: an attack on the fragility of female chaste constancy; mockery of the counsellor, who, as he is old and foolish, is illegitimate and not deserving of respect; and his desire to die. Immediately afterwards he tells Rosencrantz and Guildenstern that Denmark is a prison—a cage full of illegitimates—and moves to the theme of illegitimacy. He announces, almost with surprise, that "then are our beggars bodies, and our monarchs and outstretch'd heroes the beggars' shadows" (II, ii, 263–264). Soon afterwards, he refers to himself as a beggar.

Loss of faith in the inlaw feminine principle leads to loss of faith in male legitimacy, and thus to suspicion of male pretensions. But Hamlet's whole world is built on male pretensions. Seeing male prerogatives as pretensions, however, leads to his sense of Claudius as a diminished thing, his abuse of the old counsellor who was his father's advisor as well, and his disrespectful treatment of his mother. It leads also to his sense of himself as being weak as a peasant, wordy as a whore, as helpless as an infant to put the times in joint.

Hamlet's real hate for Claudius is not for the fact of the murder, but for his illegitimacy: Claudius is, he claims, a slave, a cutpurse, a "king of shreds and patches" (III, iv, 102). In this way, the seemingly digressive scenes with the players are central to the play. In a world where everyone is vicious, everyone is a player. What is important in such a world is *how* you play the game; Hamlet's instructions to the players are a parallel to Polonius' directions to Laertes, and to Hamlet's own orders to his mother to assume a virtue she does not possess.

The appearance of the actors is preceded by a discussion of the inconstancy and low standards of a city audience willing to take children in place of men (which Hamlet compares with the willingness of the Danes—and implicitly of his mother—to take his uncle in place of the real thing). Hamlet asks the players to perform an esoteric piece, a passage describing a situation somewhat like Hamlet's own: a man avenges his father's killing by killing the father of the man who killed him. The language, however, describes the destruction of the feminine principle—Priam is old and physically powerless; he is reverent, his head is milky; at his fall, the heavens should cry milky tears; Hecuba is constant, worn out by childbearing—by a "painted tyrant," who is momentarily paralyzed in his slaughter by an accident that "takes prisoner Pyrrhus' ear" (II, ii, 480, 477), an allusion that reminds us of the "leprous distillment" poured into the ear of Hamlet's father, paralyzing him by posseting his blood; and the poison poured in Hamlet's ear by the ghost, paralyzing him.

The relations between appearance and reality are not simple in this play—or elsewhere in Shakespeare. For the players' expressions, offering an acted despair, seem realer than Hamlet's expression of his real despair. He mistrusts everyone around him (except Horatio), but some of what occurs around him is real in some way. Ophelia is part of a trap, but she is innocent; Claudius feels guilty despite his assurance. Hamlet's "mad" seemings are as real as, or perhaps more genuine than his calmer behavior. Certitude resides only with legitimacy, which seems to have vanished from the earth.

Challenge of the very notion of legitimacy informs Hamlet's confrontation with Claudius after his murder of Polonius, as he derisively tells the King "your fat king . . . may go a progress through the guts of a beggar" (IV, iii, 23; 30-31). And challenge of legitimacy reaches its climax in the graveyard scene, when Hamlet traces the transformation of the most legitimate of legitimates, the world's greatest conquerors, through to the loam used to stuff bungholes. He does not, in this scene, come to terms with his mortality, as much as he discards finally the entire notion of legitimacy.[19]

Nevertheless, he claims it on occasion. He uses his father's ring to seal the substituted letter Rosencrantz and Guildenstern bear with them to England; he challenges Laertes in Ophelia's grave, crying "It is I, Hamlet the Dane!" And his final act, his request that Horatio remain alive to tell his story, is another motion toward legitimacy: he cares about his name, fame, honor, immortality.[20]

This split in attitudes towards male legitimacy is of a piece with many other of Hamlet's attitudes. His language is alternately lofty or vulgar—or at least, slangy—if always eloquent.[21] His behavior alternates between rash cruelty, savage action, and gentle, melancholy reflection.[22] He vacillates between thinking he must avenge his father by killing Claudius, and wanting to avenge himself by injuring Gertrude. He frequently exhorts himself to anger against the King; but he must exhort himself to control his anger against his mother.

For, if Hamlet's primary intellectual response to the information given him by the ghost is to question legitimacy, his primary emotional response is outrage at his mother's failure in chaste constancy.[23] Hamlet passes Claudius in the chapel, missing his chance and rationalizing this with a religious "reason." But Hamlet would surely know that repentance for sins like Claudius' requires penance more substantial than prayer. He does have bloody thoughts, but they are not directed at the King. They are directed at Gertrude, and despite his attempt at control, he does physically assault her to the degree that she thinks he is about to kill her. Within moments, he stabs Polonius, taking him for the King, although he has just seen Claudius in the chapel. It is unclear whether Hamlet is being illogical or simply unthinking: what is clear is that in his mother's closet he is emotionally fevered enough to act, furious enough to kill, and could have killed Claudius—*there*.

The central act of the play opens with a court scene involving plotting to discover Hamlet's problem by setting Ophelia out as a trap. In their encounter, Hamlet savagely attacks Ophelia. At the end of the act, he savagely attacks his mother. The central act of the play is thus framed by Hamlet's attacks on women, underscoring the centrality—and failure—of chaste constancy in Hamlet's moral universe.

Hamlet begins to attack Ophelia by suggesting that she may be chaste, but will not be for long because even his mother is not—"the time gives it proof" (III, i, 114).[24] He moves immediately to a satiric estimation of his own illegitimacy and viciousness. He ends with a scathing attack on Ophelia, and all women, as false, wanton, and able to turn men into monsters. As we have seen before, failure in one woman is projected to failure in all in Shakespeare's work. Hamlet's words and rhythms in these speeches are powerful; there is nothing in the play that can compare to these speeches in hatred except those uttered to his mother.

He attacks Gertrude more directly. Her act, he says,

> blurs the grace and blush of modesty,
> Calls virtue hypocrite, takes off the rose
> From the fair forehead of an innocent love
> And sets a blister there, makes marriage vows
> As false as dicers' oaths, O, such a deed
> As from the body of contraction plucks
> The very soul, and sweet religion makes
> A rhapsody of words. Heaven's face does glow
> O'er this solidity and compound mass
> With heated visage, as against the doom;
> Is thought-sick at the act. (III, iv, 41–51)

Hamlet is outraged that Gertrude should feel desire at all:

> O shame, where is thy blush? Rebellious hell,
> If thou canst mutine in a matron's bones,
> To flaming youth let virtue be as wax
> And melt in her own fire. Proclaim no shame
> When the compulsive ardure gives the charge,

> Since frost itself as actively doth burn,
> And reason panders will. . . .
>   Nay, but to live
> In the rank sweat of an enseamed bed,
> Stew'd in corruption, honeying and making love
> Over the nasty sty! . . .
> Let the bloat king tempt you again to bed,
> Pinch wanton on your cheek, call you his mouse,
> And let him, for a pair of reechy kisses,
> Or paddling in your neck with his damn'd fingers,
> Make you to ravel all this matter out.
>   (III, iv, 81–88; 91–94; 182–186)

Like his ghost-father, Hamlet barely mentions Claudius in this scene, and his references are diminishing rather than angry or hating: Gertrude, Hamlet says, has stepped from a man who combined the qualities of the gods, to a "mildewed ear" (III, iv, 64).

The scene with Gertrude is, on one level of the play, the climax. After Hamlet has persuaded his mother to refrain from Claudius' bed, he becomes a somewhat different person. He is openly flip and derisive to Claudius, which he has not been before. He seems to feel he has accomplished his real task, as indeed, if the ghost's words at the beginning of the play are examined carefully, he has. He accepts without demur the decision to send him to England. And upon his return, knowing Claudius sent him abroad to be killed, he goes back to the court easily, without pressure, seemingly without anxiety.

Whatever Hamlet may say to himself (and to us), there is no escaping the conclusion that Hamlet does not want to kill Claudius: Claudius the King is not important to him. Claudius the King is man dressed in a little brief authority, mere shreds and patches on a stick whose head will someday be a skull lying in the ground beside Yorick's. Like Pyrrhus, Claudius is a "painted tyrant." Hamlet is not interested in power-in-the-world. He knows legitimacy is a delusion, a pretension.

Claudius, Gertrude's husband, is another matter. The root of Hamlet's feeling about his mother's sexuality may perhaps be Oedipal jealousy, but it has been transformed into something very different. The play is full of clues to the source of his outrage as Hamlet feels it: it lies in a sense of humankind as vicious, and of sex as disgusting, loathsome, and bestial, as a giving up of the control necessary to distinguish man from animal. Woman, the link between these two realms, must therefore renounce sexuality, and this act is *absolutely necessary* to purify, sanctify any human claims to humanness, to difference from, transcendence of the beast. A chaste constant woman would not feel desire, would do "but duty," and would firmly corset her man, and guarantee a line of legitimate males.

The placing of so much moral weight on the state of a vagina is rationally absurd, and charges of insufficient objective correlatives to Hamlet's emotional state are understandable. But chaste constancy is the cornerstone of Shakespeare's moral universe throughout his work. Hamlet's feelings are understandable only in the context of this fact, understandable perhaps only through immersion in the entire canon. For Shakespeare, without chaste constancy, nothing is real except death, because only death endures when women are not constant, and in a world of appearances, only what endures is real.

The central segment of *Hamlet* opens with the plot and the attack on Ophelia, closes with the attack on Gertrude. Between these is the visit of the players and the performance of "The Mouse-Trap." The entire spoken portion of the play-within-a-play concerns constancy, and is implicitly a reproach to inconstant women. The King insists constancy is difficult and perhaps impossible; the Queen insists it is possible and swears herself to it. Hamlet comments: "If she should break it now!" (III, ii, 224). He arranges for the play to catch the conscience of the King, he says; but that conscience, which is moved to prayer (or its attempt), seems of little interest to him once it is caught. It is rather the conscience of the Queen that Hamlet is fishing for.

The two crimes that have been committed in Denmark are murder and "incest." Both acts are permissible if performed with license —with ceremonial purification by the state operating under what are claimed to be divine sanctions (Henry VIII married his brother's legal wife). The state (or its military or judicial agents) may kill those called enemies or criminals, and may even praise its own acts. Copulation is permitted in marriage (and tolerated in men who use women who have been isolated and segregated in a special class designed precisely for this purpose—demimondaines and prostitutes). Murder is the extreme of the masculine principle; copulation is the foundation of giving birth, the extreme of the feminine principle. Of the two, copulation without sanctification, by a woman, is the worse crime. This is suggested in *Much Ado*, and is explicit in both the design and the plot of *Hamlet*. In *Measure for Measure*, the subject is debated by Angelo and Isabel. They disagree on most things, but agree on this.

Because of the importance of chaste constancy in *Hamlet*, the intellectual level (plot) of the play conflicts with the emotional level (design). The split apparent in Hamlet's sensibility and behavior is built into the very structure of the play. The linear plot—Hamlet's bond to avenge his father—is irrelevant to his real priorities. Thus, his path *is* blocked, his paralysis is real—he is uninterested in doing what he thinks he should do, and wants to do what he knows he should not do. And nothing can repair the situation. The Queen's failure in chaste constancy cannot be altered; it can be remedied, and is, although early in the play Hamlet does not conceive of ordering his mother to refrain from sex. But even so, its fatal work has been done: Gertrude's failure has inspired Claudius to kill his brother: God is dead, a creature of shreds and patches sits on the throne. And indeed, when Hamlet does finally kill Claudius, he does not kill a king, he kills an "incestious, murd'rous" man (V, ii, 325), the man who "whor'd" his mother (V, ii, 64).

On the mythic level, *Hamlet* is about a young man growing into adulthood. His memories of the past are idyllic—his father is full of both power and "divine" virtues, is a perfect synthesis of masculine and feminine principles. He is the full incarnation of the ideal and legitimate male: God, King, Father. And, like the ideal Henry V, and the ideal fathers who follow him in haunting the first tetralogy, he is dead. He exists as memory, tradition, and above all, certitude. He haunts, with knowledge of a prelapsarian virtue and certitude, the imagination of an idealist unlucky enough to stumble on sexuality in his mother and murder in his father.

Claudius and King Hamlet have performed the same acts. Both are devoted to Gertrude and have made love to her, one after ceremonial purification, the other without it. Both have killed, one in a ceremonially purified way (war), the other independently and for himself (murder). On the mythic level, the dead King and his loving wife are the idyllic creations of childhood; the murderous King and his ardent wife are the parents the young man returns to discover after years spent away at school. The disguise convention that permits Hero to die and be resurrected is here internalized and reversed: the play opens after both funeral and wedding. The old King and his wife have died and have been resurrected in Claudius and Gertrude.

Hamlet's primary response in action to the discovery or realization that all human experience is bounded by its two most profound acts— killing and giving birth (with the implicit corollary that birth requires sexual intercourse)—is to meditate upon and feel its implications. It is because of this tendency that Hamlet is seen as sensitive, intellectual, and feminine.[25] Actually, his actions are more violent, and rasher than those of any other character. He is as malicious (to Rosencrantz and Guildenstern) as Claudius, as savage as Laertes, as given to plots (the play-within-the-play) as Polonius. And like Hamlet, the play is formally and in content divided between the gender principles.

To meditate on and consciously feel experience is "feminine." Such behavior never moves in a linear way, but occurs in clusters which may be static and are essentially associative rather than logical. Thus, the structure of *Hamlet* is at times "feminine," comedic, and seems digressive for a tragedy. There are loose connections, many delays, and full stops during the soliloquies which are devoted to Hamlet's sensations/emotions/thoughts.[26] The rigorous causal logic of action-oriented plays is lacking, as Tillyard complains.[27] Rather, the play "creates so marvelous a sense of the actual improvisation of life that we can find no simple logic in its sprawling action."[28]

In addition, the play has a more multiple focus than most of the tragedies, and resembles comedy in this. It casts attention on Polonius, his family, and servant; on Claudius with a series of characters; on Gertrude and Ophelia, as well as the protagonist. And it shows the effect, not just in behavior, action, but in feeling and thought, of a thought pattern or set that is rooted in a belief in the inherent viciousness of humankind. The series of son-father vengeances that appears in the larger play and the play within demonstrate the impossibility of right action in an illegitimate world. G. W. Knight suggests that "the question of the relative morality of Hamlet and Claudius reflects the ultimate problem of this play."[29] But that relativity embraces others too—Laertes, Fortinbras, and the female figures as well. *Hamlet*, along with *King Lear*, directly confronts the void in which we live if we permit ourselves to penetrate the carefully erected curtain of significance that normally obscures it. Incertitude about the purpose of life leads to incertitude about any code of behavior.

In this play, Shakespeare challenges, examines, probes his own ideals—male legitimacy and female chaste constancy—which, like all ideals, are based on faith rather than knowledge, and finds them shaky and untrue to actual human life, which is based on sex and killing. To do such a thing requires enormous moral courage—a willingness to cut away the foundation from under one's own feet. Shakespeare's probing led him into pain so severe as to appear in the play as despair. *Troilus and Cressida* carries his imaginative challenge of the ideal a further step from a hellish purgatory Hamlet is relieved to leave, finding death "felicity," into full hell.

Troilus and Cressida

The same failure of the inlaw feminine principle that informs *Hamlet* lies at the heart of *Troilus and Cressida*. It has been suggested that the love theme of this play rests on an assumption of female infidelity.[30] However, in this play the responsibility for that failure rests with the males. The situation described in the previous section as contributing to Hamlet's despair—a sense of emptiness and purposelessness, a loss of the sense of the ends of life—is the basic condition of the world of *Troilus and Cressida*. Claudius kills, but his end is at least partly pleasure—Gertrude. In *Troilus and Cressida*, the masculine principle has become its own end.

Inconstant women are central to male rhetoric, and the moral "worthlessness" of Helen and Cressida is symbolic of the futility of the war. But in fact there is a chaste constant woman in the play—Andromache—and she is held in little esteem. There are five female characters in *Troilus:* Cressida, Helen, Andromache, Cassandra, and Polyxena, who is only mentioned. Of these, four are at some time described by males as being central to their action, as being "causes." Helen, of course, is supposed to be the cause of the war itself, which daily paints her fair; Cressida is the "cause" of Troilus' leaving the battle in the opening scene, his impassioned speeches in the council scene, and his attack on Diomedes in the conclusion. Both these women are clearly unchaste in mind from our first glimpse of them: Theodore Spencer has shown that images associated with women in this play are violent and harsh.[31] Troilus only laughs at hearing that his brother has been wounded: he claims Paris was gored by Menelaus' horn. Cressida's bawdy banter with her uncle in I, ii, her calling him a "bawd," and her soliloquy inform any member of the audience who does not know her legend, of her moral stature. Helen is powerfully condemned by characters on both sides of the war, and by the running commentary of Thersites. Yet these are the women most highly valued by the males of the play.

The other three women are different. We know nothing about Shakespeare's Polyxena except that Achilles claims to love her, and claims also that she is the "cause" for his inaction, through a letter in which she urges him to stay out of the battle. He respects her wishes even though he is growing anxious about his status and reputation. But she is thrust instantly into insignificance by Patroclus' death. Patroclus, who asks Achilles to return to battle because *he* is being blamed for

Achilles' indolence, and whom Thersites refers to as Achilles' male whore, is far more important to Achilles than Polyxena.

Cassandra is a minor figure, but she is of course never believed, and is not therefore available for use as a "cause." Andromache, whose legend has remained untarnished, appears only once, but seems loving and mild to Hector. Yet it is announced in the first act that "Hector chid Andromache and strook his armorer" (I, ii, 6) in rage at having been knocked down by Ajax. In the last act, Hector treats Andromache with angry contempt, barely answering her concerned implorings, and dismissing her: "You train me to offend you, get you in" (V, iii, 4). He dismisses Cassandra almost as curtly, although he does finally offer her a brief and cold explanation of his insistence on going into battle. He is fully expansive and explanatory only to his father. His treatment of his wife is slighting and disdainful. Yet it is this same wife whom he names as "a lady, wiser, fairer, true, / Than ever Greek did couple in his arms" (I, iii, 275–276) in his "cause," his challenge to the Greeks to single combat.

In *Troilus and Cressida*, some women uphold chaste constancy and others do not; it is the men, who control the world and use women for their own purposes, who devalue the inlaw feminine principle and the ends it is designed to uphold, who value the inconstant women. *Troilus and Cressida* is one of Shakespeare's envisionments of a world in which the inlaw feminine principle is eradicated because of devaluation; *Macbeth* is the other. Both plays focus on war and on status; in both, power is not the greatest, but the only good. The importance of status—called honor here—is as great in *Troilus* as prowess is in *Macbeth*. A much lesser value is sensation, which is different from pleasure in that it is strictly bodily: the inconstant women function to provide this. Because of this, women are central although they are only pawns. Helen, the ultimate cause, is shown merely as silly and flirtatious. Cressida, however, is intelligent. She is aware of the nature of the world she moves in, and tries to maintain herself within it. She is a piece of merchandise, a pearl, an object to be purchased and possessed which will be prized according to the price extracted for her. The more she costs in emotional turmoil, the more she will be valued, although she will inevitably lose value once she has been "had." [32] She is correct about this. The lovers' morning dialogue is edgy and verges on argument. Troilus' lines "I prithee now to bed," and "O Cressida!" seem irritable, and Cressida's lines tend towards reproachful clingingness. In addition, her complaint "You men will never tarry," seems the conclusion of a woman much versed in mornings after, and well aware of male devaluation after satiation (IV, ii, 7, 8, 16).

Robert Ornstein writes: "To view Cressida's infidelity as a cynical traducement of the ideal of courtly love is to miss the larger commentary which Shakespeare makes upon the masculine ego . . . What are women but as they are valued *by men*?"[33] Women, in both Troy and Greece, are mere counters, objects to be bought and sold, won or traded, bragged about, fought over, or demeaned, according to the owners' momentary needs. *Troilus* is really about a totally male world; it ranges from the locker room to the battlefield to the Senate chamber. Women appear in it as instruments of male will. Their names, advanced as "causes," are simply a masking shorthand, euphemisms for the men's own motivations.[34]

It has been advanced that *Troilus* is about men's failure to live up to their ideals. But the presentation of those "ideals" is so satirical that it is evident that the play is really concerned with the delusive nature of the ideals themselves. In this, it is a further probing of the central questions of *Hamlet*. Attitudes important in the tragedy crop up here too in somewhat different form. Here, too, sex is a filthy and disgusting business when Thersites alludes to it. In Troy, which has a frivolous court life, the pleasures of Helen and Paris are subject for jokes that have a prurient edge to them. Troilus has a strong sensual appetite which he calls love but which has none of the desire to give that Shakespeare elsewhere identifies with love.[35] Ornstein claims Troilus' sensuality is rooted in a sense of sin.[36] Both sexual unions are surrounded by the trivializing running patter of Pandarus. That of Helen and Paris, Helen and Menelaus, Achilles and Patroclus, are commented upon by Thersites. Pandarus' view of sex is as sensuality, delicious gossip, and because he seems to speak as a substitute for acting, there is a prurient tone in his remarks. Thersites is scornful and scourging; sex for him is mere lechery for whores, filth and abomination. Since between them, Pandarus and Thersites have more lines than anyone else in the play, their comments loom large in the overall structure.

In *Hamlet*, the world *is perceived* by the protagonist as a perversion of an ideal he had accepted and cherished. In *Troilus*, the world *is presented* as a perversion of ideals shown to be delusive in the first place. The ideals mouthed by the characters are satirized once by their form of expression, and again by the actions those same characters perform. The elaborate, overblown, self-serving speeches of the Greek council; the tortured, labored, violently tuned speeches of Troilus in love; the ludicrously formal and hyperbolic exchanges between Greeks and Trojans: all mock themselves. And the achievements of these characters add a further layer of mockery: not only Troilus is mocked by what he has accomplished. On a third level, the "burden" of the melody level, runs the comment of Pandarus and Thersites, who mock by trivialization and scurrility, respectively. There is no minority voice in this play, no set of values that differs from the dominant values, as there is in the comedies. The design of the play, therefore, is not one of contrast and parallel, or of degrees of some central stance, but rather one in which the minority voice is implicit in the majority voice, in a pattern of inflation/deflation. It is built like a series of waves, each in turn rising, gathering height, not volume, rising too high, then because of their own hollowness, crashing down immediately upon a very rocky seabed. Both small linguistic units and the larger scenic structure are built this way.

This pattern is adumbrated in the Prologue, in which aggrandizing pompous diction and long periods are suddenly truncated by curt rhythms, plain diction.[37]

> In Troy, there lies the scene. From isles of Greece
> The princes orgillous, their high blood chaf'd,
> Have to the port of Athens sent their ships
> Fraught with the ministers and instruments
> Of cruel war. Sixty and nine, that wore
> Their crownets regal, from th' Athenian bay
> Put forth toward Phrygia, and their vow is made
> To ransack Troy, within whose strong immures
> The ravish'd Helen, Menelaus' queen,
> With wanton Paris sleeps—and that's the quarrel.
> To Tenedos they come,
> And the deep-drawing barks do there disgorge
> Their warlike fraughtage. Now on Dardan plains
> The fresh and yet unbruised Greeks do pitch
> Their brave pavilions. Priam's six-gated city,
> Dardan and Timbria, Helias, Chetas, Troien,
> And Antenorides, with massy staples
> And corresponsive and fulfilling bolts
> Sperr up the sons of Troy.
> Now expectation, tickling skittish spirits,
> On one and other side, Troyan and Greek,
> Sets all on hazard. (Prol., 1–22)

The orotund *orgillous, fraught, ministers and instruments* (for soldiers and weapons), *crownets regal, immures, disgorge, warlike fraughtage, massy staples and corresponsive and fulfilling bolts* all operate to turn the concrete into the abstract, the simple into the inflated. The rhythms also inflate these lines: the long period beginning "From isles of Greece" mounts with each verse, then suddenly falls flat in the middle of a line with "Of cruel war." The same thing happens in the next sentence, which ends suddenly with the homely: "And that's the quarrel."

The content of the Prologue shows a similar inflation/deflation. The first seven verses are inessential to the play: it is not necessary that we know the Greeks met at Athens. But these lines do aggrandize the Greeks, make them sound terribly dangerous and "high," social and physical powers. The names of Troy's gates are equally unnecessary, but offer a gradual accumulation of wonderful syllables mounting to the incredibly inflated *massy staples and corresponsive and fulfilling bolts*, all of which falls on its face with the curt, sharp *sperr up*. The early section of the Prologue aggrandizes war and the men who fight it; lines 20–22 trivialize both, turning the men into boys ("sons") who are titillated by gambling ("hazard"). The conclusion of the Prologue deflates the matter even further. After all his pomposity, the speaker shrugs: he doesn't care whether the audience likes the play or not. It is not an opening calculated to gain sympathy for the play.

The rhythms of inflation/deflation inform the opening scene, with its alternation of speeches by Troilus and Pandarus. Troilus heightens his emotion, embroidering it with hyperbole: "But I am weaker than a woman's tear, / Tamer than sleep, fonder than ignorance, / Less valiant than the virgin in the night, / And skilless as unpractic'd infancy" (I, i, 9–12). He even catches himself in his own exaggeration: "When fair Cressid comes into my thoughts— / So, traitor, then she comes when she is thence" (I, i, 30–31). Pandarus' replies to him are written in homely, matter-of-fact prose, using the homely metaphor of bread baking (part of the subtexture of imagery of love and war as appetite and feeding that pervades this play). When Troilus betrays himself, suggesting he may not be quite as obsessed with Cressida as he pretends, his "friend" tries to whet his appetite further, which angers the Prince. But Troilus does not want to hear about Cressida; he says Pandar's descriptions of her beauty are wounds. Troilus wants to talk about himself and his feelings and sensations. But Pandarus is not especially interested in Cressida either. He dismisses her finally with the admonition that she go paint if she is not fair. This is a parallel to Troilus' first description of Helen, and the motif of painting runs through this play as it does through *Hamlet*, as an emblem of false appearance, disguise of failure of chaste constancy. Finally, Pandar accuses Troilus of believing that Cressida is less fair than Helen because she is kin to him.

This dialogue is psychologically revealing. When people love, they strongly desire to hear the beloved talked about and praised. But Troilus wants no such thing; he is far more interested in his own state of mind/feeling than in Cressida.[38] He is like the Romeo who loves Rosaline and spends his time creating oxymoronic verses and mooning about. If Troilus is interested essentially in Troilus, so is Pandarus. He wants Troilus to pay attention to him, to woo him, to *see* him; his angry accusation against the Prince has nothing to do with what Troilus has said; it has to do with the self-involvement of Pandar's pandering.

After Pandarus leaves, Troilus utters an inflated soliloquy in which he specifies his goal—not Cressida's love, her affection and respect, nor even knowledge of her as a person, but a process of commercial exchange which lands him in her bed. And his soliloquy is followed immediately by a dialogue with Aeneas in which the Prince disparages and mocks Paris, Menelaus, and implicitly, Helen.

The next scene, showing Cressida and her world, is written entirely in a low style. Cressida shows herself easy in the world and knowledgeable about sexual matters in a way no other Shakespearean heroine is; not even Cleopatra is shown in such a light. Cressida's banter with Pandarus and her soliloquy show that she understands love to be war. In a "masculine" world in which ends are devalued, love is either a purchase of sensation, or a power struggle—or both. (Thus the many allusions in the play to merchandise, to consumer and consumed.)[39] This sense of love pervades *Troilus*, *All's Well*, and *Measure for Measure*. Cressida, Helena, and Isabel all see the same characteristic of their worlds; all three are defined by their response to this kind of situation. Of the three, only Cressida accepts what she cannot change.

Cressida's "low" scene is followed by a "high" one, the self-important, self-glorifying bombast of the Greek nobles. The pompous grandiloquence of Agamemnon; his aggrandizing, even apotheosizing by Nestor; the sententious, platitudinous righteousness of Ulysses (which manages to stab Nestor and Agamemnon with gossip disguised as reportage), all lead to nothing more than a schoolboy plot to manipulate Achilles, and one that fails, to boot.[40] This scene is immediately followed by one of the lowest of the "low" scenes, a dialogue, if one can call it that, between Ajax and Thersites. Again, a high: the Trojan council scene; then a low: Thersites alone, then with the other Greeks,

and the ugly manipulation of the boorish stupid bully Ajax by the two
exalted Greeks, Agamemnon and Ulysses. Their treatment of the boor
is a parody of the courtesy and nutritiveness demanded of the legitimate in dealing with their inferiors.

Thus the play proceeds. The wave of words (and a few actions)
rolls in, rises, then falls.[41] The Trojan council scene, less pompous
than the Greek, points to the theme of relativity that is important in
the play; it contains lofty debate which suddenly collapses as Hector
gives in to the appeal of "honor."[42] Hector's challenge to combat, with
its praise of Andromache, is a mockery given his real treatment of his
wife, and the combat itself comes to nothing. Troilus' exaggerated
sentiments and Cressida's exaggerated promises (echoing "The Mouse-
Trap") are another tidal wave that ends as a puddle.

In no sense, however, can one find this alternation a movement
between high ideals and human failure to live up to them.[43] It is,
rather, between human self-aggrandizement (the transcendence implicit in the masculine principle carried to a ridiculous extreme) and
human self-vilification and trivialization. The inflation is arrogant and
delusory, *vanitas* in its original sense. Ulysses, at least, is not blindly
and stupidly vain, yet he is as guilty of this behavior as the others. Self-
inflation is inherent in totally masculine worlds. It is a glorification of
men and the power they have turned into their form of procreation,
passing on the mantle, the tradition, as if they were passing on godhead.

> With due observance of thy godlike seat,
> Great Agamemnon. . . .
> Which is that god in office, guiding men?
> Which is the high and mighty Agamemnon?
> (I, iii, 31–32; 231–232)

Agamemnon may indeed stupidly believe he deserves such address,
but Ulysses and Nestor know better. They show they understand the
uses of such language in the complex scene, III, iii, in which the Greek
nobles simultaneously inflate Ajax with aggrandizing flattery and vilify
him in asides.

There is no center in *Troilus*. Insofar as the play contains an
upholder of a true ideal, it is Thersites, whose rancor must be rooted
in some unexpressed moral standard. Tillyard has suggested that Ulysses' speeches—not his character—provide the moral norm of the
play.[44] Because the "degree" speech reflects sentiments found elsewhere in Shakespeare, it is tempting to believe this. But it is difficult to

imagine the playwright placing notions for which he has respect in the
mouth of so hypocritical and unprincipled a character. It seems more
likely that, as E. K. Chambers claims, a "disillusioned Shakespeare
turns his back upon his own former ideals . . . and questions them."[45]
The belief in order based on degree, hierarchy, is an element in the
earliest plays (although it is never asserted without a contrary motion
of question), and in those plays Shakespeare insists that such a social
structure requires volitional subordination (the feminine principle) in
everyone. The powerful must restrain their power; the powerless must
subordinate themselves with grace. Ulysses is suggesting no such thing,
although he does describe the central power as a hive of honey, and as
containing a "med'cinable eye." But he is not correcting the behavior
of Agamemnon, who offers neither honey nor cure; he complains only
about those who are subordinate to him and the other generals.

Indeed, the plays written at about the same time as *Troilus* all
challenge the notion of legitimacy; the despair in their tone comes
partly from the awareness that legitimacy is a fake, but the playwright
can conceive of no other form of political and social structure. "Degree
being vizarded, / Th'unworthiest shows as fairly in the mask" (I, iii,
83–84), Ulysses claims, evading the real problem—that degree *is* a
mask, a seat, a crown, that there is no way of guaranteeing worthiness
in those in power. Ulysses' speech on degree has been given so much
emphasis because it is more eloquent, less inflated, and more seemingly reasonable than the speeches that surround it. As such, it is the
ultimate seduction—the seemingly rational appeal to preconceptions
and unquestioned values that leaves unexamined the deceits and irra-
tionalities of the assumptions that underlie them. Ulysses persuades
his hearers; he wins his point. And what does all his exalted rhetoric
lead to? A petty prank for peer manipulation. This is, of course, more
than all the inflated vapidity produces.

Because there is no center in the play, and because the inflations
are so clearly satirical, the deflations come to seem, if not the moral
norm, at least closer to reality.[46] It is possible at least to enjoy the
vituperative scurrility of Thersites, the salacious superficiality of Pandarus. The two clowns are a refreshing change from the windy bombast and empty self-assurance of high legitimacy found in the other
male characters. But what we enjoy about them is their deflation of
self-proclaimed gods among men. Theirs is just as extreme as the inflated view. The world they present is trivial or scabrous, and much
more unpleasant than what most of us recognize as everyday reality,
even the everyday reality of war. Love and loyalty and friendship and

compassion and nutritiveness do exist, are elements in the larger whole. But not in this play. And it is only in immersing us, the audience, in a world we recognize to be lacking, to be worse than our own rotten Denmarks, that Shakespeare provides a moral center for the drama. Just as our response of sympathy to certain characters in the comedies permits us to accept the literary conventions that revoke the unacceptable, our response to the ugly world of *Troilus* provides the balancing gender principle. We must manufacture or assert the norm. This is a characteristic of a certain kind of satire, a kind Shakespeare attempted only twice—in *Troilus* and in *Timon of Athens*. It is satire without a clear norm, and it issues from relativistic thinking in that it depends on reader or audience response for its affirmations. Swift and Joyce wrote this sort of satire; it is always problematic because it is inevitably dependent on its responders for its very core.

An all-male world, a world in which the inlaw feminine principle has been neglected, forgotten, or devalued, may be a tyranny, or it may have what has come to be called a "locker-room" sensibility. *Troilus* has the latter. This sensibility is essentially homosexual, but homosexual in a particular way. Single-sex relations can involve love, compassion, mutual support, and flexibility, as well as power; all-male worlds can contain females who are as accepting of the masculine principle as a single standard as its males are. (Because Shakespeare so insistently identified females with the feminine principle and males with the masculine, it is easy to forget that these principles, as I analyze them, are not gender-specific.)

The homosexuality of worlds which respect only the masculine principle has an ugly cast. This is inevitable because inlaw feminine qualities are not valued; only power—in one or another form—has value, and those "feminine" qualities that adhere are transformed into "masculine" equivalents. Thus love and emotion and sensation become matters of purchase, commodities. The serving qualities—compassion, support, nurturance—are also commodities to be bought, or coerced from others. Power is the only desirable end; thus those who possess power are the desirable people.

The world of *Troilus* is a single-sex world, and that sex is male. The men hate each other, love each other, respect, have contempt for, fear, unabashedly magnify, and vilify each other. Polyxena's love, which has been made out to be important by Achilles, is cast aside like a cobweb hanging in his way as he tears out to avenge Patroclus. Being knocked down by Ajax can turn Hector against his subordinate wife and servant. Contempt for Helen, the very cause of the war, is uttered by many characters in the play. Pandarus' response to hearing that Cressida has been traded to the Greeks is to vilify *her*, and to wring his hands for Troilus. He wishes she had never been born: "I knew thou wouldest be his death. / O poor gentleman!" he laments (IV, ii, 86–87). Troilus' constant love for Cressida seems to be a deviation from this tendency in the play. But Troilus is not constant in the way of Julia, Helena (*Midsummer Night's Dream*), Hero, or Viola, who are constant in the face of rejection, betrayal, undeserved hatred, or threat. Cressida's inconstancy does not turn Troilus into patience on a monument; it shifts his focus from Cressida to Diomedes. Thus, clearly, his love was a matter of possession rather than devotion, and is of a piece with the rest of the play. Indeed, the root of the situation implies such a value structure: the war is being fought, not over Helen's love, nor over her choice: it is a battle for the possession of a body.

In a world in which the inlaw feminine principle is not seen as the bearer of the highest values of society, its ends, tyranny (might makes right) and relativism, are rife. The theme of relativity that haunts *Hamlet* hangs here as well, never to be resolved. Troilus' "What's aught but as 'tis valued?" (II, ii, 52) is countered by Hector, but Hector's argument is based on the notions of bonds which he sees as essentially rights of possession. Ulysses eloquently, if sententiously, informs Achilles of the inconstancy, the relativity of fame. Knowing Shakespeare's insistence, in the sonnets for instance, that certain things are not relative and will not be eroded by time; knowing the great weight he places on female chaste constancy in the plays; one is aware that Ulysses' speech challenges the playwright's deepest article of faith. Or perhaps it is truer to say that Ulysses' speech expresses the grounds of the fears Shakespeare's faith was an attempt to control. But within the play, there is no countering force to this speech. The countering force is the play itself and the legend and poems on which it is based. That Shakespeare was depending on his audience's knowledge of the story is clear in the scene in which Troilus, Cressida, and Pandarus swear oaths of constancy. And the audience knows Achilles was a great warrior partly *because* he refused to fight—which is the basic situation of *The Iliad*.

There is, then, something besides death that is fixed, that endures —literature. But the relation of literature to reality is just as burdened with relativity as anything in the play. Shakespeare's re-vision of the matter of Troy casts a cynical eye on that, just as Hamlet's response to a speech made on the matter of Troy casts a cynical eye on real versus literary renderings of emotion. In the problem plays in general, moral relativism is unacceptable and idealism (seen as delusory and self-aggrandizing) is unacceptable. The two valences are equal in strength, and so great is the pain of the conflict and its unresolvability that Shakespeare can only touch it in *Hamlet* and *Troilus*. He tries again in the two problem comedies, using a different method, but he does not deal directly with this conflict until *Antony and Cleopatra*, the one play in which he allowed himself fully to embrace sexuality.

Indeed, sexuality is at the crux of this issue. Because masculine pretensions to be more than animal, transcendent of nature, are rooted in feminine control of sexuality, idealism is founded in the purgation or repudiation of that quality. Thus, the loathing attitude towards sex that is characteristic of the problem plays is of a piece with their loathing of male pretensions. As we have seen, when chaste constancy does not hold (and of course it does not), male legitimacy does not hold either. In this way, illogically, irrationally, the disparagement of sex, the sense of sex as sin, underlies the schizophrenic value-system that informs worlds like Troy.

All's Well That Ends Well

In *Hamlet*, the world is perceived as a perversion of an ideal; in *Troilus*, the ideal itself is shown to be perverse. In both plays, a suggestion of moral relativism hangs over the events like the vague memory of a bad dream. In the tragedy, chaste constancy fails in one woman, leading Hamlet to damn all women and therefore doubt the values he has adhered to; in the satire, chaste constancy appears to exist (in Andromache), but is insignificant because of the unilateral values of the males. When chaste constancy, the cornerstone of the absolute for Shakespeare, falters or is devalued, masculine legitimacy is called into question. And it is questioned, despairingly and satirically in *Hamlet*, savagely and satirically in *Troilus*. *All's Well That Ends Well* picks up the same themes and concerns.

In this play, chaste constancy is reasserted: it exists, and it and its value are recognized by most of the characters. It is an existing quality, it takes up room in the world; thus, it has power. Male legitimacy is also asserted, but in this comedy, it is seen as either an exclusively worldly quality possessing no moral value, or a moral quality possessing little worldly power. In the second case, Shakespeare reverts to his sense of Henry VI, who, towards the end of the first tetralogy, shows himself to be in possession of "feminine" values. In *All's Well*, the King and Lafew have moral excellence as well as power, and thus blend male legitimacy with "feminine" values, but as in all such cases in Shakespeare, they are ultimately powerless.

In *All's Well*, Shakespeare pits an exemplar of the legitimate masculine principle, Bertram, who is capable of juggling morals to suit his own purposes, and who is therefore perverse, against an exemplar of chaste constancy, Helena, who is illegitimate, powerless, and morally absolute. Thus, he posits an all-out war between the inlaw feminine and the masculine principles. This war tests the power of the former and the tether of the latter: how far will the unmodified masculine principle go in its effort to be free of the restraints of inlaw feminine values?

The moral relativism of the two earlier plays appears here as a series of hypothetical conclusions which are superseded by an absolute and final conclusion that satisfies few readers. This same device is used again, in *Measure for Measure*, and is related to the disguise and mistaken-identity conventions.

Bertram exemplifies the masculine principle in all its worldly virtues and fallibilities. Unlike the feminine principle, which is always suspect and is thus divided to castrate it, the masculine principle is always good, always right in itself. If a male abuses his power, no one pronounces "Frailty, thy name is man!" But individual males do, continually in Shakespeare, abuse their power, and in this play, he seems to have been viewing the gender principles in more or less abstract terms. Bertram's refusal to be guided or modified in any way by inlaw feminine values seems more the characteristic of a class of males than a personal trait. So, too, Helena's self-sacrificing insistence on inlaw feminine values seems more an element out of fairy tale and legend than a personal characteristic. This play, with its folktale sources, is close in approach to the romances.

Thus, Shakespeare pits his own ideal—female chaste constancy —against his own ideal—male legitimacy (which includes a paternal tradition). He posits chaste constancy as a reality, and places it within a strong female character. The action of the play is an examination of the power of strong and insistent and enduring chaste constancy to influence or modify the male who is legitimate but not concerned with "feminine" ends. Chaste constancy fails.

Much has been said about Shakespeare's deviations from his

sources. The folktales he used as bases for the play had one thing in common, and it may have been this that triggered his imagination. The healer of the King was a poor or despised person; the fulfiller of tasks was a woman, often a wife. In other words, both tales dealt with illegitimates attempting to achieve legitimacy. So, unlike her proto-types in Boccaccio and Painter, Helena is poor. She is not, like Giletta, easily, comfortably competent, ruling a duchy and outwitting the op-pressive husband who denies her legitimate status.

In truth, Helena is drenched in illegitimacy, and her guilt, her sense of wrongness, is one of Shakespeare's alterations of his sources.[47] It is the sense of unworthiness which pervades all her thoughts and feelings about her relations with Bertram which has led critics to con-demn her for aggressiveness. She is no more aggressive—although differently so—than Julia, Imogen, Beatrice, or Portia. If a bouncy, gay, high-spirited Rosalind pursued Orlando to Arden with a gleam in her eye and a happy determination to get what she wanted, she would most likely be viewed with delight; she would not be felt to be some silent reproachful implacable Thurberesque incarnation of the life-force hounding some poor excuse for a Shavian Don Juan. Helena's own sense of illegitimacy spreads by contagion to her critics, leading them to search for the flaw they feel must underlie feelings of worth-lessness.

As we have seen, women can never be fully legitimate in the division of experience by gender principles. Legitimacy is a male pre-serve. However, if women maintain chaste constancy and support the male establishment by obedience and nutritiveness, they may be granted a degree of protection by father or husband. The greatest legitimacy a female character can achieve is marriage, the "right" Leonato demands for his "niece." But often, women must prove them-selves worthy of this "right," earn it, as do Julia, Katharina (*Taming*), Viola, Hero. Still it is always a conditional legitimacy; it may be threat-ened, as Mistress Ford feels her status threatened by Falstaff (status in that case being reputation for "virtue"); it may be suddenly and vio-lently rescinded, as it is for Desdemona and Hermione. Helena's prob-lem is that she isn't sure she has the right to attempt to earn the "right." In her debate with herself in I, i, she tells herself that external difference between her and Bertram stands in the way of what she believes to be an emotional, internal rapport between them. Within the value structure of this play, even Helena's feelings must be justified and permitted, as they are when the Countess assures Helena (and us) that feeling is what it is and cannot be helped.

Every character in the play considers Helena worthy except Bertram (and possibly Parolles) and Helena herself. However, to make her equal in worth to Bertram, the playwright found it necessary to surround her with a halo of divinity. In order to approach Bertram's worldly status, Helena must be superhuman; yet even then, for both of them, she is unequal. Both children inherit their worldly legitimacy from their fathers (both of whom have the halo of full divinity so common in dead fathers in Shakespeare—both are remembered as perfect syntheses of the gender principles); but Helena's is not a county, it is a few recipes for medicines. Helena has moral excellence and the ability to heal; Bertram has energy and power. Their marriage, consummated, is symbolic of the synthesis of the gender principles. Bertram is unwilling to participate in this.

Whatever he may be internally, morally, Bertram is absolutely legitimate. No defects of character can remove his status. As Count of Rossillion, he has rank, wealth, and power enough to do as he pleases. Although he might not be able to get away with the murder of an aristocrat (that right being reserved for kings), he could get away with murder if the victim were lowly enough, and he can get away with just about everything else. The only way to eradicate Bertram's legitimacy is to remove him: nobles can be executed for acts construed as treason. Thus, in the last scene of the comedy, a court full of nobles, most of whom have been shown to have high moral values and some of whom have power, stands in judgment on Bertram and finds him not guilty because of his behavior, but pitiful because of his loss of Helena. He is fully restored to favor (despite the Countess's earlier emotional disinheriting of him) and the court decides to give him another wife, Lafew's own daughter. There is little else they can do: Bertram is intransigeant, but legitimate.

This privilege of his operates all through the play. The faceless lords in Florence may deplore Bertram's treatment of Diana, but they do not confront him with their disapprobation, nor do they treat him with scorn or dislike. Their motive in unmasking Parolles is concern for Bertram. The strong moral line of these lords, of the Widow and her daughter, in fact, of everyone in the play except its two clowns and Bertram, is extremely unrealistic. So is the unanimity of opinion regarding Helena. These things, however, are very much to the point of the play.

Most people praise the qualities located in the inlaw feminine principle; most of us agree that nutritiveness, compassion, ability to heal, willingness to serve, voluntary submission of self to the whole, and (for some people) moral flexibility are goods superior to all others. Most of us also, however, prefer them in the receiving rather than in the giving, and instead of attempting to return them, put them on another level, call them divine. Diana and the lords, who have only heard about Helena, grant her almost divine status. Since their unrealistic unanimity undercuts the psychological realism of the play, its function must lie in another dimension. To some degree, it emphasizes Bertram's intransigeance. But partly, it functions to dramatize what is largely undramatizable. We are quite rightly skeptical when we hear claims of sainthood for mere mortals; nevertheless, we recognize our own benefit from inlaw feminine behavior in others. Often, however, when such gifts are proffered to us, we simply take them as our due because of the lowly worldly status of subordinate behavior. We do not recognize the cost incurred by the giver. The almost instant respect granted Helena is a dramatic device designed to underscore the admirable nature of inlaw feminine qualities, and their embodiment in Helena.

Thus, the situation shapes up as a conflict between a good that is almost divine offering to merge itself with worldly power and a young man surrounded by every pressure to accept it, who instead utterly repudiates it. Insofar as Bertram too is symbolic or incarnational of a way of thinking and feeling, Bertram is ineradicable. But the Bertrams of the world hold considerable power: what is the world to do? Little sympathy is granted Bertram in the play as a whole, but his point of view is expressed: he has energy, youth, ego, assertiveness, sexual desire. He wants freedom. He feels clogged by the restraint and self-subordination inherent in the inlaw feminine principle. This is understandable, and it is a real problem for all of us, not something drummed up to fill two hours on the stage.

Bertram disobeys the King and goes off to the war in Florence. This striking out for political and social freedom (from the King's commands) could be construed as treason, but within the framework of the play it is a minor infraction, understandable in a young energetic male, and since Bertram behaves creditably in the war, it would probably not warrant more than brief displeasure on his return. But Bertram wants sexual freedom as well.

In *Much Ado*, Shakespeare envisioned the consequences to society of sexual freedom in unmarried women, and found them devastating. In *All's Well*, he examines the consequences to society of sexual freedom in a legitimate male, and finds them just as devastating, although in both cases the victims are the women.

It is the women and the two clowns who provide the sexual strand of the play. In scenes sometimes objected to by critics, Parolles with Helena, Lavatch with the Countess, the reality of sexual life is laid down.[48] The significantly named Diana, in conversation with Bertram, establishes the ideal of sexual life, the inlaw feminine standards. The last dialogue is part of the plot, but the two former conversations have no place in the causal sequence, and exist to establish the theme.

The first scene, a segment of I, i, occurs after a soliloquy in which Helena informs us of her love for Bertram and the difficulty in it: "The hind that would be mated by the lion / Must die for love" (91–92). Before Parolles speaks, she informs us of his low moral status, but claims (like the Countess later, speaking of Lavatch) to love him for the sake of the man she loves. Both these statements are significant. The inlaw feminine principle, which both Helena and the Countess embody, is antagonistic to sexuality as desire, but with its harmonizing subordination to the whole and its flexible morality, it can accept male sexuality for the sake of the males to whom it is devoted. Helena and Parolles exchange recognition of each other's illegitimacy:

> " 'Save you, fair queen!"
> "And you, monarch!"
> "No."
> "And no." (I, i, 106–109)

They are equals.[49]

The conversation which follows is ostensibly about virginity; in fact it is about sexual politics, the power relations between men and women in the area of sex. And on another level, it is an examination of the nature of chaste constancy.

Maintenance of virginity is, Parolles claims, against "the rule of nature"; it is also, however, a "vendible" commodity. His familiar Renaissance arguments against virginity are undermined by his equally familiar bias: virginity may not be a good in itself; it may be used as a salable object. But as a man, Parolles is interested and cannot be trusted to debate honestly. He speaks entirely from a male position: males want to remove the virginity of females and males have all the power, he says. "There is none," he replies to Helena's query about ways for females to resist male desire.[50] Like Cressida, Helena sees sexual politics as merchandizing, herself the merchant and the merchandise, aiming for the highest possible price; she accepts the fact that sexual politics is war. But instead of considering how she may best manage to maintain her market value in this war, how she may up her own price (which is equivalent to accepting an external estimation of her worth and seeing herself as an object in the world of men), she instead moves to question how she may remain autonomous in such a battle. If it is true, as Parolles tells her, that her virginity is doomed by the superior power of males, and if she is to be blown up, she wants also to "blow up" a man. Parolles tells her that once virginity is lost, men will more easily be "blown up," and that there is no purpose to "blowing [them] down again" lest the city be lost. The multiple meanings and puns on the phrase "blow up" may obscure the serious moral train of thought. Helena, accepting that sexual relations are a war between women and men, wants, if she is impregnated, to impregnate her man, to inseminate him as well, to implant her spirit in him so that he gets bigger as she does. On the military level, the lovers destroy each other, die, and are reborn as new people, mother and father instead of woman and man copulating. Parolles implies that male potency is increased once the barrier of the hymen has been removed, and that if women were to cool their men, they would lose everything, the power of impregnation and the worldly power man can extend to them. In answer to Helena's third question: "How might one do, sir, to lose it [virginity] to her own liking?" (I, i, 150–151), Parolles insists that women have simply no choice: they must sell when they can, they are not for all markets. Women must submit to any man who wants them.

Parolles thus expresses a sexual-political view that grants women no power at all—no defense against male aggressiveness, no ability to demand recompense or to retaliate, and no power of choice. His points are part of the design of the play, which pits an utterly powerless inlaw female against a powerful and legitimate and unbending male. Helena's responses to the seeming facts Parolles lays out are quiet insistences on autonomy. Sex may be a war and she may lack power, but she will not accept an externally dictated estimate of her worth. She will guard her virginity; she will use its loss to "blow up" the man she grants it to; and she will dispose of it to her own liking. From this angle, chaste constancy is a woman's insistence on the only power she has, and is thus an assertion of the integrity of self. Helena feels unworthy, a hind to Bertram's lion, but she values herself and her life enough to control it in the one area where she has some control.

Immediately after this dialogue, Helena considers Bertram's different situation without envy, with only devotion. Bertram has the "teder" Polonius denies to Ophelia; a male of rank and wealth, he has the freedom to move, scope. He will have a "thousand loves," a thousand experiences. She is powerless, can only wish him well. The inlaw aspect has not even any substance: " 'Tis pity . . . that wishing well had not a body in't, / Which might be felt" (I, i, 179, 181–182). She, "the poorer born," is "shut . . . up in wishes," but she too, like Bertram, desires to act, desires also "thanks," recompense, a mutuality in love (I, i, 182–183, 186).

Thus the dialogue between Helena and Parolles that occurs right at the beginning of the play articulates half of the problem: Helena's desires. On the most abstract plane, these desires constitute a projection—not quite an assertion—of female power, of the autonomous self contained within the selfless and male-oriented inlaw aspect. Within the constrictions of her position, Helena too wants freedom. On the dramatic level, the conversation reveals to the audience and to Helena herself the rationale on which she can and will proceed. She may allow herself to act for herself on this one issue; war made in the cause of nature and love is permissible. Both Helena and Parolles assume that sex is natural and that women's main function is to be broodmares. The question they debate is how to control this natural inclination. Parolles insists that men control it through will—desire and physical power. Helena insists that she will control it through will—chaste constancy.

The threads of this conversation are picked up by Lavatch in his conversation with the Countess, and twisted into an unravelable knot. He too assumes sex is part of nature, but he concerns himself not with natural process, but human nature, really male human nature, which he calls "flesh and blood." He too remarks on male antagonism to virginity, but he emphasizes the urgency of male sexual desire and its inconstancy. The tone of his comments is bitter and unhappy; these are the facts of nature, but they grieve him. Desire and inconstancy are in service to the devil. The only salvation, a good woman, is hard to find, and if one were found, that would be grievous too: "That man should be at woman's command, and yet no hurt done!" (I, iii, 92–93). Lavatch thus articulates Bertram's "side" of the battle—the resentment of the free and powerful at having to subordinate themselves in any way. The rest of this passage is opaque, and a subject of critical confusion:

> Though honesty be no puritan, yet it will do no hurt; it will wear the surplice of humility over the black gown of a big heart. . . . The business is for Helen to come hither. (I, iii, 93–97)

The figure seems to describe Helena, whose entrance is indicated at the end of the speech although it does not immediately occur. Helena is honest (chaste), although she, like the Puritans, does not find celibacy good for its own sake. Yet she intends no harm by her chastity, and no harm in the losing of it, when that occurs. She wears the Catholic (procelibacy, humble) surplice over her Puritan (anticelibacy) black suit because of pride—her pride and willfulness in wishing to dispose of her virginity according to her own will. Her heart is big not only with pride, but with generosity towards the man she loves. Nevertheless, the tone of Lavatch's remarks is ambivalent. There is resentment in his suggestion that a man should have to bow to a woman and in the suggestion that a woman could have a "big heart" —could be proud. This resentment is of course a parallel to Bertram's that he should be expected to wed himself to an illegitimate, to espouse her and her values.

The sense of sex as sinful, disgusting, and filthy that informs all four of the problem plays appears in All's Well in two major forms— the plot surrounding Diana, and the comments of Lavatch. The assumption underlying All's Well (unlike Measure for Measure) is that sex is natural and human; the play examines modes of sexual behavior. Lavatch's sense of sex as sinful and ludicrous, his bitter misery, his perception of man as an unhappy victim of his own drives, provide the basis for the behaviors that occur on and pervade the surface level of the play.[51] Lavatch's attitudes are the ground out of which the surface behaviors grow, and articulate the problem those behaviors attempt to contain or express. The clown presents a vision of men as utterly consumed with indiscriminate desire, desire that is continual, insatiable, and promiscuous: for him, life without sex is impossible. But sex without marriage is sin. The wickedness of sex can be redeemed through consecration ("I do marry that I may repent"), but married sex leads to boredom, and thus to infidelity—sin, again—on both sides. The clown utters the theological argument for the sinfulness of sex, and the wrongness of any sexual behavior but married chaste constancy.

But this ideal does not exist, for him at least, and he murmurs against it even as he proposes it. Lavatch is miserable and bitter because of sex; both freedom and constraint in sexual life lead to misery in the form of guilt or frustration. He speaks of all this to the Countess, who, presumably, is beyond such things. The two of them represent the extremes of sexual response. The major characters can be ranked between these two. Helena, closest to the Countess, is sexual and desires a degree of freedom, but only freedom of choice; meanwhile she will remain chaste. Diana (who on the mythic level of the play does sleep with Bertram) also wants choice but does not wait for ceremony, thus carrying her desire for freedom too far. Bertram achieves sexual freedom, and does not seem to feel Lavatch's guilt, but he pays the price of moral integrity (in our eyes at least).

In the ideal, strong desire does not exist in women unless they are outlaw. Diana enunciates this when Bertram urges her to adopt the standard of conduct he desires: "You should be as your mother was / When your sweet self was got." Diana replies "She then was honest." Bertram, taking the word as meaning true to her feelings, rather than purified by ceremony, counters "So should you be." Diana corrects him: "No; / My mother did but duty" (IV, ii, 9–12). Helena, being introduced to the court before she makes her choice of a husband, insists her greatest virtue is that she simply is a "maid" (III, iii, 67). The notion of chaste constancy is gradually taking on an additional connotation—one that will be probed in depth in *Measure for Measure*, and that will be taken as a given in the characters of some of the romance heroines—of a certain coldness, or at least coolness. It is a strange or perhaps only unfamiliar emotional condition: the heroines can love, seemingly sexually (as Imogen seems to love Posthumus), but they do not have sexual passion. Helena is a border figure in the development of this notion: she is capable of romantic love and yet would retain her virginity if she could. Since she cannot, she will lose it to her own liking. When that too seems impossible, she becomes a virginal pilgrim. In this state, chaste constancy becomes nearly an annulment of human sexuality, a transcendence of desire itself and not just a control of sexual expression: it becomes sex as duty.

On the surface level of the play, the Widow and Diana are parallels to the Countess and Helena.[52] On the mythic level, these four figures are intricately interwoven. Diana, who like Helena is genteel but impoverished, is seduced by Bertram because she lacks Helena's "big heart." She may lose her virginity to her liking, but she does it without recompense, without achieving the legitimacy of marriage by her act. She sells cheap, and Bertram treats her cheaply; later she suffers the consequences of such a defeat in the sexual political war. The unleashed masculine principle will not bow to the feminine, will not be at woman's command, unless it is forced to. Thus Bertram remains unreconstructed, and Diana falls into the outlaw aspect and becomes the camp follower Bertram so easily accuses her of being.

Lavatch carries not only part of the sexual theme of the play, but part of its political theme as well, attacking, mocking the pretensions of both the legitimate (the court, the army) and the illegitimate (Parolles). He satirizes himself on both counts, as well. But for the most part, in this play, the legitimate males are genuinely so. The King and Lafew synthesize the gender principles, are men of power who concern themselves with "feminine" ends—the welfare and felicity of the whole society. But as usual in Shakespeare, the full synthesis (which is always male since women cannot possess worldly power) is aged, dying, or already dead before the play opens. The King and Lafew have little more power than the aged, dying Countess. It is suggested that both men are impotent, and this impotence is emblematic of their inability to restrain the masculine principle as it appears in the young bloods of the court. Nevertheless, even the young lords who act as a chorus for Bertram, who show him the truth about Parolles and comment on his morality, cannot modify him. True morality cannot be codified; since it is spirit, feeling, it cannot be legislated and imposed without losing its character.

Bertram, like most of the other young men, like Fortinbras, has nothing better to do than fight. The cause of the war, an eggshell here too, is unimportant. War serves as a "nursery": it offers the reward of "fame." The subject of the exploit Parolles volunteers to undertake—a drum—is a good symbol for the cause of the war. Parolles, that parody of soldiers, swaggers and blusters and offers to risk his life for what Bertram calls an "instrument of honor"!

War and male prowess are not attacked in All's Well with the savage contempt found in Troilus and Cressida; rather, they are dismissed, shrugged off with scorn for their pretentious meretricious triviality. Parolles functions in the play generally as a scapegoat. The unmasking of his cowardice is an unmasking of soldiers in general as hollow, swaggering, and fake. Parolles is thoughtlessly blamed for Bertram's behavior, although Shakespeare makes it clear in the play that he does not inspire it and sometimes (as with Diana) even acts to counter it—although never in an inlaw direction.[53] He is boastful and a liar, a kind of Braggadocchio, but he is not really harmful because he has no power, worldly or moral. He may play the man of the world with Helena, but he is small potatoes compared to the young men who bow and nod their "delicate fine hats, and most courteous feathers" (IV, v, 104–105) and draw attention to their scars, the very young men who shrink away from Helena as she passes them to make her choice of a husband. (It is not just Helena's sense of unworthiness that causes her to see them rejecting her; Lafew also sees it and deplores it.)

Parolles is a parallel to Helena because like her he is illegitimate, being a male without property or title. He attempts to gain legitimacy in the world by attaching himself to a legitimate male; so does Helena. But Parolles can only pretend to the virtue (courage and prowess) of the fully legitimate male; Helena maintains the virtue (chaste constancy) of the legitimated female. Bertram's choice of Parolles as a companion, his rejection of Helena as a wife, demonstrates that it is not just Helena's social status that leads Bertram to reject her: after all, the King has elevated her. He rejects what Helena represents. What he wants in a woman is sex, and sex alone—like the men in *Troilus*. He does not want a clog on his spirit, a restraint on his egotism, he does not want to be "blown up" by Helena's values. His choice of Parolles over Helena is both a moral choice and a subtle suggestion of the single-sex nature of male-dominated worlds in which women are body and nothing more.

Parolles is a parallel to Bertram as well as to Helena. He behaves like an example of the unleashed masculine principle and pretends to a control and power he does not have (no human does). But because he is illegitimate, he cannot get away with his acts, and is easily seen through by Helena, Lafew, and the lords—as Bertram would be if he were not shielded by his rank and wealth. Parolles is easily unmasked, easily destroyed—socially. But he refuses to be destroyed utterly: "Simply the thing I am will make me live." His insistence on life, on survival with or without legitimacy, makes him comic, admirable, and pitiable. Like the lords overhearing his outrageous and irrepressible statements during the interrogation, we "begin to love him for this." Like Helena, Parolles is a victim of the value structure of his world.[54] He functions as a comment on those whose qualities and behavior do not entitle them to the privilege they are born with.

Lavatch is also a scapegoat, not for other characters' behavior, but for the underlying human situation of the play. He is a rebel, not only against codes and hierarchies and the pretensions of status, but against the laws laid down for human sexuality, and even against life itself. He lunges and thrusts, only half-comically, insisting on the reality, the power, and the sinfulness of sex: he bears the burden of human guilt in this play. He is the burden in the sexual motet: he utters the basic unpalatable unhappy truth about the constrictions of the human condition. Parolles is an ironic comment on legitimacy; Lavatch is a grim comment on sex. Together, they provide the "perverse" level of the play; Helena and Bertram provide the ideal.

Bertram may seem a strange ideal, but he is one in a worldly way.

It is generally agreed that he is "goodly." He has every external virtue. The point of view of the play obscures the fact that Bertram has everything the world desires, the goods it really wants rather than the goods it gives lip service to. He is young, beautiful, energetic; he has prowess, wealth, rank, and the privilege of legitimacy. The conclusion of this play makes explicit that without some magical means, Bertram cannot be stopped. He will whisk through the world doing as he pleases, getting what he wants, and in the process destroy the inlaw feminine principle.

But the comedy puts him in a moral perspective, in which light he is rather spotted; his moral ugliness shrinks his virtues into insignificance. M. C. Bradbrook comments that no other hero receives the open condemnation that Bertram gets.[55] But only a handful of characters in Shakespeare openly reach for sexual freedom, and all the males who do so are humiliated in some way. Proteus is shamed; Ephesian Antipholus is severely punished by being driven nearly mad; Falstaff undergoes a variety of physical punishments; and Angelo suffers public humiliation and the threat of death. Bertram, who goes on "winning," who "wins" in all but one of the endings devised for the play, suffers less than any of these figures. His suffering is suggested by the rhetoric of disapproval that surrounds him, and by the suffering of Lavatch who functions in this like an older Bertram who has discovered that sexual freedom does not open the gates to paradise any more than sexual constraint does.

The conclusion of *All's Well* is played surrealistically, or perhaps, cubistically.[56] One conclusion occurs, then is superseded by another which is superseded by another. Each of these conclusions is possible; all of them are more probable—in actuality—than the final one. The audience is forced to live through each as if it were the final one, and to experience the statement about life each one makes. In most of these conclusions, Helena is dead. But audience sympathy lies with Helena. Thus, Shakespeare forces the audience to desiderate the resurrection of Helena and her legitimation. By doing this, he forces the audience to affirm the values that Helena represents, and to wish for their incorporation with the values Bertram represents.

In the first conclusion, Helena really dies. Defeated by her sense of unworthiness and Bertram's refusal to consummate the marriage, she goes off as a pilgrim and dies of grief. Bertram is easily forgiven: his youth, his own loss of Helena (a loss of which he is unconscious), but above all his status, make such forgiveness inevitable. It is not as though Helena were Lafew's daughter; she was a nobody, and if her virtues are insisted upon, Bertram's treatment of her is not a serious offense because it has not violated the hierarchies of power. Her funeral elegy is pronounced by the Countess (in IV, v), and by the King (in V, iii): and that is that.

So completely is Bertram forgiven that the elders—even Lafew—are willing to entrust him with another wife, Lafew's daughter. Implicit in this conclusion are the facts that often in actuality, love and suffering like Helena's bear no fruit; such excellence may be remembered, even praised, but self-sacrifice is futile, suffering pointless, love ineffectual, and a woman's control of her own sexuality impossible: Lafew's Maudlin presumably has no such illusions about her own life. This ending testifies to the illegitimacy and powerlessness of the inlaw feminine principle when the masculine principle is unwilling to respect and recognize it, unwilling above all to assimilate it. This ending occurs: we live through it.

It is, however, superseded. Helena's ring, a token of the King's power, inexplicably appears in Bertram's hands. A charge of murder is made against him on extremely thin and circumstantial grounds. On the mythic level of the play, Bertram's possession of the ring does indicate murder—the murder of the feminine principle implicit in his seduction of Diana, his rejection of Helena. Bertram is arrested. Helena is dead, her sufferings useless, but at least there is some justice in the world. Bertram, her real destroyer, is destroyed for his crime.[57] This is a grim ending, but not as grim as the first. Humans generally find eye-for-eye justice harsh, but not as intolerable as absurd futility, the implication that there is no justice whatever in life.

Another supersession: a letter from Diana appears; Bertram is resurrected and returned to court, and Diana and her mother appear. This is a different trial, although it deals with the same matter. Diana is a different Helena, one who lost the sexual-political war in another way. It is clear that Bertram's legitimacy and his accusation of whoredom against Diana are sufficient, despite the evidence of Parolles, to gain Diana the name of whore and to open her to the charge of murder. For Diana and her mother are triply illegitimate: they are women; they are impoverished; and they have no rank. Diana's admission that she was seduced by Bertram damns her more than him. If the play ended here, Bertram might be somewhat tarnished, but Diana would be ruined for "respectable" life, and might possibly be charged with Helena's murder.

The conclusion of All's Well, like that of Measure for Measure, makes explicit in a new way Shakespeare's use of disguise in earlier

plays. The final scene in each play is essentially a trial scene, or series
of trials. And all the participants are guilty on the mythic level, not
guilty on the surface through the convention of revocability.[58] The
audience is asked to entertain a series of possibilities that resemble real
life far more than the final "happy" ending does.

But even in actual life, there is revocability; there are tolerance,
repentance, forgiveness, forgetfulness, and simple ignorance. Helena
herself appears. Having died in several ways, as she knew the hind
must who loved a lion, she (or some incarnation of the inlaw feminine
principle) is resurrected. What she has suffered is more than personal
decease; she has been rendered utterly invisible, which is to say utterly
powerless. Thus the principle she embodies has been annulled. She
has been personally invisible in her pilgrim disguise; personally invisible in the bed trick (which testifies to the facelessness of women, to
their existence as body alone); and entirely invisible in her attested
death. The exile (pilgrim journey) of the feminine principle was not
sufficient to make Bertram recognize its worth; the bed trick (Helena's
way of gaining her "right") has not led him to recognize her. And,
harking back to the early discussion of the nature of male sexuality,
Helena comments with some bitterness on the subject: "But O, strange
men, / That can such sweet use make of what they hate, / When saucy
trusting of the cozen'd thoughts / Defiles the pitchy night" (IV, iv,
21–24).

Even her death is not enough to make Bertram appreciate her
worth, regret her loss, or change his behavior. But her triumphal reap-
pearance is. She has won the sexual-political war in the world, yet
without forgetting her true ends, her function. She has won the ring
—legitimacy—and conceived a child. In the face of her mere resurrection, Bertram begs pardon: she and what she represents do have
power, cannot be destroyed. In the face of her substantial evidence,
he capitulates entirely. The inlaw aspect, warily guarding masculine
standards, carefully avoiding direct confrontation, has trod narrowly
through to wrest its end, legitimate procreation, from an inflexible
antagonist. In the process, it has asserted its own independent, autonomous power. That Helena's purpose is "divine" is suggested throughout the play. Without her endurance, her fidelity, her uncompromising
determination, there would be "deadly divorce" between the two gender principles.

Helena's divine status is not necessarily a religious statement. The
inlaw feminine principle is called divine because it requires such self-
effacement, dedication, and pain, but receives poor rewards. Still, for

Shakespeare, it is a worldly, not an afterworldly value: it cannot be left to heaven. *All's Well* tests the power of chaste constancy on earth, and in its earlier conclusions, finds it ineffective against its antagonist. On the mythic level of the play, for Helena, chaste constancy is futile; for Diana, the giving up of chaste constancy reaps punishment. This is the way it is in the world; there is no suggestion in the play that Helena will get her reward in heaven. Shakespeare is concerned with moral categories in this world.

The structure of *All's Well* reflects its value structure. It is "masculine"—linear and causal, intricately plotted, but interspersed with many "feminine" scenes, segments which cluster around the central idea and are essential to the plot. The first of these segments, which are significatory rather than causal, is the conversation between Helena and Parolles; the second is that between the Countess and Lavatch. The third, and central one, is that between Helena and the King, with its ritualistic and incantatory tone, its continual reference to a divine realm, and its use of rhyme. The inlaw feminine principle insists on its ability to heal society; if, given the chance, it fails, let it be destroyed and lumped together with the outlaw feminine principle— called "strumpet"—and totally illegitimated. If it succeeds, let it be married to the masculine principle so it may synthesize society. But for the inlaw aspect even to be given the chance to heal, the King must be sympathetic to it, must be able to perceive the "blessedness" of the qualities it contains.

There is no causal reason for the length of this scene. Its length, its heightening by rhyme and allusions to the divine, all work to emphasize that the powerful in the world must submit to the powerless, the lowest, if the world is to be restored to health. Moreover, although the cure of the King is causally important, his argument with Helena is not the real battle of the play: the scene is a "shrine" scene. It intimates what is at stake in Helena's war with Bertram.

After this scene, there are only sections, parts of scenes, devoted to the significatory level: the dialogue between the Countess and Lavatch after his return from court; Lafew's comments on the unhappiness of the young lords at the prospect of marrying Helena; and all of Lavatch's later dialogues. After the long, highly marked scene between the King and Helena, the plot takes over and in that plot the masculine principle maintains dominance until the final scene.

The overall shape of the play is "feminine" because it opens with death and ends with promised birth; in that sense, it fulfills its description as a comedy. But Bertram's acceptance of Helena, the title, and the King's statement at the end of the play are all qualified by the tone and by the comments of Lavatch. In II, iv, he says the Countess is healthy and merry and not in want, but is not well; or rather, he adds, she is well but for two things: that she is not in heaven and that she is on earth. Hamlet begs Horatio to absent him for a while from the "felicity" of death; Thersites sees life as an outrageous filthy joke; Lavatch sees life as unending punishment. Helena and Bertram are reconciled, but the cost in pain is so great that we wonder if the prize is worth it. "As we are ourselves, what things we are!" "All yet seems well," the King says, tentatively. Human nature in these plays is "a mingled yarn" (IV, iii, 71)—rebellious, deceitful, cowardly, boastful, aggressive, egotistical, intransigeant, and above all, sexual, which is to say sinful. These qualities must be restrained if life is to be bearable, if the race is to survive. But they can be restrained only by the powerless inlaw principle, which holds only if humans support it. It is a precarious formula.

Measure for Measure

Measure for Measure is concerned with issues similar to those found in All's Well. Again chastity is pitted against a form of legitimacy, but instead of social prerogative and invulnerability, it is the legitimacy of political authority, justice. Attitudes towards sex found in All's Well exist in the later comedy too, but rather than place such attitudes in the consciousness of one or more characters, as he does in the other problem plays (Hamlet, Thersites, Lavatch), Shakespeare sets the entire play in an atmosphere of sin and filth. The Vienna of the background seems to be a city of brothels and bawds; the outlaw characters revel in sexuality, yet not freely—their speeches contain a note of prurience and lip-licking lasciviousness (like those of Pandarus). The other characters suffer to varying degrees from a sense of the sinfulness of sex: that there is something utterly disgusting and loathsome inherent in this dimension of life is a donné of the play. Indeed, it is not just authority (justice) which is tried in Measure for Measure: it is sexuality itself that is on trial.

In Hamlet, sexual disgust appears mainly in the Prince. The ghost who gives him his information is disgusted too, but only (so far as we can tell) with the "incestuous" sex of Gertrude and Claudius. Hamlet carries this feeling into the world at large, clobbers Ophelia with it, and lets it poison his imagination to the degree that all humans seem polluted. In *Troilus*, Thersites' moral imagination pollutes the atmosphere, but many characters express disgust at sexuality. The many slighting references to Helen, Ulysses' contempt for Cressida, Troilus' horror at Cressida, and the background events—the foreknown loss of the war and destruction of Troy because of Helen—bear out Thersites' attitudes. In *All's Well*, sexual disgust is subdued; it appears in Lavatch; it is reinforced by Bertram's treatment of Diana; and by Helena's acknowledgment that sex is a war between men and women. But *Measure for Measure* exists almost totally in what feels like a sewer.[59]

Discussing the origin of the notion of the holiness of chaste constancy and its relation to male legitimacy is unfortunately like discussing a chicken-egg affair. But it is possible (if not likely) that chaste constancy could have become a value simply because of its crucial position in guaranteeing male legitimacy, a male line, a male tradition, and without any necessary sense of sexual guilt. Nevertheless, the positing of chaste constancy as a good, even if such an arrangement did not arise out of sexual guilt, would inevitably lead to sexual guilt. If the value fundamental to human civilization involves renunciation of ordinary sexuality, there has to be something taboo about that quality. Shakespeare, as we have seen, placed increasing significance on chaste constancy. Parallel with this (although probably caused by actual events, and not simply his literary development), he suffered increasingly from sexual disgust and guilt. These attitudes and feelings reached their climax in the period in which he wrote the problem plays, all of which contain strong tendencies towards despair, and are pervaded by a sense of corruption, disease, and the impossibility of human (civilized) life. *Measure for Measure* brings to the surface the sexual revulsion that bubbles just below it in the other three. It confronts directly Shakespeare's own most elemental fears, attractions, prejudices, and challenges directly his own ideals. Although sexual disgust and loathing are elements in later plays, they dominate no later play. Sex has been tried and found guilty but human, and therefore unpunishable.

The corruption of Vienna is established in the second scene, which also intimates the secondary theme—the legitimacy of authority. The major theme of the play is often alleged to be a questioning of human justice, or the relations of justice and mercy. If this is true, it is strange indeed that the only crime with which justice has to deal is sexual "crime." Barnardine is a murderer, but his crime is neither questioned nor taken seriously; at the end, he is freed. Angelo and Escalus have a conversation that includes mention of thieves: but we never see them. Sexual behavior is the only act considered in this play: Claudio, Juliet, Pompey, Overdone, Froth, Angelo, Lucio, and even the Duke are accused of such acts. And *accused* is the word: sexuality itself is a crime, right from the opening of the play. It is significant when we attempt to delineate the theme that Angelo is condemned in the final scene, and then forgiven for a sexual act he intended but did not commit; there is no mention of the subornation of justice he clearly did commit, whether or not Claudio lives. *Measure for Measure* does challenge the legitimacy of authority, but it does not examine justice itself.

All of the characters agree that sex is a crime. Even Claudio, who has been sentenced to death on a technicality, admits that his crime was "too much liberty," and compares human sexual appetite to that of rats who eat poison and then drink themselves to death. He also unquestionably challenges the demigod Authority, and derides the pompousness of that merely human authority taking on itself the power to judge and to kill that should be left to heaven. He attacks also the capriciousness of authority, a capriciousness that Angelo later admits but justifies. But Claudio does not—nor do Escalus, Isabel, or the Duke—deny that his sentence is *just*. In Isabel's last speech in the play, she says, "My brother had but justice, / In that he did the thing for which he died" (V, i, 443–444).

Even among the illegitimate characters there is little disagreement about the moral status of sex. Elbow's comic malapropism does not diminish his horror at the accusation that his wife was "respected with him before he married her." Even Pompey the bawd admits there is nothing wrong with his business except that it is not lawful. Although the bawds and Elbow are comic, their dialogue is far from lighthearted; indeed in none of the problem plays is there the lighthearted sexual banter found in the earlier comedies.

There is a wide gamut of positions on sex in *Measure for Measure*. At one pole are Pompey and Overdone, who see male desire as ineradicable (whether or not it should be morally), as necessary to populate the city, and as beneficial because it enables them to make a living. They have no guilt about sex per se, but are uncomfortable with its illegality. There is Lucio with his two gentlemen friends, who exchange the witty clichés of the day. One might expect bawdy banter a la Pandarus from these men, and they do deliver something like it— but they talk exclusively not about prostitutes or cuckolding, but about venereal disease, the worst consequence of sex. Lucio is an extremely complex figure, as changeable as the Duke is. He is so like the gentlemen of Vienna that there is "but a pair of shears between" (I, ii, 27–28) him and them. With Claudio, he is concerned, worried for his friend, and he is surprised at the sudden importance of "a game of ticktack" (I, ii, 190–191): sex does not seem serious to him. With the Duke, Lucio is sensible and accepting, insisting that sexuality is as ineradicable as the human race itself, but at the same time, he is slanderous in a gossipy bawdy way, full of delight in malice. With Pompey, he is comic and bawdy. In all of these relations, however, Lucio is essentially *distant*. He cracks a joke and moves on. He does not feel tied to anyone, and above all, he accepts no responsibility for the world around him.

With Isabel, Lucio is at his best, insisting that Claudio's act is natural, organic, and beneficial to society; urging her to speak further to Angelo; seeing her as a thing "enskied and sainted." Nevertheless, this same Lucio implies, after Isabel's admission of having been forcibly seduced by Angelo, that she is a whore and undeserving of any but physical "handling." He frequents prostitutes but does not look down on himself for that; he has contempt rather for *them*. He fathers a child but refuses to take responsibility for it. All in all, Lucio is a bundle of attitudes (as most people probably are) which are not necessarily cohesive. The single characteristic that informs them all, however, is detachment: Lucio takes no responsibility for anything.

He is witty and light, and his lightness and wit come as a relief in this heavy play, so it is easy to like him, to find him refreshing among all the passionate and serious characters. But since he is human and sexual and takes no responsibility for that, he is a threat to the basic premise of this play, which is that sex is extremely serious. Thus, he is punished by being forced to take sex seriously—by being married to a "punk." As a central character, Lucio expresses a set of different attitudes to sex that cover the range of most ordinary men.

To the other side of Lucio stand the more inlaw figures. Claudio and Juliet emphasize the pleasant and loving side of sex. Both agree it is sinful, but its sinfulness is less important to them than its joys, and they engage in it without full ceremonialization. Escalus and the Duke find sex sinful but permissible if properly ceremonialized: they emphasize the other side of the coin bearing Claudio and Juliet. Angelo and Isabel represent the extreme pole of renunciation or repudiation of sex, Angelo because he is cold and has never felt desire; Isabel—who is the complement and opposite of Angelo—because she treasures and values chastity above any other quality. All of Shakespeare's heroines in the middle and late comedies are chaste: Isabel is fiercely so.

Except for the position of Lucio with Isabel, which may be seen as the central, or normal position on sex, every other stance contains some sense of sex as tainted. Escalus deplores Angelo's intention to execute Claudio, but when the Justice murmurs "Lord Angelo is severe," he replies "It is but needful" (II, i, 282). The Duke manipulates events to save Claudio, but in his conversation with Juliet, he assumes sex is a corruption (and a greater corruption in a woman than in a man). One of the grounds of his attraction to Isabel is her "goodness," her inflexible chastity. Even Lucio, who in some moments has the broadest and most tolerant attitude towards sex of any of the "respectable" figures, speaks of the "rebellion of a codpiece," as if sex were a kind of mutiny. Indeed, marriage is seen as punishment in *Measure for Measure*: Angelo and Lucio are punished by it, Lucio crying that marriage to a prostitute is "pressing to death, whipping, and hanging" (V, i, 522–523). They are both punished more severely than Barnardine the murderer.

The entire stratification, or hierarchy, of characters in this play is based on attitude towards sexuality. Angelo's former engagement was obviously based on desire for wealth, rather than desire for love or sex. He is cold by nature, and unaware of feelings of lust until he meets Isabel. But what makes Angelo a villain is not that he suddenly becomes aware of desire; rather it is his method of handling that desire. His proposal to Isabel amounts to rape; he seems to succeed in this; and he betrays Isabel by ordering Claudio's execution despite her apparent submission. He uses his office and reputation to cover up his own indulgence in the very act he is punishing so severely. Yet all of this is forgiven, indeed, is negligible in the final judgment on him. That judgment finds him guilty of one thing: sex. This is important in that Angelo has been the pillar of the antisex forces; his "fall" into sexuality is a significant element in the trial of this quality.

It is not very fruitful to analyze the character of Isabel apart from her society, or apart from the cumulative definition found in the plays of the nature and purpose of chaste constancy. Isabel enters a convent; presumably this suggests her devotion to some transcendent principle of existence, to deity or at least, religious life. However, the only characteristic of this convent of which we are informed is a sexual—or antisexual—one: a woman may not show her face and speak to a man at the same time. Lucio, whose tongue is "far from heart" (I, iv, 33), holds Isabel sainted because of her "renouncement" of sex alone. Thus the convent functions in this play as a sanctuary from the element that poisons and corrupts all the rest of Vienna. As it happens, efforts to exclude something always involve obsession with it. The convent is as obsessed with sex as Vienna except that its emphasis is negative.

Responsibility for control of sex always in Shakespeare lies with women. In this world of sexual pollution, bawds and baths, venereal disease, and laxity of morals, the only escape is the convent. Juliet accepts that her "sin" was of heavier kind than Claudio's (although he is to be executed—an unusual event. One wonders what Shakespeare would have done with a situation in which the female, but not the male—as is more usual in the world—was punished for a sexual act. His next play, *Othello*, presents somewhat this situation, but it is not directly relevant because Desdemona has not in fact performed adultery.). Elbow's outrage at the treatment of his wife in the brothel shows a fear that simply the way she is treated by the world is enough to defame her. Sexual standards being as they are in Vienna, a woman who wishes to be "good" must be unquestionably so, above even the faintest imputation of sexuality. In *Much Ado*, Hero is destroyed by a rumor of her unchastity. Angelo, wishing to break off his affiancement to Mariana, pretends "in her discoveries of dishonour" (III, i, 227). He attempts to do the same with Isabel, to attribute to her the responsibility for his desire: "Is this her fault or mine? / The tempter or the tempted, who sins most, ha?" (II, ii, 162–164). Isabel is so fiercely chaste that Angelo cannot by any rationalization accuse her of trying to tempt him; nevertheless she feels partly responsible for his "fall": "I partly think / A due sincerity governed his deeds, / Till he did look on me" (V, i, 445–447). In *All's Well*, Bertram's word, despite the amorality of his character, is enough to cast Diana in a bad light. It takes only her equivocation with the King about the ring to send him leaping to the conclusion that she is indeed a whore.

In Shakespeare's world, a woman must be chaste and constant or else she is a whore—which is to say, a beast, subhuman, lacking any "human" rights. But being chaste and constant is not enough; not even possession of a hymen can protect a virgin from being called a whore. What is required is the saintliness of a Helena, or the ferocious abhorrence of sex as pollution of an Isabel, to guarantee the chastity demanded of women. In a play in which sex itself is on trial, the heroine must be utterly beyond question. Isabel's hatred of sex is not something that endears her to modern audiences, but it is her creator's hatred of sex she expresses, and, more to the point, her abhorrence of it is dramatically necessary. She represents and maintains the chastity Angelo only pretends to. She provides the extreme pole in this survey of sexual attitudes.

Thus, a judgment of Isabel which finds her humanly wanting is also a judgment about the proper approach to sex. Shakespeare cannot have been unaware of this. As Lavatch intimates, in the sexual area of life, all stances fail. Isabel, the exemplar of chaste constancy, which is Shakespeare's basic ideal and for him the foundation of civilization, maintains her integrity in a tormentingly difficult situation. She would, she claims, and we believe it, gladly lay down her life for her brother if that were asked, if that would help. But she will not lay down her chastity, and indeed she speaks of it as if it were not her possession, but an element in a larger whole: "More than our brother is our chastity" (II, iv, 185). She does what Shakespeare implicitly suggests women should do: she maintains her chaste constancy. And she is a tremendous figure, full of energy and passion and intellect. Yet there is something wanting in her humanly.[60] This cannot have been lost on her creator. There is no way out for "flesh and blood."

The link between the two themes of sexuality and justice (authority) is the Duke, whose character is as ambiguous as the play as a whole. He admits that he has been lax in restraining sexuality although he believes sexuality must be restrained; he offers the most contemptuous condemnations of sexuality of anyone in the play in his reprimand of Pompey (III, ii). Although he himself and others report him to have been a temperate and kind governor, given to withdrawal, Lucio accuses him of hidden license. On the surface level, this is a parallel to the easy accusations made in the final scene against Mariana and Isabel, made by Angelo years before against Mariana, of whoredom: men too can be slandered. But because of the frequent association of the Duke with Lucio, and the nobleman's fury at the rake in the final scene, the two are associated on the mythic level. There, regardless of his behavior, the Duke is as lascivious and licensed as the city itself.[61] Lucio is his other half, detached and irresponsible (consider his words to Isabel after Claudio's "execution"), and promiscuous. The surface Duke is involved and responsible—but just as cruel to Isabel about her brother's execution—and sexually restrained. Yet under his skin, he may be Lucio.

The Duke is also ambiguous in the area of justice. The logic in the authority/justice plot is severely flawed, although obviously Shakespeare could plot logically when he chose to. The uneasiness of the causal links indicates their unimportance to the dramatist in this play. In fact, both *All's Well* and *Measure for Measure*—but the latter far more—are experimental plays, experiments Shakespeare was not to repeat. What he was attempting to create was a kind of cubist drama which provides several levels or modes or approaches simultaneously. If these plays are less than complete successes (which I am not sure is true), the problem may lie with the unyielding constrictions of the proscenium stage and dramatic genre.

Shakespeare's interest in, even fascination with, disguise of various sorts was far more profound than simply his use of a dramatic convention. He had been an actor, and probably produced the plays he wrote. Daily, he must have seen a bit of rag, a bit of cardboard (or whatever they used then), transform a lowly actor into a king more regal than the present holder of the throne. Daily he saw males become females using postures, walks, and gestures considered "female" by nature. He heard language he had written uttered with deep feeling, sending out into the theater expressions more profound, and truer, than most of the people in that theater would be capable of in actual life. He had to see that appearance was reality, and reality was appearance.

Early in his career he wrote plays which implied that personal identity was conferred by social role; at the same time, he was using the disguise convention to stretch that constricting definition, to allow his characters to live out more of their possibilities. A Christopher Sly has it in him to accept aristocratic treatment, Bottom has it in him to accept the love of the Fairy Queen: both without blinking an eyelash. Katharina is both an intractable fury and a docile wife. In All's Well, Helena is a Diana seduced by Bertram, a dead, unloved wife, a woman attempting to get her "right" who is hauled off to prison and accused of being a whore, and a triumphant and pregnant wife. The same thing is true of Isabel and Mariana in Measure for Measure; and the same thing is true of the Duke, although with him, the machinery creaks a bit. It is, I think, impossible to make psychological sense out of him. He is less a character than a force—an active mind. Feeling that sexuality must be controlled in some way, he experiments with one kind of restraint. He is deeply involved in the consequences of the experiment, deeply responsible, suggesting deep immersion in the quality he seeks to rein.

Let us examine the causal sequence of the authority/justice theme. The Duke first implies, to Escalus and Angelo, that urgent business calls him away from Vienna. His words to Angelo are very strong: "In our remove be thou at full ourself" (I, i, 43). Angelo and the Duke, then, are one. Next he tells Friar Thomas that he wishes to see the sexual laws enforced but feels unjust doing that himself because of his previous laxness. Quite apart from anything else, this is an unlikely and illogical way to handle such a thing. It would be much easier to announce that the city had become too corrupt—placing the blame on others, not himself—and as a result he was appointing a commissioner in charge of regulating sex. He could do this without leaving the city. Then he asks the Friar to outfit and instruct him so he may be a "true friar" (I, iii, 48), and indeed he is a friar for most of the play. Finally, he tells the Friar that another reason for his action is that he is experimenting to see the effect of power on a rigidly principled man. This is immoral on many grounds: an entire city should not be made a guinea pig to test one man's moral strength. The Duke's explanation of why he allows Isabel to believe Claudio dead is not only weak, it is hideously callous. The Duke's various motivations and his character cannot be integrated. Whether one chooses to see him as a figure of providence or a manipulative playwright, or attempts to make a realistic figure of him, he will not cohere.

Yet he is central to the play, the lynchpin on which the themes depend. The Duke is many things because we are watching more than one play. The Duke is all the things he pretends to be—sequentially. He extends over the gamut of the testing of authority and the trial of sex. Lucio is his double in one area; Angelo is his double in another; he is the friar he pretends to be. (The words *deputy* and *substitute* are frequently applied to Angelo.) His disguises function to make irrevocable events revocable. He sprawls across the play occupying all the power roles: he is an unjust justice; an irresponsible fornicator; a plotting, eavesdropping friar. He does not tell Isabel about Claudio's being spared because in one of the plays we see, Claudio is *not* spared. He dies, and Lucio and Isabel and Angelo respond to that fact (just as in *Much Ado*, all the characters behave as if Hero were really dead). And if the Duke represents male power, legitimacy, and authority, Isabel and Mariana are aspects of one thing as well—female powerlessness and sexuality. The various plays come together in the final scene and play out several conclusions. Like the endings of *All's Well*, each prior ending is more likely in actual life than the final one.

The first conclusion presents an Isabel who has given in to Angelo's demands, in accord with Shakespeare's sources. In the sources, which are far less realistic than this ending, the Isabel figure seeks redress from some higher authority and receives it. In Shakespeare's, she is accused by the higher justice of being mad ("Who will believe you, Isabel?") and is adjudged treasonous. Authority and power support

authority and power, and in the face of that, the illegitimate and powerless female and the principle she represents are condemned for being
what they are and are defeated.

The second conclusion presents another woman bringing the
same charge against Angelo. Two identical charges would seem to
indicate there might be something to this, but Angelo resorts to a
popular political response to a charge: he claims there is a conspiracy
against him. The two women are mad; besides that they are "poor
informal women," of no account, and therefore could not have arranged this conspiracy by themselves. They must be the instruments
of some treasonous male. The Duke concurs. Again, the ending is
possible.

The third conclusion brings a male of some authority—but unworldly in kind—before the bar of authority. "The Duke's unjust," he
claims, correctly, since Angelo is the Duke. Despite his claims of im-
munity, he is threatened with torture, suspected of treasonous conspiracy, and like the women, hauled away to prison.

The Duke then asserts his benevolent power and authority, but by
then, the point has been made. "Justice" is unjust. In the many
speeches deploring Claudio's death sentence, a frequent argument is
that he had good parentage. Parentage, especially paternity, is very
important in a hierarchal male society: legitimate paternity is the seal
of the legitimacy of the son. But his parentage did not help Claudio.
In such a climate, how shall the illegitimate fare? In Shakespeare's
Vienna, the poor, the women, have no rights.

The point about justice being made, the second trial, that of sexuality, begins. Again we run through several possibilities. The sexual
behavior of both Claudio and Angelo is condemned: Claudio has been
killed for it, so must Angelo be. He is condemned first to marriage and
then to death.

Isabel begs the Duke's pardon for having "employed and pain'd"
his high rank, and the Duke grants it (such are the rights of power),
and advises her that her brother is better off dead. Isabel agrees. This
picks up a subtheme that runs through the play. Angelo says he would
prefer immediate death to the shame he is feeling; Lucio suggests he
would prefer death to being married to a prostitute. The Duke's great
speech to Claudio in prison ("Be absolute for death") begins this
strand, which resembles the death longing so prominent in Hamlet
and Lavatch's insistence that all is not well as long as one is alive. Life
denial or longing for death is linked with the repudiation and contempt
for sex that pervades these plays. Thus it is understandable that Isabel,

more than any other character, sees death as a solution to all problems.[62]

Mariana, an aspect of Isabel, has less deeply felt principle and a
greater admitted participation in human weakness—which is to say
love and eros—and pleads with the Duke for mercy for Angelo. She
begs Isabel to join with her.

Isabel, still believing Claudio dead, does so. Her plea is extremely
significant, but it is not a single act, discrete, spontaneous, or problem-
atical. It is connected to a steady part of Isabel's character that has
generally been overlooked. Angelo, standing for law and justice still,
accepts death as just; Mariana, standing for ordinary human feeling,
asks mercy; Isabel, standing for chaste constancy maintained (now), as
a thing enskied and sainted, pleads for extenuation of a "sin" we know
she abhors, really abhors, with mind, body, and principle. She is the
only character in the play who is not "tainted" with sexuality: she has
shown that her hatred of unceremonialized sexual intercourse is so
great that she is willing to see her brother die rather than engage in it.
But Isabel, much as she hates sex, the "abhorr'd pollution" (II, iv, 183),
admits to being sexual.

We could psychologize and say that her retreat to the convent in
the first place was a response to her own sexuality in the face of a city
overridden with what she sees as vice, but it is not necessary to do that.
Isabel admits to sexuality openly in her conversation with Angelo.
"Call us ten times frail, / For we are soft as our complexions are, / And
credulous to false prints" (II, iv, 127–129), she admits. In other words,
Isabel's loathing of "shame," "sweet uncleanness," and "staining"—
some of the words used in this scene to describe unceremonialized sex
for a woman—coexists with a personal knowledge of sexual desire.

In the beginning of the last scene, Isabel, trying to get justice
against Angelo, is willing to confess in a public forum that she has
yielded sexually to Angelo. If on the mythic level, in that plot, she has,
on the surface level she has not, and remains the paragon of chastity
she has been. Critics who claim Isabel is concerned above all with her
reputation seem to overlook this section. In Shakespeare's world, as
we have seen, merely the aspersion of unchastity can destroy a
woman. She opens herself to public contempt for an act she scorns
more than anyone else—and indeed, she receives it, immediately,
from Lucio, who begins to joke at the expense of a woman he himself
called enskied and sainted not too long ago.[63]

If Isabel's chastity seems fanatical, the reader must put it in the
context of the play with its sexual obsessiveness, mixed guilt, abhor-

rence, a sneering contempt for an act that appears to be the only show in town, and an act that is for some, like Angelo, utterly irresistible. Isabel the saint admits that she too is sexual; her speech asking mercy for Angelo subsumes that sex is natural and nonvolitional: "I partly think / A due sincerity governed his deeds, / Till he did look on me" is not a self-serving piece of vanity (as has been suggested), but a recognition that sexual desire comes when it comes—it cannot be willed into or out of existence. The rest of her plea seems a jesuitical quibble: he should not be punished for what he did not do although he thought he was doing it: but is, actually, a completion of the first statement. Sexuality is not within human control, but sexual behavior is. Since Angelo is not guilty of unlawful sexual behavior, he should not be punished for his feelings.

Isabel's plea for mercy for Angelo is inconceivable on a realistic plane: he has killed her brother for an act far less blameworthy than the act he thinks he has performed. Isabel is a woman of spirit and principle: she would not forgive this. What Isabel is pleading for is mercy for human sexuality itself. Allowing herself also sexual, despite her renunciation, she admits that even a "saint" has a bond with the rest of humankind, that all humans feel desire. She thereby pleads the case of humankind in a tribunal that is trying sex. If the most chaste and constant of mortals accepts the reality and force of sex—as Helena accepts Parolles, as the Countess accepts Lavatch—it is ineradicable and must be bowed to. In a division of experience along gender lines, and an attribution of dominance to one pole, sex is necessarily sinful. But since all humans are sexual, even the most chaste and constant nun, we must forgive ourselves and each other and leave it to heaven to punish this "sin."

Any other interpretation of Isabel's plea-speech will show it to be as illogical as the Duke's explanations of his motivations. Angelo did do precisely what Claudio did, and by measure-for-measure justice, should die. It is true he did not do what he was accused of doing with Isabel: he did not rape, but he did fornicate with a woman to whom he was not finally married. In addition, all the pleas for Angelo ignore the real malfeasance or subornation of justice of which he is clearly guilty. Isabel's plea is not, at bottom, for Angelo: it is for humankind against the clamorous emotions of sexual guilt.

But the values of the play remain askew. In II, iv, Angelo tells Isabel that unceremonialized sex is as bad as murder; Isabel agrees that this is so in heaven. Claudio is executed (on the mythic level); Lucio is condemned to marriage; Angelo is condemned to marriage and threatened with death; Barnardine the murderer is easily pardoned. Isabel claims that her brother's death—murder performed by the state—is preferable to her performance of fornication. Although she couches her reasoning in theological terms—"Better it were a brother died at once, / Than that a sister, by redeeming him, / Should die for ever" (II, iv, 106–108)—it bears little resemblance to actual theology, of Shakespeare's time or our own.

When Isabel cries "More than our brother is our chastity," she is uttering the ultimate logical conclusion of Shakespeare's own idealization of chaste constancy. The easy pardon of Barnardine, a barely human murderer, before the "resurrection" and pardon of Claudio, demonstrates that unceremonialized sex is a greater evil than murder, and is the greatest evil on earth. The ugly conversation between the Duke and Lucio at the conclusion of *Measure for Measure* brings up again the hideous and repellent quality sex has throughout the play. It is, it remains, evil, filthy, disgusting, diseased. It is pardoned only because everyone is guilty of it one way or another—in feeling if not in behavior. Only marriage can purify it, but in this play, marriage is seen mostly as a punishment: Lucio is sent to prison to be married.[64]

But restraint of sex is also a prison. All of the settings of *Measure for Measure* fit in with its essential dichotomy between repellent sex and the disease attendant on repression. Many scenes occur in the prison; some in the court of justice, a lesser prison, and some in Angelo's house, a lesser court. The convent is a form of prison, as is Mariana's moated grange. The only other setting is the street, which is free; anyone may walk there, anyone may speak. Justice may be demanded of authority in the street. But the street is also lined with brothels.

The weighing of the two acts, killing and copulation, is the subject of Shakespeare's next play, *Othello*, in which unceremonialized killing is set beside unceremonialized sex. But because Shakespeare cannot bear to make Desdemona guilty of the act of which she is accused, that play does not resolve his conflict. The resolution of it appears finally in *Cymbeline*, when Posthumus judges himself wrong for having killed Imogen, even if she was guilty of inconstancy. Still, all the way through the canon, sex remains the great threat; indeed, it remains a great threat in literature generally until the early twentieth century.

But Shakespeare is never simple, that is to say, single-minded. In each of the problem plays there is a countering force to the dominant value structure. Hamlet's fury at his mother's failure, his disgust with sexuality that extends to women in general, his "mad" and "sane" challenges of male legitimacy, are countered by glimpses of Ophelia's fragility, Gertrude's love for her son, Claudius' despair at events, and his inability to pray. There is not much in *Troilus and Cressida* to affirm any norm, except perhaps the magnificent ugliness of the play as a whole, which leads the audience to assert a different set of values, but there are two tendencies—the inflating and the deflating—that counter each other.

Helena's values are dominant in *All's Well That Ends Well*, but they are undercut and countered not so much by Bertram's rejection as by the rebellion against goodness of Lavatch and Parolles. And all of *Measure for Measure* is a protest against its initial situation—condemnation of humankind for sex which at its best is "sweet uncleanness."

One thing does change as a result of, or after, the writing of these plays: Shakespeare appears to lay the problem of relativity to rest. Hamlet says bitterly, "there is nothing either good or bad, but thinking makes it so," and Troilus asks, passionately, "What's aught but as 'tis valued?" In *All's Well*, Lavatch alone carries the burden of a multiple vision, but the serial conclusion embodies it. The same thing happens in *Measure for Measure*, but in this play, the multiple roles of the Duke demonstrate what Hamlet and Troilus talk about. In the plays written after these, Shakespeare *himself* never seems to question what his ultimate values are. His characters may be blind to them, or ignorant, but there is none of the tortured probing of the value and strength of the inlaw feminine principle that occurs in these plays.

In the tragedies, the inlaw feminine principle is exiled or destroyed; in the romances it endures and triumphs: in both, it lies behind the action as an absolute good. However, this does not solve Shakespeare's real problem. For the inlaw feminine principle is only *half* a principle: it lacks the power its sexual base contains, and therefore it gives rise to characters who are not at all like actual people. The division of experience into gender principles is a falsification of actual experience in the first place; to divide one of them further is to create unrealizable ideals. But Shakespeare's greatness lies in the fact that he was not only a great poet, but he never lost touch with either the actual or the ideal vision.

V

CHAOS COME AGAIN:
IDEALS BANISHED

10

The Late Tragedies

Although it may sometimes appear in a "masculine" form, that is, linear, highly plotted, Shakespearean comedy is a feminine mode. It is concerned with an entire society rather than an isolated individual; it moves towards harmonious integration of all elements of that society, and the promise of continuation through marriage and implicit new birth. The marriages with which most Shakespearean comedies end are syntheses of the gender principles, but are dedicated to the ends of the feminine principle—felicity and procreation.

In the problem plays, which are written in a mixed mode, the gender principles are at war. In *Hamlet*, the Prince, representing the inlaw feminine principle, declares internal war against the outlaw feminine (and all women), and against the pretensions of the masculine principle. The other three problem plays show the masculine principle devaluing, repudiating, or attempting to repress one or another part of the feminine principle. The survival of inlaw values is tenuous in all of these plays, and in fact does not occur in two of them—*Hamlet*, and *Troilus and Cressida*.

The tragedies after *Hamlet* are generally in a masculine mode. (*Antony and Cleopatra* is in a class by itself.) They are linear in structure, focus on a major character, always a male, who lives out an individual life and dies, like all individual humans. However, although a single male protagonist dominates the foreground in a way no single character does in comedy, he shares the focus with the background, his culture. In all the tragedies, the culture (or some aspect of it) is nearly equal in importance with the hero.[1]

This is not true of comedy, which may seem strange since comedy is more concerned with society than tragedy is, and more concerned with society than with the individual. But precisely because of that concern, comedy presents a generalized, universal picture of society. It offers a set of diverse elements that make up *any* society, that are discordant in some way, and creates a perspective broad enough to contain, to tolerate all of them. The societies depicted in the various comedies are not *essentially* different from each other. The cultures of Othello, Lear, Macbeth, and Antony are: they are particularized. We have a sense of Macbeth's Scotland and Lear's England in a way we do not of Messina or Illyria. The background of the comedies, be it Navarre or Arden, is simply a space large and free enough to allow the characters to be themselves. The background of the tragedies is a place; it comes complete with its own demands, its own character, a set of values that impose themselves on those who live in it. And the protagonist of tragedy invariably expreses those values; he grows out of them, is part of them, whether or not he finds himself at some point in opposition to them.

Although each culture that figures in the tragedies is different, they all have certain common features. The worlds of Othello, Lear, and Macbeth, as well as the other tragic heroes, are utterly "masculine"; they are dominated by men who place supreme value on the qualities of the masculine principle and to varying degrees, slight, deny, or are ignorant of the value and importance of its complement. The kind of blindness to or rejection of "feminine" values varies from tragedy to tragedy, but reaches its extremest form in the last two plays, *Coriolanus*, and *Timon of Athens*.

Because the tragedies concentrate on "masculine" values, which are dominant in the world at large in our own time as well as in Shakespeare's, and because the male heroes of the plays (who incarnate the values of their culture) are also to some degree antipathetic to that culture, what occurs in the dramas is a war, a conflict between an individual and a cultural encapsulation of the same value. It is internecine war, and amounts to a trial of a value in much the same way that *Measure for Measure* is a trial of sex. Thus, the tragedies are among the most radical criticisms ever written of the values of Western society.

Because the tragedies concentrate on "masculine" values, they have been considered, by generations of critics, more serious and more realistic than the comedies. They are neither. They deal with much the same material, the same concerns, and use many of the same techniques and devices. There is use of folktale, supernatural elements, and disguise in both genres. The difference is that in tragedy, not only acts, but even words are irrevocable. If in comedy, a serious act or speech is saved by the disguise convention, the bed trick, or a fairy potion, in tragedy, acts or words that need not necessarily lead to irrevocable consequences always do. The tragedies seem more realistic because they deal with the masculine principle, that is, they deal with structures, power, possession, and action, all of which are palpable, substantial, whereas the comedies deal with feelings, attitudes, reflections—the fluid and generative and nonsubstantial dimensions of human life. Indeed, so difficult is it (especially in our period—a time when emotion and pleasure are viewed with great disdain and contempt) to discuss the inlaw feminine principle that critics are forced to resort to terms like "irrational," "mythic," or "divine" to describe it, making it sound mysterious and unearthly in a way it is not.[2] There is nothing whatever irrational about the inlaw feminine principle (except cutting it off from its roots in the outlaw aspect); it only *seems* irrational to people whose notion of rationality is a narrow and sterile view of life as logical, linear, and self-interested. It is fortunate that most of us live more broadly than we think.

In both comedy and tragedy, the characters may be easy or uneasy, satisfied or unsatisfied, happy or unhappy in their society. Comedy concentrates on ways in which they can be assimilated. They may discover their true identity (their ordained place in society), or their emotional center (true love). By removing themselves from the power world to a place apart or "green world" (which is a metaphor for rejecting "masculine" standards, or ignoring them; turning one's back on power and structure and looking instead at feeling and sensation), and by learning to reject a value—for example, Jaques' melancholy, Sir Toby's dissipation, Katharina's shrewishness—without rejecting the person: in other words, by tolerance, the characters discover a way to live together and an enriched, enlarged world.

In tragedy, the concentration on the individual automatically creates distance between the hero and his society. The anguish implicit in tragedy is rooted in the paradox of being part of a culture, even expressing to a high degree some of its values, and yet increasingly rejecting or being rejected by it. Tragedy presents a tearing away like the original act of birth; in the course of that wrenching separation, the protagonists discover their true natures, their basic identities. But this is not necessarily pleasant: much of our lives is spent in hiding our "true" identities, from ourselves and sometimes even from others— although the latter is very difficult. This situation is true of all the tragedies, including *Hamlet*. Hamlet incarnates the schizophrenia of his world: he worships the inlaw feminine principle and respects to the point of awe, legitimacy, the masculine principle. From the first moment we see him, he stands—or sits—looking gloomily, then with disgust, then with horror, at the other side of things, rampant sexuality, the pretensions of power, the trivial or serious corruption found in human action. But he himself is capable of just such action, and he is not free of his melancholy until he indulges in it. Lear's progress is from centrality in his world to a place outside it; in all his phases he provides ground for radical criticism of it. Antony, Macbeth, Coriolanus, and Timon are living expressions of a quality highly valued in their cultures, which they carry to a more intense or different development than is permitted within that culture. Othello and to some degree Macbeth are victims of their own cultures, which is why we are able to feel sympathy (and in Othello's case, condescension, to judge from many critics) for them.

In all the plays, we are looking at the full-plumed masculine principle, Bertram made more serious, intense, profound, or deeply feeling, at powerful males who own rights, privilege, possession, and transcendence of the "feminine," who have few or no worldly boundaries placed upon them. In most, there is none can call their power to account; for harmonious society to exist, they must therefore do so themselves. Their failure or inability to do so provides the story that unfolds.

Othello

Nowhere in Shakespeare are relations between males and females more searchingly, painfully probed. *Othello* is the last play in which this occurs; with it, the concerns that are central in *Comedy of Errors*, *Taming*, *Much Ado*, and *All's Well* are finally laid to rest.

The dominant culture of the play is that of Venice, which is shown here as similar to the Venice of *Merchant*, but in a more positive light. Venice is worldly, powerful, moneyed, and mannered. It is not just a place but an influence, and its mores are implanted in all the characters, even in those who, like Othello and Cassio, are not native Venetians. Venice is civilization, a civilization the characters carry with them to primitive, wild, wartorn Cyprus.[3] The graft is as uneasy as the overlay of civility on any basic human core.

The scenes in Venice present the masculine principle in two aspects. The Senate scene shows it at its finest, possessed of honor, lawfulness, decorum, knowledge, and power, yet "feminine" in its protective and consolatory inclinations. The city is dominated by reason, and the council scene (I, iii) exemplifies reason in action, whether the issue is a set of conflicting reports of an enemy's movements or a father's hysterical attack. Reason is a form of control, and it is control above all that is the ideal of this culture. Control is essential to a culture which views natural humanity as depraved and vicious: thus Hamlet values Horatio, and Polonius lectures Laertes. It is also essential to a culture which views natural humanity as bestial and voracious, which is closer to the view of this play. The shocked Lodovico laments:

> Is this the noble Moor whom our full Senate
> Call all in all sufficient? Is this the nature
> Whom passion could not shake? whose solid virtue
> The shot of accident nor dart of chance
> Could neither graze nor pierce? (IV, i, 264–268)

Control over others is power. Control over self is invulnerability, transcendence over nature and the contingencies of natural life. In "Venetian" cultures, control is an absolute good. But belief in the existence of control is belief that reason, which leads to control, can be separated from and dominate feeling.

From a Venetian perspective, self-control is desirable in all people, necessary in males, and most valuable in soldiers, who must frequently undergo physical discomfort and danger. Othello must sleep on "the flinty and steel couch of war" (I, iii, 230), and survive "disastrous chances" (I, iii, 134) of battle, accident, and capture. Othello shows a strong self-control from his first appearance in the play. He is ideally calm, reasonable, and rooted in a sense of legitimacy. He does not fear Brabantio; he knows his lineage to be more royal than and as wealthy as that of the Venetians. He remains calm and in control even when suddenly encompassed by naked swords. Attacked in the Senate, he speaks mildly, moderately, and brilliantly, never responding to Brabantio's wild charges. Although when during his wedding night, a melee breaks out in Cyprus, he warns that "passion, having my best judgment collied, / Assays to lead the way" (II, iii, 206–207), he remains calm throughout the disruption. Othello represents an ideal control.

Iago too is controlled, although his self-control is used for dissembling, as he announces in the first scene and repeats frequently. Loss of self-control makes Brabantio appear a fool in the council scene; it causes Cassio to lose his lieutenantship. Important as this quality is, every major male figure loses self-control at some point in the play *except Iago*.

The values of Venice are shared by all of the characters. The values most important in this play are power (of various sorts), control (which means believing in the possibility of the supremacy of reason over emotion, and thus in the control, or repression, of emotion), and possession.

There is, however, inevitably in a culture that respects control, an "underside" to the Venetian culture. It is Venice unclothed, lacking ermine robes and gold seals of office. This sphere has the same values as the world of senator and aristocrat, but its members lack some of the cushions legitimacy grants. It is occupied by males with lesser legitimacy, but it is foreign to no male figure. It is rawer and cruder than Venice; the assumptions which can be sugared over, or spread with velvet in aristocratic circles, are glaringly open here. And it is this sphere that we see first as the play opens.

It is the world of the streets, the locker room, the pool hall. It is dominated by concern about money, and by male competition, which may take the form of envy or hatred. The opening scene (as well as all of Iago's scenes with Roderigo) presents its terms, as Iago bilks Roderigo of his money, and spits hatred at Cassio and Othello.

The aristocratic Venetians do nothing like this. They don't have to. Those with wealth do not have to con a man of his purse—they have subtler means, means they have legitimated by law. Those with political power do not have savagely to manipulate one man: they can impersonally manipulate an entire army. Although Shakespeare does not explicitly identify the two worlds (one senses, indeed, that he would prefer to believe them different), their kinship is demonstrated when members of the aristocratic world—Othello, Cassio, and Brabantio—accede to the terms of the second, and even use those terms themselves.

Because both of these spheres are based in a desire to transcend nature, in control, both are profoundly misogynistic. Their fear and contempt for the feminine principle is expressed not just in contemptuous treatment of women, but in disdain for "feminine" qualities like loyalty, obedience, and above all, emotion. Women are seen largely as functions, and trivialized; there is general belief in male right to own women and control them. In this kind of thinking, there is disdain for bonds that do not advance one (in a linear way) in the world, for any subordination of self, and for sex.

There is a third sphere in the play, although its character is not as firmly delineated as the two Venetian spheres. This is Cyprus, which can be reached only by immersing oneself in nature, risking drowning. It is a space, rather than place, and thus like the "places apart" found in comedy. It is a space where those things normally kept in control and hidden can—and do—grow and appear in the light. In Cyprus, where there is, symbolically, no real civilization, only that brought by the Venetians, a man may be his own judge and jury and executioner, a woman may be inconstant, and the underlying assumptions of a culture may be glaringly displayed. And, most important, in Cyprus, the conventions of civilization which permit revocability are lacking. In reversal of the comedic device of using equivocating language to suggest the ambivalence of human affairs and to permit revocability, *Othello* shows words as deeds, and as irrevocable as murder.

The character who symbolizes the upper crust of Venice, despite his different nativity, is Othello; the character who bears the lower burden is Iago. But they are two crusts of one pie, and thus do not just intersect, but share the same base, like the imprintings on two sides of a coin.

Iago is unadulteratedly "masculine." He believes in control, reason, power, possession, and individualism; he holds any manifestation of the feminine principle in contempt. It is significant that Iago opens the play: it is his terms that dictate its events throughout. The language of that opening is indicative: Roderigo speaks of money; Iago says "Abhor me," and Roderigo speaks of hate. Iago replies "despise me," and proceeds to attack Cassio. He claims his rival is "almost damn'd in a fair wife," and knows no more of war than a "spinster" or "toged consul." Essentially, Iago is calling Cassio a sissy, effeminate, as containing "feminine" qualities.[4] He blames Othello for choosing his lieutenant by "affection" (which is sometimes glossed to mean "favoritism," although the OED lists no such meaning for Shakespeare's period, which contains pejorative connotations not present in Shakespeare's term) rather than by "old gradation"—seniority, a coded hierarchy. The conversation moves to assertion of self, individuality at the expense of a social whole, and again Iago shows contempt for loyalty, subordination of self, service based on love, and equates such qualities with bestiality: a duteous servant is his "master's ass," and earns but "provender" for his pains.

What Iago lacks are the rewards of masculinity—wealth and status; his actions at the opening seem designed to gain these. He does bilk Roderigo of his fortune, and in time, he does supplant Cassio. But these achievements do not seem to satisfy him; they seem utterly insignificant. Like Richard III, Iago is cut off by his nature from the feminine principle. He not only scorns "feminine" qualities, but wishes to destroy them in others. He is not such an anomaly as he has been made out. His character is not unlike that of some historical figures who have gone into the world carrying the banner of a religious or political cause, wiping out pleasure, mercy, and sexual love.

Iago is totally rational—and I use that word as critics use it who call the feminine principle *irrational*—and his means is his end.[5] Control is his absolute good, but it gets him nothing: he goes round and round, at every step inventing new reasons to exercise control. In the hollowness of those without satisfying ends, he wills the destruction of those who have them; he wants to "poison the delight" of those who, like Cassio, have a "daily beauty" in their lives.[6] The only thing that makes Iago unbelievable is that he does this in the name of his own individuality, and not in the name of some "higher" cause.

Iago's weapons are his unremitting hatred of the feminine principle and his brilliance at articulating that hatred. This hatred appears in the first scene (thus completing the statement of values that dictates the events) when Iago cries out to Brabantio. He first describes Desdemona as if she were one more possession: "look to your house, your daughter, and your bags"; "sir, y'are robbed" (I, i, 80–85). Then he presents the marriage of Desdemona and Othello in these ugly images: "an old black ram / Is tupping your white ewe"; "You'll have your daughter cover'd with a Barbary horse, you'll have your nephews neigh to you; you'll have coursers for cousins, and gennets for germans"; Othello and Desdemona, he says, are "making the beast with two backs" (I, i, 88–89; 111–113; 116).

Iago consistently uses animal images—that is, images from nature —to describe sexuality and generation. He goes always directly to the heart of things, even if they are prejudices. Roderigo and Brabantio use political terms to describe what has occurred. Brabantio too sees his daughter as his possession: "She is . . . stol'n from me" (I, iii, 60). Roderigo says that Desdemona has made a "gross revolt"; Brabantio calls it "treason of the blood." Both men mean not only a revolt against her father's lawful possession and control, but also a revolt against the "laws of nature," as she moves to the "gross clasps of a lascivious Moor."

Both kinds of descriptions of what Desdemona has done are "masculine," and both betray the values of this culture. But Iago's way of speaking moves the case from the particular to the general. He casts filth not just on the coupling of Desdemona and Othello, but on coupling itself. All sexuality is "making the beast with two backs," if one has contempt for sex and sees it as bestial.[7]

Othello at first appears to be his ensign's opposite. That he is noble and that Shakespeare intended him to seem so appears to me to be unquestionable. His demeanor is authoritative and calm, his language intelligent and beautiful, and only rarely inflated. He appears in a particularly shining way because he appears *after* Iago. Iago's revelations about his own character "blacken" him instantly; his hatred for the Moor serves to exalt the general, and to "whiten" him. And in all the early scenes, Othello is steadily admirable, Iago steadily despicable. On the surface, the two present a clear contrast. Underneath, however, another current moves. For Othello, magnificent as he is, is also as egotistical as his ensign; moreover, his gentility and magniloquence tend to dull. Although it does not happen in the play, Othello *could* become tedious, boring; Iago is never that. The point is that Iago has the energy and wit and delight in himself that Shakespeare associates with the unleashed masculine principle. Hateful as he is, Iago is fun (in the way Richard III is fun) to listen to.

Othello's values are those of aristocratic Venice; Iago's are those of its underside. Iago has contempt for the feminine principle, for women, and feeling, and sex. Othello, without his awareness, shares this contempt. The first clue to this is his behavior in the Senate chamber. Othello swears that "as truly as to heaven / I do confess the vices of my blood, / So justly to your grave ears I'll present / How I did thrive in this fair lady's love" (I, iii, 122–125). The comparison seems inept, but Othello is never inept. Unconsciously, he is associating love with vice. In his effort to persuade the Senate that his commission will take priority over his marriage, he uses terms that could be Iago's: if he neglects his work for love, he says, "Let housewives make a skillet of my helm" (I, iii, 272). In response to the order to leave immediately, before the consummation of his marriage, he says "With all my heart." He accepts the commission for Cyprus with "a natural and prompt alacrity." He seems to have no regret whatever about leaving Desdemona. When she demurs and asks to go with him, he seconds her, but assures the Senate that he wants her "not / To please the palate of my appetite . . . but to be free and bounteous to her mind" (I, iii, 261; 262; 265). We might assume from this that Othello has a weak or undemanding sensual nature—indeed, one critic has so concluded—but this is the same man who later tells Desdemona she is "so lovely fair and smell'st so sweet / That the sense aches at thee" (IV, ii, 68–69).[8]

Othello's denial of the erotic element in love is related to Iago's denial of the loving element in eros. Both denials emerge from a need to separate love (the inlaw aspect) from sex (the outlaw). Both attempt to control sexuality, Othello by idealizing it, Iago by demeaning it: "But we have reason to cool our raging motions, our carnal stings, our unbitted lusts; whereof I take this that you call love to be a sect or scion" (I, iii, 329–332). Both men assume that love and lust are related; Othello tries to purify the lustfulness from love, and Iago tries to rationalize the love out of lust.

Othello is almost as "masculine" as Iago. He too believes in control, reason, and the assertion of individuality. (Consider his statements: "Were it my cue to fight, I should have known it / Without a prompter" [I, ii, 83–84]; "She lov'd me for the dangers I had passed, / And I lov'd her that she did pity them" [I, iii, 167–168]. Both show a strong ego sense.) He respects power and hierarchy. Dignified and self-respecting as he is before the Senate, he acknowledges it his superior; decent and humane as he is with his inferiors, he never forgets his authority over them.[9] In addition, he shares Iago's sense of the degradation sexuality constitutes, but whereas Iago would engage in sex and then hurl contempt at the woman, assuming boys will be boys, Othello attempts to idealize sex out of existence.

However, misogynistic cultures, because they need the women they despise, always contain a safety pocket. They open a very narrow gate, through which pass those women considered purified from taint, and thus elevated. Othello, Cassio, and the play itself exalt one woman, Desdemona, as being above the common run. Cassio describes Desdemona in terms that any mortal would have trouble living up to: she "paragons description"; she is so divine that even nature gives her homage. (Othello too is exalted in this section of II, i. The exaltation, coupled with the suspense attending his arrival, emphasizes his greatness. Thus the pair seems, at the moment of their meeting, two superhumans matched.) Between Cassio's hyperbolic comments about Desdemona before Othello's arrival, and Othello's hyperbolic description of his feelings about Desdemona after he arrives, is a short, odd section. It is a dialogue that would be unnecessary and irrelevant to the play if Shakespeare were not focusing on the subject of attitudes towards women.

Iago begins by castigating Emilia, and immediately extends his criticism to women in general. Desdemona challenges him on this, clearly (if implicitly) believing herself worthy, and wishing to hear some words describing worthy women. Iago dredges up a set of ancient attacks on women. Women are dissemblers; by nature they are angry, argumentative, and sexual; they pretend to competence (huswifery), and sainthood. To Desdemona's challenge he replies with a set of verses which emphasize one thing and only one thing: female (dissembling) sexuality. When she challenges him further, he admits that there may be deserving women (the very phrase betrays the assumptions of the culture), and what they deserve is to "suckle fools and chronicle small beer" (II, i, 160). For Iago, women are body, childbearers and nurturers, and housewives, none of which functions warrant any respect.

The language of Othello on his arrival is beautiful and extreme. Beside it, Desdemona's sounds pedestrian.[10] In his ecstasy, he wishes for death because "I fear / My soul hath her content so absolute / That not another comfort like to this / Succeeds in unknown fate" (II, i, 190–193). He is, of course, ironically, quite accurate, but his negligence of, or ignoring of, the sexual consummation still to come is most untypical and therefore significant. Desdemona's language is matter-of-fact and plain. She is not an enraptured idealist, but simply a happy woman expecting a happy life.

These two attitudes—one exalting, one degrading, neither able to deal with the reality—towards women, and particularly towards Desdemona, are contrasted again in II, iii, 15–29, in the dialogue of Cassio and Iago about Desdemona and sex, but they come into direct confrontation in III, iii. And in this scene, it is Othello, not Iago, who associates vulnerability to feeling with bestiality. To Iago's warning against jealousy, he responds "Exchange me for a goat" if ever he suffers from such an emotion. Iago's campaign is careful. First he impugns Cassio, then warns Othello against jealousy. His warning alone is enough to shake Othello a little; beneath his calm and assured exterior there is a sense of some kind of unworthiness. But he dismisses it: "she had eyes, and chose me."

Because male legitimacy is based on pretense, it is always shaky. Like Brabantio and others of his culture, Othello believes in his possession and right to command his wife: inconstancy would be a "revolt." But beneath this belief always lurks the suspicion that one person cannot really own another.[11] Thus the grounds on which the entire Renaissance concept of marriage is erected are shaky, and Othello is feeling the tremor.

Iago's next step is a slide onto the dangerous ground of Desdemona. He begins with a commonplace misogynistic statement—Venetian women (all of them, of course) are inconstant. Then he moves closer to home: she deceived her father, why not you? This has special force because Brabantio himself has hurled the warning—about his own daughter—at Othello. Iago adds: she even deceived you, for when she seemed frightened of you, she was most in love with you.

Just these assertions are enough to dash Othello, to undermine all his exalted love. Since for Desdemona to be worthy of his love she must be better than the common run of women, the mere suggestion that she is not the utter paragon of virtue and honesty she has been made out is sufficient to tarnish her.[12] Since she obviously could not be superhuman, Iago's suggestion that she is not has the strong force of truth: honest Iago, indeed. And seeing how the mere intimation that she *can* deceive shakes Othello, understanding that such a suspicion will lead to doubts as to whether she is really free from moral taint (with women, that means sexuality), Iago has a clear path for his next step. He trains Othello to see sex, women, and love as he does.

He accomplishes this through language, which is his greatest gift: Iago is literally a poet of hate and disgust. And in this play, language is action. Iago destroys Othello and Desdemona without lifting a finger; he uses his tongue alone. And it is a brilliant one.

Nevertheless, it would be impossible for Iago to seduce Othello if Othello did not already share Iago's value structure.[13] Othello is not dense or blind, he is not a noble savage. He is a male who lives and thrives in a masculine occupation in a "masculine" culture, the assumptions of which he shares.[14]

There are two kinds of women, one being superhuman, totally virtuous. (Even Iago believes there are such things as virtuous women: see II, iii, 360–361; IV, i, 46–47.) The other kind is a dissembler, a deceiver, because of sexuality; she is thus subhuman, bestial, capable of any degradation. And the two kinds are absolutely mutually exclusive. One can cross into the subhuman camp at any time, but once in it, one can never return. So Othello, perceiving taint in Desdemona for the first time, is deeply shaken. Her later, frightened deception about the handkerchief will clinch the case against her.

But Othello is a deeply feeling person. Unlike Iago, he is capable of dedicating himself to something or someone outside himself. Thus his fury against Desdemona is nothing like Iago's contemptuous treatment of Emilia. Desdemona has betrayed Othello in the deepest part of his being, "there, where I have garner'd up my heart, / Where either I must live or bear no life; / The fountain from which my current runs / Or else dries up" (IV, ii, 57–60). When he stops loving Desdemona, "chaos is come again."

Yet in I, ii, Othello tells Iago that he would not have confined his "unhoused free condition" except that he loves Desdemona. He does not seem to have suffered from "chaos" in the years before he loved; he did not "bear no life" before he met her.

Desdemona has seduced Othello into placing faith and trust in that unfixable, uncontrollable feminine principle; her love for him has seduced him into allowing himself to love. By submitting to the feminine principle, Othello turns his back on his training. While Iago is contemptuous of the qualities of the feminine principle, Othello feels ignorant of them. He apologizes to the Senate for his lack of polish; he thinks Desdemona may have turned against him because he is old, or black, or lacks the "soft parts of conversation" (III, iii, 264). In loving her he has opened the deepest parts of himself, allowed himself to feel, although he is unused to the "melting mood." He has freely accepted vulnerability and subordination to another. And it is Othello's ignorance of the inlaw aspect, an ignorance that in a person of mature years has to be based in fear and distrust, that makes him so vulnerable to Iago's certainty that with women, distrust, mistrust, is the only reasonable, the only rational position.

In truth, the mere suggestion that Desdemona is unfaithful is enough to send Othello into a renunciatory paroxysm that goes beyond just love and marriage and women: he renounces his career as well. It is tempting to read that passage as self-dramatization, but it is of a piece with his character generally. Othello does dramatize his emotions—consider his speech just before he kills Desdemona. He is a passionate man. And loss of faith, once he has placed it, leads to loss of the will to live. In this way, he is related to Hamlet.[15] (So is Iago, in another way.)

We are, I think, meant to find Othello a bit of an innocent, regardless of his age. He sees himself thus and so does Iago at one moment. He is emotionally deep but inexperienced, like Hamlet and (perhaps) Troilus; he is as idealistic as they are as well. His blackness is partly an emblem for this sort of difference from wily Venetians and courtly Florentines. For Othello, as for Hamlet and Troilus, the altar on which he has first placed his devotion must remain fixed, constant, else chaos is come again.

Chaos comes swiftly and it comes through language. It is the vividness and ugliness of the sexual images Iago is able to conjure that leads Othello to hell. "Would you, the supervisor, grossly gape on? Behold her topp'd?" (III, iii, 345). Othello replies, "Death and damnation!" The vividness of Iago's account of Cassio's talking in his sleep is enough to lead Othello to swear "I'll tear her all to pieces," and to abjure all his "fond love."

An essential part of the exchanges of Othello and Iago is the pervasive animal imagery. It can signify subordination, as in Iago's early characterization of a loyal servant as an *ass*; in Iago's hectoring of Brabantio, it is applied to copulation and generation. It next appears —again in Iago's mouth—when Roderigo claims he will die from love. Iago scoffs: "Ere I would say I would drown myself for the love of a guinea hen, I would change my humanity with a baboon" (I, iii, 314– 316). He then proceeds to outline what he considers to be the proper relations among human faculties; his ideas are classical and Catholic, items of accepted philosophical and theological doctrine.[16] One could read his speech and shrug about devils who can quote Scripture. But it is far more likely that Shakespeare was suggesting that the values that motivate and characterize an Iago are *accepted and respected values in the Western world*. Only his apparent ignorance of love makes his statement seem that of a villain; like Troilus, Iago identifies love as appetite (in II, i, 225–235).

Iago's associations are clear: sex, subservience, and affection are parts of the feminine principle, and are therefore not within the pale of the human because they are tied to nature, beasts, and deservedly enslaved classes, which include women.

But Othello, once his idealism is undermined (indeed his idealism is a shift made to allow love in the face of his real beliefs), shares Iago's ideas. Like the ensign, he equates love with appetite, marriage with possession, and considers less than total possession of a wife "toadlike" (III, iii, 270).[17] Iago whets him with images of Desdemona and Cassio as goats, monkeys, and wolves. Othello falls into a fit, then mutters, "A horned man's a monster and a beast" (IV, i, 62). "Goats and monkeys!" (IV, i, 263), his uncontrolled outburst at the end of his tormented speech to Lodovico, proves that Iago's poison poured in his ears has done its work.

Once Iago has poisoned sexuality itself in Othello's mind, there is nothing to be done. Desdemona as idealized woman and his exalted notion of love are dead for him whether he kills the real woman or not. If Desdemona, that paragon, is tainted, so are all women. In his rage at the destruction of his illusion, Othello treats both Desdemona and Emilia as whores. (Thus, at the end of the play, Iago calls Emilia "whore" when she tells the truth about the handkerchief.) And since Desdemona is clearly sexual—physically as well as emotionally and intellectually in love with Othello—she *is* tainted (whether unfaithful or not) once Iago has taught Othello to see sex as he does.

Nevertheless, Othello could simply turn away from Desdemona; he could divorce her; he could talk to her about the charges; he could . . . a thousand things. But he must kill her because of the prime value of his culture, his own prime value as well: control. As I said earlier, there are only two forms of control—domestication and killing. Desdemona seems unable to be domesticated, so she must be killed. Trust of the fluid feminine principle is difficult precisely because it cannot be controlled; its very nature is defined by that. Division into inlaw and outlaw aspects is a way of trying to control it, but it does not work very well. Othello must kill Desdemona because he loves her so much that if he did not kill her, he would slide into accepting her infidelity, to giving up control over her entirely.

Although he attempts, in his words over her sleeping body, to ceremonialize her murder, invoking justice and "more men" as his reasons, he cannot accomplish this. Desdemona's crime is worse than his, and this justifies his. Wakened and asked to confess her sins, Desdemona says "They are loves I bear to you" (V, ii, 40). She too sees love as sin. The murder in *Othello* is the murder of a vision of human love purified from the taint of a sexuality seen as bestial, vicious, and chaotic.[18]

That Shakespeare himself was thinking in terms like those I have described is demonstrated by his portraits of the three women in the play. They come from three moral levels: the "divine" Desdemona from the superhuman; Emilia from the realistic world; and Bianca from the subhuman, since she is a prostitute and thus, in the moral universe of Shakespeare's plays (and elsewhere as well), not deserving of human consideration or rights. Yet all three of these women are finally treated in the same way. Moreover, Shakespeare placed words in their mouths that show he was aware of the political situation of women and their personal identities apart from men.

Desdemona, the angel who has not yet experienced mistreatment, accepts her culture's dictum that she must be obedient to males. Her first words in the play express her sense of duty to father and husband, a "divided duty" (I, iii, 181). The last words she speaks before she is aware of a change in Othello are: "Be as your fancies teach you; / What e'er you be, I am obedient" (III, iii, 88–89). She cannot even conceive of infidelity to a husband; she does not struggle against Othello when he commences to abuse her. To the end she remains submissive, begging Othello to let her live one more night, one more half hour. Her last words, placing the blame for her death on herself, are self-denying in the extreme: they are the words of a martyr. With Cordelia and Hermoine, Desdemona represents the inlaw feminine principle at its most superhuman.

Yet Shakespeare also takes pains to show her human, whole, and possessed of will. She confesses, in the Senate chamber, to "violence, and storm of fortunes" (I, iii, 249). It is she who protests the separation of the newlyweds; she asserts she wants to live with Othello because she wants "the rites for why I love him" (I, iii, 257). And it is she who cries out to the senators in dismay, "To-night, my lord?" (I, iii, 278), after the order to leave immediately. She has defied and deceived her father; like Helena, she would lose her virginity to her own liking.

Desdemona is sexual. Her innocence resides not in her freedom from sexual "taint" (as does the Virgin Mary's), but in her ignorance of the bestiality others see implicit in it. She is chaste and constant by nature: she cannot conceive of infidelity; she cannot imagine that love can end; and she is ignorant of male ways of talking and thinking about sex. To the degree that she represents part of Othello's psyche, she embodies that part which exalts and idealizes love, separating it from bestial sex. But Shakespeare is at some pains to emphasize that Desdemona herself has no need of such moral schizophrenia, that in her wholeness she finds no need to redeem or idealize sex.

Desdemona has no sexual guilt because she feels no need to transcend sex. She does not claim she wants to go to Cyprus to be "free and bounteous" to Othello's mind: nor is she hesitant to assert publicly that she has sexual desires. She can jest with Iago about women without embarrassment. Although she knows that sex is sin, her own sexual acts have been sanctified by ceremony into "rites." She teases Othello about Cassio with the tenacity of a cajoling child; she lies about the handkerchief like a wary child. And yet when Othello strikes her publicly, she stands her ground with adult dignity: "I have not deserv'd this" (IV, i, 224).

In short, until the "brothel" scene, she is a sensitive and confident young woman, straitly kept, kept a dependent child, but retaining spirit nevertheless. She is whole, sexual, given to be happy. But the men in the play see her differently.

For Brabantio, she has the passivity and silence proper in women:

"a maiden, never bold; / Of spirit so still and quiet that her motion / Blush'd at itself"* (I, iii, 94–96). He thinks she is unsexual, "opposite to marriage" (I, ii, 67). Thus her elopement with Othello is doubly "unnatural": she has chosen a man of a color different from her own, and she has betrayed that she does possess sexual desires.

Roderigo idealizes Desdemona as holy, "full of most bless'd condition" (II, i, 249–250). Cassio exalts her even more than Othello does, as divine, a paragon, "our great captain's captain." For Othello, Desdemona is not fully a separate being but part of himself, the completion of himself.

But honest Iago sees her only as "fram'd as fruitful / As the free elements" (II, iii, 341–342). It is ironic that of all the men, he sees Desdemona the most accurately.

Desdemona perceives herself the way Othello perceives her—as part of him, as not existing without him; his rejection of her in IV, ii stuns her into stupefaction. She tells Iago that the removal of Othello's love will kill her "but never taint my love" (IV, ii, 161). And as she dies, she puts the blame for her murder on herself. (Interestingly, Othello sneers that she dies in sin, lying; over and again, the inflexibility of the masculine principle leads to a devaluation of the feminine.)[19]

Yet even this ideal figure complains bitterly, after Othello strikes her, of his injustice. And she sighs "O, these men, these men!" (IV, iii, 60). And that she is shown as near-ideal, and seen by most of the male characters as fully an ideal, does not keep her from being called a "land-carrack" (slang for prostitute) by Iago. Or from being treated like a whore by her husband.

Bianca echoes, with sad resignation, Desdemona's happy statement of subordination to her man: " 'Tis very good; I must be circumstanc'd" (III, iv, 201), she replies to Cassio's order to leave lest Othello see him "woman'd" (III, iv, 195). Cassio's abrupt contempt for her jealousy provides a brief but pointed contrast to the main action. Women may get jealous as well as men; but they have no power, and their jealousy is dismissed with scorn.

Bianca appears after an amused, contemptuous conversation about her between Iago and Cassio. Cassio attacks her, using animal imagery, until she retorts jealously. He retreats, and Bianca leaves in anger. Nevertheless, she is still supplicant: "An' you'll come to supper tonight, you may" (IV, i, 159–160).

It is emblematic that Iago and Cassio are discussing Bianca when

* Not Evans' reading, but Pope's emendation. Folio and Quarto read "herself."

Othello thinks they are discussing Desdemona. In this male world, all women are the same. Like Othello, Cassio exalts Desdemona; nevertheless, he shares his culture's misogyny, saying to Desdemona after Iago's satire on women, "he speaks home" (II, i, 165). And he has contempt for the woman whose body he uses. Even her most genuine love and fidelity cannot protect Desdemona from the language, the attitudes, and finally the oppression of the male view of women.

Othello treats Emelia as a bawd when he castigates Desdemona as whore; Iago treats his wife with curt contempt.[20] None of the women imagines independence of men, but Emilia is aware of her own and other women's autonomous being. And she is the spokeswoman for the females of the play. She is worldly, a little cynical, resigned. She murmurs bitterly about male dominance: "I nothing but to please his fantasy" (III, iii, 299), she says of her relation to Iago. She is bitter: men "are all but stomachs and we all but food; / They eat us hungrily, and when they are full / They belch us" (III, iv, 104–106).

In IV, iii, Emilia delivers a little sermon on the relations of husbands and wives. In context it seems almost irrelevant, since it is a defense of adultery in wives and Desdemona has not performed this act. It is a piece of moralizing, similar to other passages in Shakespeare in which the lower orders comment on the exemplary implications of the behavior of the upper classes. Here, Emilia suggests that the behavior of husbands and their treatment of their wives necessarily have consequences, and that inconstancy is, after all, a "small vice" (IV, iii, 69). She assumes that women are human—merely human, but at least human—and like men are subject to affection, temptation, and anger.

One effect of Emilia's speech is to counter the attitudes of the males in the play. Whether they idealize women or degrade them all into whores, like Iago, who says, "knowing what I am, I know what she shall be" (IV, i, 73), or whether they do both simultaneously, the thing they do not do is see women as human beings. Shakespeare does, in this play.

But on another level, Emilia's speech broadens the implications of the action. Desdemona has not been unfaithful to Othello: that is insisted upon by the play. We overhear her conversations with Cassio; we overhear her shocked conversation with Emilia; we are clearly asked to give the last drop of pity to her and to her maid as they die. In the comedies, an accusation of infidelity is tantamount to actual infidelity on the mythic level of the play. It does not function this way here. Shakespeare took too many pains to inform us at every step of the line, not only of Iago's plot, but also of Desdemona's innocence.

But he clearly wishes to consider the broader issue: if Desdemona had been inconstant, would she have deserved death? Does Othello have the right to kill her if she is guilty? He does not deal with these questions in *Othello*, because this play is about male attitudes towards women—and each other—and thus Desdemona must stand as a symbol of what men destroy. He does consider it in *Cymbeline*. But Emilia's defense of inconstancy in women brings up the question. Suppose Desdemona *had* been inconstant? Would the audience wish her dead? And Emilia's speech is a long, long way from the speech given by Luciana to Adriana in *Comedy of Errors*: a lifetime away.

Othello is a profound examination of male modes of thought and behavior, especially with regard to women and "feminine" qualities. Iago *is* honest: he speaks the ordinary wisdom of the male world. The consequences of the values he shares with the other males of the play destroy the "feminine" values held by Desdemona, above all, but also Othello, Emilia, Cassio, Roderigo.

And Iago never changes. He remains. He endures without cracking, the only character in the play who never shows a sign of emotion or passion or the weakness he despises, although his behavior clearly has to be motivated by passion. He talks about lust, but never shows any sign of it. The prime exponent of reason and control stands firm even as the world around him collapses, even knowing that he caused its collapse. Although tortures are promised, things that will make him speak word again, this brilliant verbal manipulator, this poet for whom silence is indeed punishment, stands alive at the end of the play, surrounded by bodies, and is, in our imagination, triumphant. Well, the truth is, he is.

King Lear

King Lear stands alone in the Shakespearean canon. Plunging deeply into the terrifying darkness of not-knowing that lies below the morals and accepted truths of any period, *King Lear* risks everything. It dares a late-night meeting in a blind alley with the most feared killers of mental and emotional well-being: nihilism and absurdity.[21] The meeting occurs; the killers win. For some, like Sam Johnson, that is devastating. Less courageous souls than he sweeten the play with promises of salvation. But it is not necessary to do this to find affirmation in the play. The tragedy pits the merely human—feeling, suffering, seeing, seeking for significance—against a Goliath of incertitude. Incertitude wins, as it must in any honest contest, but the contest is grand, ennobling and enlarging the human even as it is vanquished. Indeed, humanness is ultimately defined by the suffering and the effort of this struggle.

In *Lear*, Shakespeare momentarily pushes aside the gender principles to examine the original terms of their division, the split between the human and nature.[22] With steady courage, the playwright looks at human existence, and probes two opposing but equal needs— the need to accept human rootedness, participation in nature and subordination to it; and the need to distinguish between nature and the human, thus defining the latter.

The play is pervaded by natural imagery and recurrent use of terms like *Nature*, *nature*, *natural*, and *unnatural*. References to nature are wide-ranging in tone and import; so too are images drawn from natural phenomena: no one association or definition dominates the play.[23] *Nature* means *natura* and also *human nature*; at times it refers to physical, at times to psychological dimensions of a human. It is used to refer to vividness and animation, the élan of life; at other times it refers to the bonds of kinship and hierarchy, seen as implicit in "natural" law as Hooker described it. This last definition is circular: what is "natural" is what acts according to "laws of nature" which ordain certain behaviors ("offices of nature" [II, iv, 178]) as "natural" for humans according to their age, gender, and status. The word *unnatural* is flung many times, usually by parents to and about their children when the latter are perceived as not abiding by those "laws."

Thus, the term is deeply ambiguous. Gloucester uses the phrase "wisdom of nature":

> Though the wisdom of nature can reason it thus and thus, yet nature finds itself scourg'd by the sequent effects. Love cools, friendship falls off, brothers divide. In cities, mutinies; in countries, discord; in palaces, treason; and the bond crack'd 'twixt son and father. (I, ii, 104–109)

The Earl could mean wisdom or knowledge about nature, including human nature. He could also mean wisdom arising from powers of reason which, as Hooker suggested, arise out of nature itself. In this case, human wisdom is in harmony with "natural law" because that wisdom arises from nature as it exists in humans. Thus, if nature is "scourg'd by the sequent effects," something is terribly wrong with the whole conception. If "natural" reason leads to injury of human "nature," that reason itself is under suspicion.

In general, the way nature references are used imports less about the nature of nature than about the character of the user. So, Edmund uses it much as we would use *life-force*—energy, talent, and the right to existence and growth such qualities deserve. He opposes this to the "plague of custom" and the "curiosity of nations" (I, ii, 3, 4), thus setting up an antagonism between the power and "natural" right of the individual, and the traditional and hierarchical legitimacy of a class. For Lear, up through III, ii, nature is divine justice modeled of course on earthly justice, and therefore the King's subject and ally. He calls on nature to revenge him on Goneril by making her barren or giving her a "child of spleen" (I, iv, 282). Albany shares this belief of Lear in divine justice, although he terms it "the heavens," a term Lear too uses: "All the stor'd vengeances of heaven fall / On her ingrateful top!" (II, iv, 162–163). However, Lear is calling on nature in the speech in which this passage occurs. And, in fact, the continuing belief that nature is an agent of divine justice, which occurs in Edgar's and Albany's speeches through most of the play, functions after a time to diminish them. What kind of justice is it that would decree Gloucester to be blinded, regardless of his moral obtuseness? To find the hand of providence in the events of human life, one must be moralistic, pietistic, in a particularly narrow way.

There are other uses of the term. Kent claims Oswald was made by a tailor rather than by nature, which is appropriate to Kent's rather unthinking and pugnacious, if loyal, character. And Cordelia speaks directly to the benevolent and fruitful powers of earth, asking nature to reveal its "blest secrets," its "unpublish'd virtues" (IV, iv, 15, 16) to help cure the mad King. Cordelia, one moral pole in the play, asks help of the "inlaw" qualities of "feminine" nature; Edmund, to some degree representing the "outlaw" qualities, speaks to the life-force—powerful, sexual, and full of energy. Lear in the early acts, Albany, and Edgar conflate nature with divinity, which is to say they endow it with a moral character. Albany and Edgar see divine justice as an absolute set of standards; Lear's notion is more profoundly investigated.

In the beginning, the King believes in his own rightness and his own power in an absolute way.[24] Thus he identifies divine justice (manifested through natural phenomena) with his own will. Such an identification underlies his tirade during nature's storm, a storm that he at first perceives as a divine warning to his immoral daughters and others "unwhipt of justice" (III, ii, 53). It is "the great gods, / That keep this dreadful pudder o'er our heads" (III, ii, 49–50). When he goes so far as to command nature, to bid "the wind blow the earth into the sea" (III, i, 5), or orders earth to crack its molds, or reproaches it for joining with his daughters to oppress him, Lear, "in his little world of man" (III, i, 10) is as hybristic as Canute.[25]

The indifference of nature to Lear's claims is partly responsible for his breaking in this scene. But even as he calls on the storm to punish the guilty, *he* is the person the storm is punishing. He realizes, gradually (if rather swiftly), that he is a subject here, not a king, a "poor, infirm, weak and despis'd old man" (III, ii, 20). He realizes that he has sinned, even if he is more sinned against. Part of Lear's change is a result of his loss of certitude, of a sense of absolute rightness. He recalls later, near Dover, that he discovered something "when the rain came to wet me once, and the wind to make me chatter, when the thunder would not peace at my bidding, there I found 'em, there I smelt 'em out" (IV, vi, 100–103). In the beginning of the play, when Lear disinherits Cordelia and banishes Kent, he is absolute not only in power but in his sense of rightness. He begins to falter during his arguments with Goneril, not yet because he has become aware of his lack of power (he still threatens terrible revenge, still tries to command the elements), but because he cannot make his daughters see the *rightness* of his position. They do not seem to be aware of what is self-evident to the King; they shrug off indifferently a matter he sees as his natural and inalienable right. For the first time—presumably—in his long life, his will is challenged.

In fact, all three of his daughters challenge his will. Cordelia refuses to bow to his impossible demand in I, i; Goneril and Regan deny him what he has asserted as his right, afterwards. He begins to move outside the hothouse of certitude: "I did her wrong," he mutters. When the storm too ignores the rightness of his cause, defies his commands, when he finds himself exiled from all but the disinherited of the earth, wet, hungry, and cold, he cracks entirely. But what is destroyed is not the man, Lear, but the King, Lear.

Starting from a position of political—thus social and moral—preeminence, Lear topples into a class of outsiders, the dispossessed, the illegitimate every complex civilization contains. The cracking of the "masculine" mold in which Lear was formed and has lived is painful for him and pathetic to watch, but it does not in the end leave him with the "nothing" so continually threatened by him and to him, in the play. Toppling from power does not strip him of his manhood; it confers humanhood upon him. Man's life is not cheap as beast's if pity touches it, nor can tears "stain" his humanness.

Thus, the first three acts begin to create a definition of humanness by stripping away certain qualities often associated with it. Humanness is *not* power, because human power is limited; it is not privilege and right because those are only temporarily given and may at any time be challenged or denied: they are dependent upon power, not moral laws. The masculine principle, which is always identified with the human, is actually a shield against it, a protection, ermine hiding naked flesh. Attempting to strip his body to the naked skin it is, Lear does not become nothing; he becomes merely human, suddenly able to examine right and rightness from the underside, the perspective of the illegitimate. Thus a tendency perceivable in the earliest plays comes to fruition and full development in this tragedy.

The viewpoint of the illegitimate, found in the early plays mainly in clowns and women, becomes, through Lear's change, the dominant point of view in the play. From this position, the world's arrangements are not only unkind and unjust, but absurd, delusory. The poor go naked and hungry while the rich surfeit; a daughter kicks her poor old father; even the dogs bark at a beggar. "Is there any cause in nature that make these hard hearts?" (III, vi, 77–78). By the time he appears in the fields outside Dover, Lear has mulled over and seen through all human pretensions of authority and justice and found them to be merely a matter of power, of *costume*. The assumption of the early comedies, that identity is largely a matter of discovering one's true place in society and accepting it, is here completely refuted. One's given place in society is an accident, and if it is a high one, a mask for the truth of one's participation in nature. The presumption of possession of justice or authority is merely a question of being in possession of the mantle society agrees to defer to as covering nakedness.

That which is stripped away in the first acts of the play as being of the essence of humanness is presented mainly in the first two scenes. As always, the opening scene is a focusing one. The first two speeches appear to deal with affection—Lear's for Albany and Cornwall. But the language is both abstract and quantitative: "It appears not which of the Dukes he values most, for equalities are so weigh'd, that curiosity in neither can make choice of either's moi'ty." What is under discussion is affection that can be weighed, mea i4ed, apportioned like land, like the kingdom. This established, the scene moves to Edmund. This is sometimes played with Edmund standing apart, unable to overhear the dialogue of Gloucester and Kent, as is indicated by the stage directions in some editions. Nevertheless, the use of *this* rather than *that* in "Is not this your son, my lord," and "this young fellow's mother," as well as Gloucester's question of Edmund, asked without a summons, imply that Edmund is present during the entire conversation.

Gloucester's language in this segment shows a clear differentiation in moral responsibility for sex. He admits he is responsible for Edmund: he has "blush'd to acknowledge" the boy but is "braz'd to it." But the boy's mother is not in the same way responsible for the child; rather the existence of the child is a definition of *her*. Edmund is a *whore*son because his mother "had a son for her cradle ere she had a husband for her bed." Gloucester is urbane and complacent: Edmund's mother, he recalls, was "fair, there was good sport at his making."

This is a crass and insensitive way of speaking, indeed of thinking and feeling about one's child and his mother. But Gloucester's insensitivity is much compounded if he speaks thus in the child's presence. In either case, Gloucester is hardened to love and is insensitive to others. Finally, he quantifies love, claiming to love his sons equally.

Lear appears, royal, arrogant, commanding, absolute. Within a few lines, he reinforces the impression made by the opening lines of the play. But he speaks quantitatively not of his love for Albany and Cornwall, but of theirs *for him*. He commands his daughters to quantify their love for him, as well.[26] But he asks: which "*shall we say* doth love us most?" He receives his answers as he asked for them: in words alone. (In this play, unlike *Othello*, language is not identical with act, but is rather extremely cut off from it. This is inevitable in a play which questions the very foundations of human civilization, in which there is no absolute center in which language and act, tongue and heart, appearance and reality, are utterly atoned. In *Othello*, there is a single and absolute truth: Desdemona is constant.) After they challenge him and defy his power, Lear is not able to take physical revenge on his daughters, but he does so hideously in language.[27] But his real hate is as ineffectual as their pretended love: both live only in words.

There is nothing inherently "evil" (as some critics suggest) about quantification. It is a structuring, a codification of feeling; it transplants a "feminine" quality into the "masculine" sphere. This cannot be accomplished without some change in the quality, unless one is able to translate feeling into poetry. But the "masculine" is an essential human mode insofar as it structures experience; if it is not an ideal way, or even an absolutely trustworthy way of communicating feeling, it is a legitimate way, so long as it is not taken as absolute, or as the most trustworthy mode. Sensitivity to others is that—seeing, feeling the emotion of the self and of others.

Cordelia, incapable of poetry and incapable of deceit, translates her feeling for her father directly into "masculine" language, claiming to love him in accordance with the bond between them. Although Lear should know how his favorite daughter feels about him, he takes her word for the thing itself, and banishes her disinherited. Lear identifies word and act. He is old and has been King since he was a boy: for him, statements have been tantamount to realities. What the King says, the court agrees with; what the King orders is performed. "They flatter'd me like a dog, and told me I had the white hairs in my beard ere the black ones were there" (IV, vi, 96–98).

Lear has never seen himself as anything but King. Thus he confuses personal power with power-in-the-world, that is, lovableness with power. He confuses language with action, power with right, justice with will. He has never, actually or imaginatively, experienced powerlessness; thus he has never seen himself in terms of the feminine principle, as a mere denizen of earth, but only in terms of the masculine, as a wielder of power-in-the-world. Given his age, his ignorance is both arrogant and willfully blind. Where has he been all these years? How has he managed not to *see?*

Lear, however, is not alone. He represents an entire class in Western culture, and a mainstream in Western thinking. For this reason, it seems to me narrowing and fruitless to dissect him in search of his "fatal flaw." All ways of thinking contain their own blindnesses. Lear's flaw is a flaw in our society, in all societies where there is a tradition of privilege. And all people who believe in traditional privilege and inherent right exhibit the kind of blindness and arrogance we see in Lear.

When such qualities are exacerbated by rashness, however, they become dangerous indeed. Goneril and Regan will have to tame the King if they are to hold the power he has supposedly given them. He has always been rash: "I know his heart" (I, iv, 330), Goneril says, and there is no reason to doubt her. She has one like his, although she is not rash. She and Regan spring from and incarnate one side of Lear, much as he tries to disown them.[28] The sisters value power and authority, and believe in their own right to hold them; they respect control and "reason," and are utterly reasonable except in one thing— Edmund. Their reason stands in the face of Lear's passion, quietly, coolly denying it legitimacy.

But there is more to Lear. At the outset, we know this only indirectly. We know it because Kent and Cordelia, and later, Gloucester, show love for the King. Moreover, Lear has been able, at some time prior to the opening of the play, to *see* Cordelia, to perceive her essential nature. Merely to perceive goodness, generosity of spirit, and love means to be in some way in tune with them, to possess the capacity for them. Cordelia is stubborn. She stands for what she stands for; she refuses to bow to her father's approach to experience. He believes himself entitled to absolute love as well as absolute power, whereas she knows that the former at least is conditional. She grants him what he asks for, if not what he wants—a quantification, along masculine lines, of her feeling for him. It is absurd to find this a moral flaw in her.[29] Lear is asking for what he has no right to ask: even absolute power is subject to limits. Cordelia is the moral center of the play, its touchstone: she must stand fast.[30]

The consequences of Lear's mistaking the nature of both love and power are predictable. Everyone close to him knows the truth—not just the three sisters, but Kent, Gloucester, and the Fool. Even France, a relative newcomer, senses it. Lear is wrong on every count: Albany and Cornwall do not love him equally; Kent is not trying to challenge his power; his daughters' love cannot be quantified or structured into words. He banishes his loving daughter and his truest subject; he banishes love because it will not and cannot bow to power.

Everything in the play hangs on the first two scenes, not just the plot but the values as well. These scenes are in a different mode from the rest of the play—ritualistic, mythic, like fairy tale. They present an imaginative embodiment of the values of the masculine principle operating in full grandeur and power: from this set of attitudes, all the rest flows inevitably.

To pounce on Lear's guilt or flaw, to see the drama as one of sin leading to punishment, penitence, and (a very questionable) salvation, seems to me to diminish him in a way the play itself refuses to do. For we love Lear not because he is right, or even because he is more sinned against than sinning, but because of the depth of his passion, and the scope of his awareness once it is opened. The same thing is true of Hamlet: the depth of his feeling sweeps us up in him to the point where we do not question his behavior, we overlook certain savage and rash acts. And Othello too, in the depth of his dramatized feeling, takes us with him to the point where half the pity we feel over the murder of Desdemona is for him, not her. The same thing is true of Macbeth: why else do we care about him, if not for the depth and strength of his feelings? The reason-passion critics have the wrong playwright; their standards would make Iago Shakespeare's prime hero.

Lear's blindness to the limits of power, his arrogance in the face of love, is all our blindness, all our arrogance. His roarings about the indifference of nature to human concerns, about human injustice and the illegitimacy of authority, are all our roarings. No one deserves to suffer because they think as their culture thinks: but we all do.

Lear is seduced by a set of cultural assumptions, and by his own act, abandoned by those same assumptions. The same thing happens to Gloucester, and to him too, by words—by Edmund's brilliant, Iago-like speech, by the forged letter. How can it be that Gloucester does not know his sons better, that he does not deal directly with Edgar? At the root of such blindness lies power itself.

Lear is so unaware of the difference between political and personal power that he imagines he will be treated like a king after he has divested himself of the kingship. Gloucester is so jealous of his power, so frightened of losing it, that he is easily tricked: he panics. But like Lear, Gloucester has two sides. One is like Edmund, who will later treat his father with a callousness that is a savage imitation of Gloucester's callousness towards him. Edmund's furious hate for his father is similar to Gloucester's furious (and instantaneous) hatred for Edgar. The other side is like Edgar, the legitimate son, who is capable of compassion and pity, and who, in a parallel course to his father and Lear, grows and learns in the course of the tragedy.

Several elements in the play extend its implications, broaden its scope, so that it becomes not just the story of a king who disinherited himself by not understanding the nature of love, but suggests the consequences of such cultural tendencies for the society as a whole. Among these elements are Edgar's avatars, which will be discussed later, and the entire socioeconomic theme. Mere exposure to naked nature arouses pity in Lear's heart for his Fool; sending the man into the hovel first, he suddenly feels pity for a whole class of humans, the "poor naked wretches" of the earth. Gloucester has a similar awakening right after he is blinded and set on the road to Dover: he tells a poor man who tries to help him:

> That I am wretched
> Makes thee the happier; heavens, deal so still!
> Let the superfluous and lust-dieted man,
> That slaves your ordinance, that will not see
> Because he does not feel, feel your pow'r quickly;
> So distribution should undo excess,
> And each man have enough. (IV, i, 65–71)

Lear's speeches outside Dover are a final heartbroken recognition that human arrangements supposedly based on "natural law"—which

imposes hierarchy and legitimacy—and supposedly sanctified by political and religious ceremony, are in fact nothing more than power
grabbing and the imposition of an unequal standard of judgment.
Dressed in a natural crown, every inch a king now, Lear acknowledges
that he is not "ague-proof," that power can vanquish mortality as little
as it can command the elements, and that costume alone divides what
the world calls good and evil. Without the ability to see, which both
the mad King and the blind Gloucester now have, without sensitivity,
power can tolerate love only as possession, and cannot create justice.
(Thus too Othello, who listens to Iago's "reason," but not to Desdemona's unspoken love, which is evident to the eye, to the senses, to
the emotions.)

By the time Lear is captured by Cordelia's followers, a set of qualities has been rejected as being essentially human: power-in-the-world,
hierarchy, status, legitimacy, right, law and order, control, and "reason." The rejection of so many items that are part of the masculine
principle, however, is not a rejection of that principle itself. Indeed,
the masculine principle *cannot be rejected*. Its association with humanness is profound: human minds work through structure and permanencies; human civilization is based on these. (The feminine principle can
be rejected and even largely eradicated; although this results in a nightmare world, and leads to the destruction of a society from the inside,
it has been done on earth many times and within recent history.) What
is rejected in *Lear* is the *pretense* implicit within "masculine" standards
—the pretense that some people are entitled to rank or property or
rights, and others are not.

This challenge to the extremely hierarchical structure of the sixteenth century is offered repeatedly. It is implicit in the many versions
of Falls of Princes so popular before as well as during the Renaissance;
it is implicit in the pastorals. Shakespeare, however, works not by
moralizing about how even the highest fall, or how life is more pleasant on a shepherd's hillside, but by showing the consequences of belief
in "masculine" legitimacy as they might occur in a given society. In
Lear, this kind of thinking destroys not just the legitimate, but everyone, or nearly everyone; it destroys the inlaw feminine principle along
with its outlaw aspect. There is no question of watching the operations
of justice; rather what we watch is an inevitable set of events that stand
in comment on human arrangements.

There is difficulty in separating reason from passion in the characters. Lear speaks most reason at the height of a mad passion; except
for their feelings for Edmund, Goneril and Regan are eminently rea-

sonable.[31] Edmund is reasonable all the way through, given his assumptions at the beginning, until, dying with the realization that he *was* loved, he makes a gesture of love from which he has nothing to gain. Reasonableness, that is, worldly human logic, is the burden of the Fool's messages to Lear, although his behavior—his loyalty and affection—undercuts those messages even as he delivers them. And no one, no one at all, has control, although the blind King of the first scenes, and Goneril and Regan later, imagine they do.

So far, we have itemized that which is not of the essence of humanness. It is necessary now to attempt to define what is essentially human. One thing the play insists upon is human connection with nature, and to define what is human, it is necessary to examine the treatment of nature.

Nature is both benevolent and malevolent, and there is no clear distinction between those aspects. Animal, plant, and element imagery are used to describe the viciousness of Goneril, but also to articulate Lear's sufferings. Moreover, the same animals—especially bear, wolf, and dog—are used to suggest very different things. Thus, Lear says he was flattered like a dog, and Cordelia says, in tears, "Mine enemy's dog, / Though he had bit me, should have stood that night / Against my fire" (IV, vii, 35–37). Natural imagery is used to express the entire gamut of human experience. It describes human feelings, vices, and situations. Nature oppresses humans and animals, and sustains them —clothing, curing, and feeding them (however loathsomely in Tom's description).

Animals are images of natural amorality, human absurdity, human lowliness, and insignificance.[32] Penury, Edgar says, brings man "near to beast" (II, iii, 9); Lear concurs: "Allow not nature more than nature needs, / Man's life is cheap as beast's" (II, iv, 266–267). Yet the King prefers to be "a comrade with the wolf and owl" (II, iv, 210) rather than bow to his daughters' conditions. The Fool claims that horses, dogs, bears, monkeys, and men all get or deserve confinement, and compares his treatment at the hands of those in power with that of a male dog; he compares Goneril to a *brach*, a bitch dog. Albany compares the relation between parent and child to the trunk and branches of a tree, finding it organic, indissoluble. Lear wonders how life can go on, dogs, horses, and rats breathing, when Cordelia is not.

At the core is Lear's discovery that man is no more than "a poor, bare, fork'd animal," and his attempt to remove his clothes in recognition of this truth: "Come, unbutton here" (III, iv, 107, 108). His last words echo the same awareness: "Pray you undo this button" (V, iii,

310), thus suggesting that this truth is the enduring one, the ultimate one.

Thus, humans and nature are part of a continuum. Nature is a warehouse for human expression: natural imagery can serve to express any human experience and much human experience is identical to that of other animals and plants. The rain wets the wolf along with the King; a tree is an organic unit, like a family.

But the nature that dominates *Lear* is completely different from the friendly green worlds of the comedies. It is harsh and violent, a dimension of cataclysms, of ugly, deformed creatures whose entire existence seems to be devoted to poisoning or maiming life, and hideous animals and plants that serve for loathsome but necessary food. Nature in *Lear* is like that in *Timon*, predatory, cruel, and hostile to human life.

To depict nature as hostile to human life, however, is to suggest that humans are *not* part of nature, that they are a transplant, a foreign body which the planet seeks to reject. The two perceptions—that humans are intrinsically part of nature and that they are foreign to it— work throughout the play until the reuniting of Lear and Cordelia. The two ideas do not clash with each other: they coexist.

Presumably, the pain and peril nature offers humans were responsible for the earliest attempts to control, dominate it. But it is not in efforts to control nature—or delusions of control—that Shakespeare locates the specifically human. It is almost as if the playwright were explicitly challenging the traditional formula.[33] He emphasizes the absurdity of notions of control as Lear tries to command the elements, calls them his *ministers*, and strives against a storm that engenders natural fear in bear, lion, and "belly-pinch'd wolf" (III, i, 13), in all "the very wanderers of the dark" (III, ii, 44).

Mad and grand as Lear seems in this scene, he is behaving exactly as he behaved at court, arrogantly assuming that he can control human nature—feeling and behavior. *King Lear* is Shakespeare's most profound repudiation of the morality that has governed the Western world for millennia—a morality of power and control based on the relation of man to nature. The tragedy presents an agonizing picture of the consequences of such a morality.

What Shakespeare offers as the ground of humanness, as that which makes us *not* part of nature, makes us aliens in our home, is a morality based on sensitivity and responsiveness, on seeing and feeling others, on cooperation with nature which, even as it sets us off from the savage nature of the play, decreases our alienation. And power is utterly an impediment to this.

Cordelia's crime in the court is that she is not swayed by the desire for power and possession into falsifying her feelings: she does not feed Lear's delusion of control. Nor does Kent. Both are therefore deprived of power and possession, the real goods of their society, as the Fool continually reminds Lear. But the Fool, in despair, Kent, with firm confidence, and Cordelia, sorrowfully, hold to another good, another truth.

Lear is not the only one who has been blinded by power. Gloucester must be literally blinded before he can emotionally *see*. In order to see, he says, one must feel. But power is a bulwark against feelings. Powerless, Lear learns to see, and to feel, and thus to risk madness.

The turbulence of nature, its dangerous cliffs and storms, recedes from the scene when Cordelia prays to nature to grant her its benison, herbs to cure her disturbed father. Lear and Gloucester meet on a peaceful field, Lear adorned with plants and flowers, crowned with a natural crown, every inch a king. The two men speak "feelingly," seeing. Cordelia, the incarnation of the inlaw feminine principle, "redeems nature from the general curse" (IV, vi, 205) by standing for, insisting upon, values that have little to do with control. She offers her tears to water the earth from which "blest secrets" (IV, iv, 15) grow. And when she is reunited with her father, there is music and radiance, harmony and light, as if the sun had finally come out again.

I said at the outset that in *Lear*, Shakespeare probed beneath the gender divisions to examine the division—man and nature—that lies beneath. This is not to say, however, that gender divisions do not exist in the play. They do, and are extremely important on the subsurface of the tragedy.

On the surface, gender roles are blurred. Goneril is a better soldier than her husband; both she and Regan are assertive, nonnutritive, uncompassionate, interested in power, prowess, and status. Regan performs an act unique in Shakespeare: she kills, in her own person, with a sword. Goneril kills too, but in a "woman's" fashion—with poison, and offstage. Both sisters act rather than feel, and move to gain what they want in both the public and personal spheres. They are "masculine."

On the other hand, Albany and Edgar are largely "feminine." Goneril reproaches Albany for "milky gentleness" (I, iv, 341), and it is Albany who conceives of a family (or society) as organically linked. He also attempts, somewhat feebly, to create harmony between his wife and her father. Edgar's roles in the play involve considerable nutritive and supportive behavior, and from the time he meets Lear until near the end of the play he is locked into the role of suffering witness. Both

men are in some sense illegitimate: Albany because Goneril can dominate him, and thus discount him; Edgar because he is hunted and
without resources.

Gloucester and the Fool become "feminine" as they fall into being
total outsiders. (The Fool has always been illegitimate to some degree.)
Suffering and social illegitimacy invariably bring out the "feminine"
qualities of people who have any (Coriolanus and Timon, for instance,
do not).

At the beginning of the play, Edmund sounds like a representative
of the outlaw feminine principle. He seems to want to topple masculine structures; he conceives of "Nature" as vitality and verve. But he is
not really outlaw feminine. He repudiates codes, laws, and hierarchy
only because there is no legitimate place for him within them. He
rebels, not in hopeless despair and rage about structures that are foreign to his spirit, but in an attempt to usurp a place within them—as,
indeed, he does.[34] He is willing to dally with unregulated sexuality.
Since he apparently offers affection to Regan as well as Goneril, it is
unclear to what degree he loves either sister, although he takes deep
pleasure in being loved. What he wants above all, however, is power.
The three characters—Edmund, Goneril, and Regan—are not only
"masculine" but are abusers of both principles. They are willing to kill
in unsanctioned ways; they are willing to engage in unsanctioned forms
of sex.

Lear moves from "masculinity" to "femininity." In the opening
scene, dressed in majesty, he stands on power and banishes love. For
the next act and a half, he roars and rages, but begins, little by little, to
cry. And then he learns to see, to feel. He opens his mind to others—
to the poor, to his Fool's shivering, to the necessities by which all
humans are bound. By the time he meets Gloucester on the heath, he
has discovered that pomp, status, and authority are charades designed
to hide us from ourselves. By the time he and Cordelia are captured,
he is no longer concerned with power-in-the world, or with revenge.
He cares only about the quality of life, choosing to sing in the prison
that is life, enjoying the day, savoring the "mystery of things" (V, iii,
16).

Gloucester, a parallel to Lear in terms of values as well as in the
plot, also stands on power and banishes love. But his love for Lear and
his sense of human decency are strong enough to make him,
frightened as he is, challenge power when he believes it has gone
beyond the pale. Through his ordeal, he too learns to see "feelingly,"
and thus becomes "feminine," like the King.

Cordelia, of course, represents the inlaw feminine principle at its most saintly, supporting and protecting even when she has been hurt. She is constant and sensitive—she knows her sisters' natures; Edgar does not know Edmund's. Her qualities can "redeem" Lear's sufferings but they cannot sustain her in the world. Cordelian natures get destroyed.

At the penultimate moment of the play, Lear seems very large indeed. He has seen through the self-delusions of "masculine" definitions of the human, and has endured his "feminine" suffering. He remains "masculine": he does not drown in guilt, he retains will, he retains prowess enough to kill Cordelia's killer. He remains "feminine" in that he renounces power-in-the-world, and desires only felicity, love, harmony. He has achieved full humanness. But this achievement required Cordelia. His "madness" in the field outside Dover is not really madness at all: it is thwarted wholeness, perception of the delusions in society without a complementary fullness of pleasure in other things. Without Cordelia, Lear would remain in bitter cynicism.

Thus, the play suggests (again) that a chaste constant woman is necessary to transform a legitimate man into an integrated man. One critic has taken this need of Lear's as another example of incestuous feeling in a Shakespearean father.[35] But this emphasis on chaste constancy in women occurs in plays in which fathers are not very important. It is a requirement in many plays, not just for a father, or a husband, but as the cornerstone of a harmonious society.

Thus, beneath the surface, gender roles are absolute, but only for women. Men's behavior matters: an unpunished Cornwall provides a bad example for his inferiors; Lear's blind insensitivity creates a horror for him and war for his kingdom. Abuse of the masculine principle consists essentially in the refusal of males to center themselves in the feminine principle. This is one reason for the importance of chaste constancy: women must be above reproach so that men may depend upon them utterly, may trust them, may reliably serve the inlaw qualities they represent.

Men's behavior matters. But women's behavior is of the essence. Cordelia "redeems nature from the general curse / Which *twain* have brought her to" (my italics). That *twain* are, of course, Goneril and Regan. Cordelia redeems nature; Goneril and Regan are responsible for its "curse." In the rhetoric of the play, no male is condemned as Goneril is condemned. A woman who refuses to uphold the inlaw feminine principle completely topples the natural order and plunges the world into chaos.

The three major villains—Goneril, Regan, and Edmund—are, if we can quantify such a thing, about equal in cruelty to their parents, about equal in ambition and ruthlessness. Cornwall and Regan blind Gloucester; Edmund orders Cordelia's (and Lear's) murder; and all three are willing to be sexual in an unregulated way. Goneril is unyielding to her father, suggests the blinding of Gloucester, and murders Regan. It is hard to select a *worst* from among them. Yet the judgments passed on the rhetorical level of the play are very unequal.

Gloucester, upon hearing that Edgar is (supposedly) planning to murder him, cries out: "villain! . . . Abhorred villain! unnatural, detested, brutish villain! worse than brutish!" (I, ii, 75–77). Rebellion of a son against a father is both associated with nature (brutish) and separated from nature (unnatural), in line with the double strand of attitudes towards nature that inform the play. Gloucester's next decision is "I never got him." The import of all of this is that Edgar is *illegitimate*—by birth (Gloucester's wife was an adulterer), in rank (he is villain, not noble; *villain* is, of course, what Hamlet calls Claudius also), and in his morals (parricide is unnatural).

Except for the comments in the first scene which slur Edmund (as well as his mother) as a *whore*son, he is not vilified by Gloucester, not even when the Earl learns the truth. At the conclusion, Albany charges Edmund with capital treason. This is a questionable charge, since he led Goneril's forces, and she was one of the constituted rulers. But it serves the time. Edgar accuses his brother of being "a most toad-spotted traitor" (V, iii, 139). All of Edmund's horrors, then, are subsumed in this ethical term: he is a traitor.

Regan receives little verbal abuse within the play. That is reserved for Goneril, and she is abused violently, savagely, long before she does anything that can be called worse than ungrateful, unkind, and unloving. The moment she does not defer to Lear's authority and will, he calls her "degenerate bastard" (I, iv, 254), "detested kite" (I, iv, 262), and wishes hideous punishments upon her. He says her visage is "wolvish" (I, iv, 308), that she is "serpentlike" and a "disease" (II, iv, 161, 222) in his flesh.

Albany too attacks her: "Proper deformity shows not in the fiend / So horrid as in woman" (IV, ii, 60–61). "Howe'er thou art a fiend, / A woman's shape doth shield thee" (IV, ii, 66–67). Finally, as the sisters attack each other, Albany contrasts Goneril and Edmund: Edmund is a traitor; Goneril is a "gilded serpent," "monstrous" (V, iii, 84, 160).

All three characters are guilty of similar acts. Why should the judgments on them be so different? Why should Goneril bear the weight of the rhetorical condemnation of the play to such a degree that Bradley questioned whether one could even call her human?[36]

Abuse of the masculine principle was an unethical act for Shakespeare. Abuse consisted mainly in two acts of blindness: one is the forgetting of true ends—protection and fostering of the feminine principle. When true ends are forgotten, power becomes its own end and men are deluded into believing they have control over others, over nature, over their own destinies. The second is blindness to human (natural) arrangements, and thus to confusing the power of position with personal power. This leads to the deluded belief that one has an inherent right to certain prerogatives, when in fact the right to those prerogatives adheres to a particular step in the ladder of legitimacy.

Shakespeare's ideas about the masculine principle make sense. They are comprehensible in logical, realistic terms. So is the cure he urges in play after play—that men assimilate the feminine principle into themselves, remind themselves continually of the qualities power is designed to sustain. This is not true of his ideas—feelings, really—about the feminine principle. The inlaw aspect, separated from its vital, sustaining roots, seems to him almost divine. It is perfection on earth, it is the incarnation of Jesus' message (if not of the messages the churches incarnate). Inherent within it, however, is the fact that it cannot protect itself, that it must *be* protected. If it attempts to use worldly force, it loses its character and its saintliness. When it is seen for what it is, and cherished, it confers harmonious joy and radiance on the world around it.

But when women (and it must be women) do not uphold the inlaw aspect, when they attempt to move into "masculine" power and control, as do Goneril and Regan, they do not threaten the world in the way males do. They do not arouse fear of tyranny or execution or defeat in battle. Rather they emit a hideous stink of sexual pollution that is felt to be contaminating, soul-destroying, and overwhelmingly powerful *for men*. This is true in the first tetralogy, in *Hamlet*, *Othello*, and *Lear*. (It is not true in *Coriolanus*, probably because Volumnia attempts to control only her son, not the respublica itself.) Women, locked into the feminine principle, cannot abuse "masculine" qualities, cannot even have "masculine" qualities. When they abuse the inlaw aspect, they fall into the outlaw aspect of the feminine principle. Women's misdeeds, regardless of the dimension in which they occur, are always interpreted as *fiendish* (superhumanly evil), as participating in the worst uglinesses and terrors of nature, and as sexual—sexuality being seen as loathsome, disgusting.

If on the one hand the thing that divides humans from nature is the set of qualities Cordelia embodies, an inlaw feminine morality, on the other, what divides the human from nature is a pair of negatives. These annul, or regulate, the extremes of the gender principles. On the "masculine" side, based on the ability to kill, killing is regulated: it may be performed only in sanctified ways, that is, in war, or under the aegis of the state (to which the Church gives its sanction). On the "feminine" side, based on the ability to give birth, sex is regulated and may be performed only between a married woman and man, marriage being sanctioned by both the state and the Church. But for Shakespeare, a woman who attempts to move into the masculine principle violates the *feminine*. Thus, unregulated sexuality is her sin, whether it is or not.

One of the things that most crucially divides humans from animals is this attitude towards sex. This is not stated in the play; it is implicit, but all the more powerful for that. Only the characters plainly marked evil show any manifestations of sexuality—Goneril, Regan, Edmund, and perhaps Oswald. Edgar, in a moment of mean-minded moralization, asserts that "the dark and vicious place" where Gloucester conceived Edmund has now justly, in retribution, cost him his eyes. As Tom o' Bedlam, he concentrates most on desire as the vice that now torments him with guilt. The Fool mentions sexual "vice" continually, although there are no sexual events occurring in the play at the time. Both Lear and Gloucester, confronted with real or apparent betrayal in their children, leap to the conclusion that their wives were adulterers.

Finally, in the field near Dover, looking anew at nature, Lear finds it essentially copulative. If copulation is natural, he reasons, adultery should not be condemned, whores should not be whipped, especially since those whipping them are guilty of desire too. His tone is meditative, even kindly: "The wren goes to't, and the small gilded fly / Does lecher in my sight," until memory hits him, and he mutters bitterly, "Gloucester's bastard son / Was kinder to his father than my daughters" (IV, vi, 111–113; 114–115). This memory returns him to human, as opposed to animal, sexuality, and he roars in outraged abhorrence about female sexuality, which he sees as bestial, hypocritical, and demonic: hell, darkness, and "the sulphurous pit" (IV, vi, 128), which in this context becomes a metaphor for the vagina as well as for eternal damnation.[37]

Sex is not logically connected to the events of the play. The sexuality of Goneril, Regan, and Edmund is not fundamental in their treatment of their fathers. Nevertheless, it is woven deeply into the texture of the play, through image, allusion, and rhetoric, *as if* it were somehow associated with its events.[38]

Inevitably, then, there is also a strain of misogyny in the play. Misogyny invariably accompanies sexual disgust. Many of the Fool's jokes are misogynistic. Edgar is misogynistic when he reads Goneril's letter to Edmund and exclaims, "O indistinguish'd space of woman's will!" in a parallel movement to Hamlet's when he generalizes his mother's inconstancy to name woman as frail. This generalization is most emphatic in Lear's outburst in the field. There is no event that triggers his outburst. He cannot know about his daughters' desire for Edmund and the only other sexual irregularity in the tragedy is Gloucester's. Yet he roars: "Down from the waist they are Centaurs, / Though women all above; / But to the girdle do the gods inherit, / Beneath is all the fiends' " (IV, vi, 124–127).

This association of powerful (in a worldly sense) women with a sexuality felt to be abhorrent and terrifying is characteristically Shakespearean. Both Spenser and Sidney create female figures who are openly sexual and have some worldly power, but more often than not, they are comic, if also clearly deviant. Moreover, the association of women and power with filthy sexuality does not pervade their work. Duessa is singular in *The Faerie Queene*. And if the image, the emblem, of Duessa is (at the end) of a woman with filthy clotted underparts, her pollution is not sexual but intellectual: she leads the Redcrosse Knight from the one true God and the one true way into duality, duplicity, and errors of thought and belief.

Sexual abhorrence pervades Shakespeare's work and informs some of his most powerful writing. One could, I suppose, psychologize about the man. But this abhorrence is a cultural fact, and still exists—in the United States, today, it is found mainly among people who were raised in strict patriarchal churches. Discussion of the development and significance of such an attitude is out of place here and will be taken up elsewhere.

Here it must suffice to point to the sexual theme, to the consistently vile natural imagery Lear uses to assault Goneril, and to the rhetorical line of the play which implicitly lays on Goneril the blame for all the disorders of Lear's Britain. The power given Cordelia to redeem, like the power given to Mary, is balanced by the power given Goneril to damn, like the power given to Eve.[39] Since in actuality, women have neither sort of power, we must view these figures as symbolic, as references to parts of the self in disharmony, divided by a faulty conception of experience.

The rhetorical line of *King Lear* is enormously strong, so strong that it prevents any reading other than the moral direction given by it. Robert Lowell, in a Harvard seminar on Shakespeare, once shocked the class into silence by suggesting that maybe Goneril and Regan were right, maybe Lear's knights were rowdy and lecherous drunkards, and *were* disturbing the house. There are items which, if developed or described differently, would paint Goneril, Regan, and Edmund in slightly less vile colors, would offer at least ambivalence. There does seem to be love between Goneril and Edmund; his dying joy at realizing he was loved casts a pathetic light on his life until then. Oswald is as loyal to Goneril as Kent is to Lear.[40]

Lear at the opening is arrogant, rash, and willful; it is clear Cordelia has been his favorite, but he banishes her. How, then, has he treated Goneril and Regan all these years? Can their dislike for him be extenuated? Gloucester turns swiftly against Edgar, on minimal proof: what kind of father has he been all these years? Kent is loyal, but he is also pugnacious and trigger-happy. Lear's threats, offered at the slightest resistance to his will, are out of bounds.

But these questions are not permitted within the terms of the play. They cannot even be built subtly into a production of the play without violating its text. The rhetoric of *Lear*, unlike that of *Richard III*, does not rest with one major figure who damns himself, and a lamenting chorus of women who damn him also. It is woven in, line by line, and its import is unmistakable. Except for Lear and Gloucester, who err and suffer and grow, who provide the human level of the play, the remaining characters are divided almost instantly into the utterly good and the utterly evil.

What differentiates man from nature is his attempt to regulate both men and nature, the extremes of the two gender principles. Edgar, disguised as Tom o' Bedlam, *becomes* Tom o' Bedlam. A shivering, naked wretch, he *is* the bare forked animal of Lear's sudden recognition. But, part of nature, he is apart from nature. His physical sufferings are less than his psychological torment. Tom's catalogue of sins defines man as the guilty animal. And of the vices he lists, the one most emphasized is sexuality—desire and fornication, seen as filth. The second most emphasized is "pride," the kind of pride that believes ermine, civet, or a feathered hat confer on man a superiority not only to nature but other men as well, transform one into a controlling god.

These "vices" are also the foci of Lear's brilliant rage in the field outside Dover. Lear himself is, of all the characters, most guilty of the kind of pride that is really blindness; an unspecified "they," women in general, are guilty of the sin of sexuality. But because the point of view of the play resides with Lear, because we see him suffer (his suffering and Gloucester's merge to become one single human agony), his "sin" seems somehow less onerous than that of women, of Goneril and Regan, of nature itself.

It is vice that sets the human off from the animal. Inlaw feminine virtues like Cordelia's are in harmony with nature, are privy to nature's blest secrets. But humans, not animals are proud. Of all the animals, only humans flatter. In an effort to control (manipulate) the powerful, flatterers blind them as Lear was blinded. And only humans murder (as opposed to kill). In *Lear* and *Macbeth*, the ability to murder is seen as distinctively human. In a line reminiscent of *Macbeth*, the Captain accepts Edmund's commission to murder Cordelia and Lear with these words: "I cannot draw a cart, nor eat dried oats, / If it be man's work, I'll do't" (V, iii, 38–39).

A few final words about Edgar. He is a complex figure and difficult to grasp. But his complexities are all on the surface; he is not profoundly complex, like Lear. Edmund calls him "noble," and we accept the judgment, although he is a rather narrowly moralistic character.

As himself, in the opening of the play, he is easily duped by his brother, whom he seems to trust. He does *not* trust his father: it does not occur to him to try to speak to the Earl, to repair the damage. He is accurate in his estimate of his parent, at least.

He races to exile, like many characters in the comedies, but unlike them, he finds no Arden but a barren, frozen nature. His physical misery is exacerbated by his psychological misery, as he becomes Tom o' Bedlam. The exiles of Lear and Gloucester are also to nature, but lead the two older men to illumination about themselves and the world's arrangements. Edgar's leads him to a hell of guilt which illuminates little or nothing about himself, but rather offers an embroidery, a restatement of the themes of the play. His "mad" ravings present the guilt-ridden psychological dimension of the abuses performed by other characters. Thus, as mad Tom, Edgar is not himself but a testifier about the world around him.

But Edgar has many other roles to play. From Tom, the lowest possible member of his society, he becomes a Tom who is possessed of some wit and is able to lead Gloucester. In time he becomes a peasant, in which guise he convinces his father that he has survived a fall from Dover cliff, and overhears Gloucester and Lear in "mad" conversation.

Then he becomes a rustic, in which guise he saves his father and kills Oswald. Finally, he appears as an unknown knight, in which guise he kills Edmund, presently the legitimate Earl of Gloucester. And at the end, Edgar is fully legitimate once more, the new Earl of Gloucester.

Because he is victimized from the outset, he is a contrast to Lear and Gloucester, whose trials come later. Edgar *begins* at the bottom; they begin at the top. But as the powerful plunge swiftly to the bottom, Edgar begins to climb upward. His progress, then, is from illegitimacy to legitimacy, from helpless victimization to power-in-the-world. The implication is that his education in illegitimacy and sorrow will make him worthy of his worldly privilege.

Schematically, this all makes sense. But Edgar makes less sense as a character in the play. Although his main action in the tragedy is to preserve his father, his disguises actually prolong the old man's suffering. There are, of course, good dramatic reasons for this: a reconciliation between Edgar and Gloucester would dramatically undercut that between Cordelia and Lear. The one anagnorisis subsumes the other. Nevertheless, psychologically, Edgar as character is as opaque as the Duke in *Measure for Measure*. He does not function as a son to Gloucester in the scenes in which he leads him. He functions rather as a suffering witness.

And this, it seems to me, is his true role in the drama. He is not so much a character as a composite. He does not have a palpably consistent personality, as most of Shakespeare's disguised characters do— Kent, for instance, is the same man, in disguise or out.

Edgar is a composite of witnesses to events. Like Cornwall's disgusted servants, who watch the behavior of their "betters" and judge the moral nature of their world accordingly, Edgar watches, thinks, and feels. He sees Lear in the hovel, sees him mad with his Fool, hiding in Gloucester's house. He sees the blinded Earl, recognizes Oswald's—and Goneril's—moral characters, watches the two old men together in the field outside Dover. Finally, he acts, killing Edmund, but his watching is not over. With us, he must endure the bitter finale, the dead Cordelia in the old King's arms, the agony of the "promised end."

By the end of the play, Edgar has become a composite figure of illegitimate men in his culture, people who are not blinded by power, who learn to set aside narrow piety in order to see and feel and to support human decency to the limits of their power. He becomes a male parallel to Cordelia. He acts; she is. He does not possess her magical powers of healing, but he is able to fight and to kill. He personifies the quiet, unrecognized will to decency that exists in every people, every nation, as she represents the loving, constant devotion that exists in every nation, every people—in whatever proportions in individuals.

After his restoration to legitimacy, Albany tries to reorder the kingdom, but Edgar ignores this. He is concerned only with the dying King and the suffering he has witnessed (no matter how the last four lines are attributed). Albany's concern with the rule of the kingdom sounds shallow and unfeeling given the situation—the old King in despair hovering over his child's dead body. Of all the characters, Albany is readiest to find divine retribution in the events that have occurred, but we know that he has been least exposed to the horrors, and has participated least in agony. Nevertheless, his response to the sight of Lear and Cordelia diminishes him.

If I were mounting a production of *King Lear*, I would, in this final scene, slowly surround Edgar with figures like those he has impersonated, suggesting the sturdy will to decency and humaneness that is found in every community. Edgar in all his avatars should outnumber Albany at the end of this tragedy.

Macbeth

Macbeth presents another world in which the feminine principle is devalued, but in this case we see the action from the point of view of a legitimate male who gains, in a worldly way, from that devaluation. Iago seems to do the same, but in fact he derives no pleasure from all of Roderigo's money, or from getting Cassio's place. Pleasure is not possible for him. But Macbeth really wants to be king; he has thought about it and seems to have anticipated the succession being placed upon him. And he moves into the kingship with energy and firmness, at first.

This play is not about ambition per se; it is about giving up certain things for others, sacrificing seemingly unnecessary values in the course of achieving an ambition. The play is an envisioning of the consequences to a man and to his culture of casting certain values aside. In one way, *Macbeth* is more subtle than *Othello* or *Lear*: Macbeth does not dramatize his feelings as Othello does, or roar them out, as Lear does. His sufferings must be suggested by gesture as well as intonation, and understanding of the play is dependent very much on audience perception of his emotional loss and deprivation.

There is an ambiguity about gender roles in *Macbeth* as there is in *Lear*, but here it is the keynote of the play, the "myth" from which everything else springs (as in *Lear*, the values implicit in the opening dialogue and the division of the kingdom are the "myth"; and, as in *Othello*, the opening scene, with its clear contempt for "feminine" values, provides the "myth"). This ambiguity is embodied in the Witches who open the tragedy. Their chant, "Fair is foul, and foul is fair," is a legend of moral and aesthetic ambiguity, but the Witches themselves incarnate ambiguity of gender. They are female, but have beards; they are aggressive and authoritative, but seem to have power only to create petty mischief. Their persons, their activities, and their song serve to link ambiguity about gender to moral ambiguity.[41]

The reason ambiguity of gender is an element in the play is that Shakespeare did indeed associate certain qualities with the two genders. Perhaps he was shocked, and his imagination triggered by a passage in Holinshed describing women in Scotland fighting with hardiness, courage, and unshrinking bloodthirstiness.[42] But he makes Macbeth's Scotland a world of what seems to be constant war, that is, a "heroic" culture. In such worlds, the felicities of life must be put aside, and procreation is tenuous: the means by which life is sustained become all important. His sense of such worlds is demonstrated in IV, iii, when Macduff tries to convince Malcolm to raise an army and oppose Macbeth. He tells Malcolm "Each new morn / New widows howl, new orphans cry." Ross alludes to depredation of the feminine principle: Scotland "cannot be called our mother, but our grave." Malcolm's presence in the country, he says, "would create new soldiers, make our women fight" (IV, iii, 165–166, 178). In "heroic" worlds, women must become as men, and the loss such a situation entails to the culture at large is the subject of the tragedy.

The world of Scotland is one of blood and brutality. Indeed, the first human words of the play are "What bloody man is that?" The answer describes the hero, Macbeth:

> Disdaining Fortune, with his brandish'd steel,
> Which smok'd with bloody execution,
> Like valor's minion carv'd out his passage
> Till he fac'd the slave;
> Which nev'r shook hands, nor bade farewell to him,
> Till he unseam'd him from the nave to th' chops,
> And fix'd his head upon our battlements. (I, ii, 17–23)

Such a description might shock and appall an audience, might imply that the hero is not totally admirable, if not for the fact that we hear only praise for Macbeth. He is "brave Macbeth," "valor's minion," "valiant cousin," and "worthy gentleman." Most of the praise comes from Duncan, the King, the authority figure. The Sergeant's hideous description of the fighters' motivations: "Except they meant to bathe in reeking wounds, / Or memorize another Golgotha, / I cannot tell," reaps only more praise and reward.[43]

At the conclusion of this tragedy, we accept without demur the judgment that Macbeth is a butcher. In fact, however, he is no more a butcher at the end than he is at the beginning. Macbeth lives in a culture that values butchery. Throughout the play manhood is equated with the ability to kill. Power is the highest value in Scotland, and in Scottish culture, power is military prowess. Macbeth's crime is not that he is a murderer: he is praised and rewarded for being a murderer. His crime is a failure to make the distinction his culture expects among the objects of his slaughter.

A world that maintains itself by violence must, for the sake of sanity, fence off some segment—family, the block, the neighborhood, the state—within which violence is not the proper mode of action. In this "civilized" segment of the world, law, custom, hierarchy, and tradition are supposed to supersede the right of might. Although this inner circle is no more "natural" or "unnatural" than the outer one (so far as we can judge. Some people believe that aggression is profoundly "natural" to humankind. I believe humans are basically timorous, and that aggression is forcibly taught, learned under duress. Neither position however can be proven), the play insists that the inner world is bound in accordance with a principle of nature which is equivalent to a divine law.[44]

From the perspective of this study, the inner world is one which harmonizes the two gender principles. Ruled by law, inherited legitimacy, hierarchy, and rights of ownership, the inner world also demands a degree of subordination in all its members. Everyone, including the ruler, must relinquish some worldly power (increasingly as one goes down the social scale) in favor of the good of the whole, if felicity and an environment favorable to procreation is to exist. Those with great power must restrain it; those without power must accept their places gracefully. Without such relinquishment, felicities like friendship, ceremony, orderly succession, peaceful love, hospitality, pleasure, and even the ability to sleep at night become difficult or impossible.[45] An essential condition of this inviolable segment of the world is that the laws bind by themselves. They are not enforceable because enforcement is part of the larger outer sphere, the violent world. If the laws of the inner world must be enforced, that world becomes identical with the outer one. The laws therefore exist only insofar as the members of the group abide by them. Macbeth chooses to break the rules.

The factor responsible for Macbeth's doing so is Lady Macbeth. Although it is clear that Macbeth has, before the opening of the play, considered taking over the kingdom by force, it is also clear from his hesitation that he could easily be dissuaded from killing Duncan. And within the feminine/masculine polarity of morals and roles in Shakespeare's division of experience, it is Lady Macbeth's function so to dissuade him. But Lady Macbeth, a powerful person, is drawn to the role in which worldly power resides. She seems to be, by the world's standards, an exemplary wife.[46] She encourages and supports her husband in good wifely fashion; she does not undermine him; she sees, knows, and understands the terms of the world she lives in, and she accepts them.

Yet at the end of the play, when her husband earns the attribute of "butcher," she, who has not personally performed acts of violence, is called "fiend-like." In Shakespeare's eyes, Macbeth has violated moral law; Lady Macbeth has violated natural law.[47] Her reasoning, in urging Macbeth to the murder, is not unlike that of MacDonwald: he is called *traitor* and *slave*. Both of these terms refer to the ethical world of legitimacy: one suggests resistance to the currently constituted authority; the other insists on illegitimacy. But Lady Macbeth is not so judged; she is seen as supernaturally evil. Her crime is heinous because it violates her social role, which has been erected into a principle of experience: she fails to uphold the feminine principle. For her, as for Goneril, this failure plunges her more deeply into a pit of evil than any man can ever fall.

The imagery of the play is divided into masculine and feminine categories. Blood and royal robes, symbolic of male prowess, authority, and legitimacy, are opposed to procreative and nourishing images of babies, children, the female breast, and milk. Lady Macbeth informs us of her values at her first appearance: Macbeth, she says, is flawed by being "too full o' th' milk of human kindness" (I, v, 17). Laid against the view of Macbeth the warrior that we have just been given, this is an astonishing perception. It has less to do with Macbeth, however, than with his lady. She who, in Shakespeare's view, should properly encourage this milky side of her husband, resolves instead to align herself with the male principle, in a passage explicitly connecting gender to role and moral value:

> Come, you spirits
> That tend on mortal thoughts, unsex me here,
> And fill me from the crown to the toe topfull
> Of direst cruelty! . . . Come to my woman's breasts,
> And take my milk for gall. (I, v, 40–48)

In her conversation with Macbeth (I, vii), she argues from a perspective that equates manliness with killing. Macbeth protests: "I dare do all that may become a man; / Who dares do more is none." She insists: "When you durst do it, then you were a man; / And to be more than what you were, you would / Be so much more the man." The "it" in question is killing; and manliness, for Lady Macbeth, clearly *excludes* compassion and nurturing:

> I have given suck, and know
> How tender 'tis to love the babe that milks me;
> I would, while it was smiling in my face,
> Have pluck'd my nipple from his boneless gums,
> And dash'd the brains out, had I so sworn as you
> Have done to this. (I, vii, 54–59)

Both agree that manliness is the highest standard of behavior: what they argue about is what the term comprehends.[48] Macbeth's real problem is that he cannot articulate, even to himself, what is wrong with his wife's logic. He floats in vague dread, a sense of wrongness that seems to him to reverberate to the heavens (although his dread is not specifically Christian or religious—he jumps the life to come with ease), but the values he is obliquely conscious of as being in some impalpable way significant have no currency and therefore no vocabulary in his culture. At the end of their conversation, he accepts his wife's definition of manliness; it is, after all, identical to that of his —and her—culture as a whole.

> Bring forth men-children only!
> For thy undaunted mettle should compose
> Nothing but males. (I, vii, 72–74)

Still, he continues to feel uneasy, and Lady Macbeth, gazing down at the sleeping Duncan, has an intimation that there is something unpleasant about killing a father. Their trepidations heighten our sense that the inner circle, the place where murder is illegitimate, is indeed sacred.

And once the deed is done, Shakespeare suggests that the entire character of the world is changed. When the texture of the inner circle is identical to that of the outer one, the connection between means and ends is broken. Instead of procreation and felicity, the end of power becomes more power alone, consolidation and extension of power: thus, life becomes hell.[49] The porter announces the change, knowing he is in hell even though the place is too cold for it.

In Scotland, the feminine has taken to wearing beards and acting aggressively. Lady Macbeth's renunciation of her role leads to the murder of a king, father, guest. These actions lead to a new ambience, a world in which the feminine principle is being wiped out. That this is a "natural" calamity is suggested by the "unnatural" events that follow: an attack on a female falcon by a "mousing owl"; Duncan's horses "contending 'gainst obedience" and eating each other. Confusion in human gender roles leads in this play to confusion in the hierarchies of nature, as well as to the destruction of one gender principle—Malcolm and Donalbain flee a kingdom where "there's no mercy left" (II, iii, 146). Duncan's murder is called a "breach in nature" (II, iii, 113).

That the consequences of Duncan's murder involve the destruction of particularly women and children has been noted by Matthew Proser: "the content of the speech in which Macbeth plots the destruction of Lady Macduff and her brood is somewhat reminiscent of the suggestive force of Lady Macbeth's portrait of exemplary valor: the idea of the slaughter of innocents is integral to both."[50] Another critic asserts "Macbeth's destructive passion at the end of the play is directed against the innocent, especially women and children, those who hold the promise of the future."[51]

Dame Helen Gardner ties this slaughter to its larger field. She sees Macbeth's anxiety before the murder of Duncan as a fear "not that he will be cut down by Macduff, but that having murdered his own humanity he will enter a world of appalling loneliness, of meaningless activity, unloved himself and unable to love. . . . It is not terror of heaven's vengeance that makes him pause, but the terror of moral isolation."[52] Having killed his own ends, Macbeth inexorably kills them for others, with the same dogged and mindless tenacity that Don John and Iago show.

The victory of the masculine principle over the feminine is a victory of means over ends, and is an empty victory as a result. The severing of connection between means and ends has consequences for the "victors" as well as for the victims. And it is this that is ideologically important and unusual about *Macbeth*. The Thane and his wife both know there is none can call their power to account. In a world of power, linear reason, and control, there is no reason *not* to kill Duncan. The King has set the succession elsewhere, although it is Macbeth's arm that holds the country up. Lady Macbeth sees this very clearly. Macbeth, however, dreads the consequences he may unleash. "If it were done when 'tis done" it would be well, but "bloody instructions" are lessons to others, and boomerang. Beyond that, there are vague reasons for fear.

Macbeth's fears are justified. For with the eradication of pity, compassion, and "masculine" codes aimed at "feminine" ends, the felicities that make Macbeth's life worthwhile vanish. When home becomes part of the war zone, life is merely battle. Macbeth's hypocritical lament over the dead Duncan is ironically prophetic:

> Had I but died an hour before this chance,
> I had liv'd a blessed time; for from this instant
> There's nothing serious in mortality:
> All is but toys: renown and grace is dead,
> The wine of life is drawn, and the mere lees
> Is left this vault to brag of. (II, iii, 95–100)

There is another irony in the play. Duncan is almost always seen as saintly: the epithet "gracious" is continually applied to him. He combines "masculine" authority with "feminine" meekness, concern with himself with concern for the whole. He is nutritive: he tells Macbeth "I have begun to plant thee, and will labor / To make thee full of growing" (I, iv, 28–29). He combines the gender principles; he incarnates harmonious unity. When Macbeth considers the violation the murder of such a man would be, he uses masculine and feminine images:

> And pity, like a naked new-born babe,
> Striding the blast, or heaven's cherubim, hors'd
> Upon the sightless couriers of the air,
> Shall blow the horrid deed in every eye,
> That tears shall drown the wind. (I, vii, 21–25)

Nevertheless, Duncan participates in the unequal value system of his culture. His grateful approval of the hideous slaughter performed in battle, a slaughter designed after all to ensure *his* continued supremacy, bathes him as well as Macbeth and the other warriors in the blood of "reeking wounds." Like Macbeth, Duncan is destroyed by the principle to which he grants priority.[53]

The scenes following his murder swiftly and sharply depict a world gone insane from lack of balance. Murder follows murder until the entire country is a death camp. And the terms used by the characters remain sickeningly the same. Macbeth eggs on the hired murderers with the same challenge his wife threw to him.

> FIRST MUR.:   We are men, my liege.
> MACBETH: Ay, in the catalogue ye go for men. (III, i, 90–91)

True men, he claims, would murder an enemy. And so they prove themselves.

During the scene in which Macbeth is terrified by Banquo's ghost, Lady Macbeth several times turns on her husband contemptuously: "Are you a man?" (III, iv, 57). He is, she says, "quite unmann'd in folly" (III, iv, 72), and scornfully describes his terror as more suitable to "a woman's story at a winter's fire, / Authoriz'd by her grandam" (III, iv, 64–65). Macbeth insists "What man dare, I dare," and argues that only if he were to tremble facing a real enemy could he be called "the baby of a girl." When the ghost vanishes, he sighs "I am a man again" (III, iv, 98, 105).

In worlds dominated by the masculine principle, the feminine principle is partly scorned, but it is also partly feared. It is, after all, the pole of nature and feeling; it is uncontrollable in its spontaneity and its disregard for power. And most important, as the pole of procreation, it embraces the future. Thus, although Fleance is not logically a threat to Macbeth, it is the child Fleance whom the childless King fears. Why should a childless man worry about who will inherit the kingdom? Macbeth's anxiety is psychologically profound: he flails wildly, trying to secure the ends for which power is supposed to exist —which for him at this point have shrunk to the ability to sleep at night.

The very existence of Fleance prevents Macbeth from feeling secure. Moreover in the Witches' evocations for the tormented King, two infants are central. Cleanth Brooks finds the babe to be "perhaps the most powerful symbol in the tragedy."[54] The first baby to appear is bloody, symbolizing Macduff, who, born "unnaturally"—covered with blood from his mother's caesarian delivery—will perform the ritual act of killing the tyrant. (The implications of this are opaque to me. Perhaps Macduff, not being "tainted" by having arrived in the world through the female vagina, is "pure" in a special way, and able to destroy the tyrant. Or perhaps, having been born bloody, he has an imperviousness to certain fears, or a lack of certain delicacies, which make him able to defeat Scotland's greatest warrior. The implications of the vision are not essential to the play, but they are to the "myth" underlying the play.)

The second babe in the vision is clean, born naturally; he is crowned and bears a tree, which may suggest the coming of Birnan Wood to Dunsinane, but more significantly suggests a "natural" and organic line of succession—all the way to James I of England.

The play reaches its moral climax in IV, ii, with the attack on Lady Macduff and the murder of her child onstage. This horrifying scene is emblematic of the character of a world in which ends have been devalued. The horror and the pity it arouses in the audience are morally exemplary: this is what happens, what it feels like to live in a world in which power can no longer distinguish the elements it was designed to protect. But the moral climax of the play is also its moral turning point.

The next scene shows Macduff, ignorant of what has happened to his family, describing to Malcolm the scene in Scotland. G. W. Knight comments on Lady Macduff's claim that her husband's flight was caused by fear rather than love or wisdom, "It is partly true. . . . Macduff is forced to sacrifice the bond of family love."[55] Wilbur Sanders points out that in his discussion with Malcolm, Macduff actually condones the prostitution of his countrywomen.[56] It is in this scene, too, that the images of Scotland as grave rather than mother, and of women fighting, occur. It is in this scene that the real battle lines of the play are drawn. But the winning streak of the one "side" of things is broken when Macduff hears the news about his family. "Dispute it like a man" (IV, iii, 220), Malcolm urges, using the same language we have heard before.[57]

And Macduff, for the first time in the play, expands the meaning of the word *man:* "But I must also feel it as a man," he says, recalling the blind Gloucester, who without eyes sees how the world goes, sees it "feelingly." Macduff refuses either to cry or to bluster: "O I could play the woman with mine eyes, / And braggart with my tongue" (IV, iii, 230–231). He agrees finally to curtail his mourning, to Malcolm's satisfaction: "This tune goes manly."

Thus, the opening scene of the denouement, despite Macduff's definition of a man as one who feels, is still dominated by the same terms in which the play opened. And the play ends as it began, in a totally masculine world. Courage, prowess, the ability to kill, and compassion, nurturance, and mercy, are not equally valuable qualities to be held in a flexible balance. Priority continues to be given to the first set. Siward's son, for instance, who "only lived but till he was a man," is killed in his first battle. Ross tells old Siward that "like a man he died." The old man should have been played by John Wayne. He has only one question: did his son die fighting or fleeing?: "Had he his hurts before?" (V, ix, 12). This time it is Malcolm who raises a minority voice: "He's worth more sorrow, / And that I'll spend for him." The implication of this remark, plus the different tone of the dialogue at the close of this battle—saddened, heavy—compared to that of the triumphant dialogue at the close of the battle scene that opens the play, suggests that feeling will be at least an item in the new governance of Scotland.

But it will still occupy a secondary—or even lower—place. In the dialogue with Malcolm, it is Siward who has the last word: "He's worth no more." His mother might not agree. In this world, sons exist to go to war, and women exist to give birth to sons who are born to kill or be killed in battle. The language remains the same right to the end of the play. Macduff's statement to Macbeth that he was not born of woman makes Macbeth as "effeminate" as Juliet makes Romeo: he tells Macduff the announcement has "*cow'd* my better part of man" (V, vii, 18) (italics mine). And the play concludes with Macduff's entrance bearing the bloody severed head of the butcher in his bloody hands, and his triumphal, "Hail, King!"

So, although some balance is restored to the kingdom, there is no change in its value structure.[58] What is restored is the sacred inner circle, in which men are expected to refrain from applying the standards of the outer one: what is reasserted is moral schizophrenia.

Such a division may have seemed inescapable to Shakespeare. The world is continually threatened with violence and aggression; indeed, it is (either) because of this that the world grants priority to the masculine principle (or) because the world grants priority to the masculine principle that this happens. In any case, Shakespeare clearly saw the danger to society of such a priority; he examines the cost of allowing power, might, to override every other value. His conclusions are far more profound than some pious or conventional readers will allow.

It is sometimes stated, for instance, that Macbeth kills because of the "passion" of ambition, which is permitted to overcome his "reason." He kills, it is said, "order and degree": since it is a criticial truism that order and degree are good, that passion is evil and reason good, it is clear Macbeth is evil. We hardly need critics to give us this information.[59] A more sympathetic and probing critic has stated that Lady Macbeth denies the existence of "irrational values" and thus is destroyed by them.[60] But some readers have commented that Macbeth's death is an anticlimax, that he is already dead in the spirit before Macduff meets him.[61] His "Tomorrow and tomorrow and tomorrow" speech allows no other conclusion.

If passion means emotion, feeling, it is Macbeth's "passion," insofar as we see it, that makes him dread the murder. He does not kill out of passion, but out of reason. He and his wife have considered the entire political situation, and know that he has the power to seize control. They are correct in their judgment. They are what people today who admire such thinking call "hardheaded." What they forget, what Macbeth only intimates, what Heilman suggests by mentioning "irrational values," is that political considerations are not the only ones that matter. The wholeness of life matters, although humans are given to forget that. And the only rationality that is of benefit to humans is one that is aware of all of the qualities of life.

What happens to Macbeth, long before the final battle, is that he loses all reason for living. He has cut himself off from everything that makes life worth living: "honour, love, obedience, troops of friends," all life's felicities. Despite the love shown between them in the early scenes, his wife's death barely touches Macbeth. She gave up her part in his life when she renounced the gender principle she was responsible for.

Shakespeare sets the feminine principle, those values to which Judaeo-Christian culture has always given lip service and little real respect, and which Christianity projects into an afterlife, firmly within the mortal span, within everyday experience. We may not repudiate the qualities associated with pleasure and procreation, with nature and giving up of control, without injuring ourselves, perhaps even maiming or destroying ourselves. It is hardly the life to come that we breach: it is life here.

Antony and Cleopatra

It is interesting that Shakespeare would choose two figures who are remembered not only for their grand passion, but also their sexual freedom and inconstancy, on whom to build his broadest and most realistic study of constancy. *Antony and Cleopatra* is *about* constancy in a way that comedies containing a chaste constant figure are not.[62] In terms of values, the closest analogue to the tragedy is *A Midsummer Night's Dream*, a comedy about constancy that is filled with inconstant figures. And, significantly, both plays separate constancy from chastity.

Chastity, the form of constancy that seals female subordination to the male and guarantees male legitimacy, is an element in the tragedy, in Octavia. But she is unimportant to the action; like Andromache in *Troilus and Cressida*, she provides a "cause" for the males—first, to seal their compact, and second, to serve as justification for Octavius' war on his former partner. Her chaste constancy is not exalted as a quality necessary and adequate for "redemption" of the world from its own viciousness. As a result, *Antony and Cleopatra* is more realistic than many other Shakespeare plays—not that realism is necessarily more desirable than other modes.

The removal of a high value placed on chastity is concomitant with the removal of sexual guilt from one area of the play. That guilt is present, but in a very muted way: it underlies Roman values, and directs many elements of Roman behavior, many Roman attitudes. But it is missing in Egypt. As a result, a quality—sexual freedom—Shakespeare played with in an earlier play (*Love's Labour's Lost*) and worked with seriously but unsympathetically in *All's Well*, placing sexual freedom in Bertram and then proceeding to damn him—is given the only sympathetic treatment Shakespeare was ever to award it. This is not to say that Egyptian values are depicted with complete sympathy by the playwright, but that they are shown with *some* sympathy.

As a result of Shakespeare's separation of chastity from constancy in this play, constancy itself is redefined. As I discussed earlier, constancy is a "masculine" quality, a permanence; when affixed to sexual love, it effects a synthesis of the two gender principles. But in this play, constancy is totally integrated with the united feminine principle and provides what is, to my mind, the most profound vision possible of human constancy.

In most of Shakespeare's work, indeed, in most Western thinking, there is an unconscious identification between the genuine and the enduring: only that which lasts is *true*. So true love is love that does not swerve for the lifetime of the lovers. A fashion, that which passes, is automatically seen as less serious, less profound than things that endure. So institutions of various sorts are viewed with awe as incarnations of "true" values. This association is no doubt rooted in humans' needs to fix—make permanent—something or someone so as to keep their bearings in this wild world.

But the identification seems to me fallacious, unless the word *true* is defined as *enduring* (which it sometimes implicitly is). One can have a genuine and intense experience of love, hate, charity, or guilt that cannot be called anything but true, yet which does not last. Life is made up of millions of such moments, many of which contradict or overlay each other. The only human experience which lasts unalterably is death, as Cleopatra realizes, death "which shackles accidents, and bolts up change; / Which sleeps, and never palates more the dung" (V, ii, 6-7). Not only people, but empires, institutions, and even art die. This knowledge underlies *Antony and Cleopatra*.

The tragedy occurs in a vacillating world. The near chaos of the structure has frequently been noted, and in recent decades accepted as organic to the play, and not a sign of Shakespeare's diminished powers. The alternation of scenes set in Rome, Egypt, and other places that are under the influence of one or the other is paralleled by alternations in domination by Roman or Egyptian values. In addition, within this large dichotomy, there are shifts in alignments, alliances, and attitudes, accompanied by images of shift and transiency.[63] The huge scope of Shakespeare's canvas and the grandeur of the allusions —for example, repeated references to Roman rulers and possessors and upholders of the entire world, Cleopatra's identification of herself with Egypt, pervasive references to the Roman pantheon with identification of the principals with the gods—suggest that Shakespeare felt himself to be making a large, perhaps even a definitive statement, and a statement about more than the handful of characters who dominate the play.[64] More than Antony, Cleopatra, and Octavius, more than Rome versus Egypt, the play is concerned with portraying the opposition of the gender principles in the world at large.

The play is unique in the canon because it alone presents in a positive way the outlaw feminine principle embodied in a powerful female. The mature and sexual woman is rare in Shakespeare; mature women are not common, and most of those who exist seem to spend all their fruitful years in convents of some sort. There is the Nurse in *Romeo and Juliet*, but one has the sense that she is *very* mature, and that her sexual life is lived mostly in memory. At any rate, she is a comic figure. And there is Gertrude, who, in the context of the play, is guilty. Presumably Lady Macbeth has a sexual life, but she seems to renounce that when she renounces pity and compassion. So far is

Cleopatra from the idealized Shakespearean heroine, young, nubile, chaste and constant, so far also from the heavy panting Venus of the early poem, that it seems that when he wrote this play, he got up and went into a different room, one he had never worked in before, and shut the door on everything else he had done. If this were his last play, we would see it as a resolution to his conflicts. Unfortunately for those of us who like neat lives, it isn't.

For a time, then, Shakespeare put aside his ordinary demands of the female, as well as his ordinary demands of the male: no character in the tragedy is either idealized or demonized. If there is no Cordelia, no Desdemona, no Henry V, there is also no Lady Macbeth, Goneril, or Richard III. What this means is that there are no absolute values in the play.

Yet it seems to yield not an absolute, but a high good, although this is a matter of contention. On the one hand, the grandeur and beauty of the language of the lovers is a statement of value, whatever flaws we may see in their behavior.[65] On the other hand, we have seen how the beauty and power of the language of Hamlet, Othello, Lear, and Macbeth sweep us up into their values, whether or not those values are affirmed by the play. On the whole, however, I think that what the great poetry in the plays affirms is not strictly speaking a moral stance, but an approach to life. For great poetry is the language of feeling, and that is the characteristic each of these heroes most fully incarnates. Whether Hamlet is responding in shock to the world around him, or Othello is fighting off his feelings for Desdemona in order to bring himself to kill her, or Lear is satirically and savagely anatomizing the arrangements of society, or Macbeth is preparing to put his feelings aside in order to kill Duncan, each of these characters feels his experience deeply. So too do Antony and Cleopatra. Thus, on a level quite above the immediate values of the play, feeling is the quality most affirmed by it, by all the tragedies. (For this reason, Aristotelian categories seem to me quite irrelevant to Shakespearean—and even to Greek—tragedy. A fall, a flaw, a recognition: the pattern must be stretched into one-size-fits-all dimensions to fit the plays, and is not illuminating even then.) And to the degree that the poetry of this play celebrates feeling, it affirms the lovers as well.

There are two opposing motions in the surface structure: submission to Circe, a "strumpet," leading to loss of worldly power; and the triumph of love over a world well lost. The world is lost *to* Octavius, the unemotional, powerful, possessive, rational, structure-building masculine figure. The world is lost *for* Cleopatra, the shifting, variable, capricious, passionate, sexual, playful, and beautiful feminine figure. The losing, of course, is done by Antony who, because of his participation in both worlds, is a synthetic figure, blending both but in unequal and shifting, seesawing balance. In the world at large, whether in Shakespeare's time or our own, the prejudice of most people leans towards power, possession, and structure, whatever their daydreams. But the play subverts that prejudice in its presentation: there is no question of which, Rome or Egypt, is a diminished world, which richer.

Although the number of scenes set in Egypt is only slightly less than the number set in Rome or Roman territories, Roman values dominate the play. The voice of Rome opens and closes the drama. In addition, as the Roman forces slowly invade Egypt, Roman material increasingly intrudes on Egyptian material. Yet the Egyptian values never change. To see the significance of this requires comparison: consider how Iago's terms invade and poison Othello's idealized world, or how even the quiet domestic scene in Lady Macduff's castle is permeated by the fear and bitterness that have come to characterize Scotland. Increasingly, in *Antony and Cleopatra*, war becomes central to the "Egyptian" characters. Yet they are never "masculinized." There is no completely "Egyptian" scene, that is, no scene that is totally free from allusion to Rome or Roman actions or Roman values. Egyptian material finds its way to Rome as well, but it is nowhere near as pervasive, and is usually brought in in a sniggering, fascinated "locker-room" style—which is to say, Rome does not really comprehend Egypt (just as Venice cannot comprehend Belmont). And there are several Roman scenes that contain no mention whatever of Egypt, Cleopatra, or "Egyptian" values.

Roman values are strongly "masculine," concerned with power, hierarchy, ownership, and above all contest, war, rivalry. Beneath all Roman statements is the assumption that aggressive war and the establishment of a centrally ruled, constantly expanding sovereignty are good. The Romans make claims on the basis of treaties and agreements (codifications of alliances), but in fact they have no hesitation in breaking those agreements when it suits their purposes. Power does not derive from traditional and hereditary "right," but from de facto power and possession. Thus, although the notion of legitimacy functions in the tragedy as a justification for actions, it is not seriously questioned by any character because no character seriously believes in it.

Despite its concern with permanencies and structure, the defining characteristic of Rome is competition, rivalry, squabbling of all sorts. In these arguments or battles, the notion of right, of justice, sometimes appears, but it is used like food coloring, to make the claims appear more attractive. At issue in all the conflicts is power-in-the-world, dominance, and as rivals are swept aside, it becomes the single and highest good.

The Egyptian world is rooted in the feminine principle, but in this play, uniquely, it is unified. Since it is unified, wholly itself, it is powerful and not on the moral defensive. It does not have to maintain chaste constancy as a guarantee to the "masculine" world of its division of itself, its castration, and consequent subordination to "masculine" values. It is fully the pole of nature and procreation and beauty (magnetic power, as opposed to the power of force, imposition). Thus, it is nourishing and sometimes compassionate and merciful; it is also tempestuous, cruel, and variable. It is above all generative and highly erotic. It is also sensuous, anarchic (or democratic), rooted in pleasure, play, and sex. Its great threat lies in its great appeal and its lack of respect for "masculine" qualities like authority, hierarchy, order, and possession. It is thus anticivilization; yet it is the principle of life. The feminine principle rests on the ability to give birth; and many of Cleopatra's images, or allusions to her or Egypt, concern fertility, whether of the "natural" or of the "monstrous."

Like all humans, all the characters participate in the masculine principle. Cleopatra holds Egypt by power and "rights" made secure by Antony. When she is threatened, she attempts to secure some possessions. She believes in her own royal privilege; her government is hierarchical and she is an absolute ruler. But we almost never see her in such a context. We see her, or hear about her, being playful, passionate, tempestuous, variable, beautiful. She and Antony *play*—they go fishing, walk the streets incognito, switch clothes, tease, feast lavishly in a court full of luxury and games like fortune-telling. Cleopatra hops in public, or sails down the Cydnus looking like a goddess.

Although all of Shakespeare's characters contain "masculine" qualities, many demonstrate a weak or missing "feminine" side. Iago seems to have no "feminine" qualities at all; Goneril and Regan are "feminine" only in that they are sexual; Macbeth eradicates his "feminine" side and dies inwardly as a result. Coriolanus has only tenuous connections to "feminine" qualities which exist outside, not inside him, but which nevertheless destroy him. Of all Shakespeare's extremely "masculine" figures, Octavius is the only successful one. He achieves his goals; he does not destroy his world or himself. He destroys only what he sets out to destroy—Antony and Cleopatra.

Thus *Antony* has some similarity to *Macbeth*, as well as *Coriolanus*. All three tragedies contain a powerful figure who ignores or scorns "feminine" values and who is successful in the world because of this. But whereas *Macbeth* and *Coriolanus* focus on the consequences of this victory from the point of view of the victor, *Antony and Cleopatra* concentrates on portraying that which is lost.

There is a suggestion that Caesar seriously intends the establishment of "universal peace" (IV, vi, 5), the *pax romana* that was in actuality achieved during the reign of Augustus. But this is mentioned only once, and in passing. Idealistic authoritarian totalitarianism is not a strong element in Shakespeare's Octavius. Rather, the force that drives him is rivalry. He is a mechanic, a hollow man who uses trumped-up self-justifications to mask his competitiveness, his real envy of Antony. Because of the way Rome and its values gradually move in on Egypt, the overall motion of the play feels like a crusade led by a puritanical Octavius against the intractable and "sinful" feminine principle. What Macbeth kills in himself, Octavius kills in the world. With Octavia, the inlaw feminine, supporting him, he saves the world from sin.

The portrait of Octavia is as astonishing, coming from Shakespeare, as the portrait of Cleopatra. Chaste, constant, meek and mild, she is made in the image of many heroines. She is a sister to Isabel, although she lacks that figure's force; and to Imogen, although she lacks her spirit; and to Hero, although she has a bit more toughness. And as described by Enobarbus, she is "holy, cold, and still" (II, vi, 119–120): quite correctly in a wife, as Menas points out, but not very interesting. Thus Shakespeare judges—in this play—the ideal he himself has erected in a series of plays.

Within the large and definitive movement of Rome into Egypt that occurs in the tragedy are a series of seesaw motions on every level —scene structure, character alignments, behavior from moment to moment, and images as well. Variability, betrayal, and flux are the only absolutes in the play.[66] In addition, every character of any importance whatever is either betrayed or betrays others, or both. Inconstancy is this world's defining characteristic: let us examine some examples of it.

The play opens with the phrase "Nay, but," which Janet Adelman points out indicates the argumentative, dialectical mode of the play.[67] Philo's Roman judgments—Cleopatra is a gypsy and a strumpet, Antony has dwindled from his stature as a great soldier and "triple pillar of the world" (I, i, 12) into a bellows and fan—give way immediately to a teasing dialogue between the lovers. Inherent here is the motion of the whole play: Roman values dominate the world; the feeling between Antony and Cleopatra extends beyond it, into "new heaven, new earth" (I, i, 17).

Instantly appears a messenger from Rome; instantly Cleopatra is angry and challenges. Some readers interpret this passage as meaning that Cleopatra does not want him to listen to the messenger, and by challenging Antony to listen, taunts him into ignoring the message instead. Others, including myself, think she is angry about his ambivalent feelings about Rome—and about her—and taunts him about that. In any case, he ignores the messenger for a time, in her presence, and enunciates the outlaw feminine values that dominate their love:

> Let Rome in Tiber melt, and the wide arch
> Of the rang'd kingdom fall! Here is my space,
> Kingdoms are clay; our dungy earth alike
> Feeds beast as man; the nobleness of life
> Is to do thus. . . . (I, i, 33–37)

The final words of the scene are left to Rome. In sixty-two verses, the terms of the struggle have been defined.

Alternations pervade more than the scenic shifts from Rome to Egypt (and places associated with them). The entire surface of the play is a wavering series of betrayals, reversals, and realignments. Antony ignores the messenger and goes off with Cleopatra, protesting the absoluteness of their love. But suddenly he is struck by a "Roman thought" and confers with the messenger privately. The news is Fulvia's death.

He is saddened: "She's good, being gone" (I, ii, 126). He wishes he could bring back the wife he abandoned. He muses: "Thus did I desire it. / What our contempt doth often hurl from us, / We wish it ours again" (I, ii, 122–124). Cleopatra's earlier taunting of Antony: "Why did he marry Fulvia, and not love her?" (I, i, 41), or her charge that his love for her is as insincere as his love for Fulvia shows that she understands Antony's nature and his attitudes. Although she is not without some ambivalences herself, and although she is using the attack to manipulate him and keep him with her, her charges are not inaccurate. Shortly after receiving the news about Fulvia's death, Antony exclaims about Cleopatra: "Would I have never seen her!" (I, ii, 152).[68] Enobarbus ironically consoles him by reminding him that there are other women in the world. And indeed, as soon as Antony returns to Rome, he repudiates Cleopatra, describing his stay in Egypt as "poisoned hours" that "bound me up / From mine own knowledge" (II, ii, 90–91). In brief span, he marries Octavia and moves to Athens.

In time, of course, he betrays Octavia and returns to Cleopatra, but his return does not end his vacillations. He blames Cleopatra for the defeat at Actium; in this case, her tears instantly melt his anger. He moves from defeated despair to a hollow-sounding heartiness as he attempts to retrieve their fortunes; then he turns bitterly and dangerously against her again (without a clear cause) after the defeat in IV, xi. He threatens wildly to kill her. Nevertheless, news of her suicide throws him into total despair and precipitates his own suicide.

Yet when he discovers she is alive, he reproaches her for nothing. He is hauled up to her monument and the two are as loving as we have ever seen them. Antony tells Cleopatra to seek her honor and safety with Caesar, and warns her to trust none of Caesar's men except Proculeius. This is a small point, and it is seemingly irrelevant to the action. There is no question that Antony thinks he is giving Cleopatra good advice. But Proculeius does as Caesar orders, and if the Queen trusted him, she would be betrayed. Shakespeare's inclusion of this minute detail is of a piece with everything else that happens in the play: shift and betrayal—betrayal in fact, or betrayal of expectations—are the only absolutes in the play.

In contrast to Antony, Cleopatra languishes while he is away, and nearly kills the messenger who brings word of his remarriage. Oddly, the "strumpet" is faithful; it is the hero who is not. But Cleopatra is only *sexually* faithful to Antony. Politically, she is ambivalent. When their forces have been defeated, she toys with Caesar's envoy, sending Antony into an insane rage. To calm his fury after the defeat, she sends false word that she is dead. By the time she rescinds that word, Antony has stabbed himself. And even as he dies, she refuses to risk leaving the monument. After Antony's death, she hedges with Caesar, trying to feel or sense his intentions. There is little question that if she could protect herself, her children, and keep her kingdom, she would make terms with Caesar. Her suicide is a response not simply to Antony's death, but also to Caesar's intentions for her future.

Antony's suicide is of the same sort. He performs it—clumsily—after hearing of her death, but if he had won the battle, if there was a chance of mustering his forces and reengaging Caesar and winning a real victory, the chances are most unlikely he would have done any such thing. Thus, they kill themselves not entirely for love. What both assert by their deaths is that they will not live in worlds too severely diminished. Without each other, and without power over their own

lives, they choose death. Unless one has a rather idiotic view of romantic love, it is perfectly understandable that they would choose to
survive if the terms of survival were not too degrading.

The behavior of the lovers towards each other, however, is hardly
ideal. The play of Shakespeare's that most exalts mature sexual love is
also the play that least idealizes love. The lovers quarrel with real
animus, they betray each other, they move between love and renunciation, as ordinary lovers do.[69] They play together, they exchange
roles, and they remain erotically bound to each other. And they are,
at the last, faithful: if the causes of their fidelity are contingent, so are
the causes of their infidelity. They live in an unfaithful world.

Consider:

Antony speaks of the "slippery people" (I, ii, 183), the fickle populace that follows the current leader, and how the "hated, grown to
strength / Are newly grown to love" (I, iii, 48–49). Caesar speaks of the
"common body," which "like to a vagabond flag upon the stream, /
Goes to, and back, lackeying the varying tide, / To rot itself with motion" (I, iv, 44–47). For Caesar, of course, anything not fixed is intolerable, anything not permanent is rotten.

Pompey plans in II, i, to continue his war: in II, vi, he is flattered
or frightened out of that plan. He has no objection to Menas' plan to
destroy the triumvirate except that Menas consults him and he does
not want to take the responsibility for such an act. Consequently,
Menas abandons Pompey, and Caesar destroys him: two more betrayals.

Lepidus, who tries, to the amusement of the underlings, to steer
an even course between Antony and Caesar, and to conciliate the
continual wrangling and contention between them, is betrayed and
destroyed by Caesar. Yet Enobarbus' suggestion that Antony and Caesar should "borrow one another's love for the instant" (until Pompey is
disposed of), and then "return it again" (II, ii, 103–105)—which is
precisely what they do—is reprimanded.

Ventidius, in a short scene that is irrelevant to the plot, shows
how competition functions in hierarchy. He "betrays" Antony in order
not to be betrayed by him: "I could do more to do Antonius good, /
But 'twould offend him" ((III, i, 25–26). In one passage reminiscent of
Antony's feelings about the dead Fulvia, Agrippa and Enobarbus recall
Antony crying at the sight of the dead Brutus: "What willingly he did
confound, he wail'd" (III, ii, 58). After the defeat at Actium, many of
Antony's allies and soldiers abandon him. After watching even Cleopatra dally with the notion of making terms with Caesar through his
envoy, Enobarbus too decides to leave Antony.

The war vacillates: Antony is defeated, then Caesar, then Antony, again and finally. Eros "betrays" Antony by reneging on his promise to kill him. Caesar betrays Cleopatra as to his intentions. Like Antony for Fulvia and Brutus, Caesar is "touch'd" by the news of Antony's death: "I have follow'd thee to this . . . But yet let me lament" (V, i, 33, 36, 40). Cleopatra deceives Caesar about her withheld treasures and her intentions: Seleucus betrays Cleopatra, hoping to ingratiate himself with Caesar. Proculeius is not honest with Cleopatra, betraying our expectations. Dolabella, however, is, and so betrays Caesar out of pity and affection for the Queen.

Even those who attempt like Lepidus to avoid or transcend the shifting winds and seas are betrayed or destroyed. Octavia is torn between her love for her brother and her duty to her husband: "Her tongue will not obey her heart, nor can / Her heart inform her tongue —the swan's down feather, / That stands upon the swell at the full of tide, / And neither way inclines" (III, ii, 47–50).

"You must think, look you, that the worm will do his kind," says the Clown, whose speeches offer in little the contradictions and paradoxes of the play. Utter constancy is impossible: "were man but constant, he were perfect."

> Sometime we see a cloud that's dragonish,
> A vapor sometime like a bear or lion,
> A tower'd citadel, a pendant rock,
> A forked mountain, or blue promontory
> With trees upon't that nod unto the world,
> And mock our eyes with air . . .
> That which is now a horse, even with a thought
> The rack dislimns, and makes it indistinct
> As water is in water. (IV, xiv, 2–7, 9–11).

The only absolute besides inconstancy is constancy in death:

> 'Tis paltry to be Caesar:
> Not being Fortune, he's but Fortune's knave,
> A minister of her will: and it is great
> To do that thing that ends all other deeds,
> Which shackles accident and bolts up change,
> Which sleeps, and never palates more the dung,
> The beggar's nurse, and Caesar's. (V, ii, 2–8).

In such a world, and this is how the actual world is, any constancy is a miracle, a gift. Love that endures in spirit, even if not in the letter, is the greatest gift one can grant or get. Thus Enobarbus remains in the imagination as a type of loyalty despite his defection, and Eros *because* of his broken promise. In ironical fulfillment of the Sooth-sayer's prophecy, Iras and Charmian die shortly after their mistress; their words suggest they accompany her in love and admiration more than out of fear of Caesar. And so too Antony and Cleopatra, despite their alternations and removals, remain constant to each other, and take on mythic size.

Part of what makes them so large-sized is their understanding and forgiveness of alteration.[70] Despite Cleopatra's rage at hearing of An-tony's marriage, she accepts him back with no diminution of love. Although she is terrified by his threats against her in IV, xii, she for-gives him enough to risk the consequences of his rage to send word that she is really alive—once she is safely in her monument.

Antony, after his first defeat, expects and even encourages his allies to abandon him. He understands the world and does not hold up idealistic (and self-serving) demands. After his tantrum, he forgives Cleopatra for dallying with Caesar's envoy. He fully forgives Enobar-bus and sends his treasure after him. Part of his love of Cleopatra is founded on what Enobarbus calls her "infinite variety"; she expresses everything, and everything becomes her. Inconstancy may be the cause of much human sorrow, but under its other name, variety, it is the spice of life.

Thus, as in *Midsummer Night's Dream*, constancy is wrested di-rectly out of the fact of inconstancy. Like the moon images in the comedy, which offer a concrete example of constancy within incon-stancy, all elements of *Antony*—scenic structure, plot, characteriza-tion, and language and allusion—repeat in multiple ways the same notion. The Romans disapprove of Egypt; Cleopatra has contempt for Rome: but the two realms are in some way contained in each other.

Roman values and manners dominate the play in terms of time and attention devoted to them; Egyptian values dominate the emo-tional dimension of the tragedy. The activities of Rome are war and contention. The only pleasure shown or described as Roman is a male drinking bout conducted not in the sensuous abandon and pleasure of Egypt, but as a contest, which Lepidus loses. Presumably, turning the drinking session into a competition cleanses it of any associations with the feminine principle, and so purifies it. The drinking contest is a metaphor for what will happen to Lepidus: we do not need to see his destruction—it is implicit in the drinking contest.[71]

But if Roman values dominate in the plot, they do not triumph in most readers' sense of things: it is the emotional dimension of the play that matters. There is no question that the lovers are magnified. This is accomplished through the allusive level, which is idealizing; and through the poetry, which is magnificent. The use of Enobarbus as the vehicle of much praise of Cleopatra (the tough old soldier who sees her tricks still praises her inordinately) and Cleopatra's words about Antony when he is dead and she can no longer try to manipulate him —these elements function as a kind of reinforcement or validation for the large notions of the lovers themselves. In addition, the lovers are continually associated with nature, fertility, and wealth in its best sense —the heaped-up richnesses of the world. Antony is repeatedly described or shown as generous in word or deed. He is even lavish: his magnanimity is dramatically presented in his understanding and forgiveness of betrayal in "this wild world." Cleopatra is majestic and tempestuous, without shame and without guilt. Her speeches after Antony's death have a dignity, a largeness of reference, and an authority that amounts to wisdom. In drawing her idealized portrait of Antony, she makes a statement about spirit, not flesh, about largeness of being and doing and feeling.[72]

Still, the lovers are not idealized. Generous Antony takes Pompey's house in a spirit of petty greed. Both are at times unreasonable, capricious, cruel, weak, and treacherous to each other and other people. It is clear that Shakespeare's intention in magnifying them is not to create exemplary moral models, not even to idealize these particular characters. Rather, the magnification serves to exalt their feeling for each other, and to link it with eternity, the realm beyond the changes of the moon. In the process, the play exalts feeling itself, guiltless eroticism, play, free-flowing emotion of all sorts, the rich high vividness of living when experience is its own end.[73]

The pole of nature does not mask or enrobe the dung and slime of earth and flesh; it accepts the worm who does its kind, the transiency of every human experience, and accepts its participation in time, in contrast to Caesar, who wants to "possess" the time (II, vii, 99). The images associated with Egypt are alternately luxurious, fertile, and baleful; "the serpent theme culminates in a brilliant union of the fruitful and the lethal powers of the Nile."[74] They are, however, all peaceful, and they frequently link the great Queen Cleopatra with beggars, just as she herself describes herself as a milk maid: although this kingdom is ruled hierarchically, legitimacy is not a major issue in it.

One critic has claimed that love is always ambiguous in Shakespeare, and that in this tragedy, the love is a dream, the slime is the reality.[75] But Shakespeare's great triumph in this play, it seems to me, is to portray love in all the ambivalence and ambiguity it has in actuality, and to persuade us nevertheless of its authenticity and intensity. Slime is never far from love, as Yeats's Crazy Jane might say, but this does not make one real and the other an illusion.

The play is about the human conflict between seemingly contradictory impulses. Robert Ornstein writes that Shakespeare's "archetypal imagery suggests that the worlds of Rome and Egypt are eternal aspects of human experience and form a dichotomy as elemental as that of male and female."[76] I am not at all sure that these impulses are necessarily contradictory, or that the dichotomy of male and female is anything like as elemental as we have come to believe, but I will reserve such comments for the conclusion. It certainly appears that Shakespeare thought this way, however. And since he did, and since in this play he aggrandized the very pole that was seen as immoral, not just sexually, but in terms of overall response to life, he was offering a radical criticism of his culture.

Although some critics believe that Antony suffers from "a deep-seated defect of will," and that the play is "a conflict between passion and human weakness, and duty and self-denial"; or that passionate love is "sinful and dangerous," and Antony a type of Hercules in thrall to Omphale, one can only respond that the richer experience, in a life in which one may not have everything, is the more desirable.[77]

Just as the tragedy brings together the two principles at war with each other (as they were in the problem plays), but focuses equally on them, so the structure focuses on linear scenes that advance the plot, and scenes irrelevant to plot that create texture or are significatory. That it violates conventional tragic form made it seem a failure to generations of readers. A. P. Riemer claims that it violates tragic tradition in that it contains flashes of comedy, vulgarity, and swift changes of tone.[78] To challenge convention is to challenge attitude, even if that convention is a literary one. V. K. Whitaker says that only *Lear* and *Antony and Cleopatra* seriously question "the validity of the concept of universal harmony or order," and that the latter denies "that the achievement of fixity is possible."[79]

Perhaps the most daring thing Shakespeare did in the play was to present illegitimate sexuality as glorious. Many critics still find romantic or erotic love a trivial subject, not worthy of tragedy.[80] But it is impossible to deny the seriousness and grandeur of this tragedy, and impossible—largely because of Shakespeare's language—to deny that he glorified something that is seen as sinful, trivial, and contemptible by many of the characters. Once sex and sin are not seen as identical

—as they are not in Egypt—then Egypt is as hot as Rome is cold, and "as inevitably self-renewing as the other is inescapably deadly."[81] Reason, what we call reason, which is linear and goal-directed, is far less encompassing than emotion.[82] It is true that the unified feminine principle is anticivilization; but the masculine principle is antilife. In the plays that follow this tragedy, Shakespeare will pursue the second perception to its ugly and barren conclusion.

And in fact, how civilized is the civilizing principle? Roman values —order and degree, power-in-the-world, structure and possession—do not create harmonious order and a protective pale for procreation. They create contention and rivalry, one order superseding another, and a thin, pleasureless, stiff existence. The feminine principle may be doomed; it may always be defeated. But in the meantime it offers the richness of emotional and erotic dimensions of life—pleasure, play, and sex. At the end of *Antony and Cleopatra*, Caesar has the world; Antony and Cleopatra had the living.

Coriolanus and *Timon of Athens*

The two plays believed to be Shakespeare's last tragedies—*Coriolanus* and *Timon of Athens*—develop the perceptions and visions the playwright worked out in the preceding tragedies. Although they are in different modes, *Coriolanus* resembling drama of character, and *Timon*, drama of ideas, they have much in common. The ground of their similarity can be suggested in a metaphor—the image of the beast-god.

Aristotle's dictum was that "he that is incapable of living in society is a god or a beast." Shakespeare has been working, since *Hamlet* and *Othello*, towards a dichotomy within the masculine principle similar to that in the feminine. The god is that which attempts to transcend nature; the beast is that which surrenders to it. But in these plays, the deep association made by Western culture, and the playwright himself in many plays, between nature and sexuality is not important. In these plays, the qualities of nature that the heroes attempt to transcend are those of the *inlaw* feminine principle.

In *Othello*, *Lear*, and *Macbeth*, the prevailing values in the plays' cultures are masculine; the feminine principle is tainted, unrecognized, or scorned, and is eventually cast out or eradicated, although it triumphs morally at the end of *Lear*. *Coriolanus* and *Timon* occur in worlds in which the feminine principle is almost completely lacking from the outset.

Lear subverts the primacy of power values by showing the richness and depth of inner life, by showing what life is like in one who feels; like feeling itself, those who feel are exiles, outcasts, illegitimates in their world. *Antony and Cleopatra* subverts the primacy of "masculine" values by demonstrating the richness and depth of sexual life and love. *Coriolanus* and *Timon* subvert the primacy of the masculine principle by showing the texture or "feel" of life in a world in which it has absolute dominion, in which—unlike *Richard III*, *Troilus and Cressida*, and *Macbeth*—almost no trace of the "feminine" remains.

The feminine principle has little representation in these plays. In the Roman play, only the silent Virgilia has any touch of it—and she not as much as has been projected by some readers. In the Athenian play, Flavius entertains "feminine" values—indeed, Timon even calls him a *woman* when he weeps for his master. But Flavius is as ineffectual as Virgilia. There is little allusion to nature or natural events: A. C. Bradley claims nature is absent "even as background." [83] There is no sex whatever in either play: the prostitutes who appear in *Timon* are more concerned with money than with eros. In both plays, love is highly structured: in *Coriolanus*, it is hedged within hierarchy and takes the form of duty; in *Timon*, it is severely limited by the nature of the relationships Timon permits.

There is what appears to be giving in both plays. Giving, as we have seen, is a form of nutritiveness; it is also a form of love. In both cases, it is "feminine." But "feminine" giving involves granting what is needed to those who need it. The donor receives pleasure from the act, but her or his pleasure is entwined with the neediness and pleasure of the receiver. The giving done in these plays sometimes appears in this form, but is actually rooted in other feelings.

Both plays concentrate on male figures possessed of seemingly unbounded legitimacy, property, privilege, and power. The tension in the plays, since there is no significant feminine opposition, is within the masculine principle itself, divided into beast-god impulses. Thus, the tension produced in *Othello*, between Othello's and Iago's visions of the feminine principle—one idealizing, one perverting—is investigated in contexts which have nothing to do with women. In these plays, Shakespeare separates a gender principle from the gender with which it is associated, something he attempted to do also in *Lear*.

The result is that these plays, by focusing entirely on *human* (male) qualities, with no hope of a "divine," forgiving chaste constant heroine entering to redeem anything, present totally male worlds which are palpably *inhuman*. Thus Shakespeare seems to be questioning the terms of the division of experience he had inherited and examined and developed. In *All's Well*, and other plays, the feminine principle is seen as a "clog," a restraint, as indeed it is when it is seen as the principle requiring volitional subordination of the self to the whole. But because it is missing in these two plays, and because their texture is so harsh and unappealing, the feminine principle is redefined (implicitly) as a humanizing richness that enlarges life even as it restrains power and sexuality. Without the qualities of this principle, life seems as bleak as it did to Macbeth.

But "feminine" qualities, disdained as they are, are often lacking in the world. The problem Shakespeare appears to be examining in these two plays (as well as in *Macbeth*) resembles that considered by Dostoevski in a number of novels: If God does not exist, then everything is permitted. By setting his plays in pre-Christian times, Shakespeare dispensed with the necessity of including Christian beliefs in an afterlife containing a system of rewards and punishments for human behavior on earth. He can focus entirely on this world. The Russian insisted on faith in deity because he seemed to believe that, without belief in "divine" law, humans would be even more monstrous than they are. But Shakespeare usually suggests that rampant selfhood contains its own self-destruct mechanism.

All his supreme egotists (except one) contain some seed of awareness that they are missing something or that they are in some way wrong. Bertram (*All's Well That Ends Well*) has a seed of shame; Angelo (*Measure for Measure*) has a speck of conscience. Richard III and Macbeth are haunted by a vague knowledge of what they have destroyed. Only Iago remains solidly fixed, true to his values right to the end. This is perhaps why he seems a bewildering figure, although one suspects that actual human horrors, like some we have seen in our own century, never recant, never realize what they have destroyed.

But in these two plays, the case for some inner restraint or knowledge of other values is weak. The cybernetic balance that swings the powerful back towards humane rhythms does not operate. If the protagonists are stopped in their courses, they (especially Timon) are stopped by forces outside themselves. Coriolanus is goaded into the single humane act he performs, and goaded into goading others to destroy him. It is the play of others upon him, a play over which he has no control—having no restraint in this area, perhaps because he has used it all in others—that destroys him. Timon is stopped in mid-

course by an accident: his money runs out. No internal sense of wrongness exists in the man. In his second course, he is stopped by death (as
we all are): he dies because there is nothing else that can be done with
him given the terms of the drama.

It would seem that as Shakespeare aged, he came increasingly to
believe that there was nothing that could stop the Bertrams, the Iagos,
and the Coriolanuses of the world. This means, also, that his sense of
the balance of gender principles in the world was undermined. The
division of experience he believed in simply didn't work. The feminine
principle cannot restrain the masculine: there is nothing to stop the
insane, power-hungry, "masculine" figures of the world from manhan-
dling people, nature, and "feminine" qualities.

His response to this dilemma was to turn to a new mode, the
romance. Romance focuses on emotional life; in this area, the depre-
dations power works on its own humanity do show that there is a
cybernetic balance in the world. That he was right to do so is clear, for
he could not go further with his material in the tragic mode: *Coriolanus* and *Timon* are among the most unpleasant plays Shakespeare
ever wrote.

Coriolanus

Coriolanus is, like Iago, an example of the unadulterated, unmodified
masculine principle. Like Iago, he is a soldier; unlike him, he is noble.
He is called *noble*, much as Iago is called *honest*, all through the play.

There are several grounds for this nobility. Martius is an aristocrat
in an emphatically class-oriented world. His blood derives from generations of "aristocratic" blood; his inherited status confers on him
privilege, possession, and an inherent rightness. However, all his peers
in Roman society have the same prerogatives, and they are not so
persistently denominated *noble*.

The Roman's primary excellence is his prodigious prowess. But it
is not this either that is indicated by the adjective *noble*. His prowess
does give rise to his pride. So does his status. But others have the same
grounds for pride, and perhaps, a similar pride.

What distinguishes Martius from other people is that he is absolutely autonomous. Another way of putting this is to say he is utterly
incorruptible. He cannot be "bought." This sounds like a fine characteristic, and it has led many critics to admire him, and to suggest with

some bewilderment that it seems "there are certain kinds of goodness which can themselves lead to tragedy."[84] But it is necessary to examine what this incorruptibility implies, what it is based on.

Martius cannot be seduced by money. Although he may win a battle almost single-handedly, he will not accept more than his usual share of the rewards. He does not care enough about political office to "debase" himself in speaking to the common people. He scorns the reward of praise, and is curt and angry when it is offered him. Thus, he cannot be flattered into taking a position he might not take on his own.

He cares about only two things, his fame and his honor. These words overlap in meaning: both mean reputation. But *honor* suggests also a restraint founded on pride that prevents one from performing actions considered dishonorable, base. Again, this seems a fine characteristic; unlike Aufidius, Martius would never kill insidiously.

Honor has another and subtler meaning, though. It indicates a kind of privilege, a superiority to a condition most humans are subject to: unwanted imputations. Because of unwanted imputations, men fight duels, start fights in streets and bars, and in popular art forms, engage in gun duels. The attribution to a man or a woman associated with him, of some quality considered undesirable, is enough to make him fight: Smile when you say that, pardner. This is so whether the statement made is true, false, or irrelevant. The assumption behind such behavior is that a taunt unavenged is a taint, whether or not the taunt has any bearing on the person. The words alone are an action, and must be replied to by action. If it is not, the honor (or manliness) of the injured party is diminished.

This is a paradoxical arrangement. On the one hand, it arises because the man who is insulted believes himself superior—whether because of rank, wealth, or prowess—to the insults of others. He considers himself above attack, invulnerable. But on the other, his position alone opens him to utter vulnerability: he must defend his "honor" to anyone with the courage to challenge it.

That Coriolanus is tightly bound up in such a morality is clear. M. C. Bradbrook points out that Martius' mother "wins him by the means that others use to undo him, his inability to resist a taunt."[85] It is not enough to conclude, as some critics have, that Martius is adolescent: that is a judgment, not an explanation. The reason why he must reply to taunts, the reason he holds this conception of honor, is deeply rooted in the masculine principle to which he adheres.

Coriolanus fights not for friend, family, or country, but for himself, for his fame and honor. In this, he is un- or even antisocial. His highest values are located in himself alone, not in conjunction with something or someone else. Social values have too little stature in his mind to provide any moderating or balancing influence on his individualism.

He thinks about himself and is thought about by others, as a god, that is, as one who transcends nature. Not only does he not drop from wounds, he does not even feel them. He is able to function on energy alone; he is either unaware or unpossessed of bodily, sensuous, or emotional needs. He rebuffs the approval of his fellow soldiers; he refuses special reward. He denies that he needs or wants *anything*.

But need and want, things all of us feel, are part of what ties us to each other. Moreover, they remind us, daily, of our ultimate lack of control over our lives. Someone who denies any need or want, and who, in the process, disdains others who do, disdains ordinary human life. Because the circumstances of his life are such that Martius has been given—by inheritance, by rank, by accident—a social and economic position that does make him superior to ordinary human concerns, and the love of mother and wife that is unconditional and makes him superior to another set of ordinary human considerations, in fact, he does need or want for little.

He does not kill out of pleasure in killing; pleasure is another thing he does not need or want. We are never given a sense of Martius almost wallowing in blood, as we are with Macbeth. Rather, he is shown as a bloody death-bearing machine, a "mechanical juggernaut."[86] Coriolanus is as fully transcendent of nature and nature's claims as any human can be.

It is this transcendence of his that makes him appear admirable to critics raised to believe transcendence is a good. But for Shakespeare, such a degree of transcendence of the pole of nature, the feminine principle, is egotism and leads to isolation and the insanity of those who have forgotten their ends.[87] Martius' treatment of his men in battle disheartens them and leads them to fight less fiercely than they could.[88] He does not perform a single act of compassion in the play: he forgets the name of the one man he wishes to help. He reproaches his wife—tenderly and with amusement—for weeping at his return (in II, i), that is, for feeling. In IV, i, as he is about to leave Rome, he reproaches her again, and again for feeling: "Nay, I prithee, woman" (IV, i, 12). In his speeches to her in the Volscian camp, he denies her petition before she can even make it, and describes his one personal remark to her as "prating," a word his mother later uses too, when she reminds him of his bonds to her, his wife, and his son. But he denies these bonds: what moves him, finally, is the taunt that his true mother and wife are in Corioli, that his child is not his child. Coriolanus does not surrender to "great nature"; he jerks into action at the innuendo that his son is a bastard.[89]

Yet Coriolanus is a victim in the same way that Macbeth and Othello are victims of their cultures. His values are Rome's values carried to a greater degree of fulfillment than most men could achieve. He has become, as literally as one made of flesh and blood can, a fighting machine. He has, however, a fatal flaw—not in the usual sense of that term. He is uncontrollably emotional within his narrow emotional range. He is accessible to rage, and his rage can be triggered by catchwords and stereotypes. His emotionality is encoded, mechanical, and unrestrainable. All that is required is that someone name him sissy, liar, baby, and he explodes, ready to fight. He cannot be trusted in the Forum with the citizens; Aufidius can taunt him to trigger his own murder. His emotionality is the single residue of humanness in him. Without it, he would transcend completely: he would be total machine. And it is this sliver of humanness in him that earns him his human fate of death.

Without this emotionality, Martius would be the man his friends and mother wish him to be. Kenneth Burke points out that every person of good [social] standing in the play admires or loves Martius.[90] The complicity of Rome in Martius' character has frequently been remarked.[91] He learned his values from his mother, a highly respected woman of dignity, force, and pride. "The culture of which she is a representative stresses those 'masculine' qualities that range from genuine physical courage to hardness and insensitiveness in the face of life," writes L. C. Knights.[92] His wife, that "gracious silence," also shares Roman values, although some readers prefer to disbelieve that. She denies herself the pleasure of society while her husband is fighting. Her comment on her son's treatment of a butterfly—"A crack, madam"—implies amused and affectionate tolerance for a "real boy."[93] Her comments to the crowd in IV, ii, show a position identical to Volumnia's; indeed it is Virgilia who threatens what Coriolanus will later attempt to do: "He'ld make an end of thy posterity" (IV, ii, 26), she tells the tribunes. In addition, the imagery of the play is not monstrous or unusual, suggesting an aberrant world; it is realistic and everyday.[94]

Martius is disliked by the tribunes and the common people because his pride in his transcendence of nature—which comes to be

seen as a common, shared need for physical and emotional well-being
—that pride is so great that he essentially denies he is of the same
species as other people. He does not value humanness: he is "above
pity and above life."[95]

Other of the Roman aristocrats feel similarly superior to the
crowd, but they have more of a sense of their ties to it. His mother, for
instance, who has been called "Machiavellian" because she is willing
to be "ignoble" and flatter the crowd, could rather be called hypocritical.[96] But such behavior could also be seen as a recognition of the
existence of the people, and since existence alone is power, of their
power as well. Speaking to the crowd is a recognition of reality; it
acknowledges common humanity in that it accepts the limitations that
exist for all power. Bradley saw this clearly: "His mother and friends
urge him to deceive the people with false promises. But neither false
promises nor apologies are needed, only a little humanity and some
acknowledgment that the people are part of the state."[97] But neither
his mother nor his friends can articulate this to Martius because they
are aware of it only subconsciously. Their conscious superiority is identical to his.[98]

That Shakespeare saw Coriolanus as to some degree a victim of
his culture is demonstrated by his departures from Plutarch's account
of the man's life. Altering or elaborating or even contradicting his
source, Shakespeare softened the case for Martius as much as he
could. He made Volumnia far fiercer than Plutarch's figure, and Virgilia more ineffectual. The conflict in Rome is made out as one between the aristocratic and plebeian classes, rather than one between
Coriolanus and the populace. Shakespeare omits, or more precisely,
deflects Plutarch's account of Martius denying corn to starving people.
And he shows the populace as fickle in peace and cowardly in war, the
tribunes as treacherous and power-hungry.[99] (So greatly does Shakespeare strengthen Coriolanus' position that one critic believes he
meant us to find him politically right.)[100]

Without such alterations, Coriolanus would appear fully monstrous. Most important, perhaps, was Shakespeare's showing him to be
dutiful and deferential to his mother; he shows her pointing him the
moral-political way. Volumnia, a woman, would be expected to uphold
the moral right, and she is very righteous. She is a far subtler portrayal
than is Lady Macbeth, of a woman who has absorbed the dominant
values of her culture, and upholds them fiercely. And her function in
the play is to represent the best—the most moral, dignified, forceful
—Roman cultural values can attain. The best is tainted, as Hamlet

discovers: Volumnia is willing for her son to lie to gain political power. But Coriolanus is not more moral than his mother; he has simply invested his *entire* ego in his condition of transcendence. He will not lie because that is a *human* thing to do, because above all, it betrays *need*.

The consequence to the community as a whole of its values is delineated in the rhetorical line. Rome is threatened long before Martius brings an army against it. This rhetorical line is, however, associated with the warrior. There are several accounts describing him in battle, most of them praising, but their imagery and diction persistently associate him with mechanicalness and death. In addition, the rhetoric of the play persistently conflates images of love with images of death. This rhetoric comes not just from Coriolanus himself, and from Volumnia, but from Romans and Volscians as well.[101]

Love, whether tender or erotic, appears only as hate. There is human truth in this: in a world divided into gender principles, contestants in physical matches often feel more love and respect for the opponents they try to batter than for anyone else. In an echo of *Antony* and *Troilus*, Coriolanus is more concerned with Aufidius—and concern is a form of love—than with anyone else in the world. His whole purpose in life is to destroy the one man he fully respects. Aufidius' feelings for Martius are similar and equally intense.

But why not? Volumnia claims "the breasts of Hecuba, / When she did suckle Hector, look'd not lovelier / Than Hector's forehead when it spit forth blood / At Grecian sword, contemning" (I, iii, 40–43). Martius demands that all soldiers "love this [bloody] painting / Wherein you see me smear'd" (I, vi, 68–69). War is better than love, for love—or even agreeableness—is mere flattery: "I know thou hadst rather / Follow thine enemy in a fiery gulf / Than flatter him in a bower" (III, ii, 90–92).

The Volscian servants agree: "This peace is nothing but to rust iron, increase tailors, and breed ballad-makers . . . Let me have war, say I, it exceeds peace as far as day does night; it's sprightly, waking, audible, and full of vent. Peace is a very apoplexy, lethargy, mull'd, deaf, sleepy, insensible, a getter of more bastard children than war's a destroyer of men . . . 'Tis so, and as wars, in some sort, may be said to be a ravisher, so it cannot be denied but peace is a great maker of cuckolds" (IV, v, 219–229).

In the only real mention of sexuality in the play, it is seen as the opposite to war. And in a motion towards attitudes expressed in the problem plays, Shakespeare here satirizes the notion that sex is worse than murder. Sex as ravishing (rape) is better than sex as adultery, these servants claim. Better dead men than living (bastard) children; better activity than lethargy, and peace is lethargy.

It is Coriolanus who most fully articulates the scorn for "feminine" values implicit in Roman culture. His mother is constraining him to speak kindly to the common people in the Forum. He replies:

> Away, my disposition, and possess me
> Some harlot's spirit! My throat of war be turn'd,
> Which quier'd with my drum, into a pipe
> Small as an eunuch, or the virgin voice
> That babies lull asleep! The smiles of knaves
> Tent in my cheeks, and schoolboys' tears take up
> The glasses of my sight! A beggar's tongue
> Make motion through my lips, and my arm'd knees
> Who bow'd but in my stirrup, bend like his
> That hath receiv'd an alms! (III, ii, 111–120)

In this speech, Martius associates whores, castrati, virginity, tenderness to babies, hypocrisy, children's tears, and beggary. These items only seem disparate; they are all elements of the feminine principle. The virgin voice, tenderness, babies, and schoolboy tears all refer to the powerless and innocent; whoredom and hypocrisy are like beggary, in that they are a bowing, through sale of the body, sale of the mind, or powerlessness so great it has nothing to sell and can only beg, to those who do have power. For Coriolanus, these things, which represent either utter powerlessness or subordination to the power of another, are opposite to manhood.

Such standards are not his alone: the Volscian watchman asks Menenius: "Can you . . . think to front his revenges with the easy groans of old women, the virginal palms of your daughters, or with the palsied interecession of such a decay'd dotant as you seem to be?" (V, ii, 39–45). Easy groans are fake ones; virginity is trivial; age is powerless. Emotion and vulnerability are not to be taken seriously: they are illegitimate.

So, when Coriolanus sees his wife, mother, and child in the Volscian camp, he thinks "But out, affection, / All bond and privilege of nature, break!" (V, iii, 24–25). He is frightened; perhaps he is not as transcendent as he thought: "I melt, and am not / Of stronger earth than others" (V, iii, 28–29). But he wills not to bow to "Great Nature," using nature imagery in his decision: "I'll never / Be such a gosling to obey instinct, but stand / As if a man were author of himself, / And knew no other kin" (V, iii, 34–36).

This is how he has been standing all through the play. Shakespeare sees that carrying the "masculine" and human desire for control over nature too far, which means without modifying it with a complementary acceptance of human participation in nature, leads not to a desiderated humanness, but to inhumanness.

"He wants nothing of a god but eternity and a heaven to throne in" (V, iv, 23–24), says Menenius, the man who, Coriolanus believes, "godded" him. Feeling like a god, Coriolanus derides the populace and his soldiers with their beastliness. Aiming for the superhuman, he finds humans subhuman. Thus it does not matter to him whether he fights Volscians or Romans: they are subhumanly the same.

Coriolanus does have human needs, although he never acknowledges them. Given—born into—a position that grants him all he needs without his asking, he is also thrust out of it. But after his exile from Rome, he does not head into isolation or a Samsonlike retribution against the city. He heads directly for his love-hate, Aufidius, and the Volscians, the enemies of Rome from whom he again receives, without asking, welcome, adoration, support, praise, and companionship.

It has been suggested that *Coriolanus* is a satire, or that Martius is Shakespeare's Homeric hero.[102] But clearly the play is not a satire in the way *Troilus* is: satire, of course, is attack, but *all* of Shakespeare's plays attack, to some degree, the attitudes and behavior of his culture, and many attack or question ideals he himself entertained. It seems to me that satire as a mode is an attack through diminishment (although that diminishment may be accomplished through aggrandizement). *Troilus* undercuts the Homeric world by belittling and denigrating the motives of its characters. This is not the case here. Martius is never belittled: he means what he says. If some of his actions and words seem adolescent to us, that is because we have had two-hundred-odd years to think about the attitudes Shakespeare portrayed. *Coriolanus* is a serious living-out of certain cultural values, and if the hero seems perverse, it is those values, not the character, that must be indicted.

In addition, the differences between *The Iliad* and *Coriolanus* are profound enough to indicate the time span between their compositions. It is true that Homer's Greeks are just as contentious, arrogant, adolescently sullen, and trigger-happy as is Coriolanus. But the masculine principle had not progressed to the same point in Homer's time as it had by Shakespeare's. There was more of a sense of participation in nature, which had not yet come to be seen as strictly "feminine" and therefore despicable. The metaphors threaded throughout *The Iliad*, of ordinary natural events, and of the natural and poignant mortality of the warriors, emphasize the tie of Homer's heroes to flesh, nature, and human necessity. Scenes of eating and drinking, scenes in which men dying are compared to the falls of young trees, function to root the power in which men contend to the greatest power of all, that of nature. Shakespeare emphasizes exactly the opposite. One would hardly believe that Martius needed to eat, drink, sleep, or be held tenderly.

It was, I believe, not Homer, but Virgil who exerted the greatest classical influence on Shakespeare.[103] Underlying much of his work, even that which is not concerned with war and heroism—or the reverse—is a conflict of values like that found in *The Aeneid*. All his life, the playwright battled it out on the ground of his own spirit. With *Antony and Cleopatra*, and *Coriolanus*, he seems to have settled the argument. His vision was opposite to Virgil's: the establishment of empire, order, and legitimacy was not worth its cost.

Timon of Athens

Timon of Athens has been called a masque, a satire, a morality, a moral exemplum, and an unfinished play.[104] Its structure, its characterization, and its lack of an ordinary human dimension all testify to its being of a different kind from Shakespeare's other tragedies or comedies. Clearly, it is a further examination of the beast-god dichotomy, but I lean towards the opinion that it is unfinished because it is difficult to interpret. Shakespeare, in his mature years, was always so *sure*. Even when he was stretching the dramatic forms and conventions of his period, when he did things that two hundred years of critics howled about, when he attacked the beliefs of his culture, and even when he attacked his own, he had an energy and assurance that swept through the material, bringing it to life and simply drowning out pedantic objections. I do not see this assurance in *Timon*. But that may be because of my own blindness.

The problem (for me) boils down to this: Timon attempts to live as a god in the first half of the play, and as a beast in the second half. Neither, of course, succeeds. But did Shakespeare intend to show Timon as flawed in his godlike phase, operating, in all his benevolence, out of the masculine principle alone, and therefore undermining his own acts? Or did he intend to show Timon as incarnating both gender principles in the first phase, and being hybristic only in that he does not understand that men are not gods, and thus, their resources run out? I incline to the first, and will make my case out for it, but with the very lack of assurance I attribute to Shakespeare.

The situation at the opening is like that in *Coriolanus*. Timon is a powerful (through wealth, not prowess) and admired figure in his city, one who seems to live to support and protect his fellow citizens. In this play too, the god-beast imagery is pervasive, although *Timon* contains more allusions to beastliness—especially to dogs—than any other of Shakespeare's dramas.[105] (It is surely not accidental that James Joyce, that most subtle reader of Shakespeare, used the palindrome god-dog as a theme in *Ulysses*.) The critics too are pretty well split along god-dog lines: some see Timon as a noble soul attempting to create in his city the harmony and grace of the Golden Age; some find him generally reprehensible.[106]

It is my own tendency to find Timon reprehensible (mainly because I do not like the play) that worries me. Far more than any other tragic hero of Shakespeare's, Timon is not a person but a vehicle of values. It is therefore possible to see him as a well-intentioned idealizer of humankind, and then as a perverted scorner of humankind. There is no norm in the play, but there is no norm in *Troilus and Cressida*, in *Hamlet*, in *Measure for Measure*, *Antony and Cleopatra*, or *Coriolanus*, except ourselves, the values we bring with us into the theater. It is easiest, however, to see this tragedy as a savage attack on humans for not being the ideals Timon imagined they were, because the play comes most alive in his speeches of savage hatred. In other words, if the power of the poetry is considered an element in interpretation—as it must be—*Timon* is a savage attack more than it is anything else.

But, if we use the standards developed in the course of this study, *Timon of Athens* shows the texture of the best and worst the masculine principle can accomplish without a complementary principle. In this perspective, its two halves comprise portraits of the benevolent and malevolent sides of the masculine principle, thus dividing it in the way the feminine pole is usually divided in Shakespeare. And in both aspects, it is woefully lacking, and essentially antilife.

Again, the hero transcends nature. Like Coriolanus, he attempts to transcend not just *natura* but human nature. Timon himself articulates this: "Not nature / (To whom all sores lay siege) can bear great fortune / But by contempt of nature" (IV, iii, 6–8). He claims, in the first half, to give purely out of love; he insists, in the second half, that he gives purely out of hate. But whatever he feels, the consequences of his giving are remarkably the same in the two halves. The world beats a path to his door; he does some good and some harm (to the individuals involved); but the ultimate result of his giving out of love is his rejection by Athens, and the ultimate result of his giving out of hate is a real change—a revolution of morality—in Athens. Implicit in this is the notion that love, the feminine principle, cannot accomplish what power, the masculine principle, can.

But the deck is stacked. Timon finances the attack of Alcibiades upon the city. Alcibiades, accidentally, proves to have mercy and justice in his mind, but one could not count on that given Timon's misjudgment of his other friends. Just so, the ingratitude of the three men to whom Timon sends when he is in need seems accidental. It is true that ingratitude exists, but it is not found in everybody at all times. That *all* Timon's friends would refuse to help him violates probability. (Even a Spiro Agnew, a Nixon, found support in their declines.) Even given the competitiveness of Timon's bountifulness, and even if it were for all the wrong reasons—the desire to "out-god" Timon, say—someone would be likely to help him. And later on, Alcibiades and Flavius do try to do that. The events of the play seem arbitrary because they are not rooted in character.

This same complaint can be brought against other Shakespeare characters—against the Duke in *Measure for Measure*, say, or the easy forgiveness of Claudio in *Much Ado* and Angelo in *Measure for Measure*. The problem in *Timon* is that *no one* seems to have a comprehensible character except perhaps Flavius. There is no necessary connection between the Timon of the first half and that of the second.

Timon of Athens seems to be pure "myth," that is, a dramatization of a system of values quite disconnected from character, motivation, or "realistic" probability. Things happen simply because they are necessary to the mythic, the encoded vision of the playwright. Thus, the irrelevance to the city of Athens of Timon's love or hate is very significant. It survives, whatever he does. Looking at the play in this way, it seems a parable for the greater efficacy of scourging than affection and respect to create reformation.

But there are elements that challenge such a reading.

At first glance, Timon's benevolence seems utterly generous and loving. If there is a tinge of self-satisfaction at "the display of his own munificence," why should there not be? [107] It seems puritanical in the extreme to deny humans pleasure in their own actions, and "self-gratulation" for a kind act is surely more beneficial to society than for an unkind one. There is some suggestion in the text that Timon sees himself as a godlike figure whose bounty is endless, but there is nothing inherently "evil" about that either, although it is delusive. Timon seems to harm no one by his delusion. He supports painting, poetry, and the military—or at least, an underpaid soldier. He would support philosophy if Apemantus would permit it, and in fact does, by providing the philosopher with grist for his mill. He helps a friend—Ventidius—and a trusted servant—Lucilius. These are entirely laudable acts.

Some of his acts, however, seem less laudable. What is the benefit to society of forcing jewels on those who already have them, of feasting the well-fed to surfeit, of refusing to allow any gift to be reciprocated without immediately outdoing it? Timon gives unnecessary things to people who need nothing. His benevolence is not aimed at the poor (except the philosopher, whose poverty is voluntary and one senses, fashionable), although there must be poor people in Athens, and the man who wrote Lear and Coriolanus would not be likely to overlook that. In addition, there is no reciprocity possible with Timon, despite his talk of "a bond in men" (I, i, 144).[108] But the belief that one cannot be truly said to give if one also receives is the reverse form of saying what Timon says later in the play, that all of creation is a series of acts of thieving.[109] If giving is a form of taking, receiving is a form of giving. Without the possibility of reciprocity, Timon's bounty becomes for the callous merely an expected reward, and for the sensitive an act "that offers a temptation to throw off the rather stifling burden it imposes."[110]

In the second half of the play, Timon still gives. He gives gold to Alcibiades to help him in his war against Athens. But the war proves to be a beneficial act in changing the moral dimension of the city. He gives money to the prostitutes, with moot consequences. His words and gift to the thieves operate to reform them—again, despite his intentions. He does Flavius "good" but with conditions that poison the gift, and he turns away the one thing that could save him could he recognize it—loyal affection, love.

At no time does Timon seem concerned with the community as a whole, as those critics believe who see him as attempting to create a golden age of learning, charity, and ease in Athens. He is concerned with his image in his own eyes, and with his friends' relation to him— not with their relation to each other. Timon is not evil or pompous or even excessively self-aggrandizing. He is simply unaware of a vital dimension of experience. Lacking it, he does the best he can to create a substitute for it—an imitation of love and harmony and centeredness.

It is, however, impossible to be sure of Shakespeare's intentions in this matter. On the one hand, he does not show Timon's bounty corrupting the characters of his friends. He does not show Ventidius feeling crushed at Timon's unwillingness to accept a return of his gift; nor his other friends learning to take Timon's bounty for granted. But on the other hand, there are things simply lacking in the play. An entire realm of experience is missing: women, family ties, children, nature in both its splendor and in the dung so prominent in *Antony and Cleopatra*, the dung that fertilizes and stinks and prevails. There is no feminine principle in the play unless we are meant to find it in Timon. I for one do not. Neither Timon nor his friends understand that mutuality, which is equality, is a necessary condition for friendship. They understand adoration of a superior—with worship and flattery; and contempt for an inferior—with scorn and denials. In keeping with this, Timon does not recognize the true love which is offered him by his servants—perhaps because they *are* servants. Like Lear, Timon confuses personal power (lovableness) with political power. He cannot be re-formed as long as he holds political (in this case economic) power.

Because he seems to believe that he is above, beyond, ordinary human needs, Timon is like Coriolanus: he finds subjection to ordinary conditions intolerable, and will not listen to Flavius' warnings. Thus his behavior (like that of Coriolanus) is totally self-absorbed and encompassed by self. His main need is to disguise from himself that he could need anything. His real battle is with humanness itself. (The first half of the play stages itself in my mind against the glitter of foil, with shimmering metallic costumes and adornments, and nothing recognizably natural in sight. Even the food is comprised of elaborately disguised ingredients.)

Coriolanus dies without really acknowledging that he is human and has needs. His giving in to his mother is done in a grim and grudging way; she does not win him over to her position. Rather she beats him down to it because she knows his nature. His emphasis, in the speeches following his capitulation to her, is not on recognition of the women's human concern and sympathy for the city, but on how much Rome owes them, how powerful they are to have made *him*, Coriolanus the hero, "sweat compassion" (V, iii, 196) when all the swords of Rome could not stop him. He concentrates, in short, on items that are inverted self-praise. He defensively asserts his "manliness" at the moment when he feels he has surrendered it.

Timon does not die with his delusions intact. When his money runs out, and so do his friends, when he can no longer imagine that he is godly, transcending nature and human need, he has no human base to support him. He turns against the foil and glitter and the lie they represent, and turns to the very thing that underlay his delusion: fear and hatred of nature, including human nature. Thus, although no women figure significantly in the first half of the drama (the only women to appear are the dancers. They may function as an idealizing, through art, of the sexuality which the prostitutes of the second half represent in a "perverted" way [111]), nearly his first words of attack are directed to women, although his intention is to harm men: "Matrons, turn incontinent!" (IV, i, 3).

Timon moves verbally, then physically, into nature. But what a nature! It holds nothing but diseases, rot, and infection. It yields only inert gold and a mean root, nothing nourishing and pleasant. It "engenders the black toad and adder blue, / The gilded newt and eyeless venom'd worm" (IV, iii, 181–182). Women figure largely in his curses, strangely, considering their absence from the play. So do babies. The "feminine" part of humankind is seen largely as full of disgusting impurity and contagious diseases.

Men are his major objects of hate, however, as he catalogues what feels like every moral wrong ever committed. He never moves, as Lear does, to a larger perception of human wrong, to a perception of political or economic inequity as itself an injustice. He never extends his attack from human beings to human social arrangements. He probes causes less deeply than the play does.

Yet Timon's speeches in the second half of the play are the most —perhaps the only—vital things in it. With them, the play comes alive. It seems almost as if it existed in order that they might be uttered. The effect of this is to make the second half feel truer than the first. In a way it is. The shimmering, bejeweled, cultured, and graciously polite world of Athens is a disguise. Civilization was created to transcend and to mask the naked dying wretchedness that is the human condition. Timon's hate is real, deeply felt, in a way his love is not.[112]

He ends immersed in precisely what he has feared and loathed: his naked hungry body roots in hard unyielding ground for something edible; he senses all around him the terrifying and ugly elements of nature; he senses within him all the vicious elements of human nature. Trying to do good, Timon aims for godliness; trying to do harm,

Timon aims for beastliness: he achieves neither. He does not have control over the consequences of his actions in either case.

And, as with other of Shakespeare's plays, the only norm must be provided by the audience, who may see the foolishness of his first phase, who surely see the narrowness of his second. Throughout the tragedies, Shakespeare sought a way of seeing experience that was not divided in such a way as to constrict human possibilities. Failing in that, he, like Timon, proceeded to attack the value structures that did exist. That do exist.

VI
A NEW SYNTHESIS

11

The Romances

Pericles, Cymbeline, The Winter's Tale, and The Tempest

In recent decades, Shakespeare's romances, which had earlier been seen as manifesting a diminishment of his poetic powers, have been read with new attention. Gradually these plays have been drawn out from under the shadow cast by the tragedies; they are seen now not as inferior versions of earlier plays, but as existing in a mode of their own. Although there remains much critical disagreement as to the quality, unity, and major focus of these four plays, there is near universal agreement about their mood. The plays are valued for their beauty of language and a spirit of reconciliation, rather than for brilliant characterization or concise structure. They seem to represent a kind of peacemaking with the world.[1]

The elements that are reconciled in these plays are variously described. Northrop Frye sees a synthesis of the "green world" with the real one; S. L. Bethell, of the natural and the supernatural; E. M. W. Tillyard, of different planes of reality; Mark Van Doren, of "tears and integrity"; and John Danby of the "rational" and the "irrational," which he elsewhere describes as "manliness and fortitude" with "creaturely dependence."[2]

From the perspective of this study, the elements which oppose each other in these plays are of course the masculine and feminine principles, and the major effort of the plays is to rearrange the relations between them. The early and middle comedies include some "masculine" plays, which present the texture of worlds in which the feminine principle is weak or absent, but most of them deal with "feminine" worlds. The problem plays—as well as *Much Ado*—show the two gender principles as antagonistic. There is no real synthesis of the poles in these plays—in two the feminine principle is destroyed or missing; in two, it triumphs, but after struggle so bitter as to render its victory exhausted. In the tragedies, there may be antagonism towards the feminine principle, but there is no real fight: the pole is defeated quickly in the action of the play, or it is eradicated before the action even begins.

In the romances, the feminine principle is reasserted, but, as in *Antony* and the two problem comedies, it is being hounded by the masculine. The situation is one of outright war. The conclusion the playwright aims for, however, is that bitterly discussed and bitterly won in *All's Well*: the supremacy of the feminine, rather than the masculine principle. Each play provides a different form, but all of them are experiments in achieving a vision in which "feminine" values are triumphant within the world of earthly power.

All four of the romances pit males against females or "feminine" characters, and split their focus between the two groups. In all four, the male element is powerful in a worldly way, the female element is not. And the developments of plot lead to an opposition between the two that is the moral equivalent of war.

In structure too, the plays combine the linear, plotted or highly characterized form of the tragedies with the circular, associational form of the comedies.[3] In addition, all four are written in a new mode —the mode of dream. Some dream events are logical and linear, as when dream characters behave precisely as their living counterparts would, or when the dreamer, or dream self, performs actions in a detailed and chronologically realistic way, just as one would in life. More often, however, dream events are associational, illogical, circular, and disconnected from earthly necessities like the force of gravity, time and space, unchanging physical shape. The romances are shot through with dream devices like projection, surrogation, and transformation. They also have the moral simplicity of surface dream structure; that is, although a dream as a whole usually deals with an ambiguous moral and emotional situation, the figures or images on its surface are morally simple. A figure who threatens the dreamer or his / her surrogate is evil because it is *felt* as evil: no explanation for that evil

or ominousness is required, none is offered.[4] Although a dream invariably offers an emotional truth, there may be no motivation, no chain
of causalities, and no "reasonable" sequence of events. This is the form
of the romances as well.[5]

As we saw in discussing the comedies, the focus of a "feminine"
play is anarchic: no single figure dominates the rest as occurs in the
tragedies. There may be a major figure, usually a female, but she is
only major. She shares the focus with other single figures and groups.
The action is the gradual merger of these groups into a society; the
texture of the play is associational rather than linear.

In the romances, breadth of focus characterizes "feminine" segments of the plays—for example, the events at the court of Simonides
in *Pericles*, Imogen's travels in *Cymbeline*, the sheepshearing scene in
The Winter's Tale. In all of these, attention is removed from the major
character in order to introduce minor characters who have only an
oblique connection with the major figure. They may have relevance to
the plot—as does the supposed shepherd-father of Perdita, the lost
brothers of Imogen—but the attention given them and their world is
not mainly for the sake of the plot, but rather to offer a vision of a
different arrangement of society, a different texture of experience.

But there are also segments of the plays which are linear and
plotted and somewhat logical. Thus, the jealousy of Leontes is uneasily
motivated and can be called illogical—as jealousy in life often is. But
once it is accepted as a given, this jealousy and the rage and hate that
accompany it, Leontes' behavior is logical, causal; one thing follows
another realistically. In addition, the romances do contain clearly
dominant figures. In *Pericles*, the hero and Marina are really the only
important characters; in *The Winter's Tale*, Leontes and Perdita are
dominant. Imogen is central in *Cymbeline*, but the opposition of that
play is between the heroine and an entire set of males, of whom the
King is only one, and not the major one at that. And Prospero is utterly
dominant in *The Tempest*; struggling against a set of external figures,
males, and a set of internal figures, who are male in exterior ways, but
"feminine" in import.

Thus on every level of the structure, the romances combine "masculine" and "feminine" characteristics. This combining effort occurs
on the level of values as well. The major problem in each of these plays
is dual; it is the restraining of the extremes of each principle. Consequently the subject of the romances is dual: sex and power. These are
the elements most resistant to harmonious visions of society, most
assertive and intractable to expressive orders. (Expressive order, as

described earlier, is an arrangement permitting the greatest freedom consonant with living together to all members of a society. It is the opposite of impositional or oppressive order, which is decided upon by one man or group, and forced on a society.)

Sex is the most important subsurface theme in the romances. Whether it appears as romantic love or "animalistic" lust, sex must be regulated, and lust, desire, or appetite must be purged from the feminine principle if it is to be exalted into the status Shakespeare desires to give it.[6] Without its erotic component, the feminine principle is "divine," and can properly be deemed "higher" than the masculine principle with its worldly concerns.

But power too must learn to renounce, or at the very least restrain, its individual willfulness. And how the powerful learn this is the very meat of these plays. When they do, they submit themselves to the "divine" qualities of the feminine principle, thus incorporating it into themselves. This achievement is the vision Shakespeare is working towards. When it is accomplished, it comprises the best possible arrangement of moral categories, and may be called justice.

It may seem that such an integration occurs in the middle comedies as well, and this is true. But in the comedies, potentially tragic actions are made revocable by the disguise convention, and potentially destructive language is made revocable by turning it into play, equivocation. There are disguises in the romances too, and many transformations and overlays, but the potential harmfulness of sex and power is not always buffered. Tragic events do occur; unforgivable words are spoken. The full malignant capacity of power and sex is not evaded. To create a synthesis of the gender principles, to create a vision of a harmonious society under such conditions, is far more difficult.

It may seem that the power world is shown in full force in some of the comedies—*Merchant*, for instance. But this is not true. The worlds of Belmont and Venice remain separate all the way through. Shylock is a Jew, which is to say, an illegitimate; all the legitimate world of Venice is on Antonio's side. And Portia defeats Shylock not by offering a different vision of life—although she tries to do this, in the mercy speech—but by supersubtle Venetian thinking, that is, by worldly means. In the early and middle comedies, the characters can integrate their society by evading or transforming the power world. This does not happen in the problem comedies or in the romances.

In all of the romances except *Pericles*, the power world is very much in evidence and is in outright conflict with "feminine" values. The major problem facing an author, and especially a playwright, who wishes to show these two forces together, is the undramatic nature of the feminine principle. Being eternal, it is static; being interior, it does not provide much movement. Qualities of well-being, harmony, love, and elation, although they are doubtless known to most humans, are easily sentimentalized (partly because of the low status of the feminine principle).

In addition, one cannot discuss feeling without subjecting it to analytic, "rational," linear dissection which instantly destroys or transforms it. And feeling, in Shakespeare's times and in ours, is less legitimate than action. Sidney wrote in *The Apology* that poetry (which is the language of feeling) would teach proper action. In *The Arcadia*, he subjected his heroes to situations in which they would learn feeling, but the intention of their study was to become good princes. Thus, feeling is the means; proper action is the end. Shakespeare was attempting something far more difficult and unusual in these plays; he depicted worlds in which action leads to feeling which leads to action which leads to *proper feeling*. Only in this way can the feminine principle take its proper place (within the traditional division of experience) as the true end of human life.

Nevertheless, drama requires conflict, action, and does not lend itself easily to the depiction of the feminine principle. It is difficult to dramatize the nourishing, healing effects of natural beauty, compassion, and social rapport. What can provide such effects are music, dance, and lyric poetry, and significatory passages such as visions of supernatural beings, or dreams. The romances contain such elements to a greater extent than other Shakespeare plays, and their imagery is dominated by nature and sense impressions.[7] Whether or not Shakespeare was influenced by the fashion of the early seventeenth century, his use of song, masque, dream, and vision in these plays was dictated organically, by the necessities of his purpose.

If it is difficult to dramatize the beauty and (magnetic) power of a "feminine" world, it is even more so to envision a world in which that principle dominates its opposite. Dante accomplished this by brilliant and metaphoric language that radiates light and love over his masculine, hierarchical *Paradiso*. Because worldly power is so evident and so intractable, writers who wish to depict a different aspect of experience often simply turn their backs on power: the result is a sentimentalized portrait of life. What Shakespeare tried to do in these plays was show a state of being in which felicity is strived for and attained, but not through the usual means of striving, not by effort, achievement, prowess, authority, or possession. The establishment of law and order, the founding of a hierarchy, the grasping of property, rights, or rank are supposed to bring felicity, but as Shakespeare has demonstrated in the tragedies, they do not. Originally rationalized as the means to the "feminine" ends of life, the protectors and guarantors of those ends, masculine values are in fact totally antagonistic to and destructive of "feminine" ends. Thus, the action necessary to achieving the true ends of life—continuation and felicity—is the partial renunciation of masculine values, and their subordination to feminine ones.

The means Shakespeare uses to teach his male power-figures this lesson he has used before. The powerful male will learn to place second those values he has been taught to uphold—authority, status, possession, legitimacy—only by being deprived of the feminine values he has no respect for and takes for granted. In Leontes, Othello is given a second chance; less obviously, Macbeth and his ambition are given another chance through the characters of Cymbeline and Alonso. The feminine principle is exiled in the romances, just as it is in the tragedies; but in these plays, it endures its exile, while the males suffer its absence. That which is precluded from active power can manifest its power only by its absence.[8]

This device is not unique to Shakespeare. Sidney shows the two exemplary princes in his *Arcadia*, Pyrocles and Musidorus, learning to be governors by two means—acting and suffering. The major suffering each undergoes is to be forced into a position of "feminine" helplessness. They must endure the humiliation of diminished status—one as a lowly shepherd, the other as a woman. (The latter disguise would no doubt have been intolerable had Sidney not made Pyrocles an Amazon, entitled to carry a sword and use it.) Both suffer from a variety of sexual advances they cannot actively repel; both suffer from the chaste constancy of their beloveds. And they suffer from the eye cast upon them by society as a whole, from not being, for a time, the legitimate, the right, the powerful. Neither prince (within the unfinished work) *overcomes* this diminishment (although they have some time off for fun and games in a free-swinging style): they endure it.

Similarly, Spenser emphasizes the necessity of suffering as well as acting in the process of perfecting his heroes. Each hero-knight undergoes a humiliation proper to his/her particular excellence. Even his most perfect hero-knight, Britomart, the knight of chastity, is humiliated, although her suffering is an internal stroke—she learns what it is to be looked at as a sex object, and she learns how passive and helpless it is to love without requital. The male hero-knights, however, suffer externally as well—being overcome, imprisoned, feeling surrounded by a world hostile to their values. And all of them attain integrity by enduring their humiliation. They do not conquer: they survive it.

And this is the pattern in the romances: the powerful males learn the limits of worldly power by suffering. As they learn that worldly power cannot command the elements, or rather, cannot create felicity, they also learn to give respect and legitimacy to the values which can. Once they accomplish this seeing, moral life falls into balance. Except for that snake in the grass, sex. It is a snake that requires continuous scotching.

The sexually opposed figures in these plays are fathers and daughters rather than husbands and wives. Four wives—that is mature, maternal, and sexual figures—do appear, but they follow the usual Shakespearean pattern for treatment of such figures: the two "good" ones are locked away for their most fruitful years; the two "evil" ones attempt harm, are thwarted, and disappear. The benign females, Thaisa and Hermione, are precluded from having any effect beyond childbearing on their worlds; the malign females, Dionyza and Cymbeline's nameless Queen, are not locked away, and therefore move into the "masculine" principle, doing, or attempting to do grave injury.

The daughter figure is not as charged for Shakespeare; in the nubile virgin he could envision sexuality without utter horror. But the daughter figure bears another threat—that of incest. Incest is generally regarded as the "worst" sexual act (that is, if one limits the term *sexual* to those acts not involved with violence, which have another character). But incest also functions as a complex metaphor for the two "sins" that lie at the root of these plays. Since it is involved with the power and authority of the father, and his lust for his child, it combines abuse of power with abuse of sex. It thus stands as a unified symbol for both elements that threaten the moral arrangement of society, and it appears, in some guise, in every one of the romances.[9]

This is accomplished by the use of surrogates, a device that occurs in the romances to a degree unequaled in the tragedies or the comedies. Reading the plays as dream, in a gestalt manner, we find many overlappings of father and brother figures. Characters live and die for each other; they work like people in a relay race, spelling each other in pursuit of, or in the attempt to fix (permanent possession), or in persecution of the single, shining, "feminine" ideal.

Thus, although the romances contain major figures (in the style of tragedy), those figures are sometimes really only aspects of a quality or position. Imogen is opposed not just by Cymbeline, but by Posthumus, Iachimo, and Cloten as well. Prospero is troubled by, and attempts to control the entire dramatis personae of the play. What is fixed in all the romances is the essential dichotomy. And what happens in all of them is that the male, human, powerful figure learns to give up some control over what is not controllable, some will to possession over that which is destroyed by possession. This is true even of *The Tempest*, in which no female figure has importance, because Prospero has incorporated both gender principles into himself with some effort and much chagrin, and must fight off both that which is outside—the courtiers—and that which is inside—Ariel and Caliban.

In all of the romances, female chaste constancy is implicit in the idea. But the romances differ from the comedies in that responsibility for maintaining chastity is no longer placed entirely on the female. Nonetheless, the ideal moral arrangement that obtains at the conclusion of these plays is dependent upon that continuing Shakespearean ideal; indeed, he seems to carry it further in some of these plays, positing heroines who are charming and lovable, but who are essentially without desire.

In sum, what happens in the romances is extraordinarily interesting, whether one finds them aesthetically pleasing or not. (I do.) They represent, after all, Shakespeare's final approach to a dichotomy that fascinated and disturbed him throughout his career.

Pericles

Pericles, the poorest of these plays, is in some ways the most interesting. Whether Shakespeare found it, repaired it, or revised it is less important than that he used it. His hand is clearly on it. The early acts may be his own youthful effort or the work of someone else, but he let them stand. In this respect they are his: they served his purpose.

Pericles is clearly not a drama of character. It is symbolic and must be read as we read dreams. Much of the play is depiction of interior life.[10] Pericles, the human wanderer in an alien world, is male, significantly. In all of these plays, the human figure, the morally fallible and reparable, is male.

The use of Gower and his limp verse in the Prologues has a complex effect. The poet's antiquity confers legitimacy and authority on subject matter which might be considered too scandalous for the stage. His rhymed couplets and short lines frame the scenes formally, and thus lead us to see them from a distant perspective, contained in stiff

artifice. And the stiltedness of the verse, its ample use of filler, emphasize the lack of animation in the play itself. Altogether, the effect of
Gower and his verse is to locate the action in the realm of ritual and
myth, to emphasize the symbolic and traditional aspects of scandalous
material.

In his first speech, Gower underlines the age and authority of his
authors and his tale; he then moves immediately to the central fact of
the play: incest. The scene which follows, in Antiochus' court, is highly
ritualistic. The incest material is approached from a great distance,
and its realistic underpinnings are totally concealed. There is no suggestion of flesh or even sensation in the scene. There is little emotion:
the guilty fear of both Antiochus and Pericles is presented in stiff,
formal, cliché-ridden verse. There is no probing of the act such as we
would expect from the author of *Hamlet* and *Lear*. Incest exists in this
court, and incest is evil. It is evil because it is. The reasons given—and
there are reasons given—are, to say the least, peculiar. Probably, however, no one in the audience would challenge the moral condemnation. Nor does Shakespeare. He uses the stilted scene as if he found
the material too explosive to touch.

Incest is sex at its most desirable and least accessible to regulation,
despite the near-universal taboo described by Sir James Frazer and
psychologized by Freud. For that taboo was against mother-son incest,
a kind extremely rare in history or in the modern world. Since there is
not an equivalent taboo against father-daughter incest, we must deduce the other taboo to be political in nature, a forbidding of mother-
son unification seen as a threat to the power and possession of the
father.

Incest of all sorts, however, has been in bad odor for several
thousand years, and especially in Christian cultures. Nevertheless,
father-daughter incest is not infrequent, even in sophisticated societies. It would appear to be very attractive despite its taint of sin and/or
sickness. In father-daughter incest, the male is invariably the instigator; sometimes it involves very young children; often it is accompanied
by physical or moral force (authority). Thus, father-daughter incest
combines abuse of power with sexual abuse and is a prime symbol for
misuse of both gender principles.

The sense of forbiddenness increases the glamour of the scene in
Antiochus' court. The Princess, nameless and almost speechless, radiates brilliance and the glamour of forbidden fruit. The formality and
static nature of the scene make it into a set piece, a figure in masque,
a Spenserian emblem. The glittering beauty of the Princess, the forbid-

den nature of the act, and the risk—the severed heads of those who failed—all emphasize the attractiveness of incest. So does Pericles' guilty horror at discovering the secret: for he too desires the Princess and thus, implicitly, what the Princess represents.

His desire is rooted in eye and appetite. The fruit imagery with which the Princess is described, the "viol" imagery of Pericles' repudiation speech, underscore the Princess's existence as solely an instrument of pleasure for a male. This is important because it characterizes the particular appeal the act exerts: the suggestion is that in incest, beyond any other sexual act, the woman is utterly the creature of the man, created by him, formed by him, controlled by him. The highly erotic nature of this situation is suggested by a later poet, more explicitly, in the relation of Adam and Eve in John Milton's *Paradise Lost*.

The reasons given, in moralistic verse, for the unacceptability of incest are that it makes the father into a son (violation of status and role), and the daughter into an "eater of her mother's flesh." The second is peculiar, but neither reason makes much sense. The moral evil represented by incest, however, has probably never been fully analyzed, and is, to the neutral mind, difficult to fathom. It was no doubt not necessary for a playwright to explain why incest is evil to an audience already convinced of that. But it is important that the (in our terms) victim of the act—the daughter—is judged more strongly, in more abhorrent terms.

And the total effect of the scene is at odds with its explicit moral message. Father-daughter incest stands as a shimmering and utterly desirable horror, a fascinating abomination. The scene, only tenuously connected to the rest of the play through the plot, nevertheless casts its odd light on everything that follows it. Pericles' flight is supposed to be rooted in his fear of Antiochus' wish to silence him; his flight from Tyre is supposed to be rooted in his fear that Antiochus will make war against his kingdom. Not only is this behavior untypical of Shakespearean heroes, it is not especially logical. And Pericles continues to flee long after there is any necessity to fear Antiochus.

On the associational (rather than the logical, plotted) level, the entire movement of the play is a flight from the implications of the first scene. Antiochus and his daughter disappear from the play; even Thaliard ceases, within a few scenes, to be a significant factor; but the moral state depicted in the first scene is at the root of Pericles' situation.

There is critical debate about Pericles' relation to or responsibility for the incest; generally, Pericles is seen as a passive figure whose "fall" is merely an introduction to awareness of evil.[11] But such a reading negates the thrust of the entire play. If we read the play in a gestalt manner, Pericles' presence, his attraction to Antiochus' daughter, and his response indicate a complicity in the act: Pericles desires wrongly. And Pericles' later actions are performed out of guilt.

The Prince flees from what he knows will kill him (morally), but continues to live in fear and depression. The act of incest must therefore be seen as more significant than simply fornication with one's child (Pericles has no child): it is, as I indicated earlier, a prime symbol for sexual power that abuses both gender principles, and for a kind of sexuality that thrives on a position of dominance—*precisely the sort of sexuality that is inherent in the values of the masculine principle*. And Shakespeare's moral objection to this kind of sexuality is not that it dehumanizes, or depersonalizes the woman—as it is in our own time —but that it dehumanizes the man, turns him into a kind of monster who does not recognize the limits of power. Pericles' logical leap when he sees incest as near to murder as "flame to smoke" (I, i, 138)—a totally unrealistic connection, although justified in the event—demonstrates the playwright's associations. The sexuality implicit in the unmodified masculine principle is aggressive—rape. Incest is a version of rape complicated by the moral authority a father has over a child, but it is also a symbol of a kind of male sexuality which is aroused by childlike dependence and the sense of the female as merely body. It is a confusion of power and love in which power remains dominant, an effort, like Lear's, utterly to control the beloved, the love. This kind of sexuality is not uncommon, even in our own day.

If Pericles were looking only outward at the situation in Antiochus' court, fear would be a likely response. Once he has escaped from Antioch, he would be likely to feel anger, perhaps fear, but surely outrage. Instead he feels melancholy and terror: his condition seems less fearful than *tainted*: he must leave his kingdom lest it perish because of him, like the sinner who must be thrown overboard if the ship is to survive. Pericles feels guilt, and in his guilt, gives up the masculine principle, and the power it represents, entirely.

Interwoven with the action in the early acts of the drama is pedestrian moralizing on a variety of subjects. Both Gower and Pericles moralize against incest; Helicanus moralizes on flattery, and finds the flatterer more reprehensible than the flattered, the King or Prince (just as Antiochus' daughter is found more reprehensible— if less terrifying —than her father). Although this moralizing is conventional and political, it is also organic to the play: the flatterer, the subject, is guilty because he/she contributes to the delusions of power. Like the counselors leading the youthful Lear to believe he was everything, flattery and subordination of self to untrue ends are responsible for the self-aggrandizements of the powerful that lead them to forget their limitations.

There is moralizing also on grief, superfluity, and political wisdom in the first acts; there is frequent and unthinking reference to sin. The lack of imaginative and moral probing, especially in the first act, implies its composition by a mediocre mind. But something in this—and the next—act interested Shakespeare. The first act consists of a glittering vision of a violation of both gender principles, and a series of moral set pieces that sound like preceptual straws in a high wind. Pericles' behavior is consistent. He essentially abdicates the kingship of his country; he flees. At Tharsus, where he could use his Marshall Plan for the gaining of political advantage, he renounces any desire to conquer: he gives because what he has is needed; he gives out of the desire to nourish. He acts "feminine." At Pentapolis, he renounces his status, even his very identity. Evidently, conventional moralizing is not sufficient armor against the incest vision. What is required to eradicate the stain he feels is renunciation of power.

But renunciation of power-in-the-world is also the fall into mere humanness, into vulnerability and suffering. Power-in-the-world is supposed to confer on its possessor a privilege and shield against ordinary human vicissitudes. And so it does, in many areas: but not in the realm of the emotions. Departing from legitimacy, Pericles enters the world of suffering. He is sometimes described as passive, but in fact this is an active enterprise: its activeness is symbolized by his wanderings, as is typical of romance plots.

His opening speech in act II emphasizes his vulnerability, as do his remarks to the fishermen. He does not claim rank, name, or any status. He does not demand to be taken to the King, or promise future reward for present assistance. He does not in any way put himself forward: he begs as a man, a mere mortal. The fairy-tale-like discovery of the armor is also symbolic. Having given over legitimacy conferred on him by worldly hierarchy, Pericles is sustained by the legitimacy conferred on him by his "blood," his heritage. He is a prince, the son of princes. Nature provides the armor he needs to protect himself, to enter the world again. It grants him the uniform essential to such a return, but it is rusty, unknown armor, the trappings of anyman.

The competition at the court is a parallel to the competition in

Antioch, but it is purged of all abusive elements. In the first place, it is not a competition for Thaisa's hand in marriage—a kind of contest that emphasizes the object-ness of the woman who is won by the aggressiveness—whether physical or mental—of the man. This ceremony is a celebration in Thaisa's honor and its competitive aspects are minimized. No one will be killed for losing; no one will be rewarded with a female body for winning. Simonides and his motherless daughter also parallel Antiochus and his, but their relation is free of the taint of sexual connection. Indeed, Pericles' movement from the first scene through the end of act II is a movement from the perversion to the ideal, and the entire depiction of Simonides' court is a portrait of the ideal.

The ceremony is designed for pleasure, rather than for a linear goal. Thus the scene concentrates on the mottoes rather than on action or character. Each of the mottoes focuses on love and power set in proper balance. The first, *Lux tua vita mihi*, suggests that Thaisa's beauty (the magnetic power of the feminine principle) is the very source of life. *Piu por dulzura que por fuerza*, sweetness is stronger than force, can be seen as true only if one limits its application to the emotional life, but there it *is* true. *Me pompae provexit apex*, with its device, a wreath of chivalry, depicts the balance chivalry aims for—a blending of power with courtesy. (Courtesy, a bending quality, and one designed for the well-being of others, is "feminine.") The crown of triumph in chivalry requires courtesy.

The remaining mottoes refer to the paradoxical quality of love, which is aroused and extinguished by the same force; the testing of love; and the hope of the lover, Pericles. This procession is not a contest, like the testing of Portia's suitors in *The Merchant of Venice*: the mottoes are not judged right or wrong, better or poorer. As in a procession in *The Faerie Queene* or a medieval romance, the mottoes encircle the subject matter of the play emblematically. It is a ceremony designed to present the texture of courtly life at its best—concerned with pleasure, courtesy, and beauty, dedicated to love, the shorthand way of saying the ends of the feminine principle. It is fitting, therefore, that the physical contest take place offstage and be granted little attention; it is not central to the scene, although it is necessary to the plot since it demonstrates Pericles' natural excellence.

The banquet scene is written in a tone similar to that of the motto ceremony. The little it offers in furtherance of the plot is accomplished within a few lines. Like the emblem scene, it is exemplary, and depicts courtesy in action. Keeping love and power in proper balance, the

King restrains his power over the knights by affection for them; this issues in a harmonious and pleasant court—or world.

The next scene switches back to Tyre, but it is similar to the scenes in Pentapolis. Helicanus and the aristocrats of Tyre are aware of some lack, some mismanagement in the kingdom because of their absent prince. But instead of rebelling and contending out of ambition, all subordinate themselves, out of love for Pericles, to Helicanus' wise advice. Again affection and respect temper power.

The "wooing" scene, if one can call it that, has the same exemplary quality. Although Thaisa clearly loves Pericles, who presumably returns the feeling, neither has made any overture to the other. There is no manifestation of desire, no assertive courting. Both have submitted their lustful natures to regulation, have renounced willful action. They love "properly"; Pericles has learned to restrain desire. Thaisa has informed her father of her feelings; he in turn tests Pericles, who proves, despite his continuous humility, to have inner stability: he is humble but not servile; he will not be pushed to either bravado or cravenness. Thaisa on the other hand is assertive within bounds; she stretches the rule of obedience to a father only in order to claim the husband she wants. This is an act permitted to all Shakespearean heroines (implicitly). Both Thaisa and Pericles, then, carry within themselves a balance of masculine and feminine qualities suitable to their genders; both restrain the extremes of those qualities. And although Simonides as father (not as king) is a tyrant, like most Shakespearean fathers, he is also able to see and value qualities of character not dependent on status and wealth.[12]

Thus act II sets up a world that is exemplary and ideal. It is also, unfortunately, rather tame. There is nothing you can do with it except say "and they lived happily ever after." Pericles seems to have expunged the taint symbolized by incest by renouncing worldly legitimacy and willful sexuality: he finds a wife when he ceases to be a king. Thus he has achieved life in a paradise of balance. And it is at this point that Shakespeare seems to have picked up the play. He will lead the Prince back to the real world, the sea of impermanence, caprice, and power, in which his inner moral balance, achieved with suffering, will be tested against the power of nature and the power of humans who are not ideal.

From act III to the conclusion, there is a little conventional moralizing, and Gower's language becomes more vivid, less awkward, and nonmoralistic. In addition, Pericles ceases to be the major focus. The ordeal begins with a simultaneous birth and death which split apart what has been created. The particles return to their separated state. Pericles surrenders the newborn Marina to Cleon and Dionyza, and returns to his kingdom and to power; Thaisa, resurrected almost immediately, believes her husband dead, renounces the world, and becomes a votaress of Diana, implicitly renouncing sexuality. The focus shifts to the child who is the incarnation of their balance.

Dionyza and Cleon are the third (set of) parents in this play, the only one to contain a mother figure. Without foreshadowing or much logical foundation, Dionyza becomes the wicked stepmother of fairy tale. In the dream mode, the pair are Marina's parents in a different guise. The "true" parents are sensed by the girl, but they are in abeyance, invisible and unknown. Marina, child of chance, must learn to live in an unbalanced world.

And in the unbalanced world, the masculine principle is dominant; its values have extinguished those of its opposite. With only rudimentary explanation, Dionyza renounces pity, gratitude, and affection, and persuades Leonine to do the same. She brings Cleon into line as well. The murder is thwarted by an accident—the arrival of the pirates. With this event, Marina is moved into a position similar to that of her father when he arrived shipwrecked on the coast of Pentapolis: without the armor of paternal or conjugal protection, she is mere woman cast on strange shores. But it is a very different thing to be mere woman, not mere man. For the pirates and the panders to whom they deliver her, a female body is a commodity, an object to be rented and profited by. The world of commerce does not seem to be a world at war, but within it, the feminine principle is extinguished as successfully as in Macbeth's Scotland.

The language used to refer to the enslaved women emphasizes this situation: they are called *creatures*, *stuff*, *baggage*. Marina is called a *piece* and referred to as a piece of meat—*joint*. She wonders that the bawd is a woman, for Marina absolutely identifies femaleness with the inlaw feminine principle: for her the word *woman* includes the quality of *honesty*, chastity.

Marina's attitude underscores the politics of the play. The bawd in one way, Dionyza in another, have sold out the feminine principle. Without their participation, the evil that occurs would not be possible. The play suggests that women are largely responsible for the extinction of "feminine" values. Just as Antiochus' daughter is held more reprehensible than her father for their incest; just as the flatterer is held more responsible for the delusion of a prince than is the Prince himself, so here Marina's scornful sermonizing of the bawd and Boult reinforces the suggestion that the lowly are more responsible for abuses of sex (or power) than those in power. Women's job in this division of labor is to eschew sexuality.

Marina states the priorities of value women are expected to uphold. The brothel, she says, is the worst place in the world, its trade the worst on earth: she says nothing so strong when threatened with murder. Marina's stay in the brothel is a parallel to Pericles' stay in Antioch: each finds an illicit moral climate the ultimate horror. But unlike her father, Marina does not feel tainted by her sojourn in the brothel: it does not touch her because *she is not tempted by its values*, its life. There is no allure in the brothel scenes, because Marina is inviolate.

This is important, because it presumes that men and women have different sexual natures (which may be true), and that women can, by the power of will, extirpate sexuality entirely (which is not true). Or perhaps it is more accurate to say that "good" women do not have sexual natures at all: Posthumus, for instance, honors Imogen because she is cold. One has the sense that Shakespeare felt that sexuality was a door women could open or not, by will. Marina can be invulnerable in a way her father was not because she is female.

Marina retraces her father's ordeals, but with a difference. Placed in a house of illicit sex, she finds a way to escape, using considerable forcefulness rather than flight. Without station or familial legitimacy, she survives in the world on her native skills. Like her father, she dances well, but her equivalent to his ability to fight is her needlework, in which she "wounds" the cambric, but makes it "more sound / By hurting it" (IV, Prol., 24–25), an inlaw feminine transformation of assertiveness.

Above all, both Pericles and Marina stand fast, they endure, a "feminine" way of behaving, and the only way to deal with loss and sorrow. The difference between them is that Marina is not haunted by guilt, and so, although she has lost as much as her father has, she is not tormented.

The ambiguity in the character of Lysimachus cannot, I think, be resolved by the text. He is known at the brothel, he seems serious in his intention to buy sex. That he spits contempt at the bawd and Boult (and indirectly at Marina) does not mitigate against this—lust and guilt can and do coexist, and shame is frequently projected outwards as blame of the objects of lust or the providers for it. Lysimachus' later disavowal does not explain away his earlier unambiguous statements. Like the near-saint Pericles, Lysimachus is tainted. As a man, he is subject to sexual desire that it is women's responsibility to control. And so Marina does.

The last act presents the final balance of moral qualities the play is concerned with. "Thou . . . beget'st him that did thee beget" is a restatement of the accusation against Antiochus made in the opening —that he, a father, had become a son through incest. But here it is a statement of praise for Marina, salvation for Pericles. Pericles' endurance of suffering has purged him of the abusive elements of the power principle; Marina's steadfast chaste constancy purges *her father* of the taint of sexuality. Both daughter and father have dedicated themselves to the goals of the inlaw feminine principle, and Pericles is rewarded by heavenly music and a vision of Diana, the right goddess for this play. He puts aside his plans of vengeance and murder in order to obey her, and just as renunciation of power allowed him to win his wife the first time, it allows him to find her now.

Pericles never has to return to the extreme of the masculine principle, never has to kill Cleon (who bears the responsibility for his wife's act) any more than he had to kill Antiochus. The heavens take care of that. Villains die. The wages of sin is death. The suggestion strongly made is that the good do not die but live eternally in the cycle of nature and generations, happily ever after. This is the reward of those who choose to live granting highest value to the (purged—or castrated—depending on one's point of view) feminine principle. This principle can be dominant on earth because heaven takes over the role of scourger. So it is in fairy tales. So it is, often, in the inner life. Harmony within the self and with one's world can lead to a forgetfulness of injury which is equivalent to its eradication. In the inner life, love is justice.

Cymbeline

Cymbeline has less the aura of dream than *Pericles* has, but contains similar supernatural and fairy-tale elements. In many cases, motivation is scant: Cymbeline is a tyrant as a father and submissive as a husband because that is the way he is; his wife's wickedness is simply given. The feelings and state of the Belarius who kidnapped the princes are seemingly out of character with the Belarius we see, but they are also not open to question. There is one absolutely evil figure—the Queen; and one absolutely good figure—Imogen. They provide the moral absolutes of the play, but since they are both female (and the only females in the play), they also stand as exempla of female behavior. As usual, for a woman to move into power turns her into a demon; and utter goodness consists of chaste constancy combined with steadfast adherence to the male despite his behavior. The last quality is especially needed in this play.

For the males, who occupy the human realm, behave badly.[13] What a set of acts they perform! Cymbeline is dense and tyrannical and imprisons his daughter. Belarius kidnaps two children, princes. Guiderius kills a prince during a fight. Iachimo defames a woman's chastity (in a play-world in which chastity is all she has, and is the sine qua non of all excellence). Posthumus orders his wife's murder. Indeed, the entire action of the play is a series of actions performed by the Queen and various males to persecute and destroy the inlaw feminine principle—incarnated in Imogen.

Yet the rhetoric of the play does not condemn these males. Cymbeline is excused, at the end of the play, because he was under the influence of his wicked Queen, and because he, like Belarius and Iachimo, repents his deeds. Guiderius is excused because his true status is revealed. Posthumus condemns himself before he knows of Imogen's innocence, and does penance in the form of suffering. All of these males are forgiven; the condemnation of the play is reserved for Cloten, Cloten who does nothing at all.[14] (The Queen is condemned as well, but because she is not a human figure, and the condemnation is of a conventional sort, it is not very significant. It functions mainly to get Cymbeline off the hook.)

What is significant is that Cloten is damned as broadly and deeply as he is, for dense, arrogant, and ill-intentioned as the character is, he performs no act as cruel as those of the male "heroes." This is very strange: a villain, clearly marked one from the beginning, whose behavior is less villainous than that of the hero(es).

That for Shakespeare evil is the overthrow of reason by passion is a critical commonplace that has been discussed already.[15] As we have seen in discussing the tragedies, it is the most rational of Shakespeare's characters who are his villains. The single most common cause of damaging behavior in Shakespeare is a failure to respect or recognize the emotional life, the need of everyone (except Iago), no matter how powerful, for love in various forms—acceptance, respect, friendship, courtesy, and harmony. Power unsuffused by sensitivity and compassion, uncognizant of human need for community, is abusive power. In play after play, male power-figures learn to feel only when they learn to see others, and to see themselves as a result. What is emphasized, repeatedly in Shakespeare, is the human need for wholeness, remembrance of one's (and others') entire being, a being that needs power for self-protection and love for sanity, and who, in his search for invulnerability—impregnability—loses his humanness.

The behavior of the males in *Cymbeline* is in most cases dictated by feeling. Belarius kidnapped the boys in vengeance and rage; he has redeemed that act by his training of the princes, in which he has substituted natural for hierarchical legitimacy. The boys, who are idealized figures, good, noble, spontaneous, emotional, heroic, and able to recognize good from evil even when they are disguised (which both Imogen and Cloten are), are perfect incarnations of the synthesized gender principles. Given what we know of Cymbeline and his Queen, it is difficult to deplore this kidnapping, and Belarius is easily forgiven even though in actual life his crime is one of the most heinous imaginable.

Cymbeline is tyrannical, stupid, and insensitive. It is impossible to imagine him really governing a kingdom, and the conclusion promises otherwise. Since he is a father figure, he may not be criticized too severely: this is a comedy, after all. Thus surrogates are chastised for him, surrogates die for him. His tyrannical cruelty is paid for with the death of the Queen; his stupidity and insensitivity by the death of Cloten. Both are moral surrogates for the King.

Posthumus' errors are more complex. He operates out of emotion rather than reason when he marries Imogen, knowing that the King and Queen are opposed to the marriage. He operates out of reason rather than emotion, which involves love and faith, when he agrees to the bet and when he believes Iachimo's evidence. But he is responding to emotion—vengeance and possessive rage—when he orders Imogen's death. As his tirade against women shows, he kills or tries to kill not just Imogen but the inlaw feminine principle within himself. His repentance requires the reassertion of reason: female infidelity, terrible though it is in the Shakespearean world, does not deserve death. *This realization is unique in the canon.* Although the (seemingly) unfaithful Ephesian Antipholus would punish his (seemingly) unfaithful wife with only a beating, death or hell's pains are considered entirely appropriate punishment for Hero, Desdemona, Hermione, and Gertrude.

Posthumus' abuse of Imogen is redeemed partly by his self-punishment, and partly by the miscarriage of his plan: Imogen lives. It is, indeed, in her forgiveness of his order for her murder, her acceptance of his blow (Marina too forgives Pericles' striking of her), that he is fully redeemed. The price paid by females in the first three romances for the exaltation of the principle they represent is self-abasement to an extreme degree. The general treatment of Marina, Imogen, and Hermione by the power figures in their worlds is not really forgivable. The so-called divine forgiveness of these characters can be explained in not such divine terms: politically, such forgiveness is the action of utter dependents; in terms of the dramas, it is necessary to the terms in which the dramas are conceived. For in these, of all the comedies, irrevocable actions are carried out. For the gender principles to be synthesized after such actions, a superhuman forgiveness is required.

Errant or abusive as are many males in Shakespeare, no comedy except *The Tempest* contains such a collection of villainies; no play of Shakespeare's contains such a persecution of one person; and in no other play are all the worst villainies forgiven so easily. Even Iachimo, who operates totally out of the "reason" implicit in the masculine principle, is pardoned into life, which is to say, into grief and pain and the amending of conduct. Like Iago, Iachimo believes the "reasonable" worldly line that all women are basically unchaste, and functions out of competition and rivalry, out of having a goal that is linear and sacrificing truth to win it. Like Iago, he has little to gain from his effort to seduce Imogen except a cocky reinforcement of his claim that all women are unchaste, and an even more cocky assertion that it is he who can prove them so. But unlike Iago, Iachimo shows remorse and sorrow in his confession, offers the confession rather than lie, and accompanies it with expressions of torment.

Thus forgiveness is granted to those who can feel, regardless of the enormity of their behavior. The implication is that in a "feminine" world, which Cymbeline's Britain is, where the quality of life is more important than power or action, those who feel are forgivable. Cloten's sin is that he does not feel. He is dense and egotistical; he is insensitive to Imogen's feelings, to the attitudes of the courtiers, and is willing to go so far as to impose himself sexually on Imogen, to rape her. He does not see and does not care what others feel, and this is the worst sin in a feminine world. Passion, emotion, may produce terrible actions, but in this comedic world, it also produces remorse. Feeling, then, corrects its own excesses in Cymbeline's Britain. Cloten is incapable of such correction.

Feminine worlds, as we have seen, require masculine structures to protect them. In this play, that is the function of Rome. Thus, the Queen's defiance of Rome, offered out of her own ambition, is in this play "wrong." It is wrong, first, because the Queen has no business, being a woman, to act politically in the first place. The Queen is "masculine": she is ambitious, marries for status and power; takes over the power of the kingdom, and acts to preserve it and entail it to her son. She does not shrink from killing, although she attempts to do this in a "female" way (not a "feminine" way: "feminine" people do not kill at all)—through poison. Caius Lucius, as thin a character as the Queen, represents the best in "masculine" power, a Rome that encompasses and protects, tempering its power by courtesy and justice. Rebellion against Rome is equivalent, in this play, to revolt against a king.

In the foreground, Britain is feminine. The play opens with discussion of feelings—of unhappiness, love, marriage—and above all, praise for Posthumus. (Unfortunately for the play, this praise of Posthumus, which is repeated frequently throughout, and reaches hyperbolic grandeur in Iachimo's confession, is not borne out in the character, who does not appear, to this reader at least, to be especially attractive or noble or even interesting. Thus, the rhetorical line is not realized in the drama. This is true of Cloten as well. He is [rhetorically] universally damned, but the character seems hardly worth the trouble.)

Throughout the play, as throughout *Pericles*, the quality of life—feeling, sensitivity, love—matters far more than power, status, and hierarchy, and moral flexibility (within limits) is more important than "masculine" loyalty. Imogen chooses to marry below her rank; the young princes are brought up ignorant of their rank and of courtly ways; it is Imogen's self—and her chastity—that Posthumus loves, not her status. Pisanio neglects his bond of fidelity to Posthumus and evades committing murder out of feeling for Imogen; the doctor senses something awry in the Queen and lies to her; Caius Lucius is very feeling for a Roman general. Imogen's love for Posthumus leads her to retort very sharply to her father; his rage at her overflows; Posthumus nearly weeps at his parting from Imogen. It is, in short, a passionate world, a world in which a queen obsessed with power and a prince unable to feel are naturally misfits. The courtiers defer somewhat to Cloten, but unlike other courtiers in Shakespeare also speak ironically and downright insultingly to him when they advise him to change his shirt because he stinks. These courtiers are not flatterers: they value something other than power.

Because of the "feminine" nature of Cymbeline's Britain, it is necessary that it be protected by a "masculine" power. So it is that in *Cymbeline* alone of all Shakespeare's British plays, the autonomy and honor of Britain are not a major desideratum. Cymbeline, the inadequate ruler of a land of the inner life, gives over his power to his "masculine" Queen and challenges the outer structure. The conclusion, with its harmonious unison, reasserts the proper balance: Britain will be ruled in future by more sensitive princes, and pay to Rome an annual tribute that is no great sacrifice. In keeping with the overall theme of the play, that the two genders must learn to have faith in each other, and bend to the support of the other, so Cymbeline, after defeating Rome, decides to reverse himself, to submit to Caesar and pay "wonted tribute" (V, v, 462). The eagle that is Rome vanishes in the sky, just as power and power structures retreat to the fringes of emotional and personal life and stand as largely irrelevant to the radiance that is Britain.

But the radiance of Britain depends utterly on Iachimo's answer to Imogen's question—that is, on Imogen's chaste constancy.[16] Imogen totally dominates the action of this play. When she is not onstage, she is being talked about. She is the person of greatest importance to all the major characters: upon what she is and what she does depend the future of Cloten, the Queen, Cymbeline's kingdom and his happiness, Posthumus' very life, and eventually, the fates of the minor characters as well.

Her centrality to the play represents the centrality of the gender principle she represents to her world. For her world to hold, she must hold; for her to hold, her chaste constancy must hold. Thus Posthumus' long soliloquy maligning women (III, v), which seems extreme to some readers—although its sentiments should be familiar enough to readers of *Much Ado*, *Othello*, *Lear*, or *Hamlet*—is the core of the play. If this woman, who seems most honest, is not, no woman is. If no woman is, all men are bastards. Men who are bastards cannot be expected to be honorable. If those identified with the feminine principle do not uphold it, and in the process guarantee male legitimacy, there is no hope for harmony in the human race, and only tyranny will flourish.

But for the feminine principle to be central in a civilized world, it must submit itself to "masculine" fixing, making permanent. Thus, the action of *Cymbeline* consists of a series of attempts to control, manipulate, or possess Imogen and the qualities she represents. The King, the Queen, Cloten, Iachimo, and Posthumus each attempt this, and Imogen is increasingly hounded. Imprisoned first, then betrayed by Iachimo (and implicitly by Posthumus, since he loses faith in her), she escapes but is subjected to the Queen's poison, Cloten's intention to rape her, and Posthumus' order for her death. Only her brothers, raised in anarchic nature and unaware of the hierarchical aspects of the masculine principle, recognize, respect, and love her nature without trying to possess and control it.

There is a great amount of surrogation in this play. There is overlapping, in the first place. There are three father figures—Cymbeline, Belarius, and Caius Lucius; and four brother/husband figures—Posthumus, Cloten, Guiderius, and Arviragus. (Thus although incest is not prominent on the surface of the play, it lingers just below. Cymbeline's possessiveness of his daughter would be seen as incestuous if it appeared in a woman for her son.) Both Posthumus and Cloten have been raised as brothers to Imogen, and as each of the younger men adopts one side of the King—Posthumus his cruelty and Cloten his denseness—they become surrogates for him. The two people who attempt to kill Imogen are Posthumus and the Queen, who is a surrogate for Cymbeline in terms of responsibility for actions performed. And Cloten dies for Posthumus, even to the point of wearing his clothes.[17]

In sum, the play opens with a state of warfare between the gender principles. On one side are Cymbeline's power and tyranny, and his wife's ambition to secure her line, and her unscrupulousness. On the other hand is the love of Imogen and Posthumus. This warfare is so heightened and complicated and further divided that Imogen, the sole representative of the full inlaw feminine principle, is hounded and threatened, and indeed, does "die" and is mourned. If Cloten is the scapegoat for the play's moral condemnation, Imogen is the martyr to its moral ideals.

The Winter's Tale

Masculine power operates in the romances mainly in the domestic sphere. This is true of Shakespeare's work in general. Although male characters may be dukes, princes, and kings, the focus is less on their political judgments and manipulations than on their personal dealings. Only in the history plays, in *Julius Caesar* and to some degree *Antony*, is the focus significantly placed on the large outer world. Macbeth's political murder of Duncan is more significant (within the play-world) in its personal consequences than its political ones, although at the final point these become identical. Lear is a king, but his tragedy is a personal one. Like the Greek tragedians, Shakespeare identified the family and the state: conflict in the larger body is isomorphic with conflict in the smaller one.

Power-in-the-world appears in the romances in domestic and sexual situations. Antiochus, Simonides, and Dionyza are parent figures: their tyranny or benevolence is essentially familial. The same thing is true in *Cymbeline*, where the conflict rages among aspects of father and son figures against an ideal, Imogen. Although the structure of *The Winter's Tale* is very different from those of *Pericles* and *Cymbeline*, it contains similar elements. It is more popular than the other two, and this is at least partly because it seems more realistic. The motivations of the characters seem more grounded. In fact, they are not.

The Winter's Tale seems more realistic because it is made up of three acts written in the tragic mode. The remaining two acts are mythic and fairy-tale-like. Like *Pericles* and *Cymbeline*, it contains a divine message (the oracle) and a miracle—the resurrection of Hermione. Like the miraculous restoration of Thaisa and Imogen, it signals the marvel of harmony between the gender principles.

The play opens, however, with such apparent harmony. The first scenes are devoted to talk of love and children. There is conversation about status, but is is "feminine"—playful and eager to promote the other rather than the self. When the three royalties appear, they too spar in a witty and agreeable way.

The first jarring note is Polixenes' suggestion that innocence is ignorance of sexual desire, which implies that *all* sex—not just unregulated sex—is sin, and awareness of desire the fall from innocence. Hermione swiftly picks this up and makes his suggestion explicit: "Of this make no conclusion, lest you say / Your queen and I are devils" (I, ii, 81–82). Yet she then also accepts the identification of sex with sin and develops the point. Almost immediately, Leontes' jealousy appears.

It has been suggested that Leontes is sexually in love with Polixenes, and that his jealousy is of his friend, not his wife. There are clearly such overtones in the language. The problem with this interpretation, however, is that it goes nowhere. It cannot be developed. It is evident in the last act, and essential to the conclusion that Leontes wants desperately the return to his life of the feminine principle as incarnated in Hermione. It seems strange that Shakespeare, who does suggest homosexual love in other plays, and who threads such themes through *Merchant* and *Twelfth Night* and ties or cuts them off at the end, would bring in such a theme and then drop it. One can spin webs, of course, as does one critic who claims that the marriage of Florizel and Perdita resolves the attraction between their fathers through sublimation.[18] This is not the way sublimation works, but more important, there is nothing in the text to support such a theory.

However, the question arises at all only because the first three acts are written in the mode of tragedy, in which we expect some realistic motivation for behavior (which does not mean that we always get it). Leontes' jealousy is as slightly motivated as Cymbeline's tyranny, Pericles' guilt, or the murderousness of Dionyza and Cymbeline's Queen. The situation is that Leontes is jealous and he has power, just as Cymbeline is possessive of his daughter and has power, and Antiochus is sexually involved with his daughter and has power.

Leontes' power is mainly over his wife and children; like that of the other romance kings, it is essentially domestic power. Antiochus plots against Pericles, who suspects this and flees; Leontes plots against Polixenes, who discovers this and flees. Once one man in the pair is outside the domain of the other, one of them becomes unimportant, falls out of the action. The action continues, within Pericles, between Leontes and Hermione, who has no kingdom of her own to flee to.

And the main action of *Winter's Tale* is the treatment of the suspect feminine principle by a powerful male. The jealousy of Leontes, a not unfamiliar theme in Shakespeare, cannot easily be grounded in realistic elements. It is a stance adopted by many Shakespearean males in reference to women, implicitly the feminine principle. It is rooted in the need to control, to fix utterly, to possess that which cannot be possessed or fixed utterly or controlled utterly except through murder. And, as I have discussed earlier, it is deepened and made fierce by the identification of women with sex and the sense of sex as sin. Leontes, like other Shakespearean males, has recourse to the powerful strain of misogyny that is the foundation of Western culture.

This issues, as it does in *Much Ado*, *Othello*, *Hamlet*, and *Lear*, in ugly scornful slangy language expressing disgust and loathing for women and sex. Leontes orders Polixenes murdered, but he never excoriates him. He utters no anger or hurt at what he clearly sees as the betrayal of a long friendship. Neither does any other Shakespearean male. At the conclusion of *Two Gentlemen*, the bond of friendship for Proteus takes primacy over Valentine's feelings for Silvia. In *Othello*, the hero orders Cassio's death but does not anguish over his betrayal.

Part of the reason for this is a phenomenon mentioned earlier. Although there may be private hatred of man by man in Shakespeare —Hamlet and Claudius, Iago and Othello, Macbeth and Macduff— no man ever takes a generalizing, abstracting step from the behavior of one man to the behavior of men in general. Posthumus does not damn all men for Iachimo's act; nor does any other male figure. (Des-

demona and Emilia sigh about *these men:* they are the only characters
in Shakespeare to do so.) But anger at a woman invariably in Shake-
speare turns into hatred for womankind: frailty, thy name is woman.
And even in cases where the hatred exists between man and man, it is
directed towards women. Iago's hate for Othello leads him to attack
Desdemona; Macbeth's hatred or fear of Macduff leads him to kill
Lady Macduff. Hamlet hates Claudius, but the focus of his rage is
Gertrude.

This situation is involved with the double standard of judgment
exercised on the two genders. Men, being human, may err. Women
are not human, but mythic, and are therefore in some important way,
all the same. They are not women, but Woman. If one is a goddess,
she ennobles all; if one errs, she damns all. Since such a perception
requires the blunting of all sensory equipment, all actual experience
—since women are as various as men, and are certainly human—it
has to issue from inside, rather than outside. It seems to me to involve
the feminine principle as it exists within an individual man. That feminine is all the feminine a man really knows. If he allows it power
within himself; if he learns to trust, to love, to give; if he subordinates
his power to other qualities: he becomes vulnerable and able to be
humiliated. If the object of his love or trust, the person to whom he
subordinates some of his power, shows even the slightest sign of un-
dependability, his feminine side has betrayed him. He is utterly humiliated, utterly damaged; everything feminine is henceforth suspect.

In addition, Shakespeare believed deeply in the necessity of civilizing influences and seems to have believed women to be such. But
the ineradicable association of women with human sexuality undermined his perception. And because civilization is "masculine," and its
pronounced relation to nature one of dominion, misogyny is fundamental to Western culture as a whole. It is an inevitable concomitant
to that culture's obsession with power and control over, qualities that
are challenged and threatened by "feminine" values. To maintain clear
supremacy, it has been deemed necessary to derogate and scorn "feminine" values (except in church) and the gender associated with them.
The shakiness and irrationality of this arrangement are responsible for
the tremendous fear and horrified scorn that attend female self-
assertion (which seems to indicate that women are moving into the
masculine principle which in turn leads to the horror with which
Shakespeare, for instance, regarded women who presumed to exercise
power), *and* female criticism of male structures, as in radical feminism.

These remarks go beyond Shakespeare, but I think it is impossible to understand the obsession with jealousy, and the spasms of hideous misogyny and "sex nausea" in his work, without such analysis.[19] Shakespeare himself was larger than his attitudes. He *saw* these feelings—in himself and in the outer world. He saw what they meant and where they led, not in terms of ideas, but in terms of human relations, morality, and emotion. The misogyny that pervaded his culture and pervades ours is like a deep pocket full of coin which men—and women—can dig into at times of mental and moral bankruptcy. It is always available and its currency is so familiar that it is accepted everywhere as legitimate specie—irrational, illogical, and invalid as it is.

Leontes can count on all this, and does. Although Camillo and the court refuse to believe the King's specific charges, they do share his way of seeing. Antigonus swears that if Hermione is false, he'll "geld" his three daughters, segregate and leash his wife: "every dram of woman's flesh is false, / If she be," he asserts (II, i, 138–139).

Leontes silences his counselor by responding that he has the power to do as he sees fit. Thus the battle line is drawn between the power of a male and the helpless feminine principle. Leontes' rage and power sweep away all manifestations of that principle: he kills the mother and both her children, and indirectly destroys Antigonus (who has "feminine" sympathies). He empties his court of this uncontrollable attraction, this appealing set of creatures who cannot be fixed.

Paulina, of course, remains. She, like her husband, is rather androgynous: she upholds the values of the feminine principle, but uses assertion and forcefulness to do so. She is fearless and to some degree pitiless. Her behavior is dramatically necessary. Just as Antigonus dies for Leontes, Paulina lives for Hermione, speaking the truths that ideal women would not utter.

Like her daughter, Hermione is an incarnation of the inlaw feminine principle. In her renunciation speech, she itemizes the joys of that principle—love, harmony, the joy of nurturance. Without these things, she says, life is not desirable: death is no threat to one who has lost all the felicities that make it so. Her words are prophetic. Leontes, robbed of all felicities by his own hand, must discover the truth of her attitudes through suffering, through submission to mere endurance. His power cannot create what his power destroyed.

Having previously taken for granted the pleasures of the feminine principle, he has assumed they were inherent in life and that they cost nothing. But they cost a great deal. For women, who in the Shakespearean division of experience largely provide them, they cost will, independence, and power. If men wish to maintain these values, they must pay the same price. Leontes does: he subordinates his will, his authority, his independence, and his power to Paulina and her reproaches.

The qualities of the feminine principle dominate the lovely sheep-shearing scene. Perdita is a shepherdess-queen and Florizel has renounced his rank; neither of them presumes legitimacy within the shepherd world: thus, it is anarchic. It is full of play and closeness to nature and unregulated sexuality. To the extent that it has a center, or is dominated, that center of domination is Perdita's beauty, a magnetic rather than an imposed power.[20]

Until it is invaded by the power of Bohemia, the world of the shepherds is utterly joyful; nevertheless both extremes of moral experience have leashed themselves. There is bawdiness, and even Perdita makes an easy declaration of sexual feeling (not of love, like other Shakespearean heroines, but of eroticism). It is clear, though, that although she shows no sexual guilt and no association of sex with sin, that she believes sex should be regulated. She expects Florizel to participate in this regulation, and he agrees to. Sex, in the shepherd's Bohemia, is a mutual responsibility and a mutual pleasure: the exact opposite of incest.

Thievery flourishes here, but it is petty thievery that does not impoverish its victim and allows Autolycus to survive. Autolycus, the prince of dissembling and thievery, can change clothes with Florizel, the prince of constancy; nor does the character of either man change. Autolycus' new finery, however (like that of the clowns, later), allows him to attack the notion of legitimacy, and to satirize the "masculine" qualities of status, hierarchy, and power that have just destroyed the "feminine" world to which Autolycus necessarily belongs.

The joy and gaiety and freedom of this world are best expressed through lyric verse and song, and so they are. But it is after all a fragile world, like the world of Spenser's shepherds in Book VI of *The Faerie Queene*, and it is demolished upon the invasion of "masculine" insistence upon hierarchy and status. This insistence, like Leontes' insistence on possession and control, is accompanied by the worldly power to enforce.

Driven underground, driven to flight, the feminine principle continues to ripple through the world until it finds acceptance in male minds. It comes under a legitimate aegis through the discovery of Perdita's true status; her acceptance by the male powers allows the recovery of Mamillius through his surrogate, Florizel.[21] With a gasp, the world settles down: life is to be permitted to go on. So powerful is the feminine principle once it is fully accepted that it turns those who are "most marble" (V, ii, 83) to color, and returns a marble, if wrinkled statue to breath.[22] Leontes' learned wisdom is that the unmitigated masculine principle is "more stone" (V, iii, 38) than stone itself.

The Winter's Tale is the last play in which infidelity is a theme, and in it Shakespeare opens a new idea: males as well as females must take responsibility for the chastity that is so essential to male structures. He carries this notion into his next play, in which he takes up again the other half of the problem—the necessity of power and methods of regulating it.

The Tempest

It has been suggested that this last of Shakespeare's unaided comedies is concerned with the theme of justice. One critic finds in it an attempt to envision a utopia without utopianism.[23] If the play concerns the creation of justice within an unjust world, Prospero must represent deity, and he is variously admired or deprecated as a god who scourges, a celestial stage manager lacking in human sympathy; as a harsh ruler whose severity is a necessity because life is always edging into chaos; or as an eternal artist rejected by the society his art redeems.[24]

Other Shakespearean plays have been seen as concerned with justice, but in them, justice is defined negatively, defined by what it is not. Shylock, Leontes, and Othello insist that they are just—indeed, Othello seems to see himself as an agent of divine justice—when they are performing actions that are patently unjust. These men have the will, the power, and by some code or criterion, the right to act as they do. Angelo's stringent law against fornication and his harsh application of it seem just to him, inhumane as both are, but his persistence in executing (as far as he knows) Claudio even after his (seeming) rape of Isabel, shows that basically, for Angelo, justice is power. The confusion or conflation of justice with power, will, authority, or right (legitimacy) is the subject of Lear's "mad" speeches outside Dover. Thus, none of the plays in which these characters appear is actually about justice, but rather about some element which is confused with it—by people outside the play-world as well as by those within it. Property, authority, and belief in the legitimacy of male possession of women are elements in some people's notions of justice. But ultimate justice has little connection with these. Nor has it much connection with law, as Justice Holmes knew.

Indeed, ultimate justice is unimaginable: in a world in which most people are more sinned against than sinning, in a nature that is random and which carries all of us to a death that appears to be an end and a defeat, ultimate justice seems an intellectual self-indulgence, a notion with no relation to human possibility. Yet, if we are to create even a semblance of justice in human affairs, we must attempt to envision such an ideal. Stripped of its associations with property, authority, or legitimacy, all of which are variable in time and place, *justice* can only mean an arrangement of values and elements permitting to every person the room each needs or wants in which to grow and exist, consonant with not infringing too much on, not violating, the space of others. Such an arrangement may perhaps have existed in the tribal life of gathering-hunting peoples; it clearly has not existed within recorded history.

Ultimate justice is probably impossible to people who believe in legitimacy, for the notion assumes that some people have rights denied to others, that some people are entitled to more than others. Within such worlds, the idea of justice will always be connected to the grounds upon which legitimacy is conferred. In our own time, legitimacy is based slightly on inheritance of the claim, more on work of a sort that leads to power (money, physical or intellectual expertise, political power). Work that does not lead to power—serving and nutritive tasks, and for all but a few, the creation of art—is unvalued, unrewarded, and illegitimate. For Shakespeare and his contemporaries, inherited legitimacy was far more important, work was not yet the great requirement, and the creation of art (little as it was rewarded in all but a few) was considered *the* great human enterprise. Art, however, had a far broader meaning than it has now, denoting all human applications serving to transform nature. The cook dressing the fowl and the governor administering "justice" both used art.

The Tempest does seem to be Shakespeare's attempt to delineate perfect (if not ultimate) justice within the terms of his world. After a number of plays suggesting what justice is *not*, he tries to envision what it is. In keeping with his lifelong belief in the organic nature of human forms, he demonstrates the best possible arrangement of values and elements within a society by depicting that same arrangement within one man, the governor of that society. Because moral values seem, for Shakespeare, to be divided into gender categories, a proper arrangement of the former is also an arrangement of the gender principles. But unlike the other romances, *The Tempest* does not attribute "feminine" qualities to a persecuted female figure or figures. The battle fought in this play is not among a set of characters, but within the psyche of one man who contains within himself, in varying degrees of acceptance, all of the qualities of all the poles.

In describing the consciousness of this one man, Prospero, it is essential to attend to his basic sense of things. It is this that Frank Kermode suggests in describing the play as an examination of the conventional Renaissance theme of the opposition between Art and Nature.[25] Kermode sees Caliban as the "core of the play."[26] Caliban is unreconstructed Nature; Prospero's Art "is a technique for liberating the soul from the passions, from nature. . . . When [Prospero] achieves this necessary control over himself and nature, he achieves his end."[27]

Kermode's discussion assumes that nature in itself is base and must be controlled—in terms of this study, transcended—and claims that the main opposition of the play is between Prospero and Caliban, the representatives of the two realms. But Caliban is only one part of the threat to Prospero and by extension, the just society; another is offered by the ambitious, murderous courtiers; and a third by Prospero's own rage and tyrannical will, which may overwhelm tenderer feelings and destroy or punish the tenderer characters—Ariel, Miranda, and Ferdinand.

For Prospero has a puritanical sense of humanity. Like Noah's God, he finds the imagination of man's heart evil from his youth. The bitter exile has a grim view of human "nature" (women are not really seen as human) and one which is justified by the behavior of the survivors of the shipwreck. The survivors range from the untried Ferdinand to the drunken, slovenly Stephano and Trinculo (who sink into the condition of nature) to the murderous Sebastian and Antonio. The single well-meaning character, Gonzalo, is, like other well-meaning, highly placed figures in Shakespeare, essentially impotent. He is old and a bit foolish, but even when he was younger, he was unable to save Prospero despite his love for him, and could only ameliorate his casting out. The world of The Tempest is riddled with malice, cruelty, stupidity, greed, drunkenness, and disrespect for the ends of life. The men who occupy its stage are guilty of actions or intentions as ugly as those of the men in Cymbeline, but in this play, no one is "punished" by being killed, and only Alonso feels remorse. Given the behavior of these "goodly creatures" (V, i, 182), Prospero's curt response—"'Tis new to thee" (V, i, 184)—to Miranda's wonder at the beauty of the human race is understandable.

Yet strangely, The Tempest feels idyllic. Even as we watch the scrambling contention for power, the blind stumbling about of its puny

and deluded characters, or recall afterwards the unusual (for Shakespeare) ambivalence of its ending, it feels idyllic. There are a number
of reasons for this.

First, there is the poetry and the descriptions of the island: the
setting, much of the language, and even the punishments of the characters are "feminine." In addition, however, this is a play about justice
during which we are assured that justice will triumph. What we do not
know is what the terms of this final just arrangement will be. And there
is nothing more soothing to the human soul than belief in justice,
especially if it can be accomplished on earth.

The basic assumption about human nature in the play is that it is
"evil," whatever that word meant to the men who set down God's
words to Noah. Nor can humans trust to mere nature, to the qualities
of a Caliban—simplicity, amorality, lustfulness, desire for anarchy—
in building human civilization. Given such a situation, the best course
seems to be first to study the wisdom of the ages (it is, significantly I
think, not the Bible, but magic that Prospero studies) to discover a set
of standards to which humans may aspire in creating a just society,
standards that allow some freedom but also and more important, foster
the true ends of life, procreation and pleasure. For Shakespeare, pleasure (for legitimate and inlaw characters) seems primarily the avoid-
ance of conflict, and orderly communality, friendship in decorum.
Once the proper standards have been discovered, however, what is
necessary is some degree of force. Force is essential in ordering human
society for all people who believe human "nature" is inherently vicious.
Thus force, being essential, is good, and tyranny, in one who adheres
to proper standards, desirable.

Prospero demonstrates in his first appearance that he has good
and humane standards: he is (on the whole) gentle to his daughter, he
pities her compassion; he swears no one has been hurt in the storm;
and his tale of exile and usurpation gains him sympathy as much for
the way it is told as for its content. Prospero is humane, if bitter, tired,
and angry. Quickly, however, we discover that he has superhuman
powers, has indeed caused the tempest, and controls supernatural spir-
its. The configuration of the play changes: Prospero is a superhuman
figure, controlling both humans and nature, and a human figure who,
in accord with God's words to Adam, assumes the right of dominion.
The world of the play has a visibly functioning deity.

A world with a god is finite and purposive: it is thus very restful to
the human mind, which can surrender responsibility for creating purpose. A humane god assures us that his standards will be roughly like

our own, which is also reassuring. And a figure of wisdom and power will certainly be *just:* whatever we fear in the course of the play, we do not fear for righteousness. There is, throughout, little of the tension that arises from fear that the "good" characters will be undone by the "evil" ones. There is, perhaps, little tension of any sort, but if one can cast one's mind back to a first reading or seeing, what tension there is arises from the fear that the righteousness, the justice we are guaranteed, will not have the configurations we would desire.

All of these elements contribute to the idyllic feeling of *The Tempest.* The events and characters all rest comfortably in the palm of Prospero's righteous hand. We are about to see justice done. And the justice we expect is not the narrow arid sort found in courtrooms, nor simply a meting out of punishments to malefactors: it is true justice, an arrangement of all elements of life—lush, "feminine" nature; tender young romantic love; allotments of power and of freedom.

The roundness of Shakespeare's career is impressive. For however one may dismiss *The Comedy of Errors* as "mere" farce, the concern of that play is identical to that of *The Tempest.* In the early comedy as well, it is assumed that humans must be forced (by serious confusion, fear, isolation) to subordinate themselves to the limitations and roles imposed by hierarchy and the traditional division of experience. This is one theme in *The Taming of the Shrew* as well. What distinguishes Shakespeare's version of the taming of a woman is that it is not brutal: Kate is tamed by serious confusion, fear, isolation, deprivation, and capricious authority. So in *The Tempest*, the courtiers are "tamed," brought into line by a series of intimidations and coercions, none of which have fatal, or even dangerous consequences. The humbling of the Caliban crew is more physical, and comic, but again lacks fatal or fully disabling consequences. The span of years between the composition of the earlier plays and *The Tempest* has, however, resulted in a change of vision as well as greater compositional powers. For *The Comedy of Errors* and *Taming* conclude with the suggestion that subordination, when volitional (chosen as an alternative to confusion, or learned, as internalized morality), can lead to joy, to true community and love in decorum. The conclusion of *The Tempest* is less rosy.

The play opens with a storm, a disturbance of nature which ought to make those with worldly power realize the limitations of their privilege. It does not accomplish this. What it does do is overturn the order that has previously existed, separating the groups on shipboard and isolating Ferdinand. The first concern of all the survivors—after survival—is power. Alonso mourns the loss of his son, the future King; Ferdinand mourns his father, the King, and assumes he is now King; Gonzalo muses about the perfect political arrangement, decides it would be anarchic, but cannot escape or evade the necessity for a king —himself, of course. This is important and organic to the justice that will be established in the play: a king, a ruler, is necessary because force is necessary. Justice is not natural: it must be imposed. In their own ways, Sebastian, Antonio, and Stephano are also concerned with kingship: for them it is gaining control.

But control has different forms. Kingship is control over others; control of one's own life is not kingship, but freedom. It is freedom that Caliban and Ariel desire. Such desire is anarchic—outlaw feminine—and seems antipathetic to civilization. To operate without restraint or constraint can lead to violating the space of others. Shakespeare, however, distinguishes between Ariel and Caliban. The former is a compassionate, and therefore benevolent, spirit who, given freedom, would not harm others. Caliban would. It is significant, however, that Caliban's uncivilizable qualities are unrestrained erotic drive, and an unwillingness to work. Frank Kermode is, in my view, mistaken in finding the basic opposition of the play to be between Caliban and Prospero. Caliban is the core of the play because he is its most vital character: he has maintained intact his "instincts": without the civilized need for restraint, he is lustful and would rape at will; he is in touch with the sounds and smells and music of nature. He does not, however, have a drive towards power. He does not presume to the kingship; he begs Stephano to become King, imagining that the man would free him. Caliban wants merely to be free. He is a fearful creature (not having been educated to transcend that either) and is dangerous only to women. Despite the sex nausea so prominent in late Shakespeare, Caliban is not an "evil" character. Evil is a moral category, and he is amoral. He has none of the overtones of demonism possessed by Lady Macbeth, Goneril and Regan, Coriolanus' Queen, or Richard III. The will to power-over that originally toppled Prospero is found not in Caliban, but the courtiers.

Prospero's unenviable role in this drama is to teach or coerce all the elements of society to subordinate themselves to something outside, and larger than, themselves. This something is the good of the whole, the harmony of a working community. But since it is a good perceived and believed in by Prospero, and since Prospero has all the power, the something seems—to us and to the characters—to be the will of Prospero.

Prospero is barely a human figure, although the playwright has given him some touches to make him playable. Although he tells us, sotto voce, that he favors the erotic bond between Miranda and Ferdinand; although towards the end of the play, he shows kindness to Ariel: above all, throughout, he is irritable and angry. He is God, King, Father: but he is in exile. He is extremely powerful, but not powerful enough. He can coerce and control, he could presumably kill: but he cannot change hearts. He abhors much of nature (including human nature as he perceives it) and believes in transcendence over it—thus, he is "masculine."[28] But he has devoted himself to study of magic, a "feminine" form of control, and he has suffered and endured. Consequently, he combines the gender principles despite his overwhelmingly "masculine" nature—for he incarnates, above all, power.[29]

He bears his power as a burden, however, because he cannot use it freely. His study of magic, his suffering—in other words, his assimilation of the feminine principle—have taught him that the essential quality necessary to power is restraint. He despises Caliban, hates his brother, Alonso, and Sebastian; he has contempt for Trinculo and Stephano. He would enjoy destroying them, perhaps even painfully. He cannot tolerate being questioned, brooked, or disobeyed in the slightest way. He is a prima donna, and is temperamentally inclined to absolutism. But he has learned enough to know that the issue is not that he *should* not destroy those he hates, but that he *cannot*. He can destroy only persons; he cannot destroy the qualities in them that make him hate them. Thus he attempts—with the humans—to change hearts. This is a "feminine" task, requiring magnetic, seductive powers rather than coercion.

That his means are subtle does not mean he forgoes punishment. He exposes the courtiers to disorientation, and to seemingly supernatural reproach. He holds up a vision of plenty, grace, and beauty, a vision of life's feast, possible to those who eschew power for pleasure —then snatches it away, emphasizing their deprivation. He leads them into an opaque isolation, showing them themselves "when no man was his own" (V, i, 213). He impresses upon Alonso the importance of continuity, future generations, by depriving him of his son. All of his manipulations are attempts to make the courtiers recognize the true ends of life. They are not especially successful.

Towards the spirit and creature who serve him, however, he is malign and threatening. He uses "masculine" means—coercion—to dominate them. He threatens Ariel with a horrible form of imprisonment, and uses physical torment to coerce and punish Caliban and his two companions. Stephano, Trinculo, and Caliban are funny enough and stupid enough and drunk enough that we can laugh at their situations. But pinches and cramps, being left in fetid sewage, could, in other circumstances, be seen as torture (like Petruchio's treatment of Kate).

But on the whole, Prospero does restrain his impetuous and furious will. It is because he does so that he can claim to be just. Rage is his most constant companion: he is irritable even with the docile and obedient Miranda, and downright vicious on occasion to Ariel, that delightful, tractable spirit. As a god figure, Prospero is an angry god, one with frequent moments of wishing to destroy the human race. Yet much of his bad temper, his irritable moroseness, is founded in pain. He is anguished by what men do, by what men are, and frustrated that he must continually restrain his anger.[30]

Prospero has learned the proper use of power by assimilating the feminine principle, and also by learning the consequences of turning one's back on power: the abusers take over. Power, burden that it is, must be carried. If it is not borne by those with moral balance, it will be seized by those without it. Prospero's exile has been not so much from civilization (for that he brought with him) or from people (for he dislikes them), as from power he sees as "rightfully" his. On another level, his exile is emblematic of the absence from the world of a functioning god—one who controls human morality by a system of rewards and punishments called justice.

Prospero's exile has taken place in an utterly feminine world, the realm of nature, a place which has previously been governed by a queen who incarnates the entire (undivided) feminine principle, procreating and nourishing, but also fostering unregulated sexuality, magic, and anarchy. The island is entirely "natural": despite his books and hangings, Prospero lives in a cave, not a house. He has "civilized" only a tiny segment of nature's realm. The island is a world of generativeness, emotional harmony (music), spontaneity, and uncontrollable energy that has the capacity to be cruel. It has marvelous perfumes, "fresh springs, brine-pits, barren place and fertile" (I, ii, 338), "sounds, and sweet airs, that give delight and hurt not" (III, ii, 136). It contains body and bodily energy (Caliban), and spirit or emotion (Ariel), but not mind. That is what man brings. Prospero "civilizes" the island, which is to say he brings hierarchy, status, and law. Caliban, Ariel, and Miranda are his subjects in his capacities as God (Ariel), King (Caliban), and Father (Miranda). He imposes masculine structures on the island, distinguishing between degrees of power (rank), between acceptable and unacceptable behavior—moral good and evil.

Caliban, a mother's child, incarnates the outlaw feminine principle. He does not want to usurp Prospero's rank, but merely to be freed of his control. If Stephano could become King, Caliban would be grumbling about him in minutes and seeking means of escape or overthrow. His sensitivity to the beauties and music of the island, his anarchic attitudes, and his unregulated sexuality make him a morally ambiguous figure, but he is also the most vital and taking character in the play. He cannot be "civilized"—that is, he cannot be tamed, brought into "masculine" line. It is because of this that Prospero hates him, although he (and his creator) knows that this thing of darkness is in himself, and that in Caliban lies the energy of the race.

Ariel, too, is "feminine"—subordinate, generative, imaginative, and compassionate. He uses imaginative power rather than force or intellectual persuasion to achieve his effects. But he too is rebellious, resenting "masculine" control: he too wants, not rule, but freedom.

The great threat within the feminine world is, naturally, sex. Thus Sycorax is described as *littering* the island with a "freckled whelp" (I, ii, 282–283); Venus and her son are barred from the masque; and Caliban's fall from favor was caused by his attempt to rape Miranda. But the great threat within the human (masculine) world is power, and it is contention for power that the humans bring with them when they arrive. Despite Prospero's efforts, moreover, this drive or will is not destroyed in the courtiers, and is merely (predictably) thwarted in the drunks. All survive and take part in the conclusion. R. G. Hunter says, "More than any other of Shakespeare's plays, *The Tempest* insists strongly on the indestructibility of evil."[31]

Nature, indeed, does not provide a great threat to the characters, but to the ideas and customs they brought with them. Caliban, we learn, has taught Prospero the secrets of the island: it would have been possible for the two exiles to live, as Caliban presumably has, in harmony with it. This possibility, however, seems repugnant, debased, humiliating to Prospero. It means submitting entirely to the feminine principle and giving up the masculine, the principle of humanness. The link between the two realms—nature and the human—is Miranda.

Miranda represents the inlaw feminine principle: she is beautiful, subordinate, compassionate, full of pity and love, and she is chaste. She shows the only form of rebelliousness permitted the Shakespearean daughter—she will fight her father for the sake of the husband she desires to subordinate herself to, but only for that. Unlike Ariel and Caliban, she is content with unfreedom, content inside the room her father's will allows her—possibly because he hypnotizes her into sleep whenever she is in the way. The only will she possesses is totally in line with his, although she does not know that. Her obedience to "masculine" control is certified.

Chaste as she is, she is nevertheless able to love sexually, as she shows in the scene with Ferdinand. In this she moves towards the outlaw feminine. And above all, she is seen as fruitful, able to people the island with Calibans, full of the potential of nature's bounty.[32] She is a gift, a reward to the properly coerced. For, one of Prospero's tasks is to coerce Ferdinand. By serving and submitting, he learns the nature of love; by promising sexual restraint, he civilizes love. The masque is central to the definition of love Shakespeare offers, and also to the theme of nature versus the human. For the masque bars uncontrollable passion, Venus and Cupid. It promises nature's bounty without the threat of sex: thus, Prospero rather hounds Ferdinand with reminders of the necessity of ceremonializing sexual desire before unleashing it. Sex exists for procreation, as a duty performed for a beloved; it is thereby ritualized, distanced.

With this accomplished, the threat of nature is removed. What is required to civilize nature is restraint: the feminine principle must subordinate itself to "masculine" control, regulation. What is required to make power decent is also restraint: the masculine principle must be feminized. Those with power, those who desire power, must learn that volitional subordination of self to the good of the whole is essential. They must learn that without such subordination, life's feast vanishes, pleasure turns to fear and isolation. To the degree that the end of the play is a stasis, Prospero accomplishes his end. But his predictions for his own future, the suggestion that Caliban and Ariel will be free, the unrepentant natures of Antonio and Sebastian, Miranda's prediction that Ferdinand will cheat and she will forgive him—all of these suggest that the stasis is merely momentary.

Yet several things are affirmed. First, the proper balance of gender principles is delineated, and what is urged is a degree of synthesis. The "feminine" must submit to masculine control, the "masculine" must accept feminine subordination. This is less synthesis, perhaps—for synthesis would require a suffusion of the principles by each other—than separate but equal maintenance, a subordination of each principle to the other, a mutual bowing. Second, the rightness of the masculine principle is affirmed: it remains the pole of the human; its legitimacy is insisted upon. This is evident from a consideration of the relationship between Prospero and Sycorax.

Sycorax is Prospero's feminine counterpart. Both figures were sent into exile, their lives spared. Each has a child. Caliban wants mothering (see I, ii, 332–339); Miranda submissively accepts her unmotherly father. Sycorax is cruel to Ariel, imprisoning him within a tree; Prospero threatens the identical punishment and is frequently peremptory and abusive towards Ariel, calling him "dull thing," "malignant thing" (I, ii, 285, 257). But most important, both Prospero and Sycorax are identified with magic, although the female's magic is called witchcraft and associated with the ugliest things in nature. On the rhetorical level of the play, Sycorax is damned. That condemnation is necessary to justify Prospero's usurpation of her island from her "rightful" heir, Caliban. It also functions, together with the ugliness of the images associated with her and with Caliban, to suggest that without human control, nature is inherently malign.

Human control of nature is necessary for civilized life, but control over that control is also necessary. It is in the nature of control over others that one form of it begets another even to infinity. So supernatural power is required to control highly placed abusers of power. With such control, Prospero brings the world of *The Tempest* into harmony, but that harmony is only a dream rounded by a sleep. Eschewing vengeance, restraining his rage, Prospero sighs in despair at the ways of men, and gives up the control he has exercised, renounces power.

Except for Alonso, the others will go on as they were. The island will revert to nature, to Caliban and Ariel. Hated-loved-feared nature reclaims its own; man's civilization is a mere fragment shored against ruin. But man's civilization also causes its own ruin: and that, it is suggested, can be controlled only by a god.

Conclusion

Shakespeare's earliest extant work concerns itself with a set of notions that remained important to him throughout his career. I use the term *notions* because it suggests something broader and less fixed than *ideas*. The areas of his major concern were, roughly, power and sex, both of which seemed to him at once necessary and threatening, and each of which seemed to him the purview of a single gender.

Like all of us, Shakespeare began with a set of received ideas. His were naturally those of his period, although they also bear a striking resemblance to ideas and associations found in *The Aeneid*, especially the second half. But his sense of things was not primarily literary; he took his plots from literature, but the vividness of his work is the result of close observation of the life around him—of his father, mother, wife, brothers, neighbors, lovers. Certain elements in his work are biographically suggestive: the idealization of father/son relations in what is perhaps his first play, *1 Henry VI*, and the rarity of such relations in the rest of his work; the abusiveness and insensitivity of many male power figures; the helplessness and agedness of most benevolent males; the viciousness of females who were sexual and/or wielded some power in the world; the adoring idealization of inlaw feminine—motherly—qualities of compassion, nutritiveness, constancy, and givingness, although not in motherly figures.

Such elements are sometimes used to analyze Shakespeare psychologically, an activity which may provide mental exercise for the analyzer, but offers little else that is useful. These elements have significance not because of what they may indicate about Shakespeare's psyche, but because they stand in the work, reverberating meanings beyond themselves: they are fixtures in the moral landscape of Shakespeare's world.

Worldly power and moral excellence almost never coexist in one being and (with the exception of Henry V) Shakespeare's attempts to depict men with both are strained (for example, Prospero, or the Duke in *Measure for Measure*) or wooden (like Richmond in *Richard III*); the characters are manufactured to fit dramatic or moral needs and lack the felt life that comes from observation of actual beings. There is a set of figures who are vividly portrayed and who possess both moral excellence and power, but they are always, often vaguely, limited: they are aged, infirm, or impotent. They cannot set the times in joint. The very quality necessary to the proper use of power—restraint—mitigates their ability to control those who abuse power. The impression that develops as one reads through the canon is that the power of men is entirely a power to evil; attempts to do good are never good enough. Worldly power in women was for Shakespeare an abomination and bore overtones of sexual corruption.

Sex itself was an abomination throughout his career (although he seems to have had a respite from such feelings during the composition of certain plays), and because he associated sexuality with women, his hatred for the one is also hatred for the other. However, he also associated with women qualities he admired and which he came increasingly to see as necessary to the "salvation" of the human race. From this set of attitudes emerged the chaste constant heroine, purged of the taint of sexuality and of the desire for worldly power. The problem with this ideal figure was the condition of her existence: she is powerless. She cannot go out into the world and employ her healing and harmonizing qualities on men for whom they have no value, who disdain them. Men must first learn to see what the chaste constant heroine represents: when they do, they reach out to it, and feel the ecstatic sense of harmonious integration that appears in some of the middle comedies, in *Lear*, and in the romances. To the degree that these concepts function in a work, that work depicts emotional and moral life, rather than intellectual life or external events. The tragedies as well as the comedies focus on this part of experience.

Shakespeare's prime subject was disintegration, imbalance among or lack of certain values in an individual male, a community, or society as a whole. Even in those plays that center on a heroine, he was writing mainly for and about men, but he conceived of the elements that make up character as masculine and feminine. The woman is the stranger in Shakespeare because she is a part of a male's self, a pole in his psyche, whether as destroyer or restorer of harmonious wholeness. Whatever his feelings about actual women, Shakespeare was a powerful supporter of certain "feminine" values.

In most ways, his sense of life was organic. Human life is part of nature: a family is a branching tree, a community is a garden holding a variety of kinds in peaceful coexistence. The private and public were not two spheres but a continuum. The elements necessary to live a good life were identical to those necessary to a happy marriage, a harmonious and vital community, a just society. Since experience was a continuum, a single fabric, each part of it was equally important: a bad marriage can disrupt a whole community; a just society cannot exist without justice in its smallest elements. The phrase *sexual politics* would not have startled Shakespeare: he shows in *Othello* the bedroom being invaded by public attitudes about emotion and women, and in *Much Ado About Nothing*, that events in the bedroom affect the public sphere.

Nevertheless, others of his attitudes complicate or contradict this organic sense of life. Rooted in nature, humans must also transcend it —not to cooperate with it, but impose upon it. Nature is bestial and corrupt and requires art, human control, if it is not to engulf human civilization. Not just *natura*, but human nature as well is bestial and corrupt and requires moral/political control. This sense that people must be coerced into decent behavior is at odds with the perception that men cannot be coerced into decency, that they can learn only through suffering to value the true ends of life—inlaw feminine values. Further complicating the playwright's vision is the fact that although the threats to harmonious life came (as he saw it) from both gender poles—abused power threatens human life, nature threatens human civilization—his deepest horror was aroused only by the latter, by nature, sex, "corruptible" matter, the transient and unfixable. His laments (in the sonnets) for the transiency of youthful beauty, or his own aging body; his insistence on permanence in the form of children, enduring love, and poetry are tranquil expressions of a fear and hatred that appears more nakedly in some of the later sonnets and in the plays.

Shakespeare's examinations of the pole of power included questions about authority and justice, but above all, legitimacy. The question of what gives a man the right to rule others, to assume prerogatives over others was frequently raised in the Renaissance, usually as a discussion of what constitutes true nobility. Shakespeare does not formally ask this question: what he does in the first tetralogy is to demonstrate a number of forms of legitimacy, to try each out in turn. The traditionally accepted form, the passage of excellence from father to son, both holds and does not hold in *1 Henry VI*. It holds for the central figures, the Talbots, but both are killed; it does not hold in the passage from Henry V to Henry VI. The remaining plays in the set test other qualities: piety (which is respect for "feminine" ends, but also involves using "feminine" means); and might, which includes bravery, prowess, and the willingness to fight. No one of these is adequate to restore the kingdom to order or to create harmony. The good governor must have all three.

This is not a startlingly original perception. What is original about these plays is that Shakespeare clearly discovered his definition as he went along: he did not bring conventional moralizing to the work and impose it. The convulsive events of the Civil War that scourges England in the fifteenth century, compressed and somewhat altered as they appear in these four plays, teach this lesson through despair and anguish that cuts to the bone.

The first tetralogy deals with the nature of legitimacy; it does not question legitimacy itself. The plays contain the assumption that someone must rule. But Shakespeare does question legitimacy itself in later plays. The second history tetralogy (*Richard II*, the two *Henry IV* plays, and *Henry V*) returns to the subject with less anguish, more subtlety and polish, and more ambivalence. The specter that haunts the *Henry IV* plays is doubt of legitimacy itself.

Doubt about legitimacy is undermining if one believes in hierarchy as being divinely ordained and the only conceivable sociopolitical structure. Hierarchy rests on shaky premises. It is not only a codification and stratification of power, but an enshrinement of authority. Its structure incarnates what its high priests presume: that some people are superior to others. This is an indefensible claim. One person can be superior to another only in a particular and limited frame, at writing poetry, say, or throwing the discus. The claims of hierarchical institutions are not thus limited: superiors are superior in every way and are granted privileges and prerogatives deemed "rightfully" theirs because of this superiority. The awareness that such claims are unjust, empty, and vain—in the original sense of *vanitas*—leads inevitably to the suspicion that human institutions are also unjust, empty, and vain. To challenge institutions in this way is to destroy one's belief in authority; it is to destroy one's faith that moral right has any voice in the world.

Through the careful foundation provided in the *Henry IV* plays, depicting Hal's education and training in becoming a governor, Shakespeare is able to make *Henry V* a triumphant play. Hal has proven himself on all the grounds necessary to make a good ruler, including outlawing from himself the subversive aspects of the feminine principle. Like a comedy, the play ends with a promised marriage, suggestive of harmony and peace and love. Only the Epilogue reminds us that this exultant moment will vanish in a brief span and lead eventually to civil war. Questions of legitimacy are swept away in Henry's triumph. But if the play dismisses them, the playwright did not. They reappear, with new intensity and agony, in *Hamlet* and *King Lear*.

The early history plays assume the necessity of legitimacy. It is evident from his depiction of them at this time in his life that Shakespeare did not believe that women or lower-class males had the right to rights, to power. At the same time, much of the vividness and animation of these four plays issue from the very characters who are, on the moral surface of the plays, wrong. This is also true of the second tetralogy: Richard II's "feminine" meditations on power and legitimacy, Falstaff's outlaw feminine behavior provide the very heart of the plays in which they appear. This development could not have escaped the eye of the dramatist or the moralist. If vitality depends on those who challenge or undermine the constituted moral/political order, something is amiss with that constitution.

This perception is developed and built upon throughout the early and middle comedies, which focus increasingly on the underside of society, viewing it from the perspective of those denied legitimacy. The history plays look at human arrangements in their largest form, as society; the comedies look at human arrangements in their most personal form, love, marriage, and the community. In both the history plays and the early and middle comedies, however, the quality needed to harmonize the world is restraint that leads to mutual tolerance.

The two early farces, *The Comedy of Errors* and *The Taming of the Shrew*, focus on identity as it is decreed or discovered through discovery of one's proper place in the life of the community. Legitimacy is not a problem here: it is "naturally" conferred in accord with hierarchical assumptions seemingly too basic to be questioned. The father has rights over the son, the husband over the wife, the master over the slave or servant. Despite the clear-cut expectations of such relations, however, they fail. They fail because people on every social level refuse to accept the limitations on their wills or their power necessary to social order. Without such limitations, the world becomes a madhouse like Ephesus or the house of Petruchio for the newly married Katharina. Remaining outside the social order leads to the isolation and alienation felt by Syracusan Antipholus, the lonely yearning of Egeon. Establishing different conventions leads to topsy-turvy relations, like those between the two newlywed couples in *Taming*, Lucentio and Bianca, Hortensio and the Widow. Proper order, leading to peace and harmony and love, can be accomplished only through acceptance of conventional limitations. Surrender to these makes possible a surrender of the abusive and rebellious elements of the self. In these early plays, the female must give up her chafing at subordination before the male can give up his oppressive power over her, and brothers must discover their brotherhood. If these actions are performed, the society around the couple, the family, may be reconstituted and bondage turned into bonding.

All six of these early plays tend to find the best human situation within constrictions. In the history plays, freedom leads to abuse, or neglect of power, and the exercise of ego, which leads to mutual destruction. In the comedies, freedom is actually loss of structure; it terrifies the Antipholuses, confuses the secondary characters in *Comedy of Errors*. In *Taming*, it bewilders Sly, terrifies Katharina, and turns Petruchio into a moral monster.

The comedies which follow the farces introduce a new value and a new figure. The value is constancy, which swiftly becomes the highest good in Shakespeare's moral world. The figure is the chaste constant heroine. Julia, in *The Two Gentlemen of Verona*, the first of these, can function in the world dressed in boy's clothes, can take the candle that is herself out into a naughty world. She becomes a voice of moral right. The voice is soft, and never interrupts; often it speaks only in asides. But it stands immovably for inlaw feminine virtues, and through the magnetic beauty of its possessor, draws the fallible and uncertain male to good.

The female who is chaste and constant is symbolically a guarantee of moral virtue in men who remain linked with her. Whether he is father, husband, lover, or brother, a man who honors his bond to a chaste constant heroine symbolically honors "feminine" ends, and thus is devoted to the right use of power. In *Love's Labour's Lost*, constancy is opposed to fickleness which arises from ignorance of one's own emotions and to egotism. It thus becomes a shorthand way of suggesting an ultimate reality, an unswerving set of values and the faith necessary to maintain fidelity to insubstantial and powerless ends. In *A Midsummer Night's Dream*, constancy is a cosmic virtue, a larger purpose containing all human purposes, and triumphant over folly and delusion. Chaste constancy swiftly becomes the cornerstone, the pivot, the crucial element in Shakespeare's morality. It has this semi-divine nature only in women because it symbolizes "feminine" qualities of harmony, community, tolerance, moral flexibility (within limits), pity, compassion, forgiveness, and loving nutritiveness. These qualities are seen as the ultimate moral goods, the things all humans really need and want, or would if they were not blind. In Shakespeare's division of experience, however, men cannot be forced to revere these things. The process of coming to recognize these goods is a process of education in seeing.

Chaste constancy has several functions in the comedies from *Two Gentlemen* to *Twelfth Night* and *Much Ado*. If offers a reliable and immovable moral good that is visible in the world; thus it contrasts with male legitimacy, a set of men and institutions which claim to stand for moral good but which are untrustworthy and delusive. Second, it confers on females an equality of a sort with males. Males possess freedom and power-in-the-world; chaste constant women are bound to inlaw feminine ends and modes, but they possess moral superiority over men. This superiority is never offensive to male supremacists, however, because chaste constant heroines are utterly devoted to the male world, and usually to one man. That man is the center of her being, the only and wholly significant object of her desire. Because the man is so important to her, her entire existence is bent towards him. Her moral superiority is therefore not so much a power over him as it is an excellence, like her beauty or wit or wisdom, placed at his service.

Third, chaste constancy neutralizes, restrains the fearsome energies of sexuality: it is a slip leash on sex. Chaste constant heroines are "cold" until sexuality is redeemed by ceremonialization. Their natures include the ardor of Rosalind, the intense but quiet passion of Viola, the coldness of Imogen, and the profound iciness of Isabel (*Measure for Measure*). But they have an escalator clause built into their characters. Sex exists and it doesn't exist: it is affirmed and denied in the same moment. They are capable of romantic love and presumably erotic passion, these heroines: but only after marriage, and only with one man.

The chaste constant heroine provided Shakespeare with a hedge, a fence around sexuality. As long as this fixed quality holds, considerable moral flexibility is permitted. That is, as long as there is a guarantee that an absolute line is drawn forbidding physical sexual expression without marriage, other forms of sexual expression are permitted. Thus, in the middle comedies, there is a strong sense of play allowing sexual banter among other kinds.

The middle comedies play with male legitimacy as well as sexuality (always associated with the female). The males invariably err. In *Love's Labour's Lost*, the Lords are pretentious and deluded about their own emotions; the Ladies know better. From both groups, and the villagers who surround them, there flows a stream of language expressive of moral flexibility. It is "feminine" language because it undermines certitude and a linear view of experience through equivocation, pun, banter, and joke. To take a metaphor literally, or to play on several meanings of a word, is to challenge "right" meaning, and to make unification of heart and tongue impossible. In *A Midsummer Night's Dream*, this language is spoken mainly by the mechanics; it lightheartedly challenges conventional attitudes towards love (sex) and power (legitimate institutions) in parallel with the varying levels of unconventional love and power engaged in by the more prestigious and the supernatural characters.

In *The Merchant of Venice*, "feminine" language is spoken only in Belmont, and contrasts with the pompous, money- and status-centered language of Venice. "Feminine" language is less gay and bawdy in *The Merry Wives of Windsor:* soaked in a "masculine" sense of sex as commodity, emotion and love as words euphemistically used to cover legal and financial dealings, "feminine" language and the moral flexibility it represents are corseted. The idiosyncrasies of various speakers are bent in this play to competition for property. At the same time, the supposed heroine, Anne Page, is not as strong a character as other chaste constant heroines, and the wives defend their chastity as if it were a piece of property.

In the remaining middle comedies, flexible language is less lighthearted. There is sorrow, resignation, or despair in the wit and banter of many figures in *As You Like It*, and Rosalind's training of Orlando in love is largely a recitation of conventional misogynistic accusations which he must learn to overcome. Rosalind is a chaste constant heroine, but the image is weakening. In *Twelfth Night*, banter and word play appear only in the moral or social illegitimates—Toby's crew and Feste, whose wit is not comic but bitter and despairing about love and life. The banter of Beatrice and Benedick in *Much Ado* focuses on marriage, power, and fidelity but has real aminus: it is not fully play. The comic malapropisms and equivocations of the Watch and of Borachio serve to challenge the moral claims of church, state, and male legitimacy. In this play, the chaste constant ideal cracks open: Beatrice, wittily, and in language only, challenges the relations of women and men in a male supremacist world; Hero's (supposed) unregulated sexuality defies the rules of such a world. The double assault shatters the society of Messina, and culminates in Beatrice's order to Benedick: "Kill Claudio."

A new kind of language appears in *Much Ado*, in Claudio's attack on Hero. (It is not entirely new: there are fragments of it in the first tetralogy and in *Titus Andronicus*.) It is brilliant, intense, and shattering to hear, or even to read. In every play in which such language appears, it is the strongest in the piece. It is the "masculine" language of "sex nausea," expressing hatred and contempt for sex and women. A playful relation between the genders—legitimate males and neutralized but sexual females—breaks down in *Much Ado* and does not reappear in Shakespeare, except briefly, in *Antony and Cleopatra*.

In the four problem plays—*Hamlet*, *Troilus and Cressida*, *All's Well That Ends Well*, and *Measure for Measure*—Shakespeare tests his own ideals, probes his own prejudices. He has begun by assuming the rightness of male supremacy, the need for legitimacy, and the inevitability of male aggressiveness and competition. His view of women (all the major female characters in the first six plays are strong) is terrified and contemptuous at once. Quite soon—with the creation of the illegitimates Launce and Speed, and the chaste constant Julia in *Two Gentlemen*—his attitude shifts. Male legitimacy is questioned and lightly mocked; female chaste constancy and the inlaw feminine virtues it symbolizes are exalted into an ideal. With the problem plays, his attitude changes again, but not in a clear direction. The two sets of attitudes already expressed remain in uneasy balance. One does not supersede the other but rather coexists with it. The problem plays move slowly around the mysterious knot linking male legitimacy with female chastity, testing both ideals in various ways. In *Hamlet*, chaste constancy fails, and drags down male legitimacy and all possibility of human moral good with it. In *Troilus and Cressida*, it stands (in Andromache) but no one notices: the world is peopled by whores and cuckolds, self-aggrandizing males and deluded legitimacy. In *Measure for Measure*, which is a trial of sexuality itself, the world is judged sexual despite chaste constancy, and male pretensions to virtuous authority are judged meretricious. (Interestingly, the most powerful speech in the play is a lecture urging not suicide, but willingness to die.) In *All's Well*, again, chaste constancy stands (and doesn't stand), but male power nearly destroys it or makes it irrelevant.

Othello is the final play concerned with this set of considerations. In this tragedy, as in *Much Ado*, the playwright allows himself to imagine the failure of the chaste constant ideal. Gazing at the material from a predominantly male point of view, Shakespeare probes the consequences of the misogyny upon which Western culture is founded. Sex is bestial and filthy; control is an absolute good: females are sexual; males must maintain control of them. Females may be purged of the taint of sexuality only through idealization, but ideals are shaky, they fail—Othello's loss of faith in Desdemona is a loss of faith in inlaw feminine virtues—and such a loss of faith makes all other human enterprises, even war and the fine feathers of heroism, which seem unrelated to the feminine principle, pointless and hollow.

This perception is pursued further, in a nonsexual context, in *Macbeth*. It is less divine injunction—the life to come—that is jumped, but rather the life purchased in the present by violation of the laws of human community that makes such violation an error. Unless power is granted by volitional subordination of all members of a culture, it must be secured by oppressive controls. Controls beget further controls: "If it were done when 'tis done," if one deed could secure power, power would be pleasant. As it is, maintenance of imposed power automatically deprives the controllers of all the elements that make life felicitous—honor, love, trust, troops of friends, harmony.

That the feminine principle is renounced in this play is implicit in the ambiguous gender of the witches who open the play; it is explicit in Lady Macbeth's early speeches. *Macbeth* is not about ambition per se. It considers the question, why is murder acceptable in war and not at home? What is the difference? It depicts the cost to a man, a woman, eventually an entire culture, of extending to the community the masculine dominance of the public sphere, the cost of devaluing feminine ends.

Shakespeare continued to try out visions of imbalanced cultures in *Coriolanus* and *Timon of Athens*, from both of which the feminine principle is missing. The aristocracy of Coriolanus' Rome is dedicated to high-sounding, noble ends—honor, bravery, and the governing of the city in ways Menenius claims are organic and therefore just. No one speaks of pleasure or continuation: feminine ends are specifically devalued in the imagery used by Volumnia and her son, and the deathly and mechanistic language used to describe Coriolanus. Imbalance leads inevitably to excess. The imbalance of Rome's moral/political structures culminates in Coriolanus' dead end: renouncing his city (home, family), he loses any goal in life beyond the exercise of his prowess for its own sake. "Honor" and "fame," hollow as these words are when he uses them in the early acts, become utterly meaningless once he turns his sword against his home.

Similarly, in *Timon of Athens*, the hero tries to do good, to gain honor and fame and most important, love, in the first half of the tragedy. But his real end is, like Coriolanus', self-exaltation and transcendence of mortality, rather than the good of the whole, harmonious communal interaction. Timon's values are as imbalanced as the Roman's, and he too turns, when his ego and pride are thwarted, against his home city. Without rooting in others—family, community, cultures—there is only the self, and the self cannot provide its own ends.

King Lear contains these notions about balance and excess; it deals also with legitimacy and constancy and with a devaluation of feminine qualities. Lear mistrusts the feminine principle so much that he demands a linguistic quantificaton of love and discards in an instant a sensitivity to and knowledge of his most beloved daughter. Trusting not to feeling (which can mislead) but to codification (which offers a fixedness and thus, a security—or so it seems), he banishes love (Cordelia) and loyalty (Kent).

But this great play does not simply (or not so simply) play out the results of mistrust, as does *The Winter's Tale*. It probes far deeper, into the roots of power, legitimacy, authority, and finds the human creature naked and vulnerable, dressed in emperor-style ermines, deluding only itself. Legitimacy is absurd, arrogant delusion; humans are merely one part of the interacting continuum of nature. Power is might, cloaking itself in authority; humans, like nature, are sexual, but female sexuality is a sulfurous pit. If the logic is not clear, the associations are: man is evil because he seizes power and calls himself good. Woman is evil because she is sexual and pretends not to be: "but to the girdle do the gods inherit."

The consequence of Lear's education in what underlies human institutions is a renewal or perhaps first full awareness of the value of those things that are felt, not said; fluid, not fixed; and which do not presume. The mark of humanness is neither power, which the elements have, nor sex, which the animals share, but inlaw feminine virtues—loving-kindness, nutritiveness, compassion, constancy, love. The entire environment in *King Lear* is oppressive: the "civilized" courts of Goneril and Regan, the "savage" nature of cliffs and storms. All the control and transcendence of the masculine principle are spurious and delusive. Only love and bondedness make life bearable.

Cordelia does not redeem the world of the play: she dies pointlessly; Lear dies brokenhearted. But Cordelia's actions trace a pattern: they and the values they embody are all that make the play (and implicitly the world) anything but agony. Cordelia is an idealization; nevertheless the values she incarnates do exist in real people in the real world.

The greatness of *King Lear*, the greatness of any piece of literature, does not depend totally on the moral formulation that underlies it. But moral largeness—the ability to conceive of a wide range of human qualities, and complex interactions among them—and moral generosity—the ability to imagine and depict humans whose motivations are not completely, narrowly self-bound—are elements in the production of a masterpiece. Of all Shakespeare's plays, *Lear* has these qualities to the highest degree.

Lear—and *Antony and Cleopatra*. The latter is unique in the Shakespearean canon in that it presents the outlaw feminine principle incarnated in a woman, not entirely unsympathetically. (The outlaw feminine principle is incarnated affectionately in a variety of men—the most important is the Falstaff of the *Henry IV* plays.) To accept the outlaw feminine principle in a female is to accept wholeheartedly, sexuality. The only other works of Shakespeare in which he even approaches this are two early comedies, *Love's Labour's Lost* and *A Midsummer Night's Dream*. Cleopatra and the world she dominates are sexual, sensual, pleasure-loving, playful, spontaneous, changeable, powerful, nutritive, loving, and capable of pity and compassion. Cleopatra and her Egypt represent the unified feminine principle. She is the only character in Shakespeare to do so.

Because the feminine principle is unified in *Antony and Cleopatra*, it is powerful, if still not as powerful in a worldly way as Rome with its emphasis on control—power, possession, and permanencies. And in this play (along with *Troilus and Cressida*) inlaw feminine qualities are relegated to the position they actually hold in the world: they are the female contribution to the masculine world, an adjunct to it, ancilla. Octavia, who has every virtue women are supposed to possess and no others, is, like all the women in *Troilus*, not a force in herself but a mere "cause" for male behavior.

In *King Lear*, Shakespeare probes beneath the sense of right and legitimacy that informs male supremacy to reveal the emptiness on which—or against which—these things rear themselves. In *Antony and Cleopatra*, he pulls apart his ideal, chastity and constancy unified, to reveal the nature of constancy as it exists—if it exists—in the real world. Thus, he is still dealing with the subjects he focused on in his early work. But in *Lear* and *Antony*—and in only these two plays—he comes up with different results.

Cordelia is the light in darkness in *Lear* because she represents those things that make life bearable, not because she can save the world, or Lear, or herself, not because she validates male legitimacy. And Antony and Cleopatra triumph in their tragedy not because they prove the enduringness of love, or because they are constant, but because they and the play as a whole demonstrate the constancy of feeling that underlies inconstancy of feeling and circumstance, and because they demonstrate that the richer life is lived by feminine values.

Continually searching for what endures, believing that only the enduring is significant, Shakespeare violates his own sense of the gender principles by locating the enduring—love and fidelity—squarely within the mutable, fluid feminine pole. The "masculine" world, with its structures and permanencies, the world of Rome, produces as much if not more alteration, shift, betrayal, and transiency than Egypt, the world of nature. Cleopatra may shift in mood, but Rome shifts in alliances, reneges on its vows, is pervaded by rivalry and mutual betrayal. Cleopatra has loved more than one man (as Antony has loved more than one woman) but her affections remain constant for Antony even though he betrays her, first by repudiating her, and later by marrying Octavia—a thing he is not forced to do.

Both the masculine and feminine world share the characteristic of flux, uncontrollable shift and alteration. Although a masculine structure like the Roman Empire may outlast generations, the single permanency that exists within the play is one of feeling. Thus, Enobarbus remains emotionally constant to Antony despite his abandonment of him; the lovers remain emotionally constant to each other despite a variety of betrayals. Antony remains in some way constant to Fulvia, whom he has left, and Brutus, whom he hounded to death. The only true permanency is death, Cleopatra concludes: all the rest is delusion. But there is also the Nile, which like the moon is inconstant, changing, and also constant in its tides and goes on breeding life out of the slime to which we all return.

In the tragedies, Shakespeare examines from different perspectives worlds in which inlaw feminine values and the women associated with them fail, are undervalued, repudiated, scorned, or simply lacking. The consequences of such attitudes to the male who dominates the play or the world depicted in the play or both are a diminishing of life so severe as to make it no longer worth living. Whether or not *Timon* was the last tragedy Shakespeare wrote, it is a fitting conclusion to the motion of the tragedies: Timon is a suicide.

Thus, Shakespeare returns, in the romances, to a world containing both gender principles. As in the problem plays, the principles are at war: it is more precise to say that the masculine principle mistrusts, hounds, or persecutes the feminine. But in these late comedies, the feminine principle is granted a power that is almost magical, almost divine. To confer such power on the powerless inlaw feminine pole requires special means—a resort to elements of the supernatural and a gross violation of realistic probability. Such things of course occur in the tragedies as well, but they are more frequent in the romances. In the proper area of their concern, which is the emotional dimension of life, the romances are not unrealistic. Love, unsexual as well as sexual, can heal a heart, can make life seem harmonious and rich despite losses. Friendship, harmony, the desire to be part of a whole (family, community), and caring for others are still, although many of us still forget this, the qualities which make life felicitous. By granting a seemingly supernatural power to these qualities and the young women who incarnate them, Shakespeare is able to produce visions of worlds in which there is balance.

Pericles is concerned with emotional life; it dramatizes internal states of a sense of wrongness and attendant guilt, fear, purgation. Its major symbol is homelessness, uprootedness which suggests a search for emotional balance. Like Syracusan Antipholus in Shakespeare's earliest comedy (*Comedy of Errors*), Pericles is deprived of felicity by being deprived of relationship; the Prince is first guiltily haunted and second deprived of his wife and child.

It is interesting to compare these two plays, one written near the beginning of Shakespeare's career, the second near the end. Both are concerned with the problem of homelessness. In the early comedy, however, homelessness is a lack not just of family (relationship) but of a place within the context of a society. The search in *Comedy of Errors* is often called a search for identity. Identity is discovered, by all the major characters, with the discovery of family ties which confer a place within a societal structure. That is to say, identity is externally conferred.

In *Pericles*, the problem is quite different. The Prince has a place in a society; what he lacks is family, a wife, someone to love, or rather, the rest of himself. He seeks his missing integrity wrongly—in an unequal. Fleeing from this knowledge, he gives up worldly power entirely, and achieves integration with Thaisa, only to lose it again. It is restored to him by an unequal, his daughter, a young and beautiful woman whom he can look at without desire. His ability to accept love, harmony, and community without sexual desire makes him whole. Integrity is internally achieved.

Yet these two qualities, identity and integrity, seem similar, in that both involve a sense of committedness to others which allows the self to feel complete. What makes them different is that the former is posited on a degree of legitimacy, status within a structure; the second is posited on the ability to give and receive, to be accepted in one's selfhood (as Marina's acceptance of Pericles' blow suggests) and to accept others (as Pericles finally accepts Marina). The difference between identity and integrity is the awareness developed in the period when Shakespeare tested his own values, in the period when he wrote the problem plays and tragedies and allowed himself to perceive the illegitimacy of legitimacy, the hollowness of most ideals, and the nature of the true ends of life.

Cymbeline continues in this line of concern. A set of people desire to set Imogen in the center of their lives. An incarnation of the inlaw feminine principle, Imogen belongs at the center of a life. But most of those who want her approach her wrongly: they attempt to control, possess, fix her. Their efforts amount to a persecution of her. What is necessary is that she herself control herself and be permitted her own autonomy. When the world around her learns this, it arranges itself around her, in harmony.

The situation in *The Winter's Tale* is similar, and reminiscent of the situation in several earlier plays as well. The problem is male loss of faith in the inlaw feminine principle. Thus, the problem is the drive behind the masculine principle, the desire, need to control. What is not controllable becomes a threat, which many males in Shakespeare attempt to eliminate. Like Claudio in *Much Ado*, like *Othello*, Leontes eliminates the uncontrollable, fluid, vital, emotional element from his life. He must then live life out "most marble," as coldly and fixedly as stone. Like Pericles, he is healed by a daughter, a nubile woman offering inlaw feminine virtues who is seen and accepted in the beauty of her being, rather than in the heat of desire.

The Tempest, the last and finest of these plays, encompasses most as well. It is eminently a drama of emotional life, but it is about justice, the proper arrangement within one man (and thus also within a society) of the elements of experience. The threats to justice, which is also integrity, harmony, come from both "feminine" and "masculine" elements. The feminine world of the island requires constant supervision; Ariel and Caliban require continual coercion; Miranda is always within her father's eye. Anarchic, uncontrolling, these elements continually offer to slide back into mere nature, into unregulation. The masculine world of power which Prospero draws to the island is contentious, competitive, controlling, and even murderous. Using magic (feminine) and art (masculine), Prospero attempts to bring all the elements into a just and harmonious balance. What is necessary above all is restraint —of power, rage, revenge, fear, and sexuality. At great effort—and his effort is palpable in his grimness, his irritability, his occasional despair —he accomplishes this, but only for a moment. That the balance achieved is only temporary is explicit in the play, but its great beauty derives from the fact that a balance that is credible, that has the power of felt experience, is indeed achieved.

Because the focus of this study has been on poles of experience— that is, on the diverse, broad gamut of experience dichotomized, segregated, made exclusive to stated human beings—it may seem to reinforce this division. That is not my intention. I have attempted to trace and describe a disintegration in human life which I believe Shakespeare perceived and dealt with continually. Many critics have made similar attempts, and indeed there is an overlapping of concept and sometimes even terminology in a large body of criticism. But discussing moral concepts in Shakespeare leads to murkiness and ambiguity without a concomitant sense of his associational pattern and his different perception of the two genders. I lament the terms "masculine" and "feminine" when applied to an experience I myself perceive as human: but no other terms offer as consistent, comprehensive, and concise a description of the way the Western world has conceived of itself for the past two thousand years.

In addition, this study may seem to contain an animus against the masculine principle. It does. But this does not stem from lack of appreciation of the qualities associated with that pole of experience. Structures, permanencies, control, individualism are essential to all our lives and can offer at times as much pleasure as "feminine" qualities. My animus is directed against the almost total dedication to "masculine" values that is characteristic of our culture, and of most of those who make it up.

Shakespeare considered, in play after play, the consequences to men and to the worlds they dominated, of undervaluing the fluid, insubstantial, and emotional dimension of experience. In play after play, those consequences were emptiness, insanity, and suicide. The values of the world have changed since Shakespeare's time, but they have not changed direction. They have carried further the process he diagnosed, to the point where the destruction of the planet is conceivable.

For Shakespeare, the greatest threat lay in nature. Perhaps it is more accurate to say that intellectually he perceived threats to human harmony and continuation as arising out of both abused power and the power of nature, but emotionally he feared nature and those things he associated with it to a degree that seems pathological to some of his twentieth-century critics. If his horror of sex, powerful women, and the sloth and bestiality of a Caliban was pathological, the disease was not his alone. It was part of his culture and it is part of ours. But if the emotional emphasis in his work expresses this horror, the intellectual emphasis—that is, the problem considered in play after play—is on the failure of males to absorb, express, or even value inlaw feminine qualities.

In our own time and in our part of the world, nature seems a poor enough threat. It is being slowly extinguished by a belief in control and possession that does not realize that everything costs something. For Westerners of the twentieth century, it is the masculine principle and its total dedication to power and control in every area of existence that threatens to extinguish not only human felicity but the human race itself.

Shakespeare urged synthesis, integration. The difficulty lay in the impossibility of synthesizing qualities with such unequal appeal. Two thousand years of Christianity have not succeeded in persuading people to adopt "divine" virtues, even using the threat of hell pains as a coercive. Shakespeare was far subtler: the reason for assimilating and valuing inlaw qualities was because they make this life richer, make it, at its worst, bearable.

My attitude, beyond this study, is that the identification of moral qualities with genders is itself the root of the problem. A division of experience leads automatically to a ranking of its parts. Western culture is founded on misogyny because the urge to power requires devaluing those things it seeks power over, and those things have traditionally been associated with women. The way out of the bind—and it is a bind—the way to alter the world's suicidal course, seems to me to be to abandon these divisions, to see all of human experience as good and available to all humans. The separation of power from humane ends licenses power to be inhumane, bars those with humane values from power. To reintegrate human experience is to restore the links between action and feeling, between shaping and that which is shaped. This must be done in our minds before it can be done substantially.

The work of Shakespeare has been a major influence on all of Western culture. The world does not need me to say how much we owe him. He expressed, often in great poetry, the feel, the texture of human life on earth, the explorations and conclusions of a large, generous, and probing mind. He never settled for the received idea even in the area (sex) where it had most deeply implanted itself. He never turned his back on power, that uncomfortable subject. And he never stopped searching for a way to reintegrate human experience. But because he—and his tradition—saw experience in terms of polar opposites, his work has been important in perpetuating the very division he sought to reconcile. At the same time, because he captured in poetry the fluid, emotional moment, making it permanent; because he gave powerful expression to values found insubstantial in the world; his work itself achieved the synthesis that the moral dimension of the plays strove for.

Notes

The following abbreviations are used for the publications most often cited:

ELH   *Journal of English Literary History*
PMLA *Publications of the Modern Language Association*
RES   *Review of English Studies*
SEL   *Studies in English Literature*
SQ   *Shakespeare Quarterly*
SS   *Shakespeare Survey*
SStud *Shakespeare Studies*

Introduction

1. Benjamin Whorf, "Thinking in Primitive Communities," *Language, Thought, and Reality*, ed. John B. Carroll (Cambridge, Mass., 1967), p. 69.
2. Whorf, "Thinking," p. 69.
3. Gen. 1:26, 28.
4. Gen. 2:20.
5. Gen. 3:20.
6. See Judg. 4–5; Prov. 3:10–31.

I. THE GENDER PRINCIPLES

1. The Gender Principles

1. Leslie Fiedler points out that women in Shakespeare are defined as "superhuman or subhuman, divine or diabolic," and that they feel like strangers "in a culture whose

notion of the human is defined by males." *The Stranger in Shakespeare* (New York, 1972), pp. 44–45.
2. Robert E. Fitch, *Shakespeare: The Perspective of Value* (Philadelphia, 1970), p. 210, remarks that women are more "normative" than men in Shakespeare, and that they are always seen as functions of men.
3. G. Wilson Knight, *Wheel of Fire* (New York, 1947), pp. 47–48.
4. Knight, *Wheel*, pp. 264–265.
5. Terence Hawkes, *Shakespeare's Talking Animals* (London, 1973), p. 129. However, he continues: "True manhood . . . lies in true talking and listening which involves the *whole* range of man's potential, not part of it" (p. 132). Unless he has suddenly broadened the meaning of his term *manhood*, this leaves women presumably mute and deaf.
6. E. M. W. Tillyard, *Shakespeare's Problem Plays* (Toronto, 1949), p. 30.
7. John Wain, "The Mind of Shakespeare," *More Talking of Shakespeare*, ed. John Garrett (London, 1959), p. 159.

2. *Formal Equivalents of the Gender Principles*

1. Thus many critics believe that Shakespearean comedy presents a "woman's world."
2. John Russell Brown, *Shakespeare and His Comedies* (London, 1957), p. 39, writes that the comedies and the histories focus on more characters than the tragedies; in "The Interpretation of Shakespeare's Comedies: 1900–1953," *SS* 8 (1955): 1–13, he quotes E. E. Schelling, who says the interest of the comedies lies in "kaleidoscopic groupings."
3. "Tragedy presents a great event; there are no events in comedy; there are only 'happenings.' Events are irreversible and comedy is not concerned with the irreversible," writes Helen Gardner, "*As You Like It*," *More Talking of Shakespeare*, ed. John Garrett (London, 1959), p. 22. And Northrop Frye, discussing tragedy, explains that the tragic is rooted in time, in a one-dimensional quality of life, "where everything happens once and for all, where every act brings unavoidable and fateful consequences." *Fools of Time* (Toronto, 1967), p. 3.
4. "Shakespeare's comedy pleases by the thoughts and language, and his tragedy for the greater part by incident and action." Milton Crane, "Shakespeare's Comedies and the Critics," *SQ* XV, 2 (1964): 67–73. M. C. Bradbrook finds the comic form in the language: "The characters are defined by their individual accent and idiom . . . The contrast of different characters in terms of their different idiom . . . constitutes the 'form' of the comedy." *Shakespeare and Elizabethan Poetry* (New York, 1952), pp. 214–215. Emphasizing the focus of tragedy on action and comedy on language are Ludwig Borinski's observations that in the comedies, nouns and adjectives predominate over verbs (in the prose passages). Comic prose scenes are static, in keeping with the eternal, or unmoving nature of comedy. Borinski writes: "Jests, images, allusions . . . become ends in themselves." He adds that the progress of the prose passages is not logical. "Shakespeare's Comic Prose," *SS* 8 (1955): 57–68.
5. Wolfgang Clemen, *The Development of Shakespeare's Imagery* (Cambridge, Mass., 1951), p. 33, describes Shakespeare's puns as fine instruments "for the deliberately ambiguous interpretation of a situation." And Maynard Mack, writing on *As You Like It*, explains pun this way: "Instead of single-mindedness, pun presupposes multiple-mindedness; instead of preoccupation with one's present self and purposes, an alert glance before and after; and instead of loss of intellectual and emotional maneuverability, a gain, for language creatively used is freedom." "Engagement and Detachment in Shakespeare's Plays," *Essays on Shakespeare and Elizabethan Drama in Honor of Hardin Craig*, ed. Richard Hosley (Columbia, Miss., 1962), p. 289.
6. H. B. Charlton, *Shakesperian Comedy* (New York, 1938), p. 292, writes that Shakespearean comedy "is the setting up of harmonious and beneficent relationships with human beings. It is an active membership in the society of man. . . . Of all virtues, that

which best promotes its well-being is the passion for serving the world, the instinct for sacrifice in the cause of the general good." Comedy is not moral, but accepting: "the comic muse is an earthly muse," claims Edward Hubler, "The Range of Shakespeare's Comedy," *SQ* XV, 2 (1964): 55–66. "In the comic vision of experience, the effort to transcend human limitations can never be regarded as other than folly or worse." Cyrus Hoy, *"Love's Labour's Lost* and the Nature of Comedy," *SQ* XIII (1962): 31–40.

7. Because it deals with the eternal present, comedy is essentially timeless. This has been discussed by many critics, including Helen Gardner, *"As You Like It,"* Northrop Frye in numerous works, and Jay Halio, "No Clock in the Forest: Time in *As You Like It,"* *SEL* II (1962): 197–207.

8. Frye, *A Natural Perspective* (New York, 1965), among others; Susanne Langer, *Feeling and Form* (New York, 1953).

9. Mary Lascelles explains: "Where none is known until he chooses to disclose himself, the odds are strongly in favor of an unknown champion proving a woman—or if a man, one alienated from his rights, or his very name." "Shakespeare's Pastoral Comedy," *More Talking of Shakespeare*, ed. John Garrett (London, 1959).

10. C. L. Barber claims that in the tragedies, love is presented in unique destinies; in the comedies, what is shown is love's effect on a group. *Shakespeare's Festive Comedy* (New York, 1967), p. 130.

11. Frye calls linear form "progressive narrative." *A Natural Perspective*, pp. 28–29.

II. RECEIVED IDEAS

3. *Power: The First Tetralogy*

1. E. M. W. Tillyard, *Shakespeare's History Plays* (New York, 1946), p. 160. In order to support this reading of *1 Henry VI*, however, Tillyard is forced to label some of its scenes "inorganic." Andrew S. Cairncross, ed., Arden *Henry VI, Part One* (London, 1962), calls the entire tetralogy an "epic of England" (p. xli).

2. John F. Danby, *Shakespeare's Doctrine of Nature: A Study of "King Lear"* (London, 1961), p. 124.

3. Frye, *A Natural Perspective* (New York, 1965), p. 89, writes that in the histories, the theme that makes for a reconciling conclusion is the "principle of legitimacy." J. I. M. Stewart persuasively argues that Shakespeare was not the ardent adherent of "order and degree" that he has been made out. "Shakespeare's Men and Their Morals," *More Talking of Shakespeare*, ed. John Garrett (London, 1959). Much of the work of L. C. Knights is directed toward modifying and refining the "order and degree" theory. See *Poetry, Politics and the English Tradition* (London, 1954, *Shakespeare's Politics* (Folcroft, Pa., 1957), *Some Shakespearean Themes* (London, 1959), and *Further Explorations* (London, 1965) among others. The theme of legitimacy by birth is discussed by Ronald Berman, "Fathers and Sons in the *Henry VI* Plays," *SQ* XIII (1962): 487–497. Berman believes the plays "come to terms with the idea of inheritance." He develops his ideas in "Shakespeare's Conscious Histories," *Dalhousie Review* XLI, 4 (Winter, 1961–62): 485–495. David Riggs reminds us that the relation of "gentle birth and achieved virtue" was endlessly debated in the Renaissance. Riggs believes that in the *Henry VI* plays, Shakespeare "enlarges the central issue beyond the narrow problem of hereditary legitimacy," and that the behavior of the Talbots makes "valor . . . a test of legitimacy." *Shakespeare's Heroical Histories* (Cambridge, Mass., 1971), pp. 69, 83, 104. Don M. Ricks, *Shakespeare's Emergent Form* (Logan, Utah, 1968), also discusses these notions, and suggests that the very notion of inherited legitimacy is responsible for the behavior of the characters (p. 90). See also Danby, p. 75.

4. L. C. Knights, *Shakespeare's Politics*, Annual Shakespeare Lecture of the British Academy (1957), pp. 123–124.

5. Knights, *William Shakespeare: The Histories* (London, 1962), p. 15.

6. Geoffrey Bullough, ed., *Narrative and Dramatic Sources of Shakespeare* III (New York, 1960), p. 39.

7. Raphael Holinshed, *Chronicles* [600/2/2] in Bullough, p. 75.

8. Holinshed [604/1/55] in Bullough, pp. 76–77.

9. Tillyard, who sees the struggle between Joan and Talbot as the main motive of the play, explains: "Joan is not allowed to kill [Talbot]; that would be unseemly." *History Plays*, p. 168.

10. Joan is compared to Astraea when the Dauphin first meets her: Astraea is a noble figure, but she is the *female* equivalent of male legitimacy—she represents justice in a "pagan" vision, and this comparison soon after Henry V is compared with Christ. She is also compared with the "nine sibyls of Rome" (I, ii, 56), to the courtesan Rhodope, to Hecate and to Circe. Male comparisons are with Hannibal, who is seen as a witch and a strategist, and to Mahomet, whose name appears frequently as an evil god in Spenser, and who is deemed, says David Riggs (p. 101), as "a magician and a religious charlatan."

11. Tillyard, *History Plays*, p. 158, says the scenes "could be spared from the play." Don Ricks sees the scene with the Countess as simply another example of French treachery, but adds that the witchcraft theme is "not integrated . . . with the central idea . . . of 'civil broils' and their destructive effects." *Form*, p. 49.

12. Tillyard believes this scene is inorganic; Cairncross, disagrees with him, asserting that the Margaret-Suffolk scene "ensures the dominance of the disastrous French influence" (p. xlix).

13. See Berman, "Fathers and Sons," and Ricks, *Form*.

14. C. S. Lewis, *English Literature in the Sixteenth Century* (Oxford, 1954), p. 381. H. T. Price calls these "Mirror Scenes," *J. Q. Adams Memorial Studies*, ed. J. McManaway (Washington, D.C., 1948), pp. 101–114.

15. This is pointed out and discussed by Leo Kirschbaum, "The Authorship of 1 *Henry VI*," *PMLA* 67 (September 1952): 809–822. Kirschbaum finds the climax of 1 *Henry VI* in the Talbot scenes, and sees them as "order," contrasted with the "disorder" of the father-son scene in 3 *Henry VI*.

16. Bullough, p. 72.

17. Danby, p. 59, writes: "Henry VI is as nearly blameless as a king can be." But many critics disagree, among them Irving Ribner, *The English History Play in the Age of Shakespeare* (Princeton, N.J., 1957), and James Winny, *The Player King* (London, 1968).

18. See Bullough, p. 100.

19. Gareth Lloyd Evans writes "order must not be shaken," *Shakespeare* I (Edinburgh, 1969), p. 27. Many critics agree. Among those who discuss this point are Ribner, Tillyard, Ricks, Danby, and Lily B. Campbell, *Shakespeare's 'Histories'* (San Marino, Calif., 1958). This position seems too simple for Shakespeare. How can humans prevent presently constituted authority from dying, or assure a desirable succession? If Hitler is the presently constituted authority, does one refuse to shake his order?

20. Shakespeare "was not a political writer in the sense in which Milton and Dryden were sometimes: . . . he had no cause to support," writes L. C. Knights, *Poetry, Politics, and the English Tradition* (London, 1954), p. 24. I think we must discriminate between support of a party and support of a philosophy: both are political acts, and both have a set of beliefs that can be called dogma. Shakespeare had a vision of the proper organization of society that did not essentially change. In *Shakespeare's Politics* (Folcroft, Pa., 1957), Knights writes that "Shakespeare's political plays are creative explorations of conceptions such as power, authority, honour, order, and freedom, which only too easily become objects of 'idolatry' " (p. 15) and (speaking of the *Henry IV* plays) "the assumptions of the dominant groups are by no means taken for granted" (p. 3) and are even subtly challenged.

21. In Berman's terms, England must suffer because no one has the "right combination of power and piety" ("Fathers and Sons").

22. Cairncross, p. li.

23. Edward Hall, *Union of the Noble Houses of Lancaster and Yorke* [c/v], in Bullough, p. 105.

24. Bullough, p. 94.

24. Hall [clvi^v], Bullough, p. 115.

26. Tillyard, *History Plays*, p. 201, believes each of the plays in the tetralogy has a center expressing proper order. He lists Talbot doing homage to the King in *1 Henry VI*, Iden in *1 Henry VI*, Henry's idyll on the molehill in *3 Henry VI*, and Richmond's final speech in *Richard III*.

27. Tillyard, p. 188.

28. Riggs, p. 129.

29. Bullough, p. 167.

30. Lloyd Evans comments, "The whole scene gives a strange impression of being on a different time-scale from its context. This impression is partly created by the ritual language and the antiphonic structure of the speeches." Intro., Arden *1 Henry VI*, p. 59.

31. "Some write that the duke was taken alive and in derision caused to stand upon a molehill, on whose head they put a garland in steed of a crowne," adds Holinshed (Bullough, p. 210). In this account too, his head was struck off and then presented to the Queen.

32. Hall [ccxviii], Bullough, p. 203.

33. Dover Wilson, *The Essential Shakespeare* (Cambridge, 1932), p. 118.

34. Riggs, p. 144, discusses the widespread critical opinion that Richard is a "self-fulfilling exercise in anarchy and evil, utterly divorced from any plausible human motivations."

35. Danby, p. 75.

36. Shakespeare begins to launder Edward's character as early as *3H6*, II, vi, when he spares the prisoners after the battle of Towton. In fact, Edward ordered the execution of all captives. This continues into *Richard III*, where his part in the assassination of Clarence is minimized.

37. Danby, p. 59.

38. Bullough, p. 250.

39. Tillyard, p. 214. Bullough remarks that there are more major characters in *Richard III* than in the other parts of the tetralogy, and that they have larger parts. He attributes this to Shakespeare's desire to write a Senecan tragedy. See pp. 235–242.

40. Hall [ii. liii], Bullough, p. 293.

41. Hall [ii. lv], Bullough, p. 295.

42. *Ibid*.

43. Bullough, p. 38.

44. Berman, "Fathers and Sons."

45. Ricks, p. 14.

46. Winny, pp. 41–42; 29.

47. Leslie A. Fiedler, *The Stranger in Shakespeare* (New York, 1972), pp. 15; 51.

48. Virgil's *Aeneid* attempts, as Shakespeare attempted in this tetralogy, to legitimate the "masculine" values of Rome. In the first half of the epic, Aeneas' wife Creusa simply drifts away into the void; Aeneas alone has the responsibility for his young son and his aged father Anchises, whom he carries on his back. Males, then, have full control and full responsibility for legitimacy, the father-son tradition, and for the feminine principle (continuity) as well. Dido can offer Aeneas biological continuity, but not the continuity of a unilaterally masculine tradition. In the second half of the epic, the opposition is between two males who claim the territory. The land over which they fight is symbolized —indeed, comes with—a woman, Lavinia. But Lavinia herself cannot claim the land she presumably owns. She is seen as identical with it: her body and the territory require the *control*—not the cooperation—of a male. Woman = territory: Lavinia represents the inlaw feminine principle. The only other representative of the inlaw feminine principle

in this part of the poem is the piety of Latinus. Latinus, however, uses his piety to communicate with Jove, who finds in favor of Aeneas. Thus the inlaw feminine principle is, as it is supposed to be, in service to the masculine.

Both Turnus and Aeneas represent the masculine principle, which will win in any case. But Turnus is supported by a group of female figures who are furious and raging but (as in Shakespeare) ultimately impotent: the mad Amata, the sneaky Juno, the hideous Alecto. Misogynistic remarks are sprinkled through this part of the poem: females, whether mortal or immortal, are passionate, mad, crafty, unstable, and moody.

Aeneas, who incorporates the feminine principle within himself because of his powerful mother, Venus, and because he takes responsibility for the "feminine" end of continuation, has the support of two fathers, Latinus and Jove. Thus it is clear who has the *right*. Some critics read *The Aeneid* as a poem which laments the sacrifices (*lacrimae rerum*, the tears of things) necessary to build an empire. But there is little lament in the depiction of female power in the second half of the epic, which fulfills its "masculine" purpose as a national monument designed to celebrate Rome's transcendent worldly power and linguistic tradition.

4. *Marriage*

1. These plays are frequently dismissed because they are farces, claims John Russell Brown, "The Interpretation of Shakespeare's Comedies: 1900–1953," *SS* 8 (1955): 1–13.
2. Thomas Marc Parrott, *Shakespearean Comedy* (New York, 1949), p. 106, finds "the passionate and jealous Adriana" the only "firmly conceived and realistically developed" character in the comedy.
3. There are frequent references to sorcery in Ephesus. These are listed by Bertrand Evans, *Shakespeare's Comedies* (Oxford, 1960), p. 2.
4. See Harold Brooks, "Themes and Structures in *The Comedy of Errors*," *Early Shakespeare* (London, 1961), p. 68. Brooks believes the climax of the play is reached with the Duke's statement: "I think you've drunk of Circe's cup."
5. John Russell Brown, *Shakespeare and His Comedies* (London, 1957), p. 54, claims there is general recognition at the end of the play that love is ownership.
6. For a slightly different analysis of these images, see Ralph Berry, *Shakespeare's Comedies* (Princeton, N.J., 1972), p. 35.
7. Richard Henze, "*The Comedy of Errors*: A Freely Binding Chain," *SQ* XXII (1971): 35–41.
8. Harold Brooks, "Themes."
9. F. P. Wilson, *Shakespearian and Other Studies* (Oxford, 1969), p. 56, writes that *Taming* is "part of the paper war between the sexes which flourished . . . during the later Middle Ages and the Renaissance, a war in which all the shots were fired by the male sex. This is the only comedy of Shakespeare's in which the hero outwits the heroine."
10. Frye, *A Natural Perspective* (New York, 1965), p. 80.
11. C. L. Barber, *Shakespeare's Festive Comedy* (Princeton, N.J., 1959).

III. THE INLAW FEMININE PRINCIPLE

5. *Constancy*

1. John F. Danby, "Shakespeare Criticism and *Two Gentlemen of Verona*," *Critical Quarterly* 2 (1960): 309–321.

2. See Ralph M. Sargent, "Sir Thomas Elyot and the Integrity of *The Two Gentlemen of Verona*," *PMLA* 65 (1950): 1166–1180.

3. John Russell Brown, *Shakespeare and His Comedies* (London, 1957), p. 83, asserts that the commonest form of recognition of love in the comedies is the perception of beauty.

4. Thus he altered his source, Montemayor's *Diana*, with its Felix and Felismena, in which, after Felix leaves her, Felismena follows him and seeing a knight set upon, kills two men with her arrows to assist him. For full discussion of Shakespeare's changes of the source, see Thomas Marc Parrott, *Shakespearean Comedy* (New York, 1949), pp. 114–116.

5. Caroline Spurgeon observes that unlike his contemporaries, Shakespeare drew nearly half of his class images from the poor and oppressed, from prisoners, idiots or madmen, from gypsies, beggars, peddlers, and slaves. *Shakespeare's Imagery* (Boston, 1961), p. 33. Juliet Dusinberre, *Shakespeare and the Nature of Women* (London, 1975), p. 114, writes that women are related to the fools in Shakespeare because "both stand on the periphery of the serious world of men, assessing its wisdom from the perspective of not being of any account."

6. C. L. Barber claims verbal play is "almost an end in itself" in the comedy. *Shakespeare's Festive Comedy* (New York, 1967), p. 96. M. C. Bradbrook points to the "consistent . . . linguistic interest." *Shakespeare and Elizabethan Poetry* (New York, 1952), p. 213. Northrop Frye (*A Natural Perspective* [New York, 1965], p. 95) claims "verbal play . . . is the main subject"; and Thomas M. Greene, *"Love's Labour's Lost:* The Grace of Society," *SQ* XXII (1971): 314–328, sees grace and civility as central and believes the play is about language cut off from feeling. See also Ralph Berry, *Shakespeare's Comedies* (Princeton, N.J., 1972), p. 72.

7. Cyrus Hoy believes the play is a satire on fine manners and pedantry. *"Love's Labour's Lost* and the Nature of Comedy," *SQ* XIII (1962): 31–40. Harley Granville-Barker, *Prefaces to Shakespeare* (London, 1933), p. 2, writes: "The play is a satire, a comedy of affectations."

8. Nature and animal images dominate the play. Spurgeon, p. 271.

9. J. R. Brown, *Comedies*, p. 135, complains that "bawdy jokes and double entendres . . . run throughout the comedies. Allusions to horns, tails, geese, savage bulls . . . constantly touch upon the essentially beastlike element of love."

10. Berry, *Comedies*, p. 80. He adds, "The women play games with words but never devalue them, although the men confuse oaths and jests."

11. D. A. Traversi, *An Approach to Shakespeare* I (Garden City, N.Y., 1969), p. 96, points out that at the conclusion of the play, the lords are forced to go in reality into the "austere" and "insociable" life they originally vowed.

12. Thomas M. Greene argues that one source of dislike of the play is a lack, which Greene finds unique to this play (of Shakespeare's), of "any firm social underpinning—an authority, a strong wise center of political power." *"Love's Labour's Lost."* I think it is difficult to find a strong wise center of political power in most of the comedies.

13. Bobbyann Roesen, *"Love's Labour's Lost," SQ* (1953): 411–426. She asserts, "Only through the acceptance of the reality of Death are life and love in their fullest sense made possible for the people of the play."

14. Thomas M. Greene, *"Love's Labour's Lost."*

15. Barbara Everett, *"Much Ado About Nothing," Critical Quarterly* 3 (1961): 319–335, alluding to *Love's Labour's Lost*, writes that "dignity comes through the acceptance of folly."

16. C. L. Barber asserts the play is about the role of imagination in experience, seeing imagination in a positive way. Frank Kermode believes that imagination leads to "disorders of fantasy," and Charles R. Lyons finds the play shallow because imagination leads to an illusion of "love's triumph over death." Barber, *Festive Comedy*, p. 157; Kermode, "The Mature Comedies," *Early Shakespeare* (London, 1961), p. 214; Lyons, *Shakespeare and the Ambiguity of Love's Triumph* (The Hague, 1971), p. 42.

17. The importance of perception as a theme is emphasized by the frequent occurrence of the images of *eye*, *sight*, and compounds of these. For discussion of these, see Berry, *Comedies*, p. 86; and R. W. Dent, "Imagination in *Midsummer Night's Dream*," *SQ* XV, 2 (1964): 115–129.

18. The frequency of the image of the moon has been pointed out by Spurgeon, p. 259, and discussed by David P. Young, *Something of Great Constancy* (New Haven, 1966), pp. 25–26. R. W. Dent, "Imagination," sees the moon as a symbol of inconstancy and a parallel to the inconstancy of the males in the play.

19. Frank Kermode, "Mature Comedies," believes the theme of transformation is connected with the experience of divine love (p. 219). David P. Young writes that transformation, change, mutability, and transience pervade *Midsummer Night's Dream*, and are part of nature. He finds the element that provides "coherence and constancy" is "the poet's art." *Constancy*, p. 160.

20. "The ridiculous and the beautiful grow so close together in *Midsummer Night's Dream* that it is harmful to try to separate them." Barbara Everett, "*Much Ado*." David Young discusses the profusion of references to natural phenomena and the many lists found in the play and suggests that they work to create a "fully realized world," a "cornucopia of sensuous experience." *Constancy*, pp. 81–82.

21. Nevertheless, one critic is able to extrapolate from the play the fact that the males, Theseus and Oberon, represent reason, whereas the females, Hippolyta and Titania, represent passion. Paul A. Olson, "A *Midsummer Night's Dream* and the Meaning of Court Marriage," *ELH* 24, 2 (June 1957): 95–119.

22. Charles R. Lyons, *Ambiguity*, believes the play intends to celebrate that folly by celebrating "the illusion of an infinite happiness which arrests the natural disintegration of time and death" (p. 42).

23. David Young, *Constancy*, p. 80.

6. Money

1. C. L. Barber, *Shakespeare's Festive Comedy* (New York, 1967), p. 184.

2. Thus, W. H. Auden points out that in Belmont, time stands still; in Venice, it is real. *The Dyer's Hand* (New York, 1962), p. 235; and Barbara K. Lewalski writes, "Belmont is the land of the spirit, not the letter." "Biblical Allusion and Allegory in *The Merchant of Venice*," *SQ* XIII (1962): 327–343.

3. Ralph Berry, *Shakespeare's Comedies* (Princeton, N.J., 1972), p. 113, points out that the most frequently repeated words in the play—venture, hazard, thrift, fortune, lottery, and advantage—are all concerned with gain.

4. J. W. Lever claims the play is about love and usury. "Shylock, Portia, and the Values of Shakespearean Comedy," *SQ* III (1952): 383–386. John Russell Brown suggests that Shakespeare saw love as a kind of usury. *Shakespeare and His Comedies* (London, 1957), p. 62.

5. Harley Granville-Barker, *Prefaces to Shakespeare* (London, 1930), p. 90.

6. In line with such an attitude towards the play, Bertrand Evans sees Portia's announcement of the saved ships as having the effect of implying that she saved them. *Shakespeare's Comedies* (Oxford, 1960), p. 67.

7. A. D. Moody, *The Merchant of Venice* (London, 1964), p. 9, writes that Shylock and his judges have an "essential likeness." J. R. Brown, ed., Arden *Merchant of Venice* (New York, 1964), p. lvi, points out that both Portia and Bassanio use commercial terms and have transactions.

8. J. R. Brown, Arden *Merchant*, is unhappy with the bawdy talk, finding it "not apposite" (p. lii). He writes that "it is irrelevant to ask for themes and meanings in a play that ends with a bawdy joke about the chastity of a waiting woman" (p. xlix).

9. Lever, "Shylock."

10. Sylvan Barnet, ed., *Twentieth-Century Interpretations of "The Merchant of Venice"* (Englcwood Cliffs, N.J., 1970), claims the play is about giving.
11. John Hazel Smith, "Shylock: 'Devil Incarnation' or 'Poor Man . . . Wronged'?" *Journal of English and Germanic Philology* LXI (January 1961): 1–21.
12. Caroline Spurgeon, *Shakespeare's Imagery* (Boston, 1961), p. 270.
13. Berry, *Comedies*, p. 148, finds revenge the subject of the play.
14. Northrop Frye, *A Natural Perspective* (New York, 1965), p. 36, claims that this scene has been "dragged in merely to fill up time."
15. Frye, *Perspective*, p. 89, writes that Fenton becomes the "technical hero," and that, as part of Prince Hal's world, he merges two societies.

7. The Realm of Emotion

1. It has a fully "feminine" form. Helen Gardner, "*As You Like It,*" *More Talking of Shakespeare*, ed. John Garrett (London, 1959), p. 20, writes that "story was not Shakespeare's concern in this play." Harold Jenkins finds this a disadvantage: "it is in the defectiveness of its action that AYLI differs from the rest of the major comedies." He complains that the play lacks even logical cause and effect, and that "the confusions of identity in *As You Like It* have no influence whatever upon the ultimate destiny of Rosalind or Orlando, of the kingdom of Duke Senior or the estate of Sir Rowland." "*As You Like It,*" *SS* 8 (1955): 40–51.
2. M. C. Bradbrook, *Shakespeare and Elizabethan Poetry* (New York, 1952), p. 220, calls the play a literary satire.
3. M. C. Bradbrook discusses this practice in the comedies in general. *Shakespeare*, p. 181. Shakespeare seemed to have a reluctance to show gentlemen chiding gentlewomen in the comedies; when they do so, as in *Much Ado* and *The Winter's Tale*, the scenes are very strong, and function to damn the *speaker* in the audience's eyes. In general, he reproves female behavior through female characters. Since the women who are being reproved are invariably being told to behave as males would have them behave, Shakespeare's delicacy lies in not placing the demand in the mouths of those who will gain from it, but rather in the mouths of their sisters, who seem to be uttering higher truths of *nature*.
4. Jenkins, "*As You Like It.*"
5. The images that dominate the play are drawn from nature, agriculture, and animal life. Such images appear with greater frequency in *As You Like It* than in any other Shakespeare play. Caroline Spurgeon, *Shakespeare's Imagery* (Boston, 1961), p. 279.
6. For an interesting discussion of Jaques, see Bradbrook, *Shakespeare*, p. 225.
7. C. C. Seronsy points out that Petruchio's method of taming Kate is to "suppose" qualities in Kate no one suspects she has, and that "supposes" means "as if." " 'Supposes' as the Unifying Theme in *The Shrew*," *SQ* XIV (1963): 15–30. "As if" could be denominated as the principle on which all Shakespeare's comedies work.
8. Albert Gilman, ed., Signet *As You Like It* (New York, 1965), pp. 840–841.
9. Among the critics who so describe it are C. L. Barber and Charles R. Lyons.
10. Barnet, Signet *As You Like It*, p. 39.
11. As does Charles R. Lyons, *Shakespeare and the Ambiguity of Love's Triumph* (The Hague, 1971), p. 45.
12. C. L. Barber, *Shakespeare's Festive Comedy* (New York, 1967), p. 252. Bertrand Evans, however, finds Viola the most "feminine" of Shakespeare's comic heroines— whatever that means. *Shakespeare's Comedies* (Oxford, 1960), pp. 118–142.
13. Discussed by Bradbrook, *Shakespeare*, p. 230.
14. Charles Lyons, *Ambiguity*, who seems to believe that only what endures is real (as

well as good), and that there is a hierarchical ascendence of reason over emotion, finds
Malvolio a "ritual scapegoat" (p. 61). In a sense, he is right: the villain in a Shakespearean
comedy is not he who has done or said the most repulsive things; it is he who provides
the greatest threat to the values that dominate the particular play. Thus, Cloten, who
does nothing much, is the villain of *Cymbeline*.

15. Bradbrook, *Shakespeare*, p. 229.

8. Chaste Constancy

1. Northrop Frye, *The Secular Scripture* (Cambridge, Mass., 1976), p. 73.
2. Norman Council, speaking of Shakespeare's view of female honor, in *When Honour's at the Stake* (London, 1973), p. 17.
3. *Ibid.*
4. Juliet Dusinberre, *Shakespeare and the Nature of Women* (London, 1975), p. 37.
5. I am indebted to Professor Hilde Hein for some of these arguments.
6. Northrop Frye, *A Natural Perspective* (New York, 1965), p. 136.
7. John F. Danby, *Poets on Fortune's Hill* (London, 1952), p. 145.
8. Patrick Cruttwell, *The Shakespearian Moment* (New York, 1955), p. 51.
9. Charles R. Lyons, *Shakespeare and the Ambiguity of Love's Triumph* (The Hague, 1971), p. 193.
10. "Lust is, to Shakespeare, apparently the chief element in humanity that drags men and women (particularly women) down to the level of animals in the natural hierarchy." Theodore Spencer, *Shakespeare and the Nature of Man* (New York, 1942), p. 144.
11. Dusinberre, *Women*, p. 37.
12. James Smith, "*Much Ado About Nothing*," *Scrutiny* XIII, 4 (Spring, 1946): 242–257, writes that Beatrice scolds "the male sex in general," but without personal malice, but that Claudio and Benedick use what Smith calls "conventional, affected" misogyny as a weapon against women.
13. Although of all the characters Beatrice may be presumed to know best her cousin's character, and thus have *knowledge*; and although Benedick is swayed partly by his own perception and partly by Beatrice's conviction of Hero's innocence, T. W. Craik, "*Much Ado About Nothing*," *Scrutiny* XIX (1952–53): 297–316, writes that the church scene represents a triumph of emotion over reason, but he does not mean Claudio's emotion, but Beatrice's. Because of his experience (of what sort it is not clear), the Friar, Craik writes, has more *authority* than Beatrice. Her faith in her cousin is a matter of *intuition*. The Friar balances reason and emotion, he says, and is more to be trusted than Beatrice in this matter. But Benedick is ludicrous, Craik writes, because he allows Beatrice (and her "intuition") to persuade him that "the guilt is Claudio's" and to override his own "reasonable certainty" that it is Don John's. The difference between Beatrice's *intuition* and Benedick's *reasonable certainty* would seem to be located in their genitals.
14. Barbara Everett, "*Much Ado About Nothing*," *Critical Quarterly* 3 (1961), observes that the worlds of men and women are different. She adds that *Much Ado* is the first play in which the clash of the two worlds is treated seriously.
15. Walter R. Davis, ed., *Twentieth-Century Interpretations of "Much Ado About Nothing"* (Englewood Cliffs, N.J., 1969), p. 3, believes language to be the major theme of the play.
16. R. G. Hunter, *Shakespeare and the Comedy of Forgiveness* (New York, 1965), p. 102, describes the repudiation scene as extremely strong, and observes that Claudio's terms "betray a revulsion against sexuality itself."
17. This is observed by John Russell Brown, *Shakespeare and His Comedies* (London, 1957), p. 116, n. 3.
18. Smith, "*Much Ado*."

19. John Crick, "*Much Ado About Nothing*": *The Use of English* (London, 1965), p. 225, writes that Beatrice's words don't deprive people of their lives, yet that in this play, "considerable damage is done by the mere power of words."

20. David L. Stevenson, ed., Signet *Much Ado About Nothing* (New York, 1965), p. 724, claims that the imagery of the play is concerned mainly with "the act of sex" and cuckoldry.

IV. IDEALS QUESTIONED

9. The Problem Plays

1. Frederick Boas, *Shakspere and His Predecessors* (New York, 1896), p. 345.

2. Caroline Spurgeon, *Shakespeare's Imagery* (Boston, 1961), p. 288.

3. W. W. Lawrence, *Shakespeare's Problem Comedies* (New York, 1931), p. 8. William B. Toole, *Shakespeare's Problem Plays* (The Hague, 1966), asserts that the difference between the comedies and the problem plays is that the "action is more controlled by painful complication" (p. 11).

4. E. M. W. Tillyard, *Shakespeare's Problem Plays* (Toronto, 1949), pp. 2–8.

5. A. P. Rossiter, *Angel with Horns*, ed. Graham Storey (London, 1961), p. 153.

6. This element in Shakespeare's work in general has frequently been noted. The overriding atmosphere of sexual disgust in the problem plays has not, so far as I know, been seen as a general characteristic, although Rossiter, p. 125, sees "lust" as central to the problem comedies.

7. Philip Edwards, *Shakespeare and the Confines of Art* (London, 1968), p. 11, writes of the problem plays that in them "it is not so much themes he [Shakespeare] repeats as conventions—continuing to turn them inside out to see what new possibilities they reveal." But conventions are not merely artistic instruments; they are a kind of shorthand, like DNA: they hold the encoded myths.

8. Maynard Mack, "The World of *Hamlet*," *Yale Review* XLI (1952): 502–523; Harry Levin, *The Question of "Hamlet"* (New York, 1959).

9. Mack, "*Hamlet*."

10. Mack, "*Hamlet*," points out that all the major persons of the drama are players. This notion is developed by Ann Righter, *Shakespeare and the Idea of the Play* (London, 1964).

11. That the characters are continually checking up on each other is pointed out by Robert Heilman, "The Lear World," *English Institute Essays: 1948*, ed. D. A. Robertson, Jr. (New York, 1949).

12. Many critics have suggested this or something like it. Dover Wilson was probably the first to suggest it. Wilson, *What Happens in "Hamlet"* (Cambridge, 1935).

13. These are suggested, in order, by: Theodore Spencer, *Shakespeare and the Nature of Man* (New York, 1942); Spencer, *Nature*, and H. B. Charlton, *Shakespearian Tragedy* (Cambridge, 1948); Norman Council, *When Honour's at the Stake* (London, 1973) and E. K. Chambers, *Shakespeare* (London, 1925), as well as Patrick Cruttwell, *The Shakespearian Moment* (New York, 1955), who speaks of lost ideals; Chambers, *Shakespeare*; and Erich Heller, *The Artist's Journey Into the Interior* (New York, 1976), among others.

14. Rossiter, *Angel*, p. 179, writes that Hamlet is inclined to believe in absolute good and evil but is placed in circumstances which cause him to act as if there were no absolutes. H. D. F. Kitto sees the entire play-world as polluted: "A Classical Scholar Looks at Shakespeare," *More Talking of Shakespeare*, ed. John Garrett (London, 1959). Alice Shalvi, *The Relationship of Renaissance Concepts of Honour to Shakespeare's Problem Plays* (Salzburg, Austria, 1972), and Norman Council, *Honour*, both see Hamlet as attempting to act genuinely in the face of a society riddled with outworn and conven-

tional moral precepts. It was Caroline Spurgeon, of course, who first pointed to the images of sickness, disease, and disfigurement. *Imagery*, p. 316.

15. This is discussed by Shalvi, p. 132.

16. James Joyce has not been taken seriously as a Shakespeare critic, despite the importance of Shakespeare the man and his creations to *Ulysses*. But, although Joyce seized on only those elements of Shakespeare that were useful to him, he was an incisive reader of the poet. The character of Stephen Dedalus is to some degree modeled on Hamlet. Stephen is paralyzed, fearing the consequences both of action and inaction; he desires above all certitude, a rational explanation of the cosmos that would provide him with a clear basis for right action. He also wants undying love, love for him alone. He sees Shakespeare's obsession with cuckoldry and money as a need to possess, to pin down; he associates Shakespeare with Shylock and with Othello. Stephen's fiction about Shakespeare is as much about himself as the playwright, but it has relevance to Shakespeare's work, particularly *Hamlet*. The young man describes Shakespeare thus: "Lover of an ideal or a perversion, like José he kills the real Carmen." Stephen too is filled with disgust for sexuality, and see fornication as a clasping and sundering, doing "the coupler's will," and conception and gestation as being "wombed in sin darkness." Joyce, *Ulysses* (New York, 1966), p. 212; p. 38.

17. Council, *Honour*, p. 110, discusses conventional virtue as being untrustworthy as a guide to action.

18. G. Wilson Knight, *The Wheel of Fire* (New York, 1947), p. 43.

19. Mack, *"Hamlet,"* claims that in the graveyard, Hamlet finally accepts his mortality.

20. Cruttwell, *Moment*, p. 85, points out that at the end of their lives, both Hamlet and Othello show concern with their reputations on earth.

21. Wolfgang Clemen, *The Development of Shakespeare's Imagery* (Cambridge, Mass., 1951), p. 109.

22. Robert Ornstein, *The Moral Vision of Jacobean Tragedy* (Madison, Wis., 1960), p. 235, analyzes the way the point of view of the drama allows us to accept Hamlet's brutality and cruelty without questioning it.

23. Many critics, from Boas on, have pointed out that it is "the queen's frailty" that moves Hamlet rather than the King's "villainy." Boas, *Shakspere*, p. 403. Tillyard discusses this situation at length: *Problem Plays*, pp. 22–26, as does Dover Wilson, *The Essential Shakespeare* (Cambridge, 1932), p. 119.

24. Numerous critics have suggested a connection between Hamlet's feelings about his mother and his treatment of Ophelia. Reuben Brower, *Hero and Saint* (New York, 1971), p. 263, writes of Troilus that he, "like Hamlet . . . feels that if his love is false all 'womankind,' all 'mothers,' must be so too." O. J. Campbell, however, sees in Hamlet's tirade to Ophelia (III, i) "little importance for the plot of the play," since it is "merely a familiar satiric interlude." *Shakespeare's Satire* (New York, 1943), p. 153.

25. Knight, *Wheel*, p. 307, sees Hamlet's mind as set between extremes of "extraversion and introversion, of masculine and feminine."

26. Boas, *Shakspere*, p. 389, writes that the soliloquies have little relation to the "actual progress of events" in the play. Wolfgang Clemen, *Shakespeare's Dramatic Art* (London, 1972), p. 65, finds the structure full of retarding episodes and digressions and concludes that the play is "loosely constructed."

27. Tillyard, *Problem Plays*, p. 29.

28. Ornstein, *Moral Vision*, p. 234.

29. Knight, *Wheel*, p. 28.

30. Philip Edwards, *Confines*, p. 103, writes that both the war theme and the love theme "rest upon a core of sensuality and female infidelity," and concludes that the play is about inconstancy. E. K. Chambers, *Shakespeare*, p. 196, writes: "Troilus will not have us 'square the general sex by Cressid's rule,' but indeed it is to be surmised that Shakespeare meant little else."

31. Spencer, *Nature*, p. 115.

32. Ornstein, *Moral Vision*, p. 245, describes Cressida as "a daughter of the game which

men would have her play and for which they despise her." He adds that "she sees the commerce beneath courtliness and values herself at the world's rate."

33. Ornstein, *Moral Vision*, p. 245.

34. Shalvi, *Honour*, p. 192: "The private conflict between Diomed and Troilus is an echo of the greater conflict between Greece and Troy: in both cases, the protagonists fight, ostensibly over an object whose intrinsic worthlessness they are fully aware of, motivated, in fact, by self-esteem, pride, and glory."

35. Campbell, *Satire*, p. 107, calls Troilus a "sexual gourmet."

36. Ornstein, *Moral Vision*, p. 245.

37. The inflation/deflation of the style is discussed by Tillyard, *Problem Plays*, p. 58; the inflation/deflation of the Prologue is pointed out by Shalvi, *Honour*, p. 166.

38. Ornstein, *Moral Vision*, calls Troilus a victim of "narcissistic infatuation" (p. 245).

39. Tillyard points out this characteristic of the imagery, *Problem Plays*, p. 90.

40. L. C. Knights, *Shakespeare's Politics* (Folcroft, Pa., 1957), p. 5, asserts that "statecraft, for Ulysses, is the manipulation of men." Ornstein, *Moral Vision*, p. 246, sees Ulysses as a ruthless politician.

41. Discussed by Tillyard, *Problem Plays*, pp. 58–70.

42. Tillyard, *Problem Plays*, p. 70.

43. This is suggested by many critics.

44. Tillyard, *Problem Plays*, p. 12.

45. Chambers, *Shakespeare*, p. 193.

46. Una Ellis-Fermor, *The Frontiers of Drama* (London, 1945), suggests that the audience falls increasingly into agreement with Thersites. Cruttwell, *Moment*, p. 29, suggests that Thersites *feels* right, and that the play constitutes a challenge to authority.

47. John Russell Brown, *Shakespeare and His Comedies* (London, 1957), points to Helena's guilt, but claims that she is wrong and guilt-ridden because she tries to take, rather than give, love. He adds that her self-blame is Shakespeare's addition to his sources (p. 185).

48. Boas, *Shakspere*, p. 356, complains that Lavatch's insipidity and his coarse jokes make him a "scarcely suitable" companion for the Countess; W. W. Lawrence, *Comedies*, p. 65, interprets the Clown's "That man should be at woman's command" speech as "impertinent cynicism," and not a statement of theme. Robert Hillis Goldsmith, *Wise Fools in Shakespeare* (East Lansing, Mich., 1955), p. 58, discusses the fact that Lavatch makes jokes about sex and chastity more than any other fool in Shakespeare, but adds, p. 60, "his role bears no significant relationship to the theme of *All's Well that Ends Well*. He is in no way a measure of the play's meaning."

49. Tillyard, *Problem Plays*, p. 111, points out that both Helena and Parolles are adventurers.

50. Charles R. Lyons, *Shakespeare and the Ambiguity of Love's Triumph* (The Hague, 1971), p. 107, writes that the metaphoric structure of the play suggests that "sexual union is a kind of war," and points out that there is pain in the mating of a hind and a lion. R. G. Hunter, *Shakespeare and the Comedy of Forgiveness* (New York, 1965), p. 126, finds the play "a profound and disquieting comment upon the nature of male sexuality."

51. The "disagreeable atmosphere" of *All's Well* (and *Measure for Measure*) is discussed by Lawrence, *Problem Comedies*, p. 66. Tillyard, *Problem Plays*, p. 110, feels that the play is full of suffering.

52. Harold S. Wilson, "Dramatic Emphasis in *All's Well That Ends Well*," *Huntington Library Quarterly* XIII (May 1950): 222–240, suggests that Diana is Helena's alter ego.

53. Hunter, *Forgiveness*, p. 120, discusses Parolles' guiltlessness in corrupting Bertram.

54. Rossiter, *Angel*, p. 91, suggests there is significance to the fact that Parolles is a witness to Bertram's exposure in the last act. Indeed, he is more than a witness to it, he participates in it.

55. M. C. Bradbrook, *Shakespeare and Elizabethan Poetry* (London, 1951), p. 163.

56. The ending of the play is objected to by Edwards, *Shakespeare*, p. 109; Lawrence, *Problem Comedies*, p. 76; and Rossiter, *Angel*, p. 92.

57. Toole, *Problem Plays*, p. 133, claims that Bertram dies when he goes to court, and is brought back to life by Helena.

58. Lyons, *Ambiguity*, p. 125: "The deed which consummates the marriage is, and is not, a sin; it is, and is not, fornication."

59. Boas, *Shakspere*, p. 359, describes the atmosphere as totally immuring; Rossiter, *Angel*, p. 125, sees lust as central to the problem comedies, and adds that the concerns of all the characters meet in prison (p. 156).

60. Many critics have complained about Isabel's coldness, but R. G. Hunter, *Forgiveness*, p. 206, says she is uncharitable.

61. Righter, *Idea*, p. 179, claims that Lucio haunts the play. "His irreverent voice rings through and questions the most solemn scenes." She believes he exists to counter the Duke.

62. Hunter, *Forgiveness*, p. 223, points out that Isabel turns to death constantly as a solution, for herself and for others. Lyons, *Ambiguity*, p. 128, believes the play is about a war between the "destructive energy of sexual appetite with the restraint that denies life itself."

63. Campbell, *Satire*, p. 136, can find Isabel's "elevation" and her "moral intensity" acceptable, but not her "willingness to announce . . . that she has yielded to Angelo." This is, he says, "inconsistent with her saintly nature."

64. Donald Stauffer, *Shakespeare's World of Images* (New York, 1949), p. 367, demonstrates that many Shakespearean characters associate death and marriage.

V. CHAOS COME AGAIN: IDEALS BANISHED

10. The Late Tragedies

1. Although I agree with Robert Ornstein (*The Moral Vision of Jacobean Tragedy* [Madison, Wis., 1960], p. 275) that Shakespearean tragedy does not present heroes sacrificed for the good of the community, and that Jacobean tragedy does not, on the whole, contain a community in the same way that Greek tragedy does, the British literature is not totally detached from communal values. Many Shakespearean heroes are epitomes of some characteristic valued by their cultures; in other words, they are carriers of cultural "genes," and it is these genes that define them and that eventually destroy them. A culture is a far more abstract thing than a community, and a more complex thing than the communities of Greek drama, but the two are related. To the degree that the hero is a testing ground for a cultural value or set of values, he does die *for* his culture.

2. Robert Heilman defines Shakespearean tragedy as studies of "myth in crisis," and he defines myth as an area of life with value that cannot be translated into power, will, or profit. Such a value he terms "irrational," which is problematic since it suggests that there is something inherently "rational" about power, will, and profit. See "The Lear World," *English Institute Essays: 1948*, ed. D. A. Robertson, Jr. (New York, 1949). The association of "feminine" qualities with the divine occurs in all theological interpretations.

3. Alvin Kernan describes three circles or worlds in the play: an outer world, representing "the brute power of nature"; Venice, representing reason, law, and social concord; and Cyprus, which is halfway between the two. Intro., Signet Edition (New York, 1963).

4. Samuel A. Tannenbaum sees Iago's Cassio as "effeminate." "The Wronged Iago," *Shakes. Assoc. Bull.* XII, 1 (January 1937): 57–62.

5. Many twentieth-century critics find Iago a rationalist, among them Robert Heilman, who refers to R. P. Warren's remark that Shakespeare's villains are marked by rationalism. *Magic in the Web* (Lexington, Ky., 1956), and "The Lear World." Mark Van Doren says Iago has "a heart that passion cannot rule." *Shakespeare* (Garden City, N.Y., 1953), p. 194. Alvin Kernan calls Iago "icily logical."

6. Marvin Rosenberg, *The Masks of "Othello"* (Berkeley, Calif., 1961), pp. 170–171, asserts that the ultimate motive for Iago's hatred of Othello, Desdemona, and Cassio is "his denial of the values they affirm." Elsewhere, Rosenberg describes Iago as a cool manipulator who asserts the supremacy of will and intelligence and "their power to efface emotions," and quotes to the same effect Karen Horney's description of a psychological type. "In Defense of Iago," *SQ* VI, 2 (1955): 145–158.

7. Iago's misogyny and loathing for sex have been noted by many critics, among them William Empson, "Honest in *Othello*," *The Structure of Complex Words* (London, 1951); Bernard Spivack, *Shakespeare and the Allegory of Evil* (New York, 1958); and Robert Rogers, "Endopsychic Drama in *Othello*," *SQ* XX (1969): 205–215.

8. Othello has been described as an unsensual lover by Theodore Spencer, *Shakespeare and the Nature of Man* (New York, 1942), p. 127. Kernan praises Othello for what he calls self-control, and adds that every major character except Desdemona "is in some degree touched with sexual corruption." Wolfgang Clemen, *The Development of Shakespeare's Imagery* (Cambridge, Mass., 1951), p. 124, concludes from the imagery that Othello's approach to experience is primarily sensory.

9. Sometimes Othello is blamed for these qualities. Norman Council claims that he is concerned only with his honor and himself. *When Honour's at the Stake* (London, 1973), p. 113. A. P. Rossiter accuses Othello of egotism as well as possessiveness and self-pity. *Angel with Horns*, ed. Graham Storey (London, 1961), p. 195. Egotism and self-pity are the burden also of the famous criticism of T. S. Eliot, "Shakespeare and the Stoicism of Seneca," *Selected Essays 1917–1932* (London, 1932), and F. R. Leavis, "Diabolic Intellect and the Noble Hero," *Scrutiny* VI (1937).

Yet as Helen Gardner persuasively argues, the tone of the play does not support such readings, which arise mainly because of twentieth-century distaste for authority, a code of honor, and heroic postures. See *The Noble Moor*, British Academy Lecture, 1956.

10. Desdemona's "sensible normality" contrasts with the "emotional exaggeration of Othello," writes S. L. Bethell, *Shakespeare and the Popular Dramatic Tradition* (London, 1944), p. 18.

11. Kenneth Burke writes: "In ownership as thus conceived [by Othello] . . . there is . . . forever lurking the sinister invitation to an ultimate lie, an illusion carried to the edge of metaphysical madness, as private ownership, thus projected into realms for which there are no unquestionably attested securities, is seen to imply also, profoundly, ultimately, estrangement." "*Othello:* An Essay to Illustrate a Method," *Hudson Review* IV, 2 (1951): 165–203.

12. The accusation made against Othello by Leo Kirschbaum ("The Modern Othello," *ELH* II [1944]: 283–296) is that he tries to transcend the merely human, and thus moves easily into the posture of a god and an agent of divine justice.

13. That Iago and Othello share something has been pointed out by Kirschbaum, Leavis, Frank Kermode, Intro., *Riverside Shakespeare* (Boston, 1974), and Irving Ribner in the Ribner-Kittredge Intro. to the play (Waltham, Mass., 1963), as well as J. I. M. Stewart, *Character and Motive in Shakespeare* (London, 1949).

14. The "something" that critics point to that binds Othello and Iago is the misogyny and fear of sex implicit in Western culture. John Holloway suggests this very obliquely when he writes that Iago conjures in Othello the memory of something he has heard or read about women. *The Story of the Night* (London, 1961), p. 46. Iago and Othello are "binary or double stars revolving about a common axis within a gravitational field." Brents Stirling, *Unity in Shakespearean Tragedy* (New York, 1956), p. 123. In my reading, the common axis is women=sex, the gravitational field a "masculine" way of seeing. But Helen Gardner writes that Iago's views represent a "true view of life." "*Othello:* A Retrospect," *SS* 21 (1968).

15. Robert Ornstein points out that Othello's anguish shows the profound involvement of the male ego in what I call chaste constancy. *Moral Vision*, p. 221.

16. In fact, of course, misogyny too is both classical and Catholic. Traditional patriar-

chal thinking disdains both women and the qualities (rightly or wrongly) associated with them.

17. In a way of thinking that exalts transcendence, anything merely human seems bestial, and is most easily expressed in animal imagery. Caroline Spurgeon, *Shakespeare's Imagery* (Boston, 1961), p. 335, shows that the animal imagery comes mainly from Iago, who utters over half of it, and that most of the rest comes from Othello. Other images contribute to the delineation of the characters of the two men. Iago refers frequently to bodily functions and uses technical and commercial—"masculine"—terms. Othello, the idealist, refers to the cosmos—the elements, the heavens, celestial bodies, winds, and sea. Cf. Wolfgang Clemen, *Shakespeare's Dramatic Art* (London, 1972), p. 122, and Mikhail Morozov, "The Individuation of Shakespeare's Characters Through Imagery," *SS* 2 (1949).

18. Maynard Mack claims Othello faces "two ways of understanding love: Iago's and Desdemona's," and must choose between "two systems of valuing and two ways of being." "The World of *Hamlet*," *Yale Review* XLI (1952): 502–523. But in fact there are three ways to seeing sex (not love) in the play: Iago's, which reduces it to appetite and commerce, Othello's, which idealizes it into exalted romantic love, and Desdemona's, which blends sex, love, and the everyday into what we may call married love.

19. Alvin Kernan states that his murder of Desdemona destroys in Othello "all the ordering powers of love, of trust, of the bond between human beings." S. L. Bethell writes that Othello "loses his heaven with his faith in Desdemona." "Shakespeare's Imagery: The Diabolic Images in *Othello*," *SS* 5 (1952).

20. Marvin Rosenberg remarks that critics do not notice Iago's treatment of Emilia, although it is very significant. "At best he treats her with sadistic humor, alone with her . . . he snarls orders at her as if she were an inferior being." "In Defense of Iago."

21. "To take a donnée so exceptional, to hit upon so unheard-of a set of circumstances and double them, was to call the entire moral order into question, as A. W. Schlegel pointed out," writes Harry Levin, "The Heights and the Depths: A Scene from *King Lear*," *More Talking of Shakespeare*, ed. John Garrett (London, 1959), p. 91.

22. Derek Traversi calls *Lear* an allegory of "man's relation to nature," "*King Lear*," *Stratford Papers on Shakespeare*, ed. B. W. Jackson (Toronto, 1964), p. 195; L. C. Knights says the play attempts to answer the question: "What is essential human nature?" *Some Shakespearean Themes* (London, 1959), p. 83; Robert Heilman believes the play is "an essay upon nature," *This Great Stage* (Baton Rouge, La., 1948), p. 11; and H. B. Charlton offers an important discussion of the theme of nature in *Shakespearian Tragedy* (Cambridge, 1948).

23. Many uses of the term *nature* are discussed by John Danby, *Shakespeare's Doctrine of Nature: A Study of "King Lear"* (London, 1961), and by Robert Heilman, *This Great Stage*.

24. Wolfgang Clemen reports that in the early scenes, Lear does not hear others, but speaks what are essentially monologues. *Dramatic Art*, p. 135.

25. L. C. Knights points out that many of Shakespeare's history plays are concerned with "rulers who failed because they were isolated within an arbitrary conception of power or privilege," and thus were not "linked with" the society they ruled. He is describing Coriolanus, but the description fits Lear as well. *Further Explorations* (London, 1965), p. 20. Lear, however, is cut off (as is Coriolanus) not only from his society but from his natural and inevitable place in nature.

26. He continues to quantify until the middle of the play. Russell Fraser remarks that love remains a commodity for the King as late as his choice of returning to Goneril on the grounds that twice the number of retinue equals twice the love. Intro., Signet *Lear* (New York, 1963).

27. "Lear's 'disclaiming' of Cordelia at the beginning showed an appalling violence; but that is far outdone by the positively destructive savagery of his curses on Goneril." S. L. Goldberg, *An Essay on "King Lear"* (Cambridge, 1974), p. 107.

28. W. R. Keast points to the similarity of the two sisters to one part of their father.

"Imagery and Meaning in the Interpretation of *King Lear*," *Modern Philology* XLVII (1949): 45–64.

29. The criticisms that have been directed against Cordelia are dealt with by John Danby, *Doctrine*, pp. 109–125.

30. Robert Heilman reads Cordelia's steadfastness as a withdrawal from responsibility resulting from the sin of pride; cf. *Stage*, p. 36.

31. Clemen, *Dramatic Art*, p. 135, comments that the three villains of the tragedy use few images, and speak in cool and rational ways.

32. A thoughtful analysis of the function of the animal images is found in H. B. Charlton, *Tragedy*, pp. 189–226. Charlton remarks that the world of Lear is barely civilized, that it presents a state in which "men and beasts are almost indistinguishable," in which "human nature is palpably a part of nature . . . The thin dividing line . . . is the consciousness within man of his human nature."

33. L. C. Knights paraphrases John Stuart Mill's discussion of nature and the human with agreement: "Man's progress is a continual triumph over nature." *Themes*, p. 83.

34. Ornstein (*Moral Vision*, p. 263) points out that despite Edmund's rebellion, what he really wants is honor and legitimacy.

35. Barbara Melchiori, "Still harping on my daughter," *English Miscellany*, ed. Mario Praz, 11 (1960): 59–74.

36. A. C. Bradley writes that Goneril is "a most hideous human being (if she is one)." *Shakespearean Tragedy* (London, 1918), p. 300.

37. Sex is the "subhuman ingredient in mankind . . . [It] is used almost exclusively as a symbol of evil, of the animality that is continually put before us as a definition of vicious conduct." Heilman, *Stage*, p. 100.

38. "The *cupiditas* which is the root of all evil is carnal more than it is pecuniary. *King Lear* plays in an astonishing way with the idea of sexual intercourse being the root cause of the sufferings of both Gloucester and Lear; the damage which libidinous mankind inflicts on itself is the main datum on which the Romances are built, and the main effort is to find the Desdemona-figure who is immune from the self-destroying curse of humankind." Philip Edwards, *Shakespeare and the Confines of Art* (London, 1968), p. 138. Robert H. West asserts that the act of procreation comes in this play to seem the devil's, and adds that "Lear seems in his madness to imply that sex is an insult to mankind and mercilessly alien—or that man is a beast." "Sex and Pessimism in *King Lear*," *SQ* I (1960): 55–60.

39. S. L. Goldberg offers an important discussion of Cordelia, *An Essay*, pp. 100–188 passim.

40. Arthur Sewell notices the love among the "villains," and comments, "The weeds, after all, spring from the same soil as the 'sustaining corn.' " *Character and Society in Shakespeare* (Oxford, 1951), p. 119.

41. Terence Hawkes calls the Witches *epicene*, and adds that this "exactly suits their function as obscurantist dealers in appearances." *Shakespeare's Talking Animals* (London, 1973), p. 143. Brents Stirling (*Unity*, p. 139) believes that the Witches' chant and their beards, as well as the behavior of Duncan's horses, demonstrate "inverted nature," which the critic equates with overturned hierarchy. In the Intro. to the Signet *Macbeth* (New York, 1963), Sylvan Barnet writes that it was common for Renaissance literary witches to show petty malice, to have beards and masters, but uncommon for them to speak authoritatively.

Many critics have pointed out the ambiguity and paradox of the images, and have linked them to moral ambiguities in the play. "The normal delimitations of day and night disappear, as do those of manliness and womanliness, prudence and cowardice." Marion Bodwell Smith, *Dualities in Shakespeare* (Toronto, 1966), pp. 160–161. Speaking of the Witches, Smith adds (p. 172), "that women should possess male characteristics, physical or psychological, was considered not merely unnatural and therefore deplorable; along with other 'perversions' the reversal of sexual roles was . . . taken as evidence of criminal conversation with the Evil One." J. I. M. Stewart connects the paradox of "fair and foul" with moral confusion: "But it is also the victory alone, the snatching honour by unseaming people from the nave to the chops, that is both foul and fair—a monstrous confusion from which Macbeth, imaginative and highly organized as well as a soldier, now emerges, battle-shocked. That night he kills a man for a kingdom." *Character*, p. 92.

42. "In those daies also the women . . . were of no lesse courage than the men; for all stout maidens and wives (if they were not with child) marched as well in the field as did the men, and so soone as the armie did set forward, they slue the first living creature that they found, in whose bloud they not onlie bathed their swords, but also tasted thereof with their mouthes. . . . When they saw their owne bloude run from them in the fight, they waxed never a whit astonished with the matter, but rather doubling their courages, with more eagernesse they assailed their enemies." "The Description of Scotland," prefaced to *The Historie of Scotland* (London, 1585), p. 21.

43. Most critics choose to pay attention to Duncan's remarks as bearing the legitimacy and authority of power, and ignore the implications of the tone and imagery of the Sergeant's descriptions. Thus, they accept the early Macbeth as unqualifiedly "good." E. E. Stoll finds Macbeth so good that his later deed seems psychologically implausible. *Art and Artifice in Shakespeare* (New York, 1933), pp. 77–86. G. Wilson Knight, *The Imperial Theme* (London, 1931), pp. 125–129, and Matthew Proser, *The Heroic Image in Five Shakespearean Tragedies* (Princeton, N.J., 1965), p. 91, both find Macbeth noble and courageous throughout the play because he remains true to his ideals. R. B. Heilman writes that the audience is led to sympathize with Macbeth because they are "secret sharers" in his "erring humanity," and that the play is a challenge to "our manly courage." (This seems to presume an audience of only males.) See "The Criminal as Tragic Hero," *SS* 19 (1966). But Jan Kott, who if he does not always see the trees at least sees the woods, blurts out the basic definition of the play: "A man is he who kills." *Shakespeare Our Contemporary* (Garden City, N.Y., 1964), p. 92.

44. "Scotland is a family, Duncan its head. A natural law binds all degrees in proper place and allegiance," writes Knight, *Imperial*, p. 126. Wilbùr Sanders, *The Dramatist and the Received Idea* (Cambridge, 1968), p. 267, describes Macbeth as oppressed by the bond of a moral order which he feels to have "a more than legal validity, to be involved with the great world, the cosmos, the macrocosm . . . [to be] rooted in the natural." L. C. Knights does not fall back on claims of "divine" or "natural" law to authorize his position: he sees bonds among men as a basic condition of humanness. For him, "evil . . . is a violation of those bonds that are essential to the being of man as man." *Shakespeare's Politics* (Folcroft, Pa., 1957), p. 7. See also Maynard Mack, Jr., *Killing the King* (New Haven, Conn., 1973), pp. 139 ff.

45. "Sleep, in Shakespeare, is always regarded as remedial." S. L. Bethell, *Dramatic Tradition*, p. 53.

46. She is found so by Bradley, *Tragedy*, p. 312, and R. G. Moulton, *Shakespeare as a Dramatic Artist* (Oxford, 1893), p. 156.

47. Many of Shakespeare's readers share this dual standard. From Dr. Johnson on, they have used different criteria and different language in discussing Lady Macbeth and Macbeth (Bradley and Moulton are notable exceptions), and the word most frequently used for the lady is *unnatural*. Macbeth is a good man gone wrong; he is judged ethically. Lady Macbeth violates "nature," and is judged mythically. Smith, *Dualities*, p. 172, writes that Lady Macbeth reverses the roles "appropriate to husband and wife, to say nothing of violating her *natural feminine attributes of tenderness and timidity*." Terence Eagleton, *Shakespeare and Society* (New York, 1967), p. 133n, claims Lady Macbeth desires to be transformed into a woman whose desires as well as actions are *unnatural*. Proser, *Heroic Image*, p. 60, asserts that in Lady Macbeth, "womanliness, *normally tender, apprehensive, and compassionate*, transforms itself into a cruelty that denies its *usual* characteristics." (All italics mine.) Franklin Dickey finds Lady Macbeth more of a villain than her husband, for reasons that remain murky to me. *Not Wisely But Too Well* (San Marino, Calif., 1957), p. 18. A fascinating, unconscious statement of

dual standards of judgment occurs in Francis Fergusson, *The Human Image in Dramatic Literature* (Garden City, N.Y., 1957), p. 120: "Lady Macbeth fears her husband's *human* nature, as well as her own *female* nature." (Italics mine.)

Alex Aronson, analyzing the play for Jungian symbols in *Psyche and Symbol in Shakespeare* (Bloomington, Ind., 1972), p. 237, calls Lady Macbeth "serpentlike," and relates her to Hecate, who is "emasculating, bewitching, deadly, and stupefying." He argues further that in myth the male is seen as the bringer of light, form, and order: "Both in the prehistoric myth and in Shakespeare's tragedies, the symbolism points clearly enough to the victory of the masculine, conscious spirit over the powers of the matriarchate" which are associated with darkness and chaos (p. 256). But the mythic symbology Aronson describes is in direct contradiction to the symbology of *Macbeth*, in which "feminine" symbols are aligned with concord, order, love, and trust.

48. There are several interesting discussions of the meaning of this word in *Macbeth*. However, in none of them is there any doubt that manliness, properly defined, is indeed the *single highest human standard*, and is identical with virtue. This is explicit in Charlton, *Tragedy*, pp. 148 ff. It is implicit in E. M. Waith, "Manhood and Valor in Two Shakespearean Tragedies," *ELH* 17 (1950), who identifies "feminizing" and "womanish" influences with what is "weak" and "effeminate." Proser, *Heroic Image*, pp. 56–61, like Waith, points to the narrowness of the definition the characters end with, but does not question the primacy of *manliness* in the world of the play. One critic is uncomfortable with these male supremacist notions: Terence Hawkes on one hand defines manliness as the ability to speak truly—which leaves women in a peculiar position—but on the other, finds "non-manly" traits in males "not altogether unadmirable." He adds that the play seems to argue that "to stifle . . . 'womanly' traits brings about a kind of dehumanization." *Animals*, p. 128.

49. "After Duncan's murder the tone of *Macbeth* changes . . . In the succeeding portion of the play conscience ceases to function as an agent capable of preventing further crime; nor does it promote repentance." Proser, *Heroic Image*, p. 69.

50. *Heroic Image*, p. 88.

51. William Blisset, "The Secret'st Man of Blood," *SQ* XIX (1959): 397–408.

52. *The Business of Criticism* (Oxford, 1959), p. 61. James Winny, *The Player King* (London, 1968), p. 36, claims that both Macbeth and Tarquin destroy parts of themselves; L. C. Knights points out that many of the histories and tragedies are "studies of rulers who failed because they were isolated within an arbitrary conception of power or privilege." *Shakespeare's Politics*, p. 7.

53. Francis Fergusson finds Duncan's relation to Macbeth "competitive" in "*Macbeth* as the Imitation of an Action," *English Institute Essays* (New York, 1952), p. 108.

54. *The Well-Wrought Urn* (London, 1968), p. 31. Brooks sees the baby as an image of compassion and of the future which Macbeth tries vainly to control.

55. *Imperial*, p. 142.

56. *Received Idea*, p. 262. Several critics have suggested that all the major characters seem to be touched with guilt. Smith, *Dualities*, p. 185, describes Macduff in the early portion of the scene with Malcolm as "incapable of sympathy, scorning Malcolm's tears for Scotland, and calling upon him to act instead of weeping." In *Wheel of Fire* (London, 1930), pp. 166–167, G. W. Knight suggests "All the persons seem to share some guilt of the down-pressing enveloping Evil. Even Malcolm is forced to repeat crimes on himself."

57. Speaking of Malcolm's response to Macduff's sorrow, Sanders says, "This is so near to Lady Macbeth's conception of manhood, the masculine ferocity that is really bestiality, that Macduff's quiet vindication of another kind of manhood carries immense conviction." *Received Idea*, pp. 272–273.

58. Charlton, *Tragedy*, p. 147, says the temper of the prevailing moral consciousness can be seen in the secondary characters, notably old Siward. Maynard Mack, Jr., *Killing*, p. 184, describing the "hard, somber" ending of the play, writes "The voice of almost everything human speaks in Macduff's sword, but it is still a sword." And Orn-

stein, *Moral Vision*, p. 232, claims that "though order is restored at . . . [*Macbeth's*] close, though evil is purged and Macbeth receives the gift of oblivion, there is no sense of repose or reconciliation in its final scenes."

59. Prominent among the "order and degree" critics are Irving Ribner, *Patterns in Shakespearian Tragedy* (London, 1960), and Derek Traversi, *An Approach to Shakespeare* (London, 1938). Francis Fergusson also thinks *Macbeth* is about passion "outrunning reason" (*Human Image*, p. 119). Franklin Dickey argues rather circuitously that passion is evil because it makes a man effeminate because it is "manly to rule the passions" because passion puts a man under the domination of "woman." *Not Wisely*, Chap. 2 passim.

60. Heilman, "Lear World," p. 53.

61. Notably, Helen Gardner, *Business*, p. 61 (n. 52 above), and L. C. Knights, *Themes*, p. 15: "The man who breaks the bonds that tie him to other men . . . is . . . violating his own nature and thwarting his own deepest needs."

62. John Arthos sees the tragedy as being concerned with "the manner in which love, given its range in at once the greatest and most ordinary natures, arrives at apotheosis. The drama is the preservation of constancy, in this world, and afterwards." *The Art of Shakespeare* (London, 1964), p. 62.

63. "Mutability rules *Antony and Cleopatra*." M. C. Bradbrook, *Shakespeare the Craftsman* (London, 1969), p. 117.

64. Caroline Spurgeon (*Imagery*, p. 352) points out that the word *world* occurs forty-two times, more than double its occurrence in any other play. Theodore Spencer adds that the word *fortune* also appears more frequently than in any other play. *Nature*, p. 167. Maurice Charney claims that the magnitude of the issues in the play is emphasized by the many words of cosmic reference and by the *world* theme. *Shakespeare's Roman Plays* (Cambridge, Mass., 1961), p. 80.

65. Critics who believe that Shakespeare (like Virgil) upheld the claims of Rome against the charm of Egypt must juggle or ignore the language. Brents Stirling, *Unity*, p. 169, manages to find Cleopatra's ending "comic"; Daniel Stempel, "The Transmigration of the Crocodile," *SQ* VII, 1 (1956): 59–72, explains away all the poetry. T. J. B. Spencer attempts to deal directly with the problem. He writes, "The splendour of language given to Antony and Cleopatra captures our imaginative sympathy for the . . . 'wrong' side." *Shakespeare: The Roman Plays* (London, 1963), p. 31. His statement, however, makes one wonder about his respect for the playwright, who surely used language to indicate his meaning.

66. The pervasiveness in the play of what Maynard Mack calls "mobility and mutability" has been noted by nearly all its modern readers. "*Antony and Cleopatra*: The Stillness and the Dance," *Shakespeare's Art: Seven Essays*, ed. Milton Crane (Chicago, 1973).

67. Janet Adelman, *The Common Liar* (New Haven, 1973), p. 26.

68. Antony's reversals are discussed by John Danby, "The Shakespearean Dialectic: An Aspect of *Antony and Cleopatra*," *Scrutiny* XVI, 3 (1949): 196–213.

69. John Holloway, *Night*, p. 117, describes the behavior of Antony and Cleopatra as "sometimes exalted and sometimes abject." In this play, he asserts, "the highest and the lowest, the most exalted and the base . . . [are] one" (p. 106).

70. Antony and Cleopatra "transcend their environment through their capacity for change and mutation," A. P. Riemer, *A Reading of Shakespeare's "Antony and Cleopatra"* (Syndey, 1968), p. 35. He adds that the lovers "thrive on impermanence" (p. 113).

71. Riemer, *A Reading*, p. 45, sees the drinking scene as a premonition of a "dissolving world."

72. Barbara Everett finds the language of Antony and Cleopatra "expressive of a whole radically different way of living and feeling: a language of immediate individual experience . . . Love or desolation, exhilaration or rage become their own argument." Intro., Signet *Antony and Cleopatra* (New York, 1963).

73. The play offers "transcendent justification of passion in terms of emotional value

and vitality," wrote Derek Traversi, *Approach*, p. 117. In this early work, Traversi claims that in *Antony and Cleopatra*, Shakespeare "came nearest to unifying his experience into a harmonious and related whole" (p. 127). John Arthos, *Shakespeare*, p. 62, suggests that the drama is about the transformation of love into apotheosis: "the drama is the preservation of constancy."

74. Charney, *Roman*, p. 101.

75. Charles R. Lyons, *Shakespeare and the Ambiguity of Love's Triumph* (The Hague, 1971), p. 186.

76. Ornstein, "Ethic." Philip Edwards, *Confines*, p. 121, insists on the "impossibility of single vision and simple judgment" of the play.

77. Charney, *Roman*, p. 126; Ribner, Intro. *Kittredge/Ribner Antony and Cleopatra*; Dickey, *Not Wisely*, p. 1. Daniel Stempel sees the "domination" of Antony by Cleopatra as "an unnatural reversal of the roles of man and woman," and approves the end—the "defeat and death of the rebel against order." "Transmigration," p. 63. Derek Traversi hardens his attitude against the lovers in *Shakespeare: The Roman Plays* (London, 1963). Although he continues to find the lovers an image of integration and constancy, he also continually equates Cleopatra with "mortal weakness" and "corruption" (p. 94).

78. Riemer, *A Reading*, p. 15.

79. Virgil K. Whitaker, *The Mirror Up to Nature* (San Marino, Calif., 1965), p. 111.

80. Whitaker, *Mirror*, p. 104, and Dickey, *Not Wisely*, Chap. 1, among others.

81. Danby, "Dialectic."

82. Doubting his emotions, Enobarbus follows reason and dies, suggests Janet Adelman, *Liar*, p. 123. She adds that to be convinced of love is to have "faith in what we cannot know."

83. "*Coriolanus*," British Academy Lecture, 1912.

84. H. J. Oliver, "Coriolanus as Tragic Hero," *SQ* X, 1 (1959): 53–60.

85. *Craftsman*, p. 116.

86. D. J. Enright, *The Apothecary's Shop* (London, 1957), p. 39.

87. "Self-mutilation [is] inherent in egotism and isolation." L. C. Knights, *Further Explorations* (London, 1965), p. 22. John Holloway, *Night*, p. 127, writes, "What becomes inhuman is the defiantly superhuman." Holloway sees a pattern in the tragedies: "The god-like man, pinnacle of Nature, is becoming a creature having no link with nature; then essentially foreign to it; and in the end, enemy to it." Harry Levin points out that the word *alone* occurs more often in *Coriolanus* than in any other play by Shakespeare, and traces Martius' isolation from the moment he is shut up in Corioli, through to his banishment. Intro., Pelican *Coriolanus* (Baltimore, 1956), p. 2.

88. Bradley points this out, adding that when the soldiers are treated decently by Lartius, they respond. "*Coriolanus*."

89. Both Bradley ("*Coriolanus*") and John Palmer, *The Political Characters of Shakespeare* (London, 1945), p. 306, see the hero's capitulation as a surrender to "great nature."

90. "*Coriolanus*—and the Delights of Faction," *Hudson Review* XIX, 1 (1966): 185–202.

91. Enright, *Apothecary*, p. 36; p. 48: Coriolanus' "infirmity is closely akin to the infirmity of the people"; "the tragedy is the tragedy of Rome." Traversi writes "the failure of Coriolanus is a failure in sensitivity, a failure in living, and it represents a failure on the part of a whole society." "*Coriolanus*," *Scrutiny* VI (1937). "The structure of the play . . . indicates that it is not merely one man . . . who provides the theme," writes T. J. B. Spencer, *Roman*, p. 46. And L. C. Knights believes that the protagonist of the play is the city, Rome. *Themes*, p. 150.

92. *Themes*, p. 152.

93. According to the OED, a "crack" meant "an imp" in Shakespeare's time. John Middleton Murry prefers to believe it shows contempt: then he can continue to idealize Virgilia—or her silence. See *John Clare and Other Studies* (New York, 1950), p. 227.

94. J. C. Maxwell, "Animal Imagery in *Coriolanus*," *Modern Language Review* XLII (1947): 417–421.

95. Bradley, "*Coriolanus*."

96. Willard Farnham, *Shakespeare's Tragic Frontier* (New York, 1950), p. 207.

97. *"Coriolanus."*

98. Enright, *Apothecary*, p. 42, points out that Coriolanus is, of all of Shakespeare's characters, the most talked about within the play, yet that none of the talk illuminates him. It cannot, since those doing the talking share his values too completely to be able to articulate what is wrong with them, or him.

99. In addition: Martius was denied the consulship; he was not reluctant to seek it, and was far more offensive to the people than Shakespeare shows him.

100. Rossiter, *Angel*, p. 243.

101. Enright, *Apothecary*, p. 44, claims that love appears "primarily in the aspect of . . . metaphors applied to war and warriors." Traversi, *Roman*, p. 221, says that values of war and love are equated. And Reuben Brower, Intro. to Signet *Coriolanus* (New York, 1966), writes that "warmaking, love, and marriage are . . . almost identified."

102. O. J. Campbell claims the play is a satire: *Shakespeare's Satire* (New York, 1943), p. 204.

103. This is the conclusion offered by Reuben Brower, *Hero and Saint* (New York, 1971), as well. But Brower concentrates on elements different from those I refer to, which are ideas about or associations with power, legitimacy, emotion, sex, the masculine and the feminine.

104. The first by Bradbrook, *Craftsman*, pp. 145–157; then, O. J. Campbell, *Satire*; A. S. Collins, "*Timon of Athens:* A Reconsideration," *RES* XXII (1946): 96–108; Anne Lancashire, "*Timon of Athens:* Shakespeare's *Dr. Faustus*," *SQ* XXI, 1 (1970): 35–44; and Una Ellis-Fermor, *Shakespeare the Dramatist* (London, 1961), and "*Timon of Athens:* An Unfinished Play," *RES* XVIII (1942): 270–283.

105. Caroline Spurgeon, *Imagery*, p. 342, asserts that the major image is dogs, the major allusion gold. Willard Farnham, *Frontier*, finds the beast theme central in the play. Cf. p. 68.

106. Those who see Timon as noble are Knight, *Wheel of Fire*; Collins, "Reconsideration"; Frye, *"Fools of Time* (Toronto, 1967); Peter Alexander, *Shakespeare's Life and Art* (London, 1939); and Clifford Leech, "Shakespeare's Greeks," *Stratford Papers on Shakespeare*, ed. B. W. Jackson (Toronto, 1964). Among those who find him reprehensible are Campbell, *Satire*; Farnham, *Frontier*; J. C. Maxwell, "*Timon of Athens*," *Scrutiny* XV, 3 (1948): 195–208; and David Cook, "*Timon of Athens*," *SS* 16 (1963): 83–94.

107. Campbell, *Satire*, p. 186.

108. Maxwell, "*Timon*," writes that Timon does not see the "necessary reciprocity of creation, and considers even the sun a thief." David Cook, "*Timon*," believes the play is about pride, and that Timon denies reciprocity out of presumption.

109. Frank Kermode, in the Intro. to the *Riverside Timon* (Boston, 1974), claims that the lines, IV, iii, 435 ff., "do not say . . . [that the] whole creation is a system of luxurious thieving." But they do.

110. Maxwell, "*Timon*."

111. Ivor Brown asserts that the prostitutes are in the play "for no good reason but to provide targets for Timon's loathing of sex." *Shakespeare* (Garden City, N.Y., 1949), p. 182.

112. Farnham, *Frontier*, p. 47, claims that the best poetry of the play is the poetry of hate.

VI. A NEW SYNTHESIS

11. *The Romances*

1. For a summary of critical positions on the romances, see Philip Edwards, "Shakespeare's Romances: 1900–1957," *SS* 2 (1958): 1–8. Edwards writes, however: "Though we

may be convinced, because of the constant insistence, that the Romances are important, it is hard to point to the critic who has shown where the importance lies."

2. Northrop Frye, "The Argument of Comedy," *English Institute Essays: 1948*, ed. D. A. Robertson, Jr. (New York, 1949); S. L. Bethell, *The Winter's Tale: A Study* (London, 1947), p. 107; E. M. W. Tillyard, *Shakespeare's Last Plays* (London, 1938), pp. 60–67; Mark Van Doren, *Shakespeare* (Garden City, N.Y., 1953), p. 260; John Danby, *Poets on Fortune's Hill* (London, 1952), p. 96.

3. G. W. Knight, *The Crown of Life* (London, 1952), p. 99, writes that in *The Winter's Tale*, Shakespeare tries "to pit his own more positive intuitions, expressed hitherto mainly through happy-ending romance and comedy, against tragedy." He adds that romance is not "just a reversal of tragedy; rather tragedy is contained, assimilated, transmuted" (p. 127). Northrop Frye, *Fools of Time* (Toronto, 1967), pp. 120–121, describes the romances as fulfilling both tragic and comic vision. "Death is contained by the action . . . [but] the emphasis [is] on participation in a continuous movement." See also *Anatomy of Criticism* (Princeton, N.J., 1957), p. 184, for further discussion of this point.

4. Stanley Wells, "Shakespeare and Romance," *Later Shakespeare*, ed. J. R. Brown and Bernard Harris (London, 1966), includes the ignoring of cause and effect as a characteristic of romance, but Clifford Leech, *Shakespeare's Tragedies* (London, 1950), p. 117, criticizes the lack of what he calls "environmental motivation," the fact that the moral nature of the characters is a simple given. In "The Structure of the Last Plays," *SS* 11 (1958): 19–30, Leech complains about the structure of *Pericles* as being too loose. There could have been more or fewer incidents, he claims. I do not agree. Each incident contributes what is necessary to the overall demonstration; no incident could be removed without weakening the play.

5. Patrick Cruttwell, *The Shakespearian Moment* (New York, 1955), p. 105, notes that in the romances, "the subject . . . becomes in itself of minor importance: so does the form. If this poetry uses prescribed forms at all, it stretches them to the limit." He adds that the romances do not soften or sentimentalize evil (p. 96).

6. "The damage which libidinous mankind inflicts on itself is the main datum on which the Romances are built." Philip Edwards, *Shakespeare and the Confines of Art* (London, 1968), p. 138.

7. Caroline Spurgeon describes the images of the romances as subtle and ideational rather than concrete, but she adds that nearly half the images in *Cymbeline* are nature images, that the sense of sound dominates *The Tempest*, and that the images of *The Winter's Tale* focus on "the flow of life in nature and man alike." *Shakespeare's Imagery* (Boston, 1961), pp. 291, 293, 300, 305.

8. In the romances, "the state of exile is not (as in *Lear*) an opportunity to discover the true quality of humanity; it is rather that the structure of society is seen as coming to recognize its need for the elements it has rejected. The Last Plays describe the quality of the *living*—the capacity to accept the world-as-it-is has had to be bought by a sacrifice of heroic pretensions." G. K. Hunter, "The Last Tragic Heroes," *Later Shakespeare*. Although Hunter is speaking of Leontes and Posthumus, his remarks are appropriate to all the romances.

9. For a discussion of the incest theme in Shakespeare, see Barbara Melchiori, "Still harping on my daughter," *English Miscellany*, ed. Mario Praz, 11 (1960): 59–74.

10. John Arthos, "*Pericles, Prince of Tyre*," *SQ* IV (1953): 257–270, reads the play as "a drama within a man."

11. Knight, *Crown*, and Arthos, "*Pericles*," both find the hero passive, his act a willingness to look at evil. Knight, however, also believes the scene to be a moral exemplum on the dangers of visual lust. In fact, however, in late Shakespeare, any strong sexual desire is seen as dangerous. A dissenting opinion on Pericles' character is held by Thelma N. Greenfield, "A Re-examination of the 'Patient' Pericles," *SStud* 111 (1967): 51–61, who finds the hero wily and fearful. John P. Cutts, "Pericles' 'Downright Violence,' " *SStud* IV (1968): 275–293, believes Pericles is guilty because his desire for Antiochus' daughter

is the wrong kind of love, a seeking for a daughter rather than an equal. This position is close to mine, although it neglects to consider the significance of the highly erotic quality of such love.

12. Knight, *Crown*, p. 110, asserts that Shakespeare's fathers are normally tyrannical.

13. Northrop Frye, *A Natural Perspective* (New York, 1965), p. 65, claims all the characters in *Cymbeline* are blind.

14. The male characters of the romances are forgiven by the critics as well. F. R. Leavis, *The Common Reader* (London, 1952), p. 175, claims that Posthumus is not "seriously blameable" because he is a victim of Iachimo. But it is not Iachimo who urges Imogen's murder. Knight, *Crown*, p. 140, finds Posthumus' jealousy of a piece with that of many other Shakespearean characters, and shrugs off possessiveness and jealousy as a characteristic of British "national manhood." Fitzroy Pyle, *"The Winter's Tale": A Commentary on the Structure* (London, 1969), p. 100, believes the audience is able to forgive Leontes because he is absent from the stage for a long time.

15. One critic who applies this notion to a romance is Paul N. Siegel, "Leontes as Jealous Tyrant," *RES* (1950): 302–307.

16. Hazlitt claims the fate of almost all the characters depends on one circumstance— Iachimo's answer to the question about the ring. In fact, the issue is not really Iachimo's answer, but Imogen's chaste constancy. William Hazlitt, *Characters of Shakespeare's Plays* (New York, 1845), p. 1.

17. Some of these surrogations are pointed out by William Barry Thorne, "*Cymbeline*: 'Loop'd Branches' and the Concept of Regeneration," *SQ* XX, 1 (Spring, 1969): 143–159.

18. C. L. Barber, " 'Thou that beget'st him that did thee beget': Transformation in *Pericles* and *The Winter's Tale*," *SS* 22 (1969): 59–67.

19. Clifford Leech among others, although perhaps more strongly, has described the puritanism, the passion for possession in the male characters, the obsession with infidelity, and violent revulsion from the body in late Shakespeare. *Shakespeare's Tragedies*. Dover Wilson had earlier termed this a "sex nausea" apparent in the work after 1600. *The Essential Shakespeare* (Cambridge, 1932), p. 118. Leech claims that Prospero's obsession with virginity "cannot be understood other than pathologically" (p. 152). Critics generally do not connect Shakespeare's attitude towards sex with the idealization of the heroines discussed by Patrick Cruttwell, *Moment*, and by Hazlitt, *Characters*, who finds the heroines characterless "abstractions of the affections." But Leslie Fiedler does discuss this in *The Stranger in Shakespeare* (New York, 1972).

20. The beauty of women is a major symbol for "feminine" power. This is a magnetic, drawing power that arouses the desire to please rather than fear of punishment. Throughout the Renaissance it is a prime symbol for moral excellence, as Bembo declares it to be in *The Courtier*. And of course it is found only in women.

21. Parallels among the characters are pointed out by Charles Loyd Holt, "Notes on the Dramaturgy of *The Winter's Tale*" *SQ* XX (1969): 47–51, and by Joan Hartwig, "The Tragicomic Perspective of *The Winter's Tale*," *ELH* 37 (1970): 12–36.

22. F. R. Leavis, *The Common Pursuit* (London, 1952), p. 179, and Northrop Frye, *Perspective*, passim, develop the meaning of this rejuvenation.

23. Robert Speaight, *Nature in Shakespearian Tragedy* (London, 1955), p. 154.

24. By, respectively, Clifford Leech, *Shakespeare's Tragedies*, pp. 141, 147; Leo Kirschbaum, *Two Lectures on Shakespeare* (Oxford, 1961), p. 33; and Knight, *Crown*.

25. Frank Kermode, Intro. to the Arden *The Tempest* (London, 1964), p. xxxii.

26. Kermode, p. xxiv.

27. Kermode, p. xlviii.

28. Frye, *Perspective*, p. 71, comments that Prospero treats nature much as Petruchio treats Katharina.

29. The effect of suffering on a character is a measure of his moral excellence, according to Stephen Kitay Orgel, "New Uses of Adversity: Tragic Experience in *The Tempest*," *In Defense of Reading*, ed. Reuben Brower and Richard Poirier (New York, 1962).

30. There are several interesting essays on Prospero, *The Tempest* and the romances in a generally fine collection that was published after this book had gone to print. See *Representing Shakespeare*, ed. Murray M. Schwartz and Coppélia Kahn (Baltimore, 1980).
31. *Shakespeare and the Comedy of Forgiveness* (New York, 1965), pp. 240–241.
32. C. L. Barber, "Thou that beget'st," points out that there is a tendency in later Shakespeare to identify women mainly by their procreative powers. He writes that the thing most emphasized in females is "their power to create and cherish life, their potential or achieved maternity."

Index

WOMEN:
PSYCHOLOGY'S
PUZZLE

JOANNA BUNKER ROHRBAUGH

WOMEN: PSYCHOLOGY'S PUZZLE is the first attempt to assess the scientific basis of the feminist challenge to male psychology's perception of women.

Avoiding both over-simplification and the polemics frequently found in popular writing on this emotive subject, psychologist Joanna Bunker Rohrbaugh considers whether there is any essential or inherent biological reason why female behaviour or personalities should differ from male.

Clearly distinguishing established fact from popular speculation, Dr Rohrbaugh examines the prevailing myths about female psychology and shows how such myths distort the reality of women's everyday lives. She explores new areas of female experience, previously ignored because they didn't fit the traditional image of 'femininity', including female sexuality, unmarried singles, female workers and women as members of minority groups. Finally, Dr Rohrbaugh looks at the implications of being female in a world where stereotypes determine the place of women in society.

PSYCHOLOGY/NON-FICTION   0 349 12943 6   £2.95

THE LEFT-HANDED WOMAN

Peter Handke

**In this fable of the city Peter Handke
highlights the obsessions and obstacles
that separate men and women from each
other and from themselves.**

'There are echoes of Beckett, Sartre and
Kafka in this chilly little novel by the young
Austrian writer who has been called the last
of the modernists. . . . His fiction plunges us
into a riddling counter-world which by
unsettling degrees comes to seem a mirror-
image of our own.' *Newsweek*

'Handke is widely regarded as the best
young writer, and by many as the best
writer altogether, in his language.' *John
Updike*

FICTION   0 349 11631 8   £1.50

WHEN THE EMPEROR DIES

Mason McCann Smith

In 1868 Queen Victoria's empire was at the height of
its worldly power. But one nation stood against British
dominion: in Ethiopia the mystical Emperor Theodore
held a handful of Crown subjects captive. His courage
had delivered his people from the rule of the Turks but
the heroic arrogance of the Lion of Judah was about to
bring the full strength of a British expeditionary force
crashing down on his kingdon. As General Sir Robert
Napier led 12,000 troops to the fortress at Magdala, the
Emperor prepared for the death he had grown to love.
WHEN THE EMPEROR DIES is both a remarkable
novel and a brilliant depiction of the war between
earthly and spiritual powers.

FICTION   0 349 13232 1   £3.95

GOOD BEHAVIOUR

Molly Keane

Behind the gates of Temple Alice the aristocratic Anglo-Irish St Charles family sinks into a state of decaying grace. To Aroon St Charles, large and unlovely daughter of the house, the fierce forces of sex, money, jealousy and love seem locked out by the ritual patterns of good behaviour. But crumbling codes of conduct cannot hope to save the members of the St Charles family from their own unruly and inadmissible desires.

'An extraordinary tour de force of fictional presentation . . . a masterpiece . . . a technically remarkable work, as sharp as a blade . . . Molly Keane is a mistress of wicked comedy.' Malcolm Bradbury, *Vogue*

'Excellent . . . Molly Keane brings it off triumphantly . . . a distinguished comeback.' Piers Paul Read, *The Standard*

FICTION   0 349 12075 7   £2.95

JAROSLAV HAŠEK

THE RED COMMISSAR

Truant, rebel, vagabond, play-actor, anarchist, practical joker, bohemian (and Bohemian), alcoholic, traitor, bigamist and Red Commissar, Jaroslav Hasek is best known as the creator of the Idiot of the Company, the Good Soldier Svejk. THE RED COMMISSAR shows that Svejk was not Hasek's only great comic achievement.

As well as the earliest Svejk stories, this collection contains Hasek's riotous account of the troubled life of a Red Commissar in Russia and numerous other stories satirising bureaucratic idiocy and pomposity which ring as true now as when they were written. Whether slapstick or political parody Hasek's comedy is sharp, humane and very funny.

FICTION　　　　　0 349 11645 ᴜ　　　　　£2.95

PETER the GREAT

His Life and World

The Pulitzer Prize-winning Biography by

ROBERT K. MASSIE

Peter the Great combined the advanced skills
and learning of seventeenth century Europe
with the raw material of the largest nation on
earth to forge an empire that dominated both
East and West. Despite his progressive and
enlightened attitudes towards science and the
state, Peter was a barbarous feudal tsar with a
personal love of torture. His character –
volatile, restless, far-sighted and cruel –
embodied the greatest strengths and weaknesses
of Russia. This long-awaited biography is a
superb full-length portrait of the man
in his time.

BIOGRAPHY   **0 349 12281 4**   **£5.95**

Other titles available from ABACUS

NON-FICTION

YELLOW RAIN	Sterling Seagrave	£3.25 □
MEDIATIONS	Martin Esslin	£2.95 □
NAM	Mark Baker	£2.75 □
IRELAND – A HISTORY	Robert Kee	£5.95 □
THE MAKING OF MANKIND	Richard Leakey	£5.95 □
SMALL IS BEAUTIFUL	E. F. Schumacher	£2.50 □
GANDHI – A MEMOIR	William L. Shirer	£1.75 □
HITCH	John Russell Taylor	£2.75 □

FICTION

WHEN THE EMPEROR DIES	Mason McCann Smith	£3.95 □
THE RED COMMISSAR	Jaroslav Hasek	£2.95 □
A LONG WAY FROM VERONA	Jane Gardam	£2.25 □
FREDDY'S BOOK	John Gardner	£2.50 □
GOOD BEHAVIOUR	Molly Keane	£2.95 □
MADAME SOUSATZKA	Bernice Rubens	£2.25 □
A STANDARD OF BEHAVIOUR	William Trevor	£1.95 □

All Abacus books are available at your local bookshop or newsagent, or can be ordered direct from the publisher. Just tick the titles you want and fill in the form below.

Name _____

Address _____

_____

Write to Abacus Books, Cash Sales Department, P.O. Box 11, Falmouth, Cornwall TR10 9EN

Please enclose cheque or postal order to the value of the cover price plus:

UK: 45p for the first book plus 20p for the second book and 14p for each additional book ordered to a maximum charge of £1.63.

OVERSEAS: 75p for the first book plus 21p per copy for each additional book.

BFPO & EIRE: 45p for the first book, 20p for the second book plus 14p per copy for the next 7 books, thereafter 8p per book.

Abacus Books reserve the right to show new retail prices on covers which may differ from those previously advertised in the text or elsewhere, and to increase postal rates in accordance with the PO.